# RESEARCH IN
# THE HISTORY OF
# ECONOMIC THOUGHT
# AND METHODOLOGY

*Volume 13* • 1995

# RESEARCH IN
# THE HISTORY OF
# ECONOMIC THOUGHT
# AND METHODOLOGY

*Editors:*   WARREN J. SAMUELS
*Department of Economics*
*Michigan State University*

JEFF E. BIDDLE
*Department of Economics*
*Michigan State University*

VOLUME   13   •   1995

 JAI PRESS INC.

*Greenwich, Connecticut*                              *London, England*

*Copyright © 1995 by JAI PRESS INC.*
*55 Old Post Road No. 2*
*Greenwich, Connecticut 06836*

*JAI PRESS LTD.*
*The Courtyard*
*28 High Street*
*Hampton Hill*
*Middlesex TW12 1PD*
*England*

*ISBN: 1-55938-095-0*

*Manufactured in the United States of America*

# CONTENTS

# LIST OF CONTRIBUTORS

*David R. Andrews*

Walla Walla, WA 99362

*Nahid Ashlanbeigui*

Department of Economics
  and Finance
Monmouth College

*Robert E. Babe*

Department of Communication
University of Ottawa

*Humberto Barreto*

Department of Economics
Wabash College

*Randall Bartlett*

Department of Economics
Smith College

*James F. Becker*

Department of Economics
New York University

*Peter J. Boettke*

Department of Economics
New York University

*A. W. Coats*

Department of Economics
Duke University

*John B. Davis*

Department of Economics
Marquette University

*Arthur M. Diamond, Jr.*

Department of Economics
University of Nebraska at Omaha

*Robert S. Goldfarb*

Department of Economics
George Washington University

*Robert A. Griffin*

Department of Economics
Florida International University

J. Daniel Hammond

Department of Economics
Wake Forest University

Donald R. Haurin

Department of Economics
Ohio State University

John R. Henry

Department of Economics
California State University

Samuel Hollander

Department of Economics
University of Toronto

Mordechei E. Kreinin

Department of Economics
Michigan State University

Richard B. Norgaard

Energy and Resources Group
University of California
   at Berkeley

Spencer J. Pack

Department of Economics
Connecticut College

Terry Peach

Department of Economics
University of Manchester

Mark Perlman

Department of Economics
University of Pittsburgh

Yngve Ramstad

Department of Economics
University of Rhode Island

David F. Ruccio

Department of Economics
University of Notre Dame

Andrea Salanti

Department of Economics
University of Bergamo

James D. Shaffer

Department of Agricultural
   Economics
Michigan State University

Howard Sherman

Department of Economics
University of California
   at Riverside

*James L. Starkey*                    Department of Economics
                                     University of Rhode Island

*W. Paul Strassmann*                 Department of Economics
                                     Michigan State University

*Torbjörn Tännsjö*                   Department of Philosophy
                                     University of Stockholm

*John P. Tiemstra*                   Department of Economics
                                        and Business
                                     Calvin College

*Paul B. Trescott*                   Department of Economics
                                     Southern Illinois University
                                        at Carbondale

# EDITORIAL BOARD

# ACKNOWLEDGMENTS

The editors wish to express their gratitude for assistance in the review process and other consultation to the members of the editorial board and to the following persons:

Daniel Bromley

Charles Clark

Ken Dennis

William Dugger

Giovanni Dosi

Jerry Evensky

Philip Mirowski

Pier Luigi Porta

Andrea Salanti

Jeffrey Wooldridge

# ERRATA

## An Interview with Milton Friedman on Methodology
## By J. Daniel Hammond

*An Interview with Milton Friedman on Methodology*, published in volume 10, 1992, of *Research in the History of Economic Thought and Methodology* contains a number of printer's errors.

The most serious error in the text of the interview is on p. 102, where a portion of Friedman's statement is missing. Friedman is speaking of the empirical evidence on business cycles in relation to von Mises's cycle theory. His statement should read, "On the other hand, there's a very high correlation between the amplitude of a recession and the amplitude of the succeeding expansion."

Other errors in the text are on p. 99, where meeting is misspelled; on p. 101. where there should be no comma in "I'm wrong"; on p. 106, where 1953a should be in italics; and on p. 111, where Planning Public Works and Economics of Planning Public Works should be in italics.

There are also a number of mistakes in the list of references. The publication date of R.T. Bye's book is 1940. J.M. Culbertson's 1960 article is "Friedman on the Lag in Effect of Monetary Policy." The book by P.H. Douglas and A. Director is *The Problem of Unemployment*. Friedman's 1963 book is *Inflation: Causes and Consequences*. In the title of E.W. Kitch's article, remembrance is misspelled. The publication date of Popper's *The Open Society* is 1945. The title of H. Schultz's book is *The Theory and Measurement of Demand*. The title of J. Viner's 1925 article is "Objective Tests of Competitive Price Applied to the Cement Industry."

Also, an article is missing from the list of references. It is J. Tobin's 1970, "Money and Income: Post Hoc Ergo Propter Hoc?" *Quarterly Journal of Economics* 84 (May): 301-317.

# ERRATA

## The Problem of Contest for Friedman's Methodology
## By J. Daniel Hammond

*The Problem of Context for Friedman's Methodology*, published in volume 10, 1992, of *Research in the History of Economic Thought and Methodology* contains several mistakes in the list of references.

The volume number for B. Caldwell's 1992 article is 10. M. Freidman's 1977 pamphlet, *From Galbraith to Economic Freedom*, was published by the Institute of Economic Affairs. The title of the H.A. Simon article is "Problems of Methodology—Discussion."

There is also an article missing from the reference list. It is J.D. Hammond's 1992, "An Interview with Milton Friedman on Methodology." Pp. 91-118 in *Research in the History of Economic Thought and Methodology*, vol. 10, edited by W.J. Samuels. Greenwich, CT: JAI Press.

# THE RACIAL THEORIES OF
# JOHN R. COMMONS

Yngve Ramstad and James L. Starkey

In their book, *Black History and the Historical Profession, 1915-1980*, August Meier and Elliot Rudwick assert that the approach to history of U. B. Phillips, a strong advocate of the view that the innate and inherited racial inferiority of Negroes[1] gave form to Southern history, was "decisively shaped and inspired" by Frederick Jackson Turner and the "racist labor economist, John R. Commons" (Meier and Rudwick, 1986, p. 4). It may come as a shock to many of his admirers to learn that Meier and Rudwick's characterization of Commons is not without foundation. The reality is that in a set of articles appearing in 1903-04 under the series title, "Racial Composition of the American People," later published in slightly altered form as *Races and Immigrants in America* (1907), Commons articulated views that cannot but be labeled as "racist," that is, as reflecting a belief that some races are inherently inferior to others.[2]

**Research in the History of Economic Thought and Methodology,**
**Volume 13, pages 1-74.**
Copyright © 1995 by JAI Press Inc.
**All rights of reproduction in any form reserved.**
**ISBN: 1-55938-095-0**

For example, consider the following passage regarding the Negro: "Two circumstances, the climate and the luxuriant vegetation, [have conspired] to produce a race indolent, improvident and contented.... All travelers speak of their impulsiveness, strong sexual passion, and lack of will power" (Commons, 1903-1904:3, p. 223). Or: "The improvidence of the Negro is notorious. His neglect of his horse, his mule, his machinery, his eagerness to spend his earnings on finery, his reckless purchase of watermelons, chickens and garden stuff when he might easily grow them on his own patch of ground, these and many other incidents of improvidence explain the constant dependence of the Negro upon his employer and his creditor" (Commons, 1903-1904:3, pp. 227-228). Or most significantly:

> The line between superior and inferior races, as distinguished from civilizations, appears to be the line between the temperate and tropical zones. The two belts of earth between the tropics of Capricorn and Cancer and the arctic and antarctic circles have been the areas where man in his struggle for existence developed the qualities of mind and will—the ingenuity, self-reliance, self-control, strenuous exertion, and will power—which make him befitting the modern industrial civilization. But in the tropics these qualities are less essential, for where nature lavishes food and winks at the neglect of clothing and shelter, there ignorance, superstition, physical prowess and sexual passion have an equal chance with intelligence, foresight, thrift and self-control. The children of all the races of the temperate zones are eligible to the highest American civilization, and it only needs that they be 'caught' young enough. This much cannot be said for the children of the tropical zone. Amalgamation is their door to assimilation. Frederick Douglass, Booker Washington, Professor DuBois are an honor to any race, but they are mulattoes (Commons, 1903-1904:9, p. 222).

As noted, many admirers of Commons are probably unaware that he considered Negroes to be inherently inferior to Europeans and therefore incapable of assimilation into "the highest American civilization." This is hardly surprising; except for a brief nostalgic reference in his autobiography to the period he spent in Florida during the years 1885-86 (cf. Commons, 1934b, p. 33), one cannot find even a single passage in Commons's published writings, other than those in "Racial Composition," suggestive of a racist mentality. Moreover, Commons's views regarding the Negro "race" have been ignored by all major chroniclers of his writings.[3] Indeed, we have been unable to locate a single adequate analysis of Commons's views on the race issue.[4] The tasks of summarizing Commons' racial views and determining how they fit into his scheme of thought, in short, have yet to be undertaken, much less satisfactorily accomplished. In this paper we attempt to remedy this situation.

We proceed as follows. First we delineate Commons's analysis as presented in "Racial Composition" and *Races and Immigrants*, in reality a single work;[5] because this early work has not been particularized elsewhere, we elaborate it in considerable detail. We then attempt to characterize and situate the racial views Commons espoused. As we do so, we also develop our appraisal of

Commons' core argument in "Racial Composition" and argue that it has been improperly characterized by previous analysts. We conclude with some remarks relating to the matter of whether explicit recognition of Commons's racist outlook necessitates a reinterpretation of his work as a whole.

A caveat is in order before we commence our analysis. Unfortunately, in "Racial Composition" Commons sometimes neglected to make explicit the grounds upon which he reached consequential conclusions, occasionally even failing to make evident the full meaning of a crucial pronouncement. Moreover, as we read and reread various passages and tried to grasp exactly what it was that Commons wanted to convey, we often sensed that we were receiving mixed messages with respect to his analysis of the Negro Problem. In particular, we perceived that some of Commons' "progressive" proposals were put forth without conviction and occasionally contradicted his own analysis. The reader should therefore be forewarned that much of our analysis hinges on the soundness of our interpretation of Commons's weak commitment to some of the policy measures he espoused in regard to the Negro. We of course recognize that one cannot know with certainty Commons's true intention in developing his line of argument in "Racial Compositions" exactly as he did. Given this actuality, we have endeavored throughout the analysis to make explicit and to develop at some length the ground(s) upon which we have reached our judgments.

## I.   COMMONS'S RACIAL ANALYSIS

### A.   The Background

Commons's opportunity to write about the fitness for participation in American life of the Negro and other races was thrust upon him quite by accident. In 1899, Commons had lost his position at Syracuse University for too-enthusiastically supporting the propriety of Sunday baseball for workers.[6] Soon after his dismissal, Commons was hired by George H. Shibley, a bimettalist who believed that a knowledge of specific facts about the presumed falling price level would be politically useful to construct a weekly index of wholesale prices. Commons succeeded in producing the price index, but when it began to document price movements opposite those his benefactor sought, Commons's contract was cancelled. Thus, in the fall of 1900, he again joined the ranks of the unemployed. Once more good fortune struck. Within two weeks, E. Dana Durant, a former student Commons encountered by chance, asked whether Commons would be willing to finish for him a report on immigration he had begun for the U.S. Industrial Commission. Commons immediately agreed. To inform himself of the facts, Commons toured the country for six months or so investigating firsthand the conditions of life experienced by immigrants who worked in urban sweatshops. He also visited the headquarters of roughly half the national trade unions in an attempt to gain insight into the effects of immigration on unionism.

Commons presented his findings in a report to the Industrial Commission in 1901 (see Commons, 1901), whereupon he accepted a position with the National Civic Federation (NCF). While working for the NCF, Commons wrote a series of articles, drawing extensively on the report he had prepared for the Industrial Commission, and had them published during 1903-1904 in the *Chautauquan Magazine* under the heading "Racial Composition of the American People." Even though the series as a whole was nominally designed to provide an overview of the various "races" of which the American People was then constituted, many of the individual articles in the series, as their titles suggest,[7] explored the relationship between immigration and specific social problems of concern to progressive elements of American society. Additionally, in the final article, Commons sought to assess whether or not the various races were capable of full assimilation into American civilization, that is, of being fully "Americanized." Since "the emancipation of the Negro ... added, in effect, another race to the list of immigrants," Commons apparently thought it also necessary to assess whether the Negro race was capable of such assimilation. Thus, "Racial Composition," which represented a significant extension of his work for the Industrial Commission, required a mastery of "facts" going well beyond those Commons had investigated in person in his work for the Industrial Commission.[8] When he returned to academia in 1904 as a member of the University of Wisconsin faculty, Commons capitalized on his experiences by offering a course, "Races and Immigrants in America," the title he also gave to his book based on the *Chautauquan* series.

## B.  Commons's Social Philosophy

In his later writings on methodology, Commons placed great emphasis on the relationship between an investigator's "social philosophy" and any "theory" his mind was capable of propagating or countenancing [cf. Commons, 1934a, p. 98]. Thus, before elaborating Commons's racial analysis, it may be helpful to review some of the important non-racial "habitual assumptions" rooted in his social philosophy that, *on the basis of his published writings*, can be presumed to have already implanted themselves in Commons's mind as he worked on "Racial Composition."[9]

Probably the most important element of Commons's social philosophy was his synthesis of middle-class values—the values of individual initiative and responsibility[10]—and the presumptions of the "Social Gospel" movement, which proclaimed that the Protestant churches are obligated to do more than assist the individual in achieving eternal salvation.[11] In a series of essays written early in his career, gathered together as *Social Reform & The Church* (Commons, 1894), Commons joined these elements into his own Social Gospel manifesto. Therein he declared, "Man is made in the image of God. His possibilities are divine" (Commons, 1894, p. 30). Perhaps foremost among "such [Godlike] gifts as we have, Commons went on, is the capacity to embrace and manifest in one's behavior "the noble [Christian] qualities of truth, love, honor, fidelity and manliness" (Commons, 1894, p. 37).

However, Commons continued, in the American setting at the turn of the century, the Godlike possibilities were being crushed out of the working man who, irrespective of his intrinsic capacities, consequently was anything but "noble:" "The workingman of to-day (sic) ... is slavish in his instincts.... He is distrustful, jealous, incapable of co-operation, treacherous to benefactors and fellow-laborers, and an eye-servant" (Commons, 1894, pp. 36-37). Revealing an inclination for a dichotomous accounting of individual character later given free reign in "Racial Composition," Commons traced the wage worker's "character flaws"—and the social problems emanating from them such as intemperance, crime, and corrupt city government (Commons, 1894, pp. 32, 40)—to both biology and socialization:

> But how shall this soul [individual character] unfold and develop. Sociology, based as it is upon the sciences of biology, tells us it is through that universal law of life—adaptation to environment. Adaptation is direct and indirect; the first is effected through use and disuse of faculties; the second through heredity. Thus the individual, both in his body and his soul, in the process of generations becomes fitted to his environment.
>
> Now, it is society that furnishes the environment of the individual. Society determines the conditions under which his physical and spiritual powers shall be permitted to develop. Society creates great social classes, and assigns the individual, even before his birth, and on through infancy, youth, and manhood, to one of these classes. For generations before his birth, and again through the plastic years of childhood, his particular social class is shaping and conditioning his physical and mental powers, his appetites, emotions, and ideals (Commons, 1894, pp. 33-34).

Foremost among the conditions underlying the failure of workers to realize their inherent capacities, according to Commons, were poverty (Commons, 1894, p. 37) and *"wage-slavery,* ... the dependence of one man upon the arbitrary will of another for the opportunity to earn a living" (Commons, 1894, p. 34, emphasis added). Significantly, these conditions were held by Commons *not* to reflect the operation of "so-called natural laws which man cannot modify. Social conditions are the result of the human will" (Commons, 1894, p. 14). And, if Christianity is "to reach ... a man with its noble qualities of truth, love, honor, fidelity, *manliness* [this term will take on significance below]," it must "first [create] for him those physical conditions of life and true independence out of which such qualities can spring" (Commons, 1894, pp. 36-37, emphasis added). Therefore, the Christian who desires that these

"Godlike" qualities have an opportunity to develop within the souls of wage workers and their families must work to establish conditions of life allowing for an adequate and secure income *and* a status of true equality between the worker and his employer. "True independence," in short, was itself raised to the level of a desideratum by Commons (cf. Commons, 1894, pp. 9-10). Indeed, the belief that "good" social policy must honor yet "balance" the various *independent* interests reflected in economic life is evident in practically all of Commons's subsequent policy recommendations. Moreover, it lies at the core of his theory of Reasonable Value.[12]

A second, though interrelated, element of Commons's social philosophy that was to condition the entirety of his work, and which also underlay the form of his argument in "Racial Composition," relates to his interpretation of competition. John Dennis Chasse has established in a carefully argued paper dealing with the history of the American Association for Labor Legislation that by the turn of the century Commons had come to accept Henry Carter Adams's contention that unregulated competition is a "destructive" competition, one in which the least ethical competitors are able to force those who would like to be more ethical down to their own "low level" (cf. Chasse, 1991, p. 804). In Commons's mind, for reasons made clear in *Social Reform & The Church*, the wage rate clearly was foremost among the factors requiring protection from "destructive competition." Whenever the wage falls, he reasoned, it becomes more difficult for the individual to develop fully the "noble qualities of truth, love, honor, fidelity, [and] manliness" of which he or she is capable. Thus, "destructive" wage cutting was in Commons' mind foremost among the "unethical" behaviors from which workers must be protected (cf. Commons, 1913, Chap. 18).[13]

But how could such protection be ensured? The Christian appeals to the love of man for man, but in 1894, while listening to Christian ministers preach the gospel of love, Commons "... became suspicious of Love as the basis of social reform" and "made Duty ... instead of ... Love" one of the foundations of his thought (Commons, 1934b, pp. 51-52). Of course, it is only the state, with its superior ability to use violence to enforce its "commands," which is capable of making "good" behavior a duty.[14] Thus Commons came also to accept Adams's belief that it is a central function of government to regulate competition in such fashion that "unethical" behavior cannot lower the "plane of competition," or as Commons himself later came to refer to it, to ensure that competition is "fair and reasonable." Throughout his career, accordingly, Commons saw regulation or "standards" as the positive contribution of government to orderly "non-destructive" market activity.[15] This mental reflex also played a role in shaping Commons's analysis of the immigration question.

A final element of Commons's social philosophy relates to the question of how effective representation can be assured for "independent" classes of people whose interests conflict in shaping the state's policies regarding the regulation of economic life. In *Social Reform & The Church*, Commons had argued that proportional representation was a precondition for workers gaining an effective voice in government (cf. Commons, 1894, pp. 87-96, 155-176). In *Proportional Representation*, first published in 1896, Commons developed this theme at some length and argued forcefully for the direct legislative representation of economic interest groups.[16] This scheme, he argued, embodied the substance of "representative government" as it had evolved in England (cf. Commons, 1896, pp. 12-17; 1913, p. 68). In Commons's assessment, representative government based on geographical districts, as inherited from England, had worked properly in the United States only so long as suffrage was limited, as it was by the founding fathers, to a single class (cf. Commons, 1896, pp. 28-31). When suffrage was extended to other classes whose private interests "with respect to the profound problem of the ownership of wealth and the betterment of the social conditions of the lowest classes" conflict (Commons, 1896, pp. 31-32), the fact that such interests must be represented by a single candidate led to a situation in which the "lowest classes" were not represented effectively (Commons, 1913, p. 68). Indeed, it was Commons's belief that representatives selected in accordance with geographic representation are typically "in the pockets" of lobbyists representing corporate interests. It therefore would be better for each competing interest, in proportion to its percentage of the total vote, to elect its own leaders who would then be spokesmen for its particular interests. If proportional representation was instituted, Commons concluded, the compromises hammered out by legislative bodies would more closely approximate a true compromise between the various outcomes preferred by the competing (and "independent") interests at stake in public policy decisions impacting upon the distribution of wealth (Commons, 1913, p. 70).

In *Proportional Representation*, Commons laid out a comprehensive plan for effectuating such an approach. Of central import in the present instance are two crucial presumptions evident in Commons's approach, first, that only a particular group's own freely chosen representative(s) will be able to represent effectively the interests of that group (cf. Commons, 1896, p. 171) and, second, that, historically, disadvantaged groups have achieved an equal role in determining public policy *only* upon exercising their economic power to withhold something which those who previously monopolized power have desired but could not command (cf. Commons, 1896, pp. 12-17; 1913, p. 67).

In short, Commons understood free choice of its own leaders and equality of bargaining power (the power to withhold) to be the prerequisites for effective participation by a group in determining the rules apportioning the "burdens and benefits of collective wealth-production" among the various "interests" that together make up "society," that is, the rules constituting and "regulating" economic competition.[17] However, in 1900, while occupied with the research which ultimately led to the writing of "Racial Composition," Commons changed his mind as to how effective class representation could best be secured. While attending a national "joint conference" of bituminous coal miners and their employers, he "was struck by the resemblance to the origins of the British Parliament" (Commons, 1934b, p. 72). This realization led Commons to the view that "constitutional government in industry"—that is, collective bargaining between self-selected representatives of labor and capital—constituted a practical alternative to a scheme of comprehensive proportional representation (cf. Commons, 1934b, p. 72).[18] Thus, throughout the remainder of his career Commons advocated association into trade unions as the mechanism through which *both* preconditions for "self-actualization" (development of "noble qualities") could be secured.

These deeply ingrained constituents of Commons's social philosophy—(1) the middle-class desideratum of "true independence"; (2) the belief that the state should regulate the "plane of competition," that is, act is, act to eliminate "destructive competition;" and, given his presumptions that self-selected spokesmen most effectively represent the interests of any particular class and that empowerment of disadvantaged groups to a status of "equality of bargaining power" is the mechanism through which group progress occurs, and (3) the belief that trade unionism should be promoted since it constitutes the best available mechanism for effecting an "uplifting" of the working class—gave shape to all of his subsequent work. Accordingly, Commons sought throughout his lifetime of research to identify, first, specific government actions that would actually have the effect of securing "reasonable" protection for workers from the "competitive menace" *and*, second, specific mechanisms through which "protected" workers, via actual- or quasi-collective bargaining, would be able to participate as true ("independent") equals. Determining the "correct" tradeoffs between the various, yet to some degree incompatible, individually ethical ends government action might be capable of furthering then becomes possible. These same mental predilections, rooted in his social philosophy, account for the specific way Commons formulated his analysis of race and immigration.

## C.  "Racial Composition of the American People"

The crux of Commons's argument in "Racial Composition" is that whereas sound public policy will enable the nation to make true "Americans" out of most immigrants, there is no possibility of obtaining the same result for Negroes. It was Commons's determination to develop systematically an "objective" justification for this position which accounts, in our judgment, for the particular manner in which "theories" and "facts" about race are introduced and utilized over the course of the nine segments comprising the series.

In the first article, Commons examined the question of whether the immigrant "races," including the Negro race, were equally capable of obtaining an "equal voice in determining the laws and conditions which govern all" (Commons, 1903-1904:1, p. 33), that is, equally capable of achieving "true independence" and participating as full equals in collective decision-making processes. If certain classes or races lack the capacity to participate as equals in the operation of democratic government, then, according to Commons, "democracy as a practical institution" will break down and in its place will arise a *de facto* class oligarchy or race oligarchy disguised as democracy (Commons 1903-1904:1, pp. 33-34).

Commons did not consider such an eventuality to be mere speculation. Democracy, he averred, is an institution developed by "the so-called Anglo-Saxon" race, whereas, many of the other "races" that had emigrated to the United States were "accustomed to despotism and even savagery, and wholly unused to self-government" (Commons, 1903-1904:1, p. 34). The "political boss" system so prevalent in urban areas populated by recent immigrants only showed that "we have begun actually to despotize our institutions in order to control these dissident elements [while] holding that we retain the original democracy" (Commons, 1903-1904:1, p. 34). Thus, the crucial questions regarding "non-English" immigrants were, first, do they have the capacity for acquiring the personal characteristics needed to make democracy real and, second, assuming they do, are there mechanisms capable of assimilating them into a single people of similar mental and moral character. The nation's motto, *e pluribus unum*, requires this, "for it is that union of the hearts and lives and capacities of the people which makes government what it really is" (Commons, 1903-1904:1, pp. 34-35).

As noted, Commons embraced a wholly middle-class conception of the "good." Hence he conceived of the character issue as follows:

> The true foundations of democracy are in the character of the people themselves, that is, of the individuals who constitute the democracy. These are first, intelligence—the power to weigh evidence and draw sound conclusions based on adequate information; second, manliness, ... which at bottom is dignified self-respect, self-control, and that self-assertion and jealousy of encroachment which marks those who, knowing their rights, dare maintain them; third, and equally important, the capacity for cooperation, that willingness and ability to organize, to trust their leaders, to work together for a common interest and toward a common destiny, a capacity which we ... designate as ... self-government (Commons, 1903-1904:1, p. 35).

From Commons's perspective, then, the issue boiled down to whether or not immigrants possess the capacity to develop the character ("true independence") necessary for participation as full equals in self-government (Commons, 1903-1904:1, p. 42). If, as Commons believed, the various races possess an equal capacity to become assimilated, the existence of a single language constitutes a powerful force for actually bringing such assimilation into being. What

Commons sought to determine, therefore, was whether immigrant races do in fact possess the capacity to become fully assimilated into the highest American civilization or whether they would prove incompetent "to share in our democratic opportunities" (Commons, 1903-1904:1, p. 37). In other words, the question of interest to Commons was: Are there races *lacking the capacity* to acquire the traits of intelligence, manliness, and cooperation?

Even before he undertook to write these articles, as noted previously, Commons tended to think of individual character as rooted in *both* heredity and socialization. Apparently he perceived that a majority of the educated citizenry embraced the view that character was wholly a matter of education and environment. Accordingly, he sought to direct the reader's attention in this first installment to the possible error of this presumption: "We are trying to look beneath the surface and to inquire whether there are not factors of heredity and race more fundamental than those of education and environment" (Commons, 1903-1904:1, p. 34). The crucial question, in other words, was whether the evolutionary process has produced races with different "physical, mental and moral capacities and incapacities" (Commons, 1903-1904:1, p. 35). For, if such differences exist, being "established in the very blood and physical constitution they are most difficult to eradicate and they yield only to the slow processes of the centuries" (Commons, 1903-1904:1, p. 35).

Commons acknowledged that he was employing the term "race" "in a rather loose and elastic sense" (Commons, 1903-1904:1, p. 87).[19] Through its use, he explained, he sought only to focus attention on "those large and apparent divisions which have a direct bearing on the problem of assimilation" (Commons, 1903-1904:1, p. 87). With this limited end in mind, Commons declared that mankind may be broken into "five great racial stocks," all of which have representatives in the United States: (1) the Aryan, with many branches or "races," including the Greeks, Latins, Slavs, Celts, and Teutons, the latter in turn divisible into the Germans, the Scandinavians, and, above all, the English; (2) the Semitic, with its "remarkable branch," the Hebrews; (3) the Mongolian, from which are derived the Magyar, the Chinese and the Japanese; (4) the Negro; and (5) the Malay (Commons, 1903-1904:1, pp. 39-40). Of particular significance to Commons was the fact that whereas the Aryan, the Semitic, and the Mongolian

> has in earlier time met one another and even perhaps had sprung from the same stock, so that when in America they come together there is presumably a renewal of former tie[s,] ... we find no traces [in the records of archaeology or philology] of affiliation with the black race. The separation of continents, by climate, by color, and by institutions, is the most diametrical that mankind exhibits anywhere (Commons, 1903-1904:1, p. 38).

Thus Commons clearly considered the Negro race to be fundamentally different from all the others[20]—so different, in fact, that a separate article in the series would be devoted to it. No other race received such recognition, and already it is clear why. For with respect to the question of whether education might not elevate the character of a race, Commons observed:

> "True enough," [it was] said, "the black man is not equal to the white man, but once free him from his legal bonds, open up the schools, the professions, the businesses, and the offices to those of his number who are most aspiring, and you will find that, as a race, he will advance favorably in comparison with his white fellow citizens." It is now more than thirty years since these opportunities and educational advantages were given to the negro, not only on equal terms but actually on terms of preference over the white, and the fearful collapse of the experiment is recognized even by its partisans as *something that was inevitable in the nature of the race* at that stage of its development (Commons, 1903-1904:1, p. 34, emphasis added).

One can find a suggestion here that it is actually Commons's intention to divert the educated citizen's (the reader of the *Chautauquan*) attention *away from* "the most fundamental of all American social and political problems ... the problem of the relations between the white and the negro races" (Commons, 1903-1904:1, p. 34). Indeed, he declared, it was this same race problem that now diverts attention from the treatment of such pressing economic problems as taxation, corporation, trusts, and labor organization (Commons, 1903-1904:1, p. 34), the very problems to which Commons directed his attention throughout the remainder of his lengthy career.[21]

In the second installment of the series, Commons presented information as to the "race" origins of the nation's early settlers. Relying on data accumulated by Henry Cabot Lodge about "eminent Americans" from the earliest settlements through the late nineteenth century, Commons noted that the English have been foremost among the eminent—indeed, Lodge found some 10,376 out of 14,243 eminent persons to be English (Commons, 1903-1904:2, p. 118). Commons argued, however, that eminence is not necessarily identical to ability in that it is due as much to accident of social conditions and to the social and legal environment. Thus was Commons able to point to the Scotch-Irish immigrant (the latter being the Protestants of Northern Ireland) rather than the English as "the distinctive American type"—a "type" which, while left undefined, presumably incorporates the traits of "intelligence, manliness, and cooperation" Commons found so necessary for collective self-determination, that is, representative democracy. Not incidentally, the Scotch-Irish were second on Lodge's list of eminent Americans with a total of 1,439 (Commons, 1903-1904:2, p. 118).

In the first installment of the series, Commons had advanced the view that "a nation (here apparently meaning the same thing as "race") composed of a mixed stock is superior in mind and body to one of single and homogeneous stock." Then he noted, "But it must be remembered that amalgamation requires centuries" (Commons, 1903-1904:1, p. 40). It was just such a process that

Commons found to be responsible for the superior fitness of the Scotch-Irish to the other "races" who had emigrated to America during the colonial period. As he put it, "[M]ore than any other race [the Scotch-Irish] served as the amalgam to produce, out of divergent races, a new race, the American" (Commons, 1903-1904:2, p. 125).

Commons did not suggest that the other races participating in the colonial migration were therefore at a permanent disadvantage, for the "race factor is decisive [only] when it marks off inferior and primitive races" (Commons, 1903-1904:2, p. 120). It was of profound significance, therefore, that almost the entire colonial migration "was Teutonic in blood and Protestant in religion. The English, Dutch, Swedes, Germans, and even the Scotch-Irish, who constituted practically the entire migration, were, less than two thousand years ago, one Germanic race in the forests surrounding the North Sea" (Commons, 1903-1904:2, p. 120). Not only were these initial immigrant "races" biologically capable of assimilation into the "American" race, they also had experienced conditioning to individualism through their association with the Protestant Reformation. Commons had thus set the stage for further articles by establishing that it was only the non-Teutonic races about whose capacity for "Americanization" the educated citizen must be concerned.

Especially the Negro race. Hence, in the third piece, "The Negro," Commons attempted to assess the "physical, mental and moral capacities and incapacities" of Negroes.[22] He began by asserting that the tropical climate and the luxuriant vegetation along the West African coast from which most slaves were brought to America have "produced a race [that is] indolent, improvident and contented" (Commons, 1903-1904:3, p. 223). Indeed, "The torrid heat and the excessive humidity weaken the will and actually exterminate those who are too energetic" (Commons, 1903-1904:3, p. 223). In other words, according to Commons the Negro is burdened with deficient physical and mental capacities. Equally deficient was his moral character, for along the West African coast,

> sexual purity is unknown, ... cannibalism prevailed, the people are unstable, indifferent to suffering, and easily aroused to ferocity by the sight of blood or under great fear....
> They exhibit ... certain qualities which are associated with their descendants in this country, namely, aversion to silence and solitude, love of rhythm, excitability, and lack of reserve. All travelers speak of their impulsiveness, strong sexual passion, and lack of will power (Commons, 1903-1904:3, p. 223).

Moreover, slavery had further degraded the inherent character of the Negro. Since slavery worked best, Commons held, if workers were docile rather than independent,

> slavery tended to transform the savage by eliminating those who were self-willed, ambitious, and possessed of individual initiative. [Whereas] other races of immigrants, by contact with our institutions, have been civilized—the Negro has only been domesticated. Civilization

offers an outlet for those who are morally and intellectually vigorous enough to break away from the stolid mass of their fellows; domestication dreads and suppresses them as dangerous rebels. The very qualities of intelligence and manliness which are essential for citizenship in a democracy were systematically expunged from the Negro race through two hundred years of slavery (Commons, 1903-1904:3, p. 224).

In short, environmental and historical circumstances had combined to render the Negro much less fit than "Teutons" for assimilation into the "American" race. Indeed, Commons judged the Negro, at his present stage of development, to be totally unfit for self-government. The Negro, Commons asserted, lacked the prerequisites of self-government, namely, "intelligence, self-control and capacity for cooperation" (Commons, 1903-1904:3, p. 224). The absence of these qualities, returning to the issue he emphasized in the first article, was responsible for the Negro ballot "only making way for the 'boss,' the corruptionist, and the oligarchy under the cloak of democracy.... The suffrage must be earned, and not merely conferred, if it is to be an instrument of self-protection" (Commons, 1903-1904:3, p. 224).[23] And what did this imply? "The great lesson already learned is that we must 'begin over again' the preparation of the Negro for citizenship. This time the work will begin at the bottom by educating the Negro for the ballot, instead of beginning at the top by giving him the ballot before he knows what it should do for him" (Commons, 1903-1904:3, pp. 225-226).

Such an education, of course, must be designed so as to produce a Negro with the qualities of intelligence, manliness, and cooperation. With respect to intelligence, Commons found it extremely important that the Negro was "lacking in 'the mechanical idea'" (Commons, 1903-1904:3, p. 226). The significance of this "lacking" extended far beyond the disadvantage it gave the Negro in his job competition with white workers:[24] "The foundation of intelligence for the modern workingman is his understanding of mechanics .... Intelligence in mechanics makes way for intelligence in economics and politics, and the higher wages of mechanical intelligence furnish the resources by which the workman can demand and secure his political and economic rights" (Commons, 1903-1904:3, p. 227).

Just as a lack of the "mechanical idea" precludes the acquisition of intelligence, the Negro's "improvidence"[25] serves as a barrier to independence and manliness. For

these qualities are not produced merely by exhortation and religious revivals. They have a more prosaic foundation. History shows that no class or nation has risen to independence without first accumulating property. However much we disparage the qualities of greed and selfishness which the rush for wealth has made obnoxious, we must acknowledge that the solid basis of the virtues is thrift (Commons, 1903-1904:3, p. 227).

And what about the Negro's capacity for cooperation? Here Commons suggested that there are actually two forms of cooperation, a lower and a higher. The lower is cooperation with "the chief or the boss who marshals his ignorant followers through fear or spoils"; for individuals participating in this type of cooperation, personal jealousies and factional contests prevent united action under elected leaders (Commons, 1903-19004:3, p. 228). The higher form of cooperation, that of self-government, is impossible without a prior "growth of intelligence and moral character" (Commons, 1903-1904:3, p. 229). Commons explained that Negroes were generally in the "low stage of cooperation" (Commons, 1903-1904:3, p 228). Thus, it was their own character defects that made it difficult for Negroes to organize under leaders of their own race.

As noted, Commons understood history to have revealed that real gains for an oppressed group occur only when its own members acquire sufficient bargaining strength to force those in power to include its interests among those synthesized into the "public purposes" reflected in social policy.[26] Thus he averred in this article, "liberty (for an oppressed group) has always come through (self-)organization" (Commons, 1903-1904:3, p. 229). But here the Negro was in a difficult position, as his own qualities made self-organization a dubious prospect. Even though Commons observed that "with the modest beginnings of self-organization among Negroes the way is opening for their more effective participation in the higher opportunities of our civilization," he also emphasized that "the Negro trade unionist has not as yet shown the organizing capacity of other races" (Commons, 1903-1904:3, p. 229). Indeed, it was Commons's perception that "the Negro is being organized by the white man, not so much for his own protection as for the protection of the white workman" (Commons, 1903-1904:3, p. 229). Moreover, only if the Negro "is brought to the position of refusing to work for lower wages than the white man" will he have taken "the most difficult step in organization; for the labor union requires, more than any other association in modern life, reliance upon the steadfastness of one's fellows" (Commons, 1903-1904:3, p. 229). Yet therein lay the "Catch-22" for workers. Only by "refusing to work for lower wages than the white man" could the Negro really achieve equality with other unionists. However, given his own "industrial inferiority," the Negro who did refuse would be replaced by his employer with white men. Therefore, Commons concluded that acquisition of "manual and technical intelligence ... [is] the basis for all other progress" (Commons, 1903-1904:3, p. 229).

Commons was quite direct about what he considered to be the policy implication of the foregoing assessment:

> It must not be inferred, because we have emphasized these qualities of intelligence, manliness, and cooperation as preparatory to political rights, that the Negro race should be deprived of the suffrage until such time as its members acquire these qualities. Many

individuals have already acquired them. To exclude such individuals from the suffrage is to shut the door of hope to all. *An honest educational test, honestly enforced on both whites and blacks, is the simplest rough-and ready method for measuring the progress of individuals in these qualities of citizenship.* There is no problem before the American people more vital to democratic institutions than that of keeping the suffrage open to the Negro and at the same time preparing the Negro to profit by the suffrage (Commons, 1903-1904:3, p. 230, emphasis added).[27]

The fourth and fifth articles in the series dealt with the topic, "Immigration During the Nineteenth Century." Most of the space in these selections is devoted to a recitation of facts as to who immigrated, in what numbers, and when. Attention is also directed to the circumstances that led each of the immigrant groups to leave its native land. What Commons documented was the dramatic shift in the character of immigration after the early eighteen eighties from western to southern and eastern Europe, from Protestant to Catholic Europe, from subjects of popular governments to subjects of absolute governments, from educated to illiterate, from those suited to skilled trades to those suited to primitive industry, and from Teutonic races to Latin, Slav and Semitic.

Particular emphasis was placed on the background and character of particular immigrant "races"—the Italian, Austro-Hungarian, Russian; various "minor" races such as the French-Canadians, Portugese, Syrians, Armenians; and the Chinese and Japanese.[28] Thus the reader was informed that the southern Italians, who comprised the bulk of Italian immigrants, "are nearly the most illiterate of all immigrants at the present time, the most subservient to superiors, the lowest in their standards of living, and at the same time the most industrious and thrifty of all common laborers" (Commons, 1903-1904:4, p. 340). The reader also learned that the Russian Jew, although averse to agriculture, is among the non-Teutons best fitted for self-government (cf. Commons, 1903-1904:5, p. 439); that "the Chinaman complacently refuses to assimilate with Americans, and the latter reciprocate by denying him the right of citizenship" (Commons, 1903-1904:5, p. 442); that the Syrians have the lowest of all standards of life, come from the most despotic of all governments, and, having mainly been traders and peddlers, are "intrinsically servile," tend toward ingratitude and mendacity, and prostitute all ideals "to the huckster level" (Commons, 1903-1904:5, p. 441); and so on. What do all these "facts," and the many, many others presented in these articles, imply regarding the issues uppermost in Commons's mind? It is only in subsequent installments of the series that this becomes evident.

The first of these issues is the problem referred to earlier, that of the standard of living attained by the American wage-worker. In the sixth installment of the series, an article titled "Industry," Commons explained how immigrants from the "backward races" have undermined the attainments of those who arrived prior to the 1880s or so. Indeed, it is clear from this piece that Commons perceived immigration to be in large part a consequence of "destructive competition." For

> even more important than the initiative of immigrants have been the efforts of Americans to bring and attract them. Throughout our history these efforts have been inspired by one grand, effective motive, that of making a profit upon the immigrants. The desire to get cheap labor, to take in passenger fares and to sell land have probably brought more immigrants than the hard conditions of Europe, Asia and Africa have sent us. Induced immigration has been as potent as voluntary immigration (Commons, 1903-1904:6, p. 533).

Thus, Commons suggests that even though such immigration contributes to the production of wealth (cf. Commons, 1903-1904:6, pp. 536-539), the already "Americanized" worker must be protected from the "competitive menace" of further immigration by "backward races"—a category from which he excluded "immigrants from Northwestern Europe, the Germans and Scandinavians" (Commons, 1903-1904:6, p. 542). Commons's reasoning should be familiar by now: "The future of American democracy is the future of the American wage-earner. To have an enlightened and patriotic citizenship we must protect the wages and standard of living of those who constitute the bulk of the citizens" (Commons, 1903-1904:6, p. 535). Indeed, had this same orientation been accepted from the first, "the Negro would not have been admitted in large numbers and we should have been spared that race problem which of all is the largest and most nearly insoluble" (Commons, 1903-1904:6, p. 535).[29]

But even if further immigration by "backward, thriftless and unintelligent races" (Commons, 1903-1904:6, p. 542) is prohibited by law, as he later recommended it should be (cf. Commons, 1903-1904:9, p. 224),[30] the nation must still contend with the social and industrial challenges emanating from the earlier admittance of such "races" into the country. In the seventh article, titled "Social and Industrial Problems," Commons explored how those challenges might be surmounted by developing further the line of thought made evident in the immediately preceding article. First, however, Commons focused the reader's attention back to a basic difference between the "backward" races, those that are branches of the "superior races" (Aryans, Semites, and Mongolians) versus those of the "inferior races" (Negroes and Malays) who, having "developed under a tropical sun are ... indolent and fickle" (Commons, 1903-1904:7, p. 13). In order to probe the significance of this division, Commons called attention to the four "systems of law" through which property in labor may be governed, namely slavery, peonage, contract labor and free labor. Since the "inferior races" or, as Commons elsewhere referred to them, the "non-industrial races" (Commons, 1903-1904:7, p. 15), are by nature "careless, thriftless and disinclined to continuous exertion" (Commons, 1903-1904:7, p. 15), labor markets in which such workers predominate must be organized so as to "compel a shiftless race to work" (Commons, 1903-1904:7, p. 15). Commons suggested this is why nominally free labor for the rural Negro so quickly reverted into "peonage" via the sharecropping system (cf. Commons, 1903-1904:7, pp. 13-14).[31]

Commons perceived "necessity and ambition" to be the "two grand motives" that induce the freeman to work. In typical Commons fashion, "necessity" was construed in elastic terms. What he clearly meant by the term, however, is the quality of life to which the worker has become accustomed or feels a social obligation to attain (cf. Commons, 1903-1904:7, p. 16). Thus the "necessities," that is, wage rate, required to induce members of different immigrant "races" to work will vary according to the standard of life they became accustomed to in the "old country." Equally significant, however, was "ambition, . . the desire for an improved position for one's self and family—for better quality and greater variety of material things" (Commons, 1903-1904:7, pp. 16-17).[32] In his view it is ambition that precipitates "destructive competition:"

> [A]mbition has its penalty. It is equivalent to an increase in the supply of labor. Rather than lie idle the ambitious workman accepts a lower rate of pay. His fellows see the reduction and go still lower. The see-saw continues until wages reach the level of necessities and there is nothing left for ambition.... The ambitious races are the industrial races. But their ambition brings on the momentous problem of destructive competition (Commons, 1903-1904:7, p. 17).

The remedy? "There is but one immediate and practical remedy—the organization of labor to regulate competition" (Commons 1903-1904:7, p. 17). And why is this?

> The method of organization is to do in concert through self-sacrifice what the non-industrial races do individually for self-indulgence, namely, refuse to work. Where the one loafs the other strikes. While the necessities of the workers set the minimum below which wages cannot fall, the labor union, by means of the strike or the threat to strike, sets a higher minimum which leaves room for ambition. Eventually the higher minimum becomes habitual and becomes a higher level of necessities. Gifted individuals may, indeed, rise above the wage-earning class by their own efforts, but labor organization alone can raise the class as a whole (Commons, 1903-1904:7, p. 17).

Labor organization, in short, is the "corrective to the evils of free competition" (Commons, 1903-1904:7, p. 19). In the absence of such organization, Commons insisted, employers will simply play one race against another, as indeed they often had done, and "The competition of races is the competition of standards of living.... The race with lowest necessities displaces others" (Commons, 1903-1904:7, p. 18). And should the immigration laws not be amended to prevent it, the eventual consequences of this "competition of races" were ominous in Commons's mind:

> As rapidly as a race rises in the scale of living and, through organization, begins to demand higher wages and resist the pressure of long hours and over-exertion, the employers substitute another race, and the process is repeated. Each race comes from a country lower in the scale than that of the preceding, until finally the ends of the earth have been ransacked in the search for low standards of living combined with patient industriousness.... There is but one thing that stands in the way of complete unionization in many of the industries, namely a flood of immigration too great for assimilation by the unions (Commons, 1903-1904:7, p. 19).[33]

What about other social issues linked to immigration? In the eighth installment of the series, "City Life, Crime and Poverty," Commons directed the reader's attention to problems arising from "the tendency of the (recent) foreign-born towards great cities" that impact upon "the future of democracy and the welfare of the nation" (Commons, 1903-1904:8, p. 115). Here Commons clearly portrayed "city life" as deleterious to full "Americanization:"

> The dangerous effects of city life on immigrants and the children of immigrants cannot be too strongly emphasized. This country can absorb millions of all races from Europe and can raise them and their descendants to relatively high standards of American citizenship in so far as it can find places for them on the farms, but the cities of this country not only do not raise them but are themselves dragged down to a low level by the parasitic and dependent conditions which they foster among the immigrant element (Commons, 1903-1904:8, p. 118).

Commons then took the reader through a maze of statistics regarding the criminal behavior of recent immigrants compared with those who have become more established and showed that criminal behavior is much more prevalent among the former group (the Negro is the sole noted exception). Statistics were also reviewed regarding the incidence of poverty and pauperism among recent immigrants compared with more established groups, and Commons again concluded that "in all cases it appears that the foreign born and the Negroes exceed the native classes in their burden on the public" (Commons, 1903-1904:8, p. 122). Then what are the appropriate policy actions? Here Commons was silent.

At last we come to the ninth and final, and in our view the most important with regard to the subject of this paper, of the individual articles comprising the "Racial Composition of the American People" series, one titled "Amalgamation and Assimilation."[34] It is here that Commons at last developed explicitly the implications of the racial analysis sketched out over the preceding installments.

Commons began this final article by raising the issue of "race suicide," meaning by that term the possible degeneration of "the native American stock," that is, of the "American" race (Commons, 1903-1904:9, p. 217). As Commons saw it, "This question of the 'race suicide' of the American or colonial stock should be regarded as the most fundamental of our social problems, or rather as the most fundamental consequence of our social and industrial institutions" (Commons, 1903-1904:9, p. 218).[35] The problem, in a nutshell, was that members of the "American" race were bearing fewer children than those from recently immigrated "races." This was particularly vexing since such behavior on the part of the former group was interpreted by Commons as a natural outcome of the "American" character (cf. Commons, 1903-1904:9, p. 218). Hence, he found it necessary to explore the implications of the evident fact that, on the whole,

> immigration and the competition of inferior races tends to dry up the older and superior races wherever the latter have learned to aspire to an improved standard of living, and that among well-to-do classes not touched by immigrants, a similar effect is caused by the desires for luxury and easy living (Commons, 1903-1904:9 p. 221).

Whether or not the declining birth rate of "the older superior races" actually would lead to "suicide" for the "American" race, Commons suggested, hinged on the abilities of "lesser" races to become "Americanized." In order to focus properly on that matter, Commons made clear, it is necessary to grasp the distinction between amalgamation and assimilation:

> The term amalgamation may be used for that mixture of blood which unites races in a common stock, while assimilation (here reiterating the interpretation discussed above) is that union of their minds and wills which enables them to think and act together. Amalgamation is a process of centuries but assimilation is a process of individual training. Amalgamation is a blending of races, assimilation a blending of civilizations. Amalgamation is beyond the organized efforts of government, but assimilation can be promoted by social institutions and laws (Commons, 1903-1904:9, p. 221).

Accordingly, Commons continued, "Amalgamation ... cannot attract our practical interest, except as its presence or absence sets limits to our effort toward assimilation" (Commons, 1903-1904:9, p. 221).

Given the earlier articles in the series, it is not difficult to anticipate where Commons was going. What is crucial, he posited, is the previously made distinction between "superior" and "inferior" races:

> We speak of superior and inferior races, and this is well enough, but care should be taken to distinguish between that superiority which is the original endowment of race and that which is the result of the education and training which we call civilization. While there are superior and inferior races, there are primitive, medieval and modern civilizations, and there are certain mental qualities required for and produced by these different grades of civilization. A superior race may have a primitive or medieval civilization, and therefore its individuals may never have exhibited the superior mental qualities with which they are actually endowed and which a modern civilization would have called into action. The adults coming from such a civilization seem to be inferior in their mental qualities, but their children, placed in the new environments of the advanced civilization, exhibit at once the qualities of the latter (Commons, 1903-1904:9, p. 221).

And, as already indicated in a passage quoted earlier, "The line between superior and inferior races, as distinguished from civilizations, appears to be the line between the temperate and tropical zones" (Commons, 1903-1904:9, p. 222). Accordingly, those who are from "branches" of the Aryan, Semite, and Mongolian races can in all likelihood be fully "Americanized" so long as their "new environment" includes the social institutions and laws needed for assimilation to occur.

But no longer, Commons asserted, is frontier life "the most powerful agency of assimilation," a possibility for the immigrant; neither will most immigrants find it possible to live on the farms of America, the "next richest field of assimilation" (Commons, 1903-1904:9, p. 222). And, unfortunately, while the schools can be a proper influence, the immigrant's out-of-school activities are likely to prove more influential: "[I]t is the community that gives [the immigrant child] his actual working ideals and his habits and methods of life" (Commons, 1903-1904:9, p. 223). No, Commons maintained, despite the "noble instrument" of a common language, it is unlikely that the immigrant can be "Americanized" while a child.

What institution, then, can "Americanize" the immigrant? "[T]he labor union is at present the strongest Americanizing force. The union teaches [immigrants] self-government through obedience to officers elected by themselves. It frees them from the spirit of subservience and gives them their primary lesson in democracy, which is liberty through law" (Commons, 1903-1904:9, p. 223). In short, in so far as the "superior races" are concerned, we have been taken full circle back to the position Commons articulated a decade earlier in *Social Reform & The Church*.

But what about Negroes? Unfortunately, being members of an "inferior race," they will be unable to assimilate solely through exposure to a higher "civilization." Their improvement is beyond the practical reach of social institutions and the law: "Amalgamation is their door to assimilation" (Commons, 1903-1904:9, p. 222).[36]

## II.  THE CHARACTER OF COMMONS'S STANDPOINT TOWARD IMMIGRANT "RACES"

One purpose giving rise to this paper was our desire to present, for students of John R. Commons, a carefully developed exposition of his views on the question of race. To this point we have assiduously avoided the impulse to label his stance or to assess it. Now we need to address the other issues raised earlier. How are Commons's racial views properly characterized? Where did they fall along the spectrum of views expressed at the time he wrote "Racial Composition"? What were their origins? Finally, what impact did those views have on Commons's approach to social policy? It is to the consideration of these issues that we now turn.

## A.  A Racist Posture?

As we have recounted, Commons advocated in "Racial Composition" the restriction of immigration by means of a literacy test. By championing a literacy test, Commons was hardly staking out a novel position. For while the South struggled with the problems defined by its "central theme" (Phillips, 1928), the North was embroiled in conflict over the immigration problem. At the time Commons was writing the articles comprising "Racial Composition," the principal remedy being debated was immigration restriction through the device of a literacy test. In fact, during the period 1897-1917, a literacy test was enacted by Congress on four separate occasions but vetoed successively by Presidents Grover Cleveland, William Howard Taft, and, on two occasions, Woodrow Wilson. Only after the onset of World War I did the test's supporters finally manage to marshal the votes needed to override the veto, and a literacy test became law in 1917 (Higham, 1988, pp. 104-105, 187-191).

It is widely accepted that the movement to restrict immigration into the United States had its roots during the post-Civil War years in a rural midwestern provincialism fostering a xenophobic rejection of Asians, Jews, Catholics and Negroes (Vidich and Lyman, 1982, p. 1053). During this same period, "Yankees" in most of the great cities were increasingly finding themselves "outnumbered and overwhelmed" (Hofstadter, 1955, p. 177), and their insecurity about the changes taking place was only exacerbated as the predominant sources of immigration shifted from northern Europe to southern and central Europe. Hence support for immigration restriction quickly spread from the Midwest to other areas of the nation. Not surprisingly, this new movement gave rise to a broad range of restrictionist ideologies from the Nativist to the Eugenic, that is, from the merely ethnocentric notion that immigrants pose some threat to the national interest, to the notion that immigration will lower the quality of the American racial stock. The literacy test itself was first proposed in 1888 as a measure to protect American wage earners from the competition of foreigners conditioned to a lower standard of living. However, the proposal to institute a literacy test for immigrants failed to attract much support from politicians until it was endorsed in 1897 by the Boston-based Immigration Restriction League (IRL). Since Commons testified in support of the literacy test a number of times as a representative of the IRL (Solomon, 1956, p. 132), some discussion of its orientation to the immigration problem is warranted.

The IRL was founded and supported by such patrician anglo-saxonists as Nathaniel Shaler, the Harvard naturalist, student of Louis Aggassiz, and racist (Gossett, 1963, p. 281); Francis Amasa Walker, first president of the American Economic Association and racist (Higham, 1988, p. 142); Senator Henry Cabot Lodge, sponsor of the literacy test who introduced European racist concepts to the floor of the U.S. Senate (Higham, 1988, p. 142);[37] and Madison Grant, whose "scientific" book, *The Passing of the Great Race* (1916), brought to America, in full force, the racist ideas of Houston Chamberlain and Count Arthur DeGobineau (Snyder, 1939, p. 231; Gossett, 1963, p. 357). This cultural elite, educated at such "anglo-saxonist incubators" (Curtis, 1968, p. 91) as Oxford and Cambridge in England and Amherst, Harvard, Johns Hopkins and Yale in the United States, became alarmed at the "Irish conquest" (Hofstadter, p. 178) of the police and fire departments of Boston and the mill towns and of the Democratic party in Massachusetts. While the IRL men raised all the same issues to justify their position in support of immigration restriction as nonracist restrictionists, namely, "the threat to American institutions, the American rate of wages, and the American standard of living" (Walker, 1896, p. 829), they also forwarded explicitly racist arguments.[38] As E.A. Ross put it, the leaders of the IRL were "arrogant" men with "swelled heads" who clung to the "hypothesis of an immutable hierarchy of races with the Nordics on top" (Ross, 1930, p. 203). Walker, for example, attributed urban political corruption to the "foreign element" whose members were "the ready tools of the demagogues" and also blamed immigrants for what he perceived to be the irresponsible behavior of unions. Walker further alleged that immigrants would undermine national productivity because they lacked "the English capacity for mechanical ingenuity" and had none of the inherited race traits necessary to make one assimilable into a democracy:[39]

> They are beaten men from beaten races; representing the worst failures in the struggle for existence. Centuries are against them…. They have none of the ideas and aptitudes which fit them to take up … the problem of self-care and self-government, [unlike] those who descended from the tribes that met under the oak-trees of old Germany to make laws and choose chieftains (Walker, 1896, p. 828).

What clearly most alarmed Walker and the other anglo-saxonists was their perception that racially inferior immigrants from "every foul and stagnant pool of population in Europe" were replacing the "native" anglo-saxon stock which was "wholly out of the loins of our own people" (Walker, 1896, p. 824). In other words, it was the racist desire to preserve the dominant status of "our own people" which doubtlessly impelled the ILR patricians to advocate a literacy test. But as we have seen, despite his willingness to ally himself with the ILR, this was not Commons's motivation for championing such a test.

All the same, it would not be difficult to confuse Commons with a racist on the immigration question since the position Commons took on the "race suicide" issue is, to say the least, perplexing. As noted, he contended in "Racial Composition" that "race suicide should be regarded as the most fundamental of our social problems" and argued that even though "social and industrial institutions are implicated, … [on] the whole it seems immigration and the competition of inferior races tends to dry up the older and superior races" (Commons, 1903-1904:9, p. 221). In spite of the importance he accorded the issue, however, it is not clear exactly what Commons meant by race suicide or why he considered it such a fundamental problem. Thus, the context is important.

As employed in public discourse at the time Commons was writing "Racial Composition," the term "race suicide" had many dimensions and was usually more broadly understood as a social and political issue than simply as a "race" issue. Many proponents of the race suicide argument understood it mainly as a problem of declining fertility that threatened the human race (Gordon, 1977). More generally the argument asserted that lower fertility among the upper classes, accomplished "often by sinful methods," would result in making the prolific and "ignorant masses the chief supply of the future ruling majorities" (Gordon, 1977, p. 149). Race suicide as defined by Commons is the "reduced proportion of children brought into the world" (Commons, 1903-1904:9, p. 218). One must assume that he meant a reduced proportion of children of the superior races. But remember that Commons insisted "care should be taken to distinguish between that superiority which is the original endowment of a race and that which is the result of the education and training we call civilization" (Commons, 1903-1904:9, p. 221). Thus it would appear the term "superior race" does not in this case imply racial superiority.

Commons continued his analysis by asserting that the only truly inferior races were those which evolved in the tropical zone. But immigration of Negroes and Malays was not involved in the "race suicide" issue. Indeed, Commons himself was somewhat perplexed by the absence of any evidence of race suicide in the South. He resolved this problem by asserting that race suicide requires both an inferior race and an ambitious race, and while Negroes, in his mind, were certainly inferior, he judged white Southerners generally to lack ambition (Commons, 1903-1904:9, p. 220). Commons additionally took notice of the fact that falling birth rates were observed not only for the "native stock" but for second generation immigrants as well. Indeed, he emphasized that the phenomenon was even more pronounced for this group (Commons, 1903-1904:9, p. 219). Significantly, Commons also judged that while the problem of race suicide was not so severe in the "country districts where the native stock prevails," it was "disastrous" in the case of Irish-Americans who live in the "cities and industrial centers" where they were being exposed to the relentless competition of newer immigrants. This suggests he saw the problem in terms broader than those racial anglo-saxonists who saw it in terms of the replacement of "Yankee" stock. In fact, whereas the anglo-saxonists were affronted by the success of the Irish, Commons perceived this "versatile race with distinct native ability" to be suffering the same fate as the "colonial native stock" (Commons, 1903-1904:9, p. 219).

We can infer from this that while Commons supported the goals of the Immigration Restriction League, he did not share the racist views toward immigrants of the patricians who controlled it. For, while Commons's position with respect to immigration can be understood as elitist, as we shall spell out below, it was not racist. Indeed, even though Commons made clear his belief that the "civilizations" of south and central Europe were "backward" and that immigration from these nations was increasingly from the undesirable lower classes, he made a special effort to emphasize that immigrants from these nations do *not* come from inferior racial stocks.

## B.   A Nativist Posture?

If it was not "racist" in character, how, then, is Commons's standpoint toward the immigrant to be characterized? In an analysis of Commons's advocacy of immigration restriction, Mark Aldrich has used the term "nativist" to epitomize Commons's position (Aldrich, 1985, p. 1). John Higham has opined that scholars must be alert to the "bad habit" of reflexively "labelling as nativist any kind of unfriendliness toward immigrants" (Higham, 1975, p. 106), and we judge Higham's word of caution to be especially apropos in the case of Commons. Indeed, even though Aldrich's classification of Commons as a nativist is undoubtedly defensible, we believe that when viewed in the context of Commons's work as a whole, "nativism" is an infelicitous characterization of the posture underlying his support of immigration restriction. This matter bears some additional discussion.

In its broadest meaning, nativism connotes the practice or policy of favoring native-born citizens as distinguished from immigrants. Nativism typically arises when ethnocentrism is combined with a perception that an alien group constitutes some kind of threat to the "national interest." Emerging thusly, nativism "mobilizes prejudices, feeds on stereotypes and radiates hysteria" (Higham, 1975, p. 105). Accordingly, as commonly used the term conveys an attitude of animosity toward an internal group that is rooted in the belief that it is responsible for the "major ills of a society" (Higham, 1975, p. 105).

While nativism at the turn of the century was often cast in racial terms, as reflected in the views of the ILR patricians, this usage was not prevalent. For example, in the 1840-1850s anti-Irish Know-Nothing movement, the Irish were perceived as a threat to the national interest not because they were considered an inferior race that would lower racial quality in the United States but because they were Catholics—slaves of the corrupt and totalitarian papacy and therefore of ambiguous loyalty and a threat to American democracy (Higham, 1988, pp. 77-87). Anti-Catholicism was also an important force in the movement to restrict immigration at the turn of the century. For example, the American Protective Association championed "a free public school system, immigration restriction and a slower, more rigid system of naturalization" as a means of "defend[ing] true Americanism" from the "subjects of an un-American ecclesiastical institution" (Higham, 1988, p. 83). Various other immigrant groups have similarly been declared "defective" by presumed spokesmen for the "national interest" because of a perceived tendency toward, say, anarchism, communism, intemperance, or crime (Higham, 1988, p. 51). Admittedly, there were some who addressed even these issues in racial terms, that is, considered anarchism and communism to be "blood diseases," but at least through the 1890s nativism remained predominantly nonracial in character (Higham, 1988, p. 138).

In the United States, the 1890s was a period of intense social strife exacerbated by a severe depression. Where the South used the Negro as a scapegoat for its troubles (Williamson, 1986, pp. 198-201), other regions of the country quickly focused on the immigrant as the source of class strife, crime, corruption, depression, and the other problems which threatened to tear the nation apart. Nativism thus became a "psychological palliative" used to mitigate the anxiety produced by a sense that the fabric of American life was being shredded (Lubove, 1962, p. 53). During the 1890s, this "palliative" manifested itself across a broad spectrum: Italians suspected of being "mafia" criminals were shot, striking Slavs were shot down, Catholics were accused of planning an invasion of the United States, and Jews were denounced for conspiring, through their control of gold, to take over the government of the United States (Higham, 1988, p. 93).

It will be recalled, however, that the literacy test was first proposed in 1888 *before* the perception that "American life was being shredded" by immigration was widespread. Further, its explicit rationale was to protect American wage earners from the competition of foreigners conditioned to a lower standard of living. This, as we have seen, was also the core of Commons's analysis. We have already noted the connection between Commons's early views and those of Richard T. Ely, his teacher and mentor.[40] Significantly, it was Commons's fellow student under Ely and his later associate, Edward T. Bemis, who originally proposed the test.[41] Thus one can surmise that Commons probably had a commitment to the test dating back to his student days.

Like Commons, Ely and Bemis were Social Christians who were not only motivated, not only out of the "heart of love" but possessed a knowledge of sociology "to guide [that] love."[42] As was the case with Commons, their agenda was to *reform existing institutions* so as to create an environment within which every member of the urban wage-earning class would have an opportunity to manifest their "Godlike" capacities. Beyond the strictly economic rationale already noted, these men, being attuned as "sociologists"[43] to the dangers of social disintegration, also wanted to restrict immigration because it reduced social homogeneity and made *reform* more difficult. They also understood immigration to be a mechanism for capitalists to combat unionism, thereby subverting the "uplift" mechanism—the union—they had singled out.[44] Clearly, it was a concern with these factors which initially motivated the Social Christians in 1888 to advocate immigration restriction.

To recognize this reality is not to deny that these reformers were essentially ethnocentric in outlook. Yet while clearly ethnocentric, we have not been able to unearth any information revealing that the associates who shared his perspective on immigration restrictions were any more "racist" with respect to immigrants than was Commons himself. Ross, also a fellow student of Commons's at Johns Hopkins and later a colleague of Ely and Commons at Wisconsin and similarly an advocate of "uplift" unionism,[45] used the term "culture conflict" to differentiate the ethnocentrism of the reformers from racism:

> The success of Democracy requires that a people be fairly homogeneous and like-minded. Exclusion of immigrants of an altogether different hue and culture may be motivated by people's reluctance to become a hodge-podge of diverse colors, tongues, religions, with the most discordant moral and economic standards; yet it is easy to insinuate that the policy is begotten of racial arrogance[46] (Ross, 1930, p. 201).

Some proponents, moreover, seemed well aware of the deficiencies of the Social Christian's rationale for immigration. For example, consider the statement of Richmond Mayo-Smith, another of Commons's acquaintances[47] and a fellow Social Christian, in *Emigration and Immigration*:

> We readily perceive that one population differs from another, and we are able in a very general way to characterize the difference. We can often see that national traits are changing with the passage of time, and we can indicate in a general way the direction of the evolution. But to define the difference precisely is beyond our power. Many of these things depend on relations which cannot be measured and which can only, so to speak, be felt. We feel instinctively that such and such elements are incompatible with our social life, but we are unable to produce the technical proof. We are morally certain, but we cannot make the evidence scientifically complete. It may only be national prejudice that is struck by the change (Mayo-Smith, 1890, p. 10).

It seems fair to say, then, that the impulse of the Social Christians toward immigration restrictions originated in both ethnocentricity and a concern for the national interest ("uplifting" wage workers). Strictly speaking, their posture was "nativist." The same is obviously true of Commons. But even if Commons shared the ethnocentric attitudes of his fellow reformers, a claim we have not made, it does not follow that these attitudes led him to his strong advocacy of immigration restriction. Significantly, Higham added to his previously noted assertion that the practice of attributing all ethnic cleavages to racism and nativism serves to "[take] the curse off the fact of inequality" (Higham, 1975, p. 108). The problem of which Higham takes note is that sometimes issues that are actually rooted in class conflict can take on the appearance of ethnic antagonism. This, we maintain, gets at the heart of the matter with respect to Commons and his analysis of immigrant "races." Accordingly, to return to the topic at hand, we believe the term "working-class exponent" more accurately epitomizes why Commons advocated immigration restriction than does "nativist."

That Commons had a class conflict conception of society and that, in the context of that conflict, he considered himself to be toiling *on behalf of* the wage-earning class appears beyond doubt. In an 1899 critique of President A. H. Hadley's Presidential Address to the American Economic Association, which he later gave the title "Economists and Class Partnership,"[48] Commons rejected the idea that a policy can be good for the "nation as a whole" and argued that progress actually occurs through policies explicitly intended only to improve the situation of "the excluded classes." According to Commons, "The class is the temporary means of bringing about the permanent welfare of all" (Commons, 1913, p. 69), and "the economist in working through social classes is working through the greatest of social forces" (Commons, 1913, p. 67). Thus he insisted that "the economist [who] truly represents society as a whole" will strive "to give the excluded classes a larger and more just legal share in government and industry" (Commons, 1913, p. 54). As we have already indicated, Commons had since at least 1894 argued that the wage-earning class was the "excluded" class in late nineteenth century America. We therefore surmise that Commons, without explicitly saying so, was in "Economists and Class Partnership" affirming that he was indeed in "partnership" with the working class and insisting, moreover, that he was thereby actually serving "society as a whole."[49]

In a discussion before the American Sociological Society delivered in December 1906 just as *Races and Immigrants* was going to press, Commons accentuated the importance of class solidarity to effective concerted action by wage workers.[50] He also underscored in his remarks another reason why unrestricted immigration was "bad": "[I]mmigration undermines [solidarity]" (Commons, 1913, p. 78). Going on, he outlined the impact of immigration on the course of class conflict: "First it intensifies the conflict of classes in the dominant race. Next it shatters class solidarity. Finally, when the immigrants and their children are Americanized ... they renew the class alignment" (Commons, 1913, p. 79). Thus, "While immigration continues in great volume, class lines will be forming and re-forming, weak and unstable; [however, to] prohibit it or greatly restrict immigration would bring forth (in active form) the class conflict within a generation" (Commons, 1913, p. 79). Well aware of the fact that immigrants were lured to the United States by the "captains of industry" for the express purpose of undermining labor unions and as cheap, "docile and obedient" labor (Commons, 1903-1904:6, p. 540), Commons made even more apparent in a 1911 *Chautauquan* article, "European and American Unions," that immigration restriction was for him a class issue: "It is, therefore, on this question of races and immigration that the real class conflict in American industry has occurred; for the backward or alien races have been made the instruments of employers to reduce the wages of the older nationalities" (Commons, 1913, p. 152).

In his critical appraisal of Commons's advocacy of immigration restriction, Aldrich suggests that Commons should have asserted that the real problem was "unfettered capitalism" rather than immigration (Aldrich, 1985, p. 22). In our view this criticism is misplaced. Commons's espousal of a class conflict perspective makes it abundantly clear to us that he in actuality regarded the character of "unfettered capitalism" to be the central issue. Furthermore, in making this observation, Aldrich reveals that he has missed entirely the point of all of Commons's policy recommendations, including this early one, to restrict immigration. As Commons later put it himself, "I was trying to save Capitalism by making it good" (Commons, 1934b, p. 143). What Commons sought to effect throughout his career, accordingly, were alterations in the "working rules" structuring economic activity—of which he understood the American brand of "capitalism" to be the active expression. His proposals would, he thought, produce "better" economic outcomes, that is, outcomes more in keeping with the interests of the "excluded classes." By altering the "working rules" which determined the character of the "competition" giving rise to actual wage and employment outcomes, immigration restriction was in Commons's mind a way to make competition itself "better." Commons's explicit advocacy of a protective tariff in 1908 (see Commons, 1913, Ch. 18) makes it eminently clear that his real motive was to raise the "plane of competition" in the labor market and thereby to eliminate the "destructive competition" which resulted from the actions of those conditioned to a low standard of living. In other words, Commons's proposal to restrict immigration was *in and of itself* nothing other than a proposal for reigning in "unfettered capitalism."[51]

Aldrich further suggests that instead of arguing for immigration restriction, Commons should have supported a minimum wage for immigrants (Aldrich, 1985, p. 22). Even though Commons did eventually come to embrace the idea of a minimum wage as another device for raising the "plane of competition" in the labor market (cf. Commons and Andrews, 1919, p. 43), it is true that he did not give it consideration in 1903. It must not be forgotten, however, that what Commons sought as a "partner" of labor was a practical legislative remedy to the problem of "destructive competition" in the labor market. That is to say, Commons would clearly have shunned any proposal having no realistic chance of legislative enactment. Given that widespread interest in minimum wage legislation in the United States did not arise until at least 1910

(Commons and Andrews, 1919, p. 54), a full decade after Commons wrote "Racial Composition" and at least 15 years after he began supporting immigration restriction, we consider this criticism somewhat unfair.

We surmise, then, that Commons was fundamentally concerned only with large numbers of unassimilated immigrants and the problems they posed for unions, the American standard of living and urban politics. In particular, we submit that Commons's advocacy of immigration restriction was essentially nothing more than an attack by a "partner" of the working class on an important instrument used by employers to advance their own position, to the detriment of wage workers, within the context of class conflict. A.E. Ross once noted perceptively that, in the face of actual or perceived job scarcity, it is often not the "foreigner" but the *competitor* who is actually detested; nonetheless, Ross continued, "*Hatred of the competitor* wears at times the mask of race antipathy" (Ross, 1930, p. 199). Commons himself never donned that "mask:" His posture towards immigrants was in no way a "hostile" one, that is, rooted in the belief that immigrants are inherently "defective" as compared to natives.

## C.  Summary

We have found no passage in Commons's pre- or post-"Racial Composition" writings indicating that his advocacy of immigration restriction had any purpose other than the "protective" one of lessening "destructive competition" in the labor market (cf. Commons and Andrews, 1919, p. 347) and the affirmative one of promoting genuine democracy. With respect to the latter, it will be recalled that Commons judged large segments of the urban "native stock" to be incapable of effective participation in self-government; indeed, he understood it to be a principal mission of the union to train them to properly discharge that privilege. Similarly, he maintained that not all of the Negro stock was inherently *dis*qualified. In particular, he urged that Negroes be qualified by a "fair and honest" educational test, that is, a literacy test. Given the need, on "protective" grounds, to restrict the number of immigrants entering the country, the literacy test for foreigners would appear to be nothing more than a reasonable and logical extension of this middle-class "elitist" position.

In our view, Commons supported the literacy test as a protective mechanism that could also "improve" the quality of immigrants and thereby "better the quality of our future citizenship." It would do this while performing its *principal function* of controlling the overall numbers of "low standard workers" who undermined the interests of the wage-earning class. In "Racial Composition," Commons argued for immigration restriction on the grounds that the traditional vehicle for assimilation, the frontier farm, was no longer available and its successor, the labor union, was being overwhelmed by the sheer number of immigrants. He maintained that while the new immigrant "races" were not inherently inferior, they were "backward" and an impediment to democracy. More fundamentally, however, the continuing influx of "backward" immigrants would only increase the problem of "destructive competition" with its noxious manifestations of low wages, inhibition of unionization and "race suicide." These, in turn, would perpetuate "wage slavery" and poverty and impede the development of labor leaders who, in Commons's view, are the vehicle through which laborers' genuine class interests can be expressed and their "uplifting" effected. In short, for Commons the "influx of backward races" (Commons, 1903-1904:6, p. 535) who are "unable to rapidly assimilate" was a threat to the living standard of the American worker *and therefore* to Democracy: "The future of American Democracy is the future of the American wage worker. To have an enlightened and patriotic citizenship we must protect the wages and standard of living of those who constitute the bulk of the citizens" (Commons, 1903-1904:6, p. 535).

We acknowledged earlier that in the strict meaning of the word, Commons's position regarding the issue of immigration restriction can with some justification be labeled nativist. However, to do so distorts the real basis for Commons's advocacy of immigration restriction, for, as conventionally understood and employed, the term nativism denotes a subjective *irrational* prejudice against foreigners periodically exploding as "an emotionally charged impulse ... [arising] from no compelling social need" (Higham, 1975, pp. 103-105). In other words, as Higham has emphasized, use of the nativist framework typically casts the immigrant as a victim who actually poses no real threat to natives. After all, there was never really a papal conspiracy to take over the United States, yet, in part because of the belief in such a conspiracy, the Irish were subjected to social, political and economic discrimination which cost them municipal jobs and control of school boards, police forces and fire departments (Higham, 1975, pp. 109-110).

We feel strongly that a distinction should be made between actions based on nativism as conventionally understood and actions based on rational analysis that points to a clear threat to the class interest of the American worker. Class conflict does not arise from irrational myths but from the class structure of a society (Higham, 1975, p. 107). As our analysis makes clear, Commons did *not* seek to restrict immigration in order to limit the influx of inherently "defective" people (cf. Commons, 1903-1904:9, pp. 224-225). Rather, Commons endorsed immigration restriction based on rational analysis in response to a clear threat to the class interests of the American worker. Accordingly, while Commons was both "elitist" in outlook and avowedly a "working class exponent," and while his analysis of immigration may have been "convincing only to the already convinced" and "farfetched," "contradictory" and "overdrawn" (Aldrich, 1985, pp. 21-22), we conclude that his posture toward the immigrant was neither racist nor substantively nativist.

## III. COMMONS'S STANDPOINT TOWARD THE NEGRO

In his analysis of the racial thought of economists who were embroiled in the debate over immigration restriction in the early twentieth century, Robert Cherry categorized the participants as either "genetic racialists" or "environmentalists," with the former group emphasizing the role of heredity in constituting the traits determining whether a group was assimilable or not and the latter emphasizing cultural factors (Cherry, 1976, p. 153). Among American economists, according to Cherry, the "environmental position was the majority position" (Cherry, 1976, p. 158). Cherry averred, moreover, that the prototypal environmentalist, as evidenced by "the most influential work, ... *Races and Immigrants in America*," was John R. Commons (Cherry, 1976, p. 153). Cherry argued, and we obviously concur, that Commons and other Progressives like him urged the restriction of immigration for "economic reasons," that is, the tendency of immigration to lower the wages of native workers and to exacerbate the business cycle (Cherry, 1976, p. 155), not because of any threat it posed to the quality of the American racial stock. Although absolutely correct as far as it goes, Cherry's depiction of Commons as an environmentalist may lead the casual reader somewhat astray regarding Commons' race theory. It is clear that although Commons took an "environmentalist" stance on the origins of the putative trait deficiencies among immigrants, he at the same time took *with regard to the Negro* a biological determinist, if not, strictly speaking, a "genetic racialist," position, also clearly the "majority position" at the time of "Racial Composition."[52]

We now turn to the matter of assessing the character of Commons's racial views concerning the Negro. Specifically, we will attempt to determine where Commons's posture regarding the Negro fell along the spectrum of views expressed at the time he wrote "Racial Composition" and how his views related to contemporary "scientific" thinking regarding racial characteristics. It is to the exploration of these matters that we now turn.

### A. Commons's Views on the Negro in Context

In the 1903 edition of the *Encyclopedia Britannica*, reference is made to the "inherent mental inferiority" of the Negro, his "nonmoral rather than immoral" character, and the purported fact that he smells "like a buck goat" (Bloom, 1987, p. 45). *The Encyclopaedia* goes on to note that "no full-blood Negro has ever been distinguished as a man of science, poet or an artist, and the fundamental equality claimed for him by ignorant philanthropists is belied by the whole history of the race throughout the historic period" (Bloom, 1987, p. 45). There can be little doubt that Commons, along with most Progressives, if with varying degrees of evasiveness, accepted this set of "stylized facts." Within this general agreement, however, there were a number of distinctive policy agendas and the differences were not trivial. For example, one extreme advocated the exportation of Negroes back to Africa; the other proposed programs directed toward the uplift of the race and eventually the full economic, political and social integration and equality of Negroes. Joel Williamson (1986) has employed the terms radical, conservative, and liberal to distinguish the alternative standpoints being espoused at the turn of the century.

Radicals not only presumed the Negro to be inherently inferior but also maintained that the Negro had to be eliminated because after emancipation he had begun to regress toward his "savage nature"—as was manifest in his criminal activity and, most especially, in his supposed raping of white women. Amid allegations of such heinous crimes, radicals were not often impeded in their quest for justice by the Negro's constitutional right to due process. In fact, radicals were unapologetic in their advocacy of violence and intimidation to control the savage "Ethiop" in their midst. For example, James K. Vardaman, in the Mississippi gubernatorial campaign of 1900, allowed that he could justify the "slaughter of every Ethiop on earth to preserve the unsullied honor of a single caucasian home" (Gossett, 1963, p. 271). "Pitchfork" Ben Tillman, as Governor of South Carolina, proclaimed in 1900, "To hell with the Constitution if it stood in the way of mob justice to rapists" (Gossett, 1963, p. 271). Similarly, Rebecca Felton, a leader in the Temperance and the Women's Rights movements, did not flinch at a "thousand lynchings a week if necessary" (Williamson, 1986, p. 95). Given the impracticality of returning Negroes to Africa, radicals took some solace from the predictions of men like Frederick Hoffman (1896) and Joseph A. Tillinghast (1902) that the Negro race was doomed to extinction. Radical writers asserted that in the face of competition from whites, "the Negro race is vanishing before its superior. God's law of evolution, the survival of the fittest, the extinction of the unfit, is operating and will lead to a gradual whitening of the South" (Fredrickson, 1971, pp. 257-258). Not surprisingly, radicals considered education for the Negro not only a waste of resources but fundamentally a process which only made him a more efficient criminal (Storey, 1986, p. 95). Vardaman of Mississippi, to provide a case in point, claimed that Negroes were, by a factor of three, the most criminal element of the population and that the educated Negro was the most criminal of all (Aldrich, 1979, pp. 10-11).

The radical ideas that engulfed the South between 1889 and 1915 reflected more than a new rhetorical strategy by a few members of the elite strata of Southern society. Radicalism was a popular grass-roots phenomenon engendered by the "economic circumstances and cultural predispositions" of the South, especially those related to sexuality and gender (Fredrickson, 1988, pp. 176-177). Radicals were obsessed with the alleged hypersexuality of the free Negro male and the threat it presented to white women. The traditional Southern antagonism toward miscegenation, coupled with the proposition that "no self-respecting white women in the full possession of her sense .... would ever be so lost to shame and love or race pride as to unite herself in marriage to a Negro" (Newby, 1965, p. 130), elevated the causes of the sexual integrity of white women and white racial purity to the level of hysteria.

At the opposite end of the spectrum were the liberals, who desired integration and full civil rights for the Negro. Few in number (Williamson, 1986, pp. 77-78), liberals were a heterogenous group advocating a New South where class distinctions would replace the racial caste system (Fredrickson, 1971, p. 215; Degler, 1974, pp. 354-356). Among these liberals, one of the most notable, George Washington Cable, considered the Southern caste system to be "stupid wickedness" (Turner, 1956, p. 134). Pragmatically, Cable argued that the South could not industrialize effectively unless it allowed the Negro race to develop to its potential (Fredrickson, 1971, p. 225). Cable, like many Southerners with an aristocratic and elitist bent, particularly objected to the caste system's subjugation of the "genteel" Negro to lower class whites (Fredrickson, 1971, p. 227).

Cable did not doubt the present inferiority of the Negro but was at least open on the question of its permanence (Degler, 1974, p. 307). Indeed, liberals generally rejected "fine spun theories of racial differences" and blamed the "weaknesses and shortcomings" of the Negro people on "250 years of assiduous education in submission" and on slavery "having knocked out the brains of the race" (DuBois, 1901, p. 125). They argued that the Negro was capable of advancing but had been retarded because he was "left alone and unguided without capital, landless, without skill, without economic organization, without even the bald protection of law and order or decency" (DuBois, 1901, p. 126). Liberals were impressed with the educational gains the Negro had achieved under Northern leadership during Reconstruction. Indeed, they understood education to be the principal facilitator of Negro improvement. Generally speaking, liberals were optimistic about the prospects for further gains and were willing to experiment to find the best means of achieving the uplift of the Negro race (Williamson, 1986, pp. 70-75).

The liberals responded to the persistent Southern fear that integration would lead to miscegenation by emphasizing that amalgamation was not desired by either race. Tom Watson, a leader in the interracial populist movement, wrote in 1892 that "miscegenation is further off (Thank God) than ever ... [as] neither blacks nor whites have any relish for it" (quoted in Degler, 1974, p. 350). Both to quell the fears of the lower classes and to drive home the point of the necessity of racial accommodation, liberals like Watson discredited the notions that the number of mulattoes was rising due to growing miscegenation and that the

Negro race was dying out (Degler, 1974, p. 350). In the final analysis, the liberal argument that it was in the white interest to integrate blacks into the economy of the South, and what really mattered was class not race, fell for the most part on deaf ears both in the South and in the North; this was especially true in the case of lower-class whites who had no status except what white supremacy gave them (Degler, 1974, p. 354). As a result, liberals generally lost hope in the possibility of public policy designed to implement the liberal agenda and walked away from the responsibility of seeking solutions. What Cable, who was drummed out of the South, wrote about the end of Reconstruction no doubt characterized felicitously the attitudes of most "liberally" inclined Northerners at the turn of the century: "The popular mind in the old free states, weary of strife at arms length, bewildered by its complications, vexed by many a blunder, eager to turn to the cure of other evils, and even tinctured by that race feeling whose grossest excesses it would so gladly see suppressed, has retreated from its uncomfortable dictatorial attitude and thrown the whole matter over to the states of the South" (quoted in Grantham, 1955, p. 476).

Staking out a position between these two antipodes were the conservatives. Perhaps the clearest statement of the conservative mindset was developed at mid-century by a group of Southern pro-slavery intellectuals known as the "sacred circle." Included in this group were Edmund Ruffin, James Henry Hammond and William Gilmore Simms, all of whom were self-proclaimed "[men of] genius ... possessed of great truths" (Faust, 1986, p. 47). For these men the justification of slavery was "an evangelical act, a defense of morality and truth, a sacred duty" (Faust, 1986, p. 115).[53] Based on biblical revelation and "the essential principles of human association revealed in history," they constructed a world view based on several fundamental principles. First, was the proposition that the "natural society was inevitably hierarchical and provided for appropriate and orderly differentiations among men." Each person, in this view, is "to occupy his proper place. He, only, is the slave, who is forced into a position in society which is below the claim of his intellect and moral [character]." Second, it was presumed that within the naturally-hierarchical social organism, the essential relationship is paternalistic stewardship by "educated men" who are "independent in their circumstances" and who recognize the "community of interests" among various elements of the hierarchy. It was not the role of the social leadership to "make the butcher a judge, or the baker president, but to protect them, according to their claims as butcher and baker." It was also understood, finally, that the inherent racial inferiority of the Negro both warranted and legitimated benevolent white supervision. As Simms put it, "(r)egarding our slaves as a dependent and inferior people, we are their natural and only guardians." These "men of mind" saw the Negro as having been providentially provided to do the necessary menial work of society, that is, to be the "mudsill" class.

By the turn of the century, slavery had departed the conservative agenda, but in all other respects it retained the racist and elitist elements of the apologetics of slavery. Thus conservatives advocated absolute, if paternalistic, white supremacy and race purity, the complete segregation of Negroes, education for the Negro only that befits his place in society, and restrictions on the suffrage of lower-class whites. Significantly, it was the conservative standpoint which commanded by far the greatest acceptance within educated circles and, especially, by notables within the Progressive movement such as Ray Stannard Baker, Edgar Gardner Murphy, Theodore Roosevelt, and the historian U. B. Phillips. Each of these men, as did most Progressives, accepted uncritically the inherent inferiority of the Negro. Furthermore, each believed it was in the best interest of the Negro to accept segregation under the leadership of the "wisest and justest white men of the south" (Roosevelt, 1912, p. 911) in the name of race integrity and race progress (Fredrickson, 1971, p. 299).

For example, the Progressive journalist Ray Stannard Baker wrote that Jim Crow laws were the "inevitable scaffolding of progress." Not only had they prevented "clashes between the ignorant of both races," but by forcing Negroes together they engendered the development of a "spirit of self-reliance which would not have otherwise existed" (Baker, 1907b, p. 395). Edgar Murphy, an Episcopalian minister and a prominent proponent of the Social Gospel, similarly believed it essential that Negroes be segregated so that they might find the perfect communion with their inner nature and rise to a consciousness of their unique genius—their "volksgeist" (Williamson, 1986, p. 211). From a similar perspective, Roosevelt rejected the idea of trying to "dragoon the people of Georgia and Louisiana" into giving the Negro justice and proposed that "competent, high-minded white men," motivated by their "sense of honor and justice" and their "own awakened consciousness," should act voluntarily to give deserving "colored men" the "same chance" as their white neighbors (Roosevelt, 1912, p. 911). Lynching was perceived by many conservatives to be a "disgusting" necessity to control the savage "Ethiop" for which none were inclined to apologize.[54] Indeed, even though the more sophisticated conservatives were concerned that lynching undermined respect for law and order, they nevertheless often became apologists for the practice since they were unable to identify a viable alternative to achieve the commonly held goal (Fredrickson, 1988, p. 272). In short, though clearly appalled by lynching, peonage, and unequal enforcement of suffrage restrictions, Progressive racial conservatives were generally disinterested in finding legislative solutions to the plight of the Negro and looked instead to "points of light" in the South for the remedy.

For Phillips, the central theme of Southern history was the maintenance of white supremacy in a setting where Negroes provided the principal source of labor and were "numerous enough to create a problem of race control in the

interest of orderly government" (Phillips, 1928, p. 31). Since he considered the
Negro absolutely essential as a source of labor for the South, Phillips was vexed
by the radical program favoring the exportation of Negroes back to Africa.
To him, such a program was tantamount to cutting off the hands and feet
of the Southern social organism (Roper, 1984, p. 107). Phillips perceived the
Negro in terms of the old "Sambo" stereotype (Roper, 1984, p. 8)—a "loyal,
docile, deceitful, dissembling, childlike, lazy rascal" (Elkins, 1968, p. 82) with
some "imitative faculties" but so "ignorant and slothful" the plantation was
the only mode of economic organization capable of getting work out of him
(Phillips, 1904, p. 3). Phillips believed, accordingly, that the Negro could never
survive without the supervision and protection of the "better whites." Thus,
he favored a return to the antebellum plantation model using free Negro labor,
at fair wages, under benevolent white supervision (Phillips, 1904, p. 9).

Like other conservative Progressives, Phillips clearly assumed the Negro to
be morally and intellectually inferior to whites and therefore perennially
consigned to agricultural and mechanical pursuits. He believed that the Negro
should be educated for the purpose of raising his moral character, but shared
the commonly-held opinion that such education should be limited to "manual
training...[,] whether [the Negro] intends to become a mechanic or not"
(Newby, 1965, pp. 176-177). As Phillips put it, "Negroes are less in need of
a literary education than of practical knowledge and general wisdom ... [t]hey
need to become well-developed men and women and not half-baked scholars"
(cited in Newby, 1965, p. 177). Phillips also believed it was best for Negroes
to be segregated to minimize social contacts with "crackers" who usually robbed
the Negro of his dignity and often his life.

It almost goes without saying that the radical and conservative standpoints
overlapped to a considerable extent. Nonetheless, there were two matters on
which a clear difference existed. We will elaborate in the next section the debate
at the turn-of-the-century regarding the implications of Darwinian natural
selection for the future of the Negro race in American society. Following the
1890 census, which revealed the relatively slow growth of the Negro population
in the South, speculation on the future of the Negro race ran rampant
(Fredrickson, 1971, p. 247). As already indicated, radicals generally accepted
the "pessimistic" forecast that members of the Negro race could not survive
the Darwinian "competition of the races" and, hence, that extinction was likely.
Conservatives, on the other hand, more optimistically presumed that under
white leadership the Negro could continue to carry out the functions of the
"mudsill" class.

A related issue involved the controversial question of the alleged criminality
of the Negro. As noted, radicals understood a criminal propensity to be deeply
rooted in the Negro character. Men like Frederick Hoffman, the economic
demographer Walter Wilcox, and Wilcox's protege, Joseph A. Tillinghast,

presented the spectre of a Negro with criminal propensities that were substantively racial in origin. According to Wilcox, for example, the source of Negro criminality was his "weakened grip on white man's civilization" as he retrogressed following emancipation (Aldrich, 1979, p. 5). Conservatives, however, tended to attribute the allegations of high rates of Negro crime and rape to the "deep forces of interracial suspicion" rather than tracing them to an essential Negro trait (Fredrickson, 1971, p. 288). Like Phillips, most conservatives espoused the "Sambo" notion that the Negro was intrinsically docile, submissive, tractable, fundamentally harmless and unusually inclined to turn the other cheek (Fredrickson, 1971, p. 289; Mayo-Smith, 1890, p. 65). Thus they emphasized that it was only the ignorance of the Negro that made him a menace. In their view, the Negro was not only docile but, as we have recounted, teachable, and it was the responsibility of whites to train the Negro to do productive work.

At the core of the conservative standpoint, then, was the philosophy manifest in Phillips's notion of conservative progress, which espoused neither the extinction nor the integration of the Negro but "a modified form of the old plantation system" where the "best elements of Southern whites" will give the Negro "much needed guidance ... enabling them to use their imitative faculties" to "make further progress in acquiring the white man's civilization" (Phillips, 1904, p. 8). Of course, because the core of conservatives was made up of intellectuals like Phillips, and because the South was a "profoundly anti-intellectual society" (Fredrickson, 1971, p. 297), the conservative image of the future was of limited efficacy in shaping public views in the South during the 1890-1915 period of radical predominance.

Obviously, this brief overview of salient differences evident in the views espoused by educated men around the turn of the century is neither exhaustive nor definitive. Still, it should suffice for the purpose at hand of situating Commons within his own milieu. Given his previously revealed "habitual assumptions" and his manifest environmentalism in the case of immigrants, one might think that Commons would have been predisposed to the liberal "environmental" characterization of the origins of the Negro's plight. One also would expect Commons to have supported the liberal education agenda and to have challenged the systematic denial of the Negro's civil rights. And, as we have shown, Commons did offer lip service to the "liberal" notions of fair treatment of Negroes and Negro improvement, including protection of the franchise for "qualified" Negroes. Moreover, he not only voiced support for the vocational education programs offered by Booker T. Washington but also the "liberal" demand of W. E. B. DuBois for liberal arts education directed towards producing leaders—albeit in Commons's mind they would be mulattoes—for the black race. Indeed, in his seeming endorsement of amalgamation of the Negro and white races—implicitly the only ray of hope he offered, "Amalgamation is their door to assimilation" (Commons, 1903-1904:9, p. 222)—he clearly went beyond what most liberals would have been willing to recommend.[55]

We suspect, however, that there is probably less to the seemingly-"liberal" nature of Commons' standpoint regarding the Negro than a first impression suggests. First, we believe that Commons's ostensible approval of amalgamation as a goal was somewhat disinguous. As Commons himself had earlier pointed out amalgamation, the only flicker of hope he offered regarding any improvement in the situation of the Negro, takes centuries even under the most facilitating social circumstances.[56] In truth, Commons appears to have had no real expectation that the Negro would *ever* "share in our democratic opportunities" (cf. Commons, 1903-1904:1, p. 87). Instead, he expected that race relations in the American South, where some 90 percent of Negroes still resided at the time he wrote (Jones, 1985, p. 80) would inexorably degenerate into a caste system similar to that of India: "We can see today," he declared, "the very historical steps by which in the forgotten centuries India proceeded to her system of rigid castes" (Commons, 1903-1904:1, p. 86).[57]

Additional considerations also support this interpretation of Commons's views regarding the potential benefits for the Negro ensuing from amalgamation. For example, in his discussion of amalgamation in the inital installment of the "Racial Composition" series, Commons asserted that even the "ten or more subdivisions" of the Aryan race are "so far removed by nature from one another as to render successful amalgamation an open question" (Commons, 1903-1904:1, p. 37). But if amalgamation is an open question for subsets of Aryans, how could Commons have truly believed it could proceed successfully when the separation of Negroes from Aryans by "continents, by climate, by color, and by institutions is the most diametrical that mankind exhibits anywhere" (Commons, 1903-1904:1, p. 39).[58] Certainly, the conventional scientific wisdom at the turn of the century considered the white-Negro amalgam an evolutionary dead-end (Gossett, 1963, p. 282); among Negroes even, amalgamation was considered "self-stultification with a vengeance" and was not advocated by anyone (Miller, 1908, p. 47). In fact, it was widely believed, with the support of some "scientific" evidence, that miscegenation led to a being that was inferior to both the black and the white progenitor—the mulatto supposedly had a lesser intellectual capacity than the white progenitor and a weaker physical constitution than the Negro progenitor. In this view, then, the consequences of miscegenation were understood to include a decline in the quality of the "American" race. E. A. Ross, for example, characterized the outcome of amalgamation as the "ball and chain of hybridism" (Ross, 1901, p. 85). It was also believed by many that mulattoes were either sterile—mulatto is derived from the word *mule* (Poliakov, 1974,

p. 135)—or had offspring who were weak and less likely to procreate. Although he nowhere addressed them directly in "Racial Composition," these views were well known to Commons as they were put forth in at least two publications which he cited.[59]

Second, we question whether Commons believed that education could in fact serve as an "uplift" agency for the Negro. A passage we incorporated into the earlier discussion, taken from the selection on "Race and Democracy," hardly suggests that he did:

> ... [M]ore than the present generation did [our forefathers] regard with hopefulness the educational value of democracy. "True enough," they said, "the black man is not equal to the white man, but once free him from his legal bonds, open up the schools, the professions, the businesses, and the offices to those of his number who are most aspiring, and you will find that, as a race, he will advance favorably in comparison with his white fellow citizens." It is now more than thirty years since these opportunities and educational advantages were given to the negro, not only on equal terms but actually on terms of preference over the whites, and the fearful collapse of the experiment is recognized even by its partisans as something that was inevitable in the nature of the race at that stage of its development (Commons, 1903-1904:1, p. 34).

Moreover, despite his passing endorsement of DuBois's education program, Commons's position on the nature of appropriate education for the Negro paralleled the position taken by Phillips and other conservatives. Particularly interesting are Commons's assertions that the "foundation of intelligence for the modern working man is his understanding of mechanics" (Commons, 1903-1904:3, p. 227) and his finding that the Negro, in general, is "lacking 'the mechanical idea'" and "the simplest mechanical principles, such as that of the lever" (Commons, 1903-1904:3, p. 226).

The origins of this notion are most revealing. Commons lifted this concept, without citation, out of Tillinghast (1902) who had in turn lifted it, with citation, from a Mary Kingsley who had published two books in the late 1890s about Africa. Miss Kingsley wrote that:

> The great inferiority of the African to the European lies in the matter of the mechanical idea.... The African's own way of doing anything mechanical is the simplest way, not the easiest, certainly not the quickest.... [The African] has no idea of a lever, or anything of that sort, and remember that, unless under white direction, the African has never made an even fourteenth-rate piece of cloth or pottery (quoted in Tillinghast, 1902, p. 574).

Most significant is that Kingsley had focused this discussion toward a critique of the missionary educational system in Africa which was teaching Africans how to read and write in order to turn them into clerks that, she argued, Africa did not need: "What Africa wants at present, as it will want for at least the next 200 years," she complained, is not clerks but "workers, planters, plantation hands, miners and seamen" (Tillinghast, 1902, p. 575).

Given her assessment, Miss Kingsley would no doubt have concurred with Phillips, other conservatives, *and* Commons on the importance of institutions like Tuskegee and Hampton with their "emphasis on manual training" (Commons, 1903-1904:3, p. 228). It is also worthy of mention that Commons shared Kingsley's views on the salutary effects of white supervision on Negro productivity. The census of 1890 revealed that extraordinary cotton crops were being produced by the Negroes in the "alluvial districts of Mississippi and Arkansas." Commons was quick to point out that one should not infer from this that "Negroes are better farmers than whites," for, he continued, it is clear that the superior productivity of Negroes in these areas is actually attributable to the quality of the land and "the close supervision [of the Negro farmer by] a white landlord or creditor" (Commons, 1903-1904:3, p. 230).

We would submit, thirdly, that Commons's "liberal" position on the question of Negro suffrage also is more apparent than real. The conservative social philosophy, though imbued with racism, was basically aristocratic and equally infused with class antagonism (Bloom, 1987, pp. 48-49; Roark, 1977, pp. 17-24). As a consequence, conservatives were as willing to recognize the accomplishments of the "better Negroes" as they were to disparage lower class whites. That is, while they were quite ready to allow the "better" Negro to vote they were also intent on excluding "unqualified" whites. Commons's apparently liberal stand on the issue of Negro suffrage, we believe, was at heart as much a conservative, aristocratic position aimed at limiting the suffrage of lower class whites as a liberal one aimed at helping the Negro toward full citizenship. In any case, Commons also revealed a fundamentally racist attitude in his discussion of Negro suffrage. As noted, Commons argued that the descent rule which arbitrarily defined a person with a single drop of black blood as Negro was foolish, because in the "veins of the mulatto flows the blood of the white aristocracy." Clearly, for Commons, the more "aristocratic" *white blood* in his veins, the better the Negro.

Other views of Commons's were more clearly inconsistent with the liberal standpoint. For example, Commons seemed to accept the cost of "despotizing" democratic institutions, even to the point of using violence and intimidation in order to accomplish disfranchisement of the Negro and to maintain segregation in the South. To illustrate, in his selection on "City Life, Crime and Poverty," Commons made it clear that he understood in particular the role of lynching, pogroms, and other forms of violence to maintain white control over the Negro (cf. Commons, 1903-1904:8, p. 121). Indeed, he had already acknowledged as much in his earlier selection on "The Negro": "It is not necessary to dwell upon the methods by which the whites regained and kept control of the states. Admittedly, it was through intimidation, murder, ballot-box 'stuffing' and false counting" (Commons, 1903-1904:3, p. 225). Even though one can be sure Commons found such practices "disgusting," he did not apologize (cf. Commons, 1903-1904:8, p. 121). In fact, while granting that such violence "has blackened the face of the nation," Commons, more or less "blaming the victim," opined that it was, unfortunately, "one of the penalties paid for experimenting on a problem of political and economic equality with material marked by extreme racial inequality" (Commons, 1903-1904:8, p. 122).

Other elements of Commons's analysis, especially his thoughts pertaining to the future of the Negro race and his stereotypical pejorative characterizations of the Negro's current behavior, seem to us to be rooted in the distinctively pessimistic mindset characteristic of radicals. For example, while Commons allowed that high rates of Negro mortality were in part due to "social conditions," he also declared that part was related to "race traits," in particular to deficiencies in the "moral character" of the Negro that foster "sexual immorality and debauchery" (cf. Commons, 1903-1904:3, pp. 232-233). Such remarks strongly suggest that Commons was in some sympathy with the views expressed by Frederic Hoffman, the noted statistician and social Darwinist, in *Race Traits and Tendencies of the American Negro* (1896).[60] In this work, Hoffman asserted that the high rates of Negro mortality he reported were the result of the lax moral standards of the Negro race and would eventually lead to its extinction. Indeed, according to Hoffman, high Negro mortality was caused not "by the conditions of life" but by the "race traits and tendencies" of the Negro which are manifest in "an immense amount of immorality" (Hoffman, 1896, p. 95). Thus, in Hoffman's eyes, the situation of the Negro was "hopeless" (Hoffman, 1896, p. 1). Hoffman's position was taken seriously by many, including several major insurance companies which, following Hoffman's pessimistic prognosis, refused to sell life insurance to Negroes (Roper, 1984, p. 108).

It seems to us that the radical perspective is also manifest in Commons's analysis of "Crime, City Life and Poverty," wherein he discussed the "startling preeminence of the Negro in the ranks of criminals" (Commons, 1903-1904:8, p. 119). Upon a quick glance it might be concluded that Commons attributed this "startling preeminence" to the high rate of urbanization of Negroes and the "degenerating effects of city life"—an explanation he applied to other races. However, a closer look reveals that Commons was using urbanization only to explain the higher rates of Negro crime in the urban North than in the rural South, emphasizing that even within the South itself the Negro is more crime prone than others, particularly so in the case of "public intoxication," the "extreme prevalence" of which "indicates that the race in question is not overcoming *the degenerating effects of competition* and city life" (Commons, 1903-1904:8, p. 120, emphasis added). It was fortunately the case, Commons added, that Negroes live mostly in Prohibition counties, for "were it not for the paternal restrictions imposed by such laws the downward course of the Negro race would doubtless have outrun considerably the speed it has actually attained" (Commons, 1903-1904:8, p. 120).

The phrase Commons employed in his analysis of the Negro's criminal tendencies, "the degenerating effects of competition," would perhaps appear to suggest "destructive competition" as employed by Commons in the context of labor market problems. However, we do not advance such an interpretation. To comprehend fully the meaning of these words they must be put in context. It is important to note that the alleged criminality of the Negro was a very controversial question. Many prominent conservatives such as Richmond Mayo-Smith, Nathaniel Shaler and Edgar Gardner tended to attribute the allegations of high rates of Negro crime and rape to the "deep forces of interracial suspicion" rather than the essential Negro character (Fredrickson, 1971, p. 288). These men instead proffered the notion that the Negro was fundamentally docile, submissive, tractable, and thus essentially harmless and generally prone, like good Christians, to turn the other cheek (Fredrickson, 1971, p. 289; Mayo-Smith, 1890, p. 65). The paternalistic conservatives emphasized that it was only the ignorance of the Negro that made him a menace. They considered the Negro to be teachable and argued that it was necessary, and indeed the responsibility of whites, to train the Negro to do productive work (Fredrickson, 1971, p. 296).

Commons appears to have rejected this conservative interpretation of Negro criminality and to have been influenced instead by men like the very prominent economic demographer, Walter Wilcox, and his protege, Joseph A. Tillinghast. These men presented the specter of a Negro race with criminal propensities that were substantively racial in origin. According to Wilcox, the source of Negro criminality was his "weakened grip on white man's civilization" as he *retrogressed* following emancipation (Aldrich, 1979, p. 5). As freedman, he argued, the Negro lacked "those habits of obedience, industry, self-restraint and sexual morality" necessary to be a good citizen and to be competitive with whites in agriculture and industry (Aldrich, 1979, p. 5). Following the 1890 census, which revealed the relatively slow growth of the Negro population in the South, speculation on the impending Darwinian extinction of the Negro race ran rampant (Fredrickson, 1971, p. 247). Francis Amasa Walker even asserted that blacks would become concentrated in the tropical areas of the South because they could not survive elsewhere (Fredrickson, 1971, p. 243).

In this context, given that his characterization of the Negro's inherent tendencies closely paralleled the views of men like Tillinghast, it seems highly likely to us that Commons also believed that the Negro race was, under the pressure of competition from whites, on its way to extinction.[61] Moreover, although he mentions the degenerative effects of city life and discriminatory arrest patterns (Commons, 1903-1904:8, p. 120), repeated readings of the related discussion convince us that Commons accepted the view that crimes also "spring from racial tendencies" (cf. Commons, 1903-1904:8, p. 120). We believe that with respect to the issue of criminality, Commons was much closer to the radical than to the conservative position.

In summary, while it is clear that Commons showed no genuine enthusiasm for the "liberal" standpoint, it is apparent that his views regarding the future place of the Negro within American society cannot be neatly characterized as either consistently "radical" or "conservative" with respect to the turn-of-the-century standpoints toward the "Negro Problem." Nonetheless, while fully cognizant that there are inconsistencies and ambiguities we have not completely laid to rest, we believe the term "conservative" best characterizes the general tenor of the analysis Commons forwarded on this issue in "Racial Composition."[62] This is probably not surprising, since most Progressives were in the conservative camp (Grantham, 1955, pp. 461-462), and surely, for reasons we will elaborate below, it was Progressives, already equipped with attitudes predisposed to a general line of argument, whom Commons sought to "inform" by writing "Racial Composition" with its clear "subtext." Still, "Racial Composition" was intended to be more than an appeal to prejudice and to provide a "learned" and hence "detached" overview of the challenges of assimilating or "Americanizing" *presently*-deficient "races." As a result, it was incumbent upon Commons, if possible, to root his antithetical posture toward immigrant "races" versus the Negro "race" in "scientific" arguments. We turn next, therefore, to the issue of how Commons's own racial analysis reflected then-current scientific thinking.

### B.   Commons's Use of Racial Theories

Despite the equivocation that he utilized race as a "loose and elastic" concept, Commons seems to have had a very specific framework for thinking about race when it came to the Negro. Taking note of the lengthy quotation from Commons at the beginning of this article, it is clear that he considered geography to be the true source of the Negro characteristics included in his stereotype. It is also evident that Commons believed heredity to be a major factor influencing the likelihood of assimilation. But beyond these facts, if Commons had a coherent theory of the origin of racial differences in the capacity for assimilation, he never made it explicit. It may prove illuminating nevertheless to explore how his argument reflected contemporary theories regarding the source and possible modification of racial differences.

Historically, most American racists, with the notable exceptions of Josiah Nott and Louis Agassiz, abstained from any direct assertion on the origin of the different races because they did not wish to become embroiled in the polygenist heresy. Most race theorists were able to finesse this issue by asserting that whether the races were the result of a single or multiple, separate, creation was really irrelevant. Even if all races did stem from the same parents, Adam and Eve, they have lived for so long in different environments that they are now as dissimilar as if they had been created separately. Such race thinking was rooted in a long tradition of geographical determinism.

The geographical determinist notion that differences in climate are the source of somatic and temperament differences in people, which was widely accepted by educated men in the eighteenth and nineteenth centuries, can be traced back to Hippocrates and Aristotle (Gossett, 1963, p. 6). This hypothesis was revived in 1749 by George Louis Buffon in his *Historie Naturelle*, in which he attributed race differences to a process of "degeneration" according to the "influence of the climate, from the differences in food, and the mode of living" (quoted in Greene, 1954, p. 33). A similar theme was sounded late in the eighteen century by Johann-Gottfried Van Herder, a man of letters and leader, with Goethe and Schiller, of the German Romantic Movement (Poliakov, 1974, p. 102) who was annoyed at the antipathy directed at the Negro and suggested the Negro instead be pitied for his lack of intelligence; in exchange for intellect, Van Herder argued, nature has given the Negro a climate which allows him to "spend his life void of care in a country which yields him food with unbounded liberality" (Poliakov, 1974, p. 174). The environmental hypothesis appeared again a century or so later in the work of Ellen Semple, a student of German anthropo-geographer Frederick Ratzel. Semple considered non-Europeans to be inferior races, and she avouched that the superior Anglo-Saxon monopoly on "energy, initiative, adaptability, and receptivity to new ideas" was due to the rigors and vagaries of the northern climate (Newby, 1965, p. 26).[63] By the turn of the century, the environmental hypothesis had become so accepted that it was taken for granted (Newby, 1965, p. 29).[64]

But even as geographical determinism was accepted uncritically, the process through which the effects of geography and climate become inherited traits of a race was vigorously debated. Early in the nineteenth century, Jean Baptiste Lamarck rejected the notion that the environment worked directly on the form of an organism. Instead, Lamarck asserted, an organism would be altered by the environment only to the extent that the environment altered the "habits of use and disuse" of faculties (Eiseley, 1961, p. 50). Newly acquired traits, Lamarck further asserted, are passed on through inheritance. Darwin's theory of natural selection, on the other hand, stressed environmental selection, through the struggle for existence, of beneficial variations from among random biological mutations in the form of an organism (Eiseley, 1961, pp. 53, 305).[65]

As the true nature of inheritance was not understood until well into the twentieth century, the inherent incompatibility between Darwinian natural selection and Lamarckism was not generally perceived by turn-of-the-century thinkers. In fact, few doubted that both forces were at work, and many included elements of both in their race analyses (Stocking, 1968, p. 254).[66] At issue was only the relative importance of each. What was widely perceived to differentiate the self-consciously "Darwinian" from the "Lamarckian" view, in other words, was the time it would take for environmental and social conditions to change race characteristics—the heart of the assimilation issue Commons was attempting to address in "Racial Composition." In the Lamarckian world, since each generation passes on acquired characteristics to the next through biological inheritance, it was understood to be only a matter of a few generations before socially acquired characteristics would become prevalent in a "race." However, if the inherent characteristics of a race—for example, the Negro's putative propensity for criminal behavior—are shaped solely by the forces of natural selection, it would be eons before life in a democratic environment could elevate that race to the point where its members would be worthy of full participation.[67]

But while Lamarckism still had numerous adherents at the turn of the century, especially in Progressive circles, they were unquestionably on the defensive. Despite a spirited counterattack from an American group of neo-Lamarckians led by the University of Pennsylvania paleontologist Edward Cope, who accepted Darwin's law of natural selection but considered it secondary to the effects of the environment which are passed on through inheritance,[68] Lamarckism was collapsing under the assault of German scientists armed with the recently rediscovered works of Gregor Mendel (Stocking, 1968, p. 283). Social reformers understood perfectly well what was at stake and only gradually and reluctantly gave up their Lamarckian standpoint (Stocking, 1968, pp. 253-254). Yet by approximately 1910, the Darwinist victory was complete. Thus, in 1912. Simon Patten was able to assert confidently: "[He] who thinks his efforts to help individuals are of social importance suffers from the downfall of Lamarckism" (Stocking, 1968, p. 255).

Commons, of course, wrote "Racial Composition" well before this debate had run its course, as did others who put forth racial views around the turn of the century, including figures such as J. A. Tillinghast and Nathaniel Shaler, whom Commons used as authorities in developing his analysis, and E. A. Ross, whose published views in most important respects parallel Commons's.[69] And, like Commons, these writers were far from consistent in the views they expressed.

Tillinghast, for example, proffered an eclectic view of evolution combining the Darwinian concept of natural selection with the geographical determinist view.[70] In a book published by the American Economic Association in 1902, he wrote that heredity changes in "slow and infinitesimal degree" as "modified through selection, which tends to accumulate advantageous variation in offspring and eliminate unfavorable ones" (Tillinghast, 1902, p. 408). But, Tillinghast went on, the effects of heredity are complemented by the effects of the physical environment, "which constitute a large proportion of the influences that mould human progress" (Tillinghast, 1902, p. 577).

Regarding the Negro in particular, Tillinghast noted that "The natives of west Africa live under conditions adverse to the growth of industrial efficiency; indeed few regions are so hostile to such development. Their physical environment deprives them of many motives to labor.... So abundant is nature's provision of food and other wants, that with little effort they obtain what is needed" (Tillinghast, 1902, p. 434). But even though the Negro character has been "moulded for ages in an undisturbed environment" (Tillinghast, 1902, p. 408), Tillinghast continued in the hopeful tone characteristic of environmentalists, "[o]ur climate ... has helped steadily to stimulate tropical indolence into northern activity, and the constant influence of a civilized model has tended to substitute American civilization for African barbarism" (Tillinghast, 1902, p. 576). By the time he reached the end of his manuscript, however, Tillinghast had apparently abandoned environmentalism and optimism. For now emphasizing that the Negro is "unsteady at labor and impatient of restraint" (Tillinghast, 1902, p. 632), he made clear his doubt that the "science of education" would be able to overcome the "powerful conservatism of heredity" (cf. Tillinghast, 1902, p. 634). He further insisted— and this must have fueled many a radical fire!—that not only is the Negro unable to progress further but, free from the paternal bonds of slavery and under the pressure from "able, strenuous and rapidly progressing competitors" (Tillinghast, 1902, p. 634), he is tending to "revert" (Tillinghast, 1902, p. 632) as manifest in "increasing looseness and instability" in family relations and growing criminality (Tillinghast, 1902, p. 632). We have already summarized how Commons in "Crime, City Life and Poverty" took essentially the same tack in drawing attention to the "startling preeminence of the Negro in the rank of criminals."

A perspective similar to Tillinghast's was put forth by the Harvard naturalist, Nathaniel Shaler.[71] Shaler subscribed to the modern Darwinian theory but simultaneously held on to Lamarckism.[72] Believing that each race had acquired its permanent race characteristics long ago in the geographic environment of its "cradle-land," he contended that only the Teuton had the sociobiological capacity to prosper in the environment of America (Shaler, 1890, p. 137). According to Schaler, the Aryan race developed its outstanding capacities, not in Asia as traditionally believed, but on the shores of the Baltic Sea where the winters are severe and life is a constant struggle with the long enduring cold (Shaler, 1890, p. 135). In a paragraph that epitomizes the theory of race formation that Commons presents in Racial Composition, Shaler asserted:

> In such conditions, as long as food and fuel is abundant the human body attains its greatest vigor, size, and longevity, and the mental powers are at their best; thence southward it may retain these qualities as long as the winter season brings a moderate degree of frost. When we pass into the tropics, though the frame may with certain races exhibit a moderate development, it can not endure hardships as well as where it is bred in contact with an

earth that is snow-clad, and here the mental powers appear always to be be enfeebled (Shaler, 1890, p. 136).

The Negro, in other words, had never developed the "assemblage of physical and mental motives" necessary "to survive in a temperate climate and in a democracy." Indeed, Shaler believed that the cradle-land experience of the Negro had produced a being without any significant intellectual capacity (Shaler, 1890, p.143). Moreover, according to Shaler, since the Negro race had for so long lived in a uniform climate, its present members were psychologically and physiologically resistant to change. As a result, he contended, Negroes were incapable of developing the "habits and traditions" necessary for participation in democracy. Whereas one might expect this presumption to foreshadow an argument that the Negro neither has nor can acquire the racial capacity to fully participate in democracy, Shaler insisted instead that the South was obliged to develop "a system of education that may serve to develop the saving qualities of the race." Otherwise, he predicted, the South "would lapse into barbarism" since, independent of white control under slavery, "Negro communities seldom retained those principles necessary for civilization" (Haller, 1971, pp. 175-176).[73]

A fundamentally different posture was articulated by E. A. Ross, Commons's fellow graduate student at Johns Hopkins and subsequently his colleague at Wisconsin, who late in life admitted that he had felt little sympathy for Negroes (Gossett, 1963, p. 271). Ross granted that where there is no struggle for existence, as in Africa where food was understood to have been supplied in abundance by nature and where people thus "lived from hand to mouth taking no thought of the morrow[,] ... energy, thrift, industry and self-reliance" had failed to develop (Ross, 1901, p. 75). But in seeming opposition to Darwinism, he proclaimed race to be "the watchword of the vulgar" and expressed particular disdain for Darwinists because they "exaggerate the race factor" (Ross, 1901, p. 67). Without making clear upon what grounds he could make such an argument,[74] Ross further contended that social and environmental conditions were paramount as evident especially in the "tonic selections of the frontier" and the "individualizing struggle with the wilderness" that developed "the American body, brain and character" (Ross, 1901, p. 89). Clearly, Commons's analysis of the immigrant's capacity for assimilation suggests that he shared fully Ross's evaluation of those who advocated immigration restrictions on "Darwinist" grounds. We have similarly seen that Commons shared Ross's perspective on frontier life, at least in so far as the "non-tropical" races were concerned, as reflected in his emphatic statement in "Racial Composition" that "in the earlier days the most powerful agency of assimilation was frontier life" (Commons, 1903-1904:9, p. 222).

As these summaries of various views make clear, the theory of inheritance once embraced made no difference with respect to the conclusion reached concerning the Negro's inherent inability to adapt to new conditions. It is absolutely remarkable that Commons, Tillinghast, Cope, Shaler, and Ross could approach the Negro problem from such different perspectives yet reach essentially the same conclusion. It seems that all race theorists, even as they struggled to maintain environmental causation, forwarded theories that were sufficiently "loose and elastic" to find in the case of the Negro that environmental factors are inconsequential.

Indeed, what is truly remarkable about the situation at the turn of the century is the consistency with which racists who in their general systems explicitly or implicitly advocated what is clearly Lamarckian environmentalism elevated the role of natural selection and diminished the role of environment when it came to the case of the Negro and often also the non-nordic immigrant. That is, Lamarckian environmentalists generally included a loophole in the general laws of race development which made the Negro, to modify John Haller's (1971) phrase, an outcast from Lamarckian evolution. For example, even though they were self-professed Lamarckians, Shaler and Cope both nevertheless considered non-nordics and Negroes to be irrevocably inferior. Cope referred to immigrants as "dead material in the very center of our vital organism" (Haller, 1971, p. 200) and advocated immigration restriction. Considering the Negro to have been "side-tracked" from the path of "progressive alterations" and consequently "left behind" (Haller, 1971, p. 199), Cope advocated exportation of Negroes back to Africa or to the Philippines (Haller, 1971, p. 201). Similarly, Shaler considered Negroes to be "nimble-witted" and to have lost the capacity to profit from environmental development (Haller, 1971, p. 172). He also advocated immigration restriction because Catholicism had permanently damaged the peasant stock of Europe (Haller, 1971, p. 173).

What the foregoing makes equally evident is that Commons had a wide range of theoretically dissimilar views expressed by academics upon which he could have drawn in formulating his core argument with respect to heredity and the challenges of assimilating immigrants into the "American" race. What, then, was the scientific standpoint revealed in the analysis Commons forwarded in the "Racial Composition" series? Was he a Darwinist, a Lamarckian, or simply an old-fashioned pre-Darwinian geographical determinist who was scientifically no more sophisticated than antebellum apologists for slavery? Before attempting that determination, we believe it necessary to consider briefly an earlier paper Commons wrote while still at Syracuse University, "Natural Selection, Social Selection and Heredity" (Commons, 1897).

The central point made by Commons in this brief article was that "degeneracy" (insanity, criminality, prostitution, pauperism, intemperance, and so on) was not fundamentally related to the phenomenon of intra-racial variation as incorporated into Darwin's theory of natural selection. Commons argued that with the evolution of individual self-consciousness and the advent of private property, institutionalized modes of character formation—"education" in the broad meaning of the word—became the principal mechanism through which further modifications of individual character were passed to succeeding generations. As he put it himself:

> In natural selection there is a physical environment which presses upon individuals and only those who survive are fitted to sustain this pressure. In social selection society enters between the individual and the physical environment, and, while *slowly subordinating the latter* transforms its pressure upon the individual, and he alone survives who is fitted to bear the social pressure. This pressure reaches the individual through the educational media of language and social institutions, especially the family, the state and property.... Personality is the final outcome of social selection. When once liberated it becomes a new selective principle to which all others are subordinated (Commons, 1897, pp. 90-91, emphasis added).

In short, Commons argued, "social selection" had long ago replaced "natural selection" as the fundamental explanation for the evolution of "personality" attributes.[75] Having established that point, Commons went on to attack social theories emphasizing biological heredity because they tended to charge "evils" to heredity rather than social injustice (Commons, 1897, p. 96). In so doing, of course, he was siding with the other Progressives who disdained Social Darwinism with its emphasis on natural selection and its laissez faire implications; for example, we have already seen that Ross took exactly this tack. Although he did not know it at the time, Commons was also laying the foundation for the argument he was to formulate about immigrant assimilation in "Racial Composition."

It is important to grasp that in "Natural Selection" Commons nowhere rejected the view that Darwinian natural selection or biological heredity is irrelevant to human personality or physical and mental capabilities. Neither was he rejecting the view that within a "race" there naturally occurs variation in the traits related to personality or capabilities. What Commons was trying to establish, in our judgment, was that the physical environment's dominant role in guiding the process of selection among the traits related to human character, that is, "personality," had ended eons ago. Or, to put it slightly differently, Commons was making essentially the same argument as Shaler by asserting that the traits established through Darwinian natural selection and passed on through *biological* heredity were fixed long ago.

Now, given that it was Shaler whose theory Commons agreed with in discounting the applicability of Darwinian natural selection to the ongoing process of human evolution, did Commons reveal simultaneously an affinity for the Lamarckian interpretation of biological heredity? At least one aspect of his analysis in "Natural Selection" would seem to suggest that he did. In advocating "segregation of degenerates to prevent propagation" (Commons,

1897, p. 96). Commons differentiated between "degenerates" who were "congenital" (afflicted via biological heredity) and those who were the product of "social injustice and degraded education," that is, those whose degenerate traits were acquired. Commons clearly was worried that this second group would pass its degeneracy on to the next generation (cf. Commons, 1897, pp. 96-97), which strongly suggests an acceptance of Lamarckian logic.

However, despite arguably seeming to do so, we believe Commons did *not* incorporate Lamarckian reasoning into his analysis. A more reasonable interpretation, in our view, is implicit in the question posed immediately after the lengthy passage quoted two paragraphs above: "What, then, are the social conditions which promote or retard the survival of personality [or moral character]?" In what preceded this question, as indicated in that quoted passage, Commons made clear his belief that it is a matter of proper "education," that is, of proper social experiences.[76] Clearly, the failure to maintain the "personality" which has evolved through the process of social selection, which is what Commons meant by *non*congenital "degredation," is a matter of the individual being subject to improper "education." Given that family life is a major consituent of one's "education" (social experiences), one would clearly anticipate from the perspective embraced by Commons that the offspring of a "degenerate" generally would be exposed to a similar "education" as the parent and hence develop the same "degeneracy." By this line of reasoning, "social selection," not biological heredity, accounts for the intergenerational reproduction of "degenerate" traits among biologically related individuals. Since, as we have made explicit, Commons could easily have reached his conclusion regarding the intergenerational transfer of "degeneration" upon grounds he made explicit in "Natural Selection," in our view there is no basis for imputing to him an unstated affinity for Lamarckism.

Despite the use in "Racial Composition" of the conventional Lamarckian phrase, "use and disuse of faculties" to describe adaptation,[77] Commons' core argument in "Racial Composition" accords with our judgment that he was not a Lamarckian. Even more revealing is Commons's recognition, which he made explicit in his discussion of "Additional Reading" sources on the final page of "Colonial Race Elements," that the views of Lester Ward, a Lamarckian, had been "rejected" by August Weismann in the latter's seminal article on the "germ plasm," published in 1893 (Commons, 1903-1904:2, p. 125).[78] But, of course, there is one major difference between the earlier and the later works, namely, in "Natural Selection" Commons does not address the issue of whether his "social selection" theory applies to the Negro also. It is in "Racial Composition" that he explains, *again on Darwinian grounds*, why it does not.

The core of Commons's argument in this latter work, in so far as the present matter is concerned, can be summarized as follows. Eons ago, existence in a given geographical setting fixed certain capacities through the slow process of

Darwinian natural selection. Those capacities have to a considerable extent been mixed into the biological constitution of various races in consequence of extensive amalgamation between members of non-tropical races (cf. Commons, 1903-1904:1, p. 39).[79] Thus, the basic capacities, which have been more or less unchanged through recorded history, are now part of the biological inheritance of all non-tropical immigrant races. Northern European races, with the "Scotch-Irish race" foremost among them, developed *within* those biologically-limited capacities a higher personality through the process of ("post-Darwinian"?) social selection. Since they have the same biological capacities as the "Scotch-Irish race," members of non-tropical "races" with less evolved "personalities" nonetheless have the capability, when presented with the appropriate "education" (social environment), to leapfrog to that higher personality:

> A superior race may have a primitive or medieval civilization, and therefore its individuals may never have exhibited the superior mental qualities with which they are actually endowed and which a modern civilization would have called into action. The adults coming from such a civilization seem to be inferior in their mental qualities, but their children, placed in the new environments of the advanced civilization, exhibit at once the qualities of the latter.... It is civilization, not race evolution, that has transformed the primitive warrior into the philosopher, scientist, artisan and business man. Could their babies have been taken from the woods two thousand years ago and transported to the homes and schools of modern America, they could have covered in one generation the progress of twenty centuries (Commons, 1903-1904:9, p. 221).

Unfortunately, this is not the case for the Negro: "The children of all the races of the temperate zones are eligible to the highest civilization, and it only needs that they be 'caught' young enough. This much cannot be said for the children of the tropical zone" (Commons, 1903-1904:9, p. 222). For, having evolved eons ago within the *tropical* zone, the Negro did *not* develop via natural selection the *biological* foundation necessary to leapfrog the process of social selection through which the higher personality has actually evolved. Moreover, Commons averred, there was no possibility that amalgamation of the "black race" with other races had occurred prior to slavery (cf. Commons, 1903-1904:1, p. 39). In other words, in the language Commons had employed in his earlier paper, natural selection had made the run-of-the-mill Negro a "congenital degenerate" who cannot be elevated by "education and opportunity" into the "higher forms of human character" (Commons, 1897, p. 97). Moreover, Darwinian "artificial selection" had eliminated even those whose variation within the "race" type might have made them somewhat fit to be elevated. To add the preface to a passage cited earlier:[80]

> Just as in the many thousand years of man's domestication of animals, the breechy cow and the balky horse have been almost eliminated by artificial selection, so slavery tended to transform the savage by eliminating those who were self-willed, ambitious, and possessed

of individual initiative. Other races of immigrants, by contact with our institutions, have
been civilized—the Negro has been only domesticated.... The very qualities of intelligence
and manliness which are essential for citizenship in a democracy were systematically
expunged from the Negro race through two hundred years of slavery. (Commons, 1903-
1904:3, p. 224).

Without question, to return to the point, Darwinian natural and artificial
selection were the *biological* concepts that lay at the root of Commons's
determination that immigrants had the capacity to be assimilated whereas the
Negro's only hope, even if a "slow and doubtful process," is blood amalgamation.
Lamarckian reasoning simply had no role of any kind in Commons's story.

Let us sum up. Commons shared with his contemporaries an uncritical
acceptance of a theory of geographical determinism rooted in the temperate-
versus tropical-zone dichotomy. Despite the evidence that most other writers
of his time were either confused or had "suspended judgment" (Stocking, 1968,
p. 254) regarding the relative merits of "Darwinian" and "Lamarckian"
explanations of heredity, Commons's analysis in "Racial Composition" is, in
the context of Darwinism versus Lamarckism, consistently Darwinian in
character. Thus it is Darwinian natural selection, operating under the impetus
of fundamentally different geographical influences, *and* the degree of previous
amalgamation (cf. Commons, 1903-1904:1, p. 39), which has produced a
different *biologically-rooted innate capacity* for the development of higher
character, that is, "Americanization," on the part of the Negro as compared
to the other "races" that have emigrated to the United States. To explain the
*actual development* of the higher character attributed to the "American" as
compared to the immigrant, Commons moved outside the realm of biological
inheritance and added to the Darwinian framework the concept of "social
selection." In short, to return to the framework outlined by Cherry, as
recounted as the outset of this section of the paper, while Commons was indeed
an "environmentalist" in so far as his views on the immigrant were concerned,
he was a throughgoing Darwinist when it came to the Negro. And just as the
Declaration of Independence did not mean *all* men are created equal (cf.
Commons, 1903-1904:1, p. 33), not *all* races are capable of being Americanized.
For, unfortunately, "race and heredity (are) beyond our organized control"
(Commons, 1903-1904:1, p. 42). That is, *with respect to the Negro only,* "factors
of heredity and race [are] more fundamental than those of education and
environment" (Commons, 1903-1904:1, p. 34).

## IV.   FINAL THOUGHTS

### A.   Why Was "Racial Composition" Written?

We have searched throughout Commons's major works, including the labor
volumes, for passages suggesting ill will toward Negroes, or even a concern

about their situation. We must report that we failed to find even one sign of enmity. We have also searched for passages in his other writings indicating a belief in the Negro's natural inferiority and have found only one in an essay in *Trade Unionism and Labor Problems* (1905), a collection edited by Commons shortly after his arrival at Wisconsin, about the experiences of workers from different "races" in the slaughtering and meat packing trades (cf. Commons, 1905, p. 247). In *Documentary History of American Industrial Society* (10 vol.), there is included only one document relating to the activities of Negroes, a highly laudatory account by a white unionist regarding the participation of Negro unionists at the National Labor Union meeting of 1869 (cf. Commons and associates, 1910, Vol. 9, pp. 243-256). Only a few paragraphs of *History of Labour in the United States* (4 vol.) are devoted to the problems confronted by the Negro worker, and these passages, written by Commons's associates on the project, John B. Andrews and Don D. Lescohier, present the problems encountered by the Negro as being due principally to white discrimination and secondarily to the habits of mind produced by the institution of slavery (cf. Commons and associates, 1918, Vol. 2, pp. 134-138, 145-147; vol. 3, pp. 42-45). In short, nowhere in these volumes is it intimated in any way that the Negro worker's problems result from his own inherent limitations. Of greater significance, perhaps, is the fact that one will search in vain throughout the remainder of Commons's writings for any indication of interest at all about the economic, political, or social status of Negroes in American society.

Thus it is something of a puzzle why Commons, who in his autobiography later proudly proclaimed that "Liberty, equality, and defiance of the Fugitive Slave Law were my birthright" (Commons, 1934b, p. 7), decided in 1903 even to write about issues arising from the most fundamental of all American social and political problems, much less to do so with such seeming indifference to the consequences his words might have for members of the Negro race.[81] As we have recounted, Commons in September of 1900 accidentally chanced upon an opportunity to write up a report for the U.S. Industrial Commission regarding the economic effects of immigration. According to his own account in *Myself*, Commons spent about six months studying firsthand the conditions of life suffered by urban immigrants employed in sweatshop industries, after which he took a trip to the headquarters of about half of the national trade unions in order to discover the effects of immigration on unionism (Commons, 1934b, p. 71). There is no evidence that Commons similarly studied the situation of Negroes firsthand as part of his investigation.[82] And, whereas the approximately 500-page report Commons prepared for the Industrial Commission (Commons, 1901) is replete with statistics and analysis pertaining to specific immigrant "races," we have been unsuccessful in finding any facts or analysis in the report specifically pertaining to the Negro "race" or even a hint of the racial analysis he would be forwarding in "Racial Composition." Yet it is the Negro's inherent incapacity for participation in American life as a true equal upon which Commons focuses the reader's attention both at the outset and the conclusion of his analysis and to which he devotes an entire article in the middle of the series.

As we reported earlier, Commons alluded in only one brief passage to his possible motivation for calling attention to the inherent deficiencies of Negroes. As he put it:

> [The] race question in America has found its most intense expression in the relations between the white and the negro races, and has there shown itself to be the most fundamental of all American social and political problems. For it was this race question that precipitated the Civil War, with the ominous problems that have followed upon that catastrophe; and it is this same race problem that now diverts attention from the treatment of those pressing economic problems of taxation, corporations, trusts and labor organizations which themselves originated in the Civil War (Commons, 1903-1904:1, p. 84).

It is possible to infer from these brief remarks that Commons's attempt to establish the inherent limitations of Negroes as fact was motivated by his desire that reform-minded individuals shift their focus to other matters. However, we find it highly implausible in light of extant turn-of-the-century white attitudes, as recounted above, that Commons could have believed that a preoccupation with solving the race problem actually lay at the root of middle-class reformers' putative failure to direct sufficient "attention" to the "pressing economic problems" he itemized.

To repeat, given these realities, it is a puzzle as to why Commons decided to write "Racial Composition," with its unequivocal message that—unlike other immigrant "races"—the inherent limitations of Negroes regrettably make it inconceivable that even the provision of an ideal education and environment will suffice to transform them into equal members of the American race. We find a significant clue regarding his actual motivation in Commons's explicit singling out of one line of temperate-zone evolution as an exception to the general rule of geographical determinism, namely, the line producing the other "congenitally degenerate" race in the United States, the Native American or "Indian." With respect to Native Americans, whose evolution similarly proceeded without contact—amalgamation—with the Aryan, the Semitic or the Mongolian but, unlike the Negro, whose evolution proceeded *outside* the tropical zone, Commons proclaimed: "the Indian ... [is] superior in some respects to the Negro" (Commons, 1903-1904:1, p. 39).[83] Clearly, this assessment of the Native American's capacities suggests that amalgamation was considered by Commons to have played a major role in improving the biological constitution of non-Aryan races. But more important, it also makes clear the basic *ad hoc*, if not outright *ad hominem*, nature of the apologetic argument he was constructing.

Let there be no mistake, *apologia is precisely what we believe Commons was up to in "Racial Composition."* According to Marvin Harris, "all racial identity, scientifically speaking, is ambiguous. Whenever certainty is expressed on this subject, we can be confident that society has manufactured a social lie in order to help one of its segments take advantage of another" (Harris, 1964, p. 56). Presuming Harris to be correct in this regard, the question then becomes: In the service of which of societys segments, then, was Commons's "social lie" employed? In our view, the answer is clear: In the service of the labor movement.

As we noted earlier, Commons in 1899 as much as proclaimed that he was a "partner" of the working class, whose instrument of salvation, he insisted, was the labor movement. Even though Commons's work around the time he wrote "Racial Composition" did in fact touch on *all* the issues he itemized in the passage recounted on the preceding page, it is clear that the task of educating the classes who fashion public opinion (Commons, 1903-1904:1, p. 84) about the positive potentialities inherent in the last of the four economic problems he enumerated, that of *labor organizations*, was his overriding concern at the time he wrote the series (see Commons, 1934b, Ch. IV).[84] Surely it is that actuality which accounts for Commons appending to the final installment of the "Racial Composition" series, published in May 1904, a short piece he had earlier written for the October 1903 issue of *The World To-day*—one titled "'Americanization by Labor Unions."

As we have indicated, Commons's principal message in "Racial Composition," one prefigured in his previous publications, is that once appropriate immigration restriction is in place, the labor movement can play an important role in successfully "Americanizing" immigrants who are members of "low standards of living" races. The context in which he sought to forward this message is important. Around the turn of the century, leaders from the Negro community were critical of the discriminatory practices employed by unions and the failure of the union movement to work toward organizing Negroes. For example, in 1897 Booker T. Washington charged that trade unions were inhibiting Negro economic advancement (Mandel, 1969, p. 83). Perhaps more importantly, W. E. B. DuBois in a 1902 study documented discrimination against Negroes in the American Federation of Labor (Mandel, 1969, p. 89). Washington and DuBois both were disappointed and perplexed with this situation since the official position of the AFL was that real labor solidarity required organizing all workers, most especially Negro workers (Mandel, 1969, p. 79). Indeed, at the 1893 convention of the AFL, the following resolution had been adopted: "We here and now affirm as one of the cardinal principles of the labor movement that working people must unite and organize irrespective of creed, color, sex, nationality or politics" (Spero and Harris, 1968, p. 87). As Gompers explained it in a letter to one of his Southern organizers in 1897:

If the colored man is not permitted to organize[,] ... if a chance is not given him by
which he can uplift his condition, the inevitable result must follow, that he will sink down
lower and lower in his economic scale and in his conception of his rights as a worker and
finally find himself ... absolutely dependent (worse than chattel slavery) in the hands of
unfair and unscrupulous employers.... If . . white wage workers ... will not cooperate
with him, he will necessarily cling to the other hand (that of the employer) who also smites
him, but at least recognizes his right to work (quoted in Mandel, 1969, p. 80).

In practice, however, Gompers was forced, given that the prejudices of white
workers in the South no doubt appeared to be an insuperable obstacle to
integrated unions or even separate Negro unions, to do what was "theoretically
bad but pragmatically necessary." That is, he set labor solidarity aside, caved
in to the prejudices of white workers, and took the gains to be had by organizing
only white workers (Mandel, 1969, p. 92). To do otherwise, Gompers
apparently had concluded as early as 1892, one year *before* the resolution
reproduced above was adopted, would "practically subordinate the labor
movement to the race question" (quoted in Mandel, 1969, p. 83). Accordingly,
Gompers responded in a personal letter to DuBois's request for a reaction to
his documentation of union discrimination by rather brusquely dismissing the
analysis as "neither fair nor accurate" without specifying a single factual error,
adding that "I have more important work to attend to than [to] correct 'copy'
for your paper" (quoted in Mandel, 1969, p. 89). From the union standpoint,
the single practical resolution of this problem was to organize only whites and
endorse a social and political system that effectively excluded the Negro from
the industrial labor force altogether (Mandel, 1969, p. 92). That is, most
propitiously, the Southern solution to the Negro problem—Jim Crow—was
also the union solution to the problem (Mandel, 1969, p. 92). Of course, the
official union position was to blame the situation not on white prejudice but
on the Negro himself. Thus, in testimony before the Industrial Commission
in 1899, Gompers maintained that the problem was not color prejudice but
the willingness of the Negro to be used as a "whip in the hands of employers
to cow white men and to compel them to accept abject conditions of labor"
(Mandel, 1969, p. 85). Gompers, who often began his public speeches with
"darkie" stories (Mandel, 1969, p. 91), also endorsed the view that the Negro
lacked the temperament "peculiar to most of the caucasian race, and which
alone make a ... modern trade union possible" (Mandel, 1969, p. 84).

"If the economist truly represents society as a whole," Commons had
declared in 1899, "he should strive to give the excluded classes a larger and
more just legal share in government and industry" (Commons, 1900, pp. 54-
55). Yet Commons failed to extend this maxim to the "excluded" Negro race.
Given that Commons clearly believed the Negro question to be "nearly
insoluble" and attempts to resolve it certain to divert attention and energy away
from more pressing needs (cf. Commons, 1903-1904:1, p. 34), there can be little

doubt that he agreed with Gompers that it would be a potentially ruinous mistake for the union movement also to take on the task of "uplifting" or "Americanizing" the Negro. To justify the failure to do so is of course the "subtext" of "Racial Composition," and, while clearly it is speculation, the labor movement's *interest* at the time he was working on this manuscript in obtaining such justification is the only credible reason we have been able to think of for Commons's extension of the 'immigrant question" to include the Negro.[85] We find no other credible answer to the question of why Commons decided to extend his analysis of the "immigration issue" to include the Negro than to recognize that his racial "analysis" is at core nothing other than crass apologetics in the service of "class struggle." Put slightly differently, we conclude that Commons's motive in extending his analysis in "Racial Composition" was to provide his "class partners," Samuel Gompers and others in the labor movement who shared his perspective on this matter, with a "scientific" justification of pragmatic decisions already made.[86]

## B.   Commons's Social Philosophy Revisited

In his musings about methodological issues, it was one of Commons's insights that a researcher's social philosophy is of fundamental importance to the results he obtains: "If a man starts out to prove a thing, it is wonderful how he can select the facts that prove it. It is our social philosophies that unconsciously select for us our facts" (Commons, 1934a, p. 98). It is evident that the social philosophy Commons had articulated in his previously published works accounts for the manner in which he structured his analysis of immigration in "Racial Composition" as well as his conclusion, presuming enactment of immigration restriction, that the trade union is the necessary and sufficient agency for transforming immigrants into true "Americans." As enunciated, however, Commons's social philosophy cannot account for his determined effort to establish simultaneously that the trade union should not *also* be assigned responsibility for "uplifting" or "Americanizing" the Negro, which we surmise to have been Commons's real motive for broadening the analysis of immigrant "races" to include the Negro.

As we have noted, Commons was predisposed to a framework that would emphasize social as opposed to natural selection, that is, environmentalism over heredity or, in his words, "civilization" over "racial endowment." This predisposition evinced itself in Commons's complete disregard of facts and theories espoused by other scholars regarding the inherent defects of non-Teutonic temperate-zone immigrants. But, in appropriating geographical determinism to explain the superior character of races evolving in the temperate zone and, particularly, to nullify the applicability of the social selection framework in the case of the Negro, Commons seemed to have no difficulty in brushing aside his previously revealed skepticism concerning the adequacy of racial theories embraced by authorities. Within the epistemological framework articulated by Commons himself, only one factor can reasonably be held to account for these particulars, namely, an overriding predisposition not made apparent in his earlier writings but still very much a constituent of the true social philosophy he embraced at the time he began this endeavor.

Put bluntly, the word for that predisposition is *racism*. We earlier defined racism as the belief that a particular group is inherently—biologically—inferior to other groups.[87] Racism typically occasions an indifference to or even outright hostility toward the social, political, and economic advancement of the putatively inferior racial group (Potter, 1967, p. 359). As we have shown, Commons, if not hostile—and the common ground he shared with racial radicals would certainly not allow one to dismiss this possibility out of hand— was assuredly indifferent to the interests of the Negro.[88] This actuality, as we have outlined, is evident in the callous disregard for the Negro implicit in his conclusion that "amalgamation is their door to assimilation." But not only was Commons indifferent to the plight of the Negro, he justified his failure to call for social action to remedy that plight with the argument—one, to be sure, in full concurrence with the "conventional wisdom" of his time—that the Negro is biologically inferior. This, in our judgment, is bedrock racism.[89]

Having said this, there is a related matter that we feel should be addressed. Returning to the allegation of Meier and Rudwick as recounted in the first sentence of this paper, we find it inconceivable that Commons had any effect at all, much less a "decisive" one, on his Wisconsin colleague U. B. Phillips's racial views, which almost certainly the latter learned at his mother's knee (Dillon, 1985, pp. 5-6; Roper, 1984, pp. 6-7). In fact, Phillips had already revealed his racial prejudices as early as 1901, two years before "Racial Composition" was written, when he excoriated and refused to support Theodore Roosevelt because Roosevelt had entertained Booker T. Washington at the White House. Although Phillips admired Washington, he thought Roosevelt's action provided legitimation for radical ideas of integration (Roper, 1984, p. 79). Furthermore, in a 1904 article entitled "Conservatism and Progress in the Cotton Belt," a piece that he surely began to work on well before the "Racial Composition" series was published, Phillips advocated the legal disenfranchisement of Negroes and a return to the "graciousness and charm of antebellum civilization" (Phillips, 1904, pp 7, 9). Given this timing, we find Meier and Rudwick's use of the term "racist" in reference to Commons, while accurate, entirely gratuitous. We also find it odd that they would highlight Phillips's association with Commons when in fact, by Phillips's own admission, his most prized associations at Wisconsin were with Fredrick Jackson Turner and Richard T. Ely (Roper, 1984, pp. 59, 61). In short, we find no basis for Meier and Rudwick's claim that Commons exercised a "decisive" influence over

Phillips. It is equally unlikely, we should add, that Phillips turned Commons into a racist, as Commons did not arrive at Wisconsin until mid-1904 after he had already completed his "Racial Composition" series.

## C. Conclusion

The policy position to which Commons's racism led him can hardly be described as benign. As we have recounted, Commons, without any apparent concern, condemned the southern Negro to a social system where he would be excluded from the franchise despite his qualifications, where he would be deprived of education, where he would be at the mercy of terrorists, and where he would have no secure right to property—that is, where he would be deprived of freedom and equal opportunity. By so doing, Commons effectively acquiesced in denying Negroes all of the means necessary to evolve socially into "Godlike" individuals. For, as he himself had emphasized in "Social Selection:" "Social evolution is ... the evolution of freedom and opportunity, on the one hand, and personality, on the other. Without freedom and security there can be no free will and no moral character. Without exalted personality there can be no enduring freedom. The educational environment, therefore, which develops personality must itself develop with freedom" (Commons, 1897, p. 92). But, Commons apparently convinced himself, one need not be particularly troubled by this situation since it is likely the Negro will not reflect upon his deprivation. He conveniently surmised that, like the serf, "[The negro] knows himself to be by birthright a member of an inferior class, from which he has no chance of escaping.... There is a wall between him and the higher realms of life. The imprisonment is so complete that he rarely thinks of escaping" (Shaler as approvingly quoted in Commons, 1903-1904:3, p.36). "Complete indifference" to the plight of the Negro is surely not an inaccurate way to characterize the standpoint reflected in these views.

Racism, John Stuart Mill averred, is the "most vulgar mode ... of escaping from the consideration of the effect of social and moral influences on the human mind" (quoted in Benedict, 1940, p. 7). E. A. Ross, ironically, similarly judged racism to be a "cheap explanation" of differences in "collective traits," most often used by novices who are "too stupid or too lazy to trace" them to their origins in "the physical environment, the social environment, or historical conditions" (quoted in Benedict 1940, p. 146). Despite his remarkable capacity for going beyond the "habitual assumptions" of his time, as revealed throughout his theoretical writings, in "explaining" the traits of Negroes Commons unquestionably did retreat to "cheap" and "vulgar" racism. Like so many others of his time, Commons clearly had not managed by 1903 to transcend what Eugene Genovese has referred to as the "poisonous demands of white supremacy" (Genovese, 1969, p. xx).

Were the racial views that Commons revealed in "Racial Composition" ones that he maintained throughout his life? We strongly suspect that to be the case. First of all, he allowed *Races and Immigrants* to be reissued in 1920 (Commons, 1920) without any substantive revision of his earlier analysis. In any case, what else can account for the following sentimental recollection in *Myself* of his Florida experiences circa 1885?

> It was a romantic life and the happiest I have known. I have told my Friday Niters stories of 'crackers' and their bananas, Negro hunts, Negroes brought in dead to our courthouse, or slashing each other at Christmas with razors and filling the gaps with spanish moss; of revolvers we carried, of branded cows, razor-back hogs, pine-tree squirrels bigger than cats, huge crocodiles and snakes in the swamps and shallow lakes, coon hunts with the crackers—it was a poetic pine-roofed sanitarium for nerves (Commons, 1934b, p.33).

Assuming we are right, how, then, is Commons's lifelong racism reflected in the character of his work writ large? Mainly, we believe, through omission. In our judgment, "Racial Composition" was for Commons a symbolic "washing his hands" of any responsibility for even addressing the race question. By his own account, the guiding vision underlying Commons's endeavors throughout his remarkable life was to make American capitalism "good" (cf. Commons, 1934b, p. 143). Yet, despite the enormity of his contribution to the historical "uplifting" of the American working class, Commons failed throughout the remainder of his long career to reveal even a glimmer of interest in using his talents to contribute to the economic betterment of the Negro race. And, despite his consistent advocacy of economic justice for wage workers, nowhere in his later writings is there indicated a concern of any kind with the unsatisfactory economic status of Negroes as a distinct group—or even an awareness that the manner in which the extant allocation of the "burdens and benefits of collective wealth-production" affects Negroes is relevant to the issue of the "goodness" of American capitalism.

To recognize that a racist standpoint helped to give form to the life's work of "St. John R.,"[90] whom Edwin E. Witte once characterized as "the most loveable man I have even known" (quoted in Harter, 1962, p. 81), is not to diminish Commons's monumental achievements, both practical and theoretical: He was, and remains, one of the most creative minds ever to address the fundamental issues of economic theory and its power to guide fruitful social action. Neither is it to condemn him, for Commons was in this respect wholly in harmony with his contemporaries—neither better nor worse. In short, in our judgment, John R. Commons's reputation as a scholar, if slightly tarnished by his sloppy work in "Racial Composition," remains intact.

As to our personal judgment of Commons the man, we are reluctant to presume moral superiority. If we substitute "modern scholars" for "anthropologists," Eugene Genovese's assessment of how the "modern" standpoint came to be adopted rings true to our ears: "Most anthropologists today reject racism, but we might reflect on the development of this rejection, for Adolph Hitler probably had more to do with it than Franz Boas" (Genovese, 1969, pp. vii, xv). At the same time, we should keep in mind that while "racial prejudice may spring from economic and political causes, from a particular race's superiority or inferiority complex, from biological differences, from hereditary instinct or from a combination of these causes[,] [i]n every case matters are greatly aggravated by the tendency to accept theories and hypotheses *without the slightest critical examination*" (Comas, 1961, p. 54, emphasis added). This, of course, was the essence of Commons's transgression. So, lest we proceed too far in acquittal, we might consider the words of W. E. B. DuBois, written in 1903: "We must not forget that most Americans answer all queries regarding the Negro a priori and that the least that human courtesy can do is to listen to the evidence" (DuBois, 1903, p. 130). Given the undeniable reality that America's "Negro Problem" remains to this day, as Commons put it, "the most fundamental of all American social and political problems,"and given the current revival of racially tinged politics, we should all take notice of Commons's experience. The fact that *even* so well-intentioned and open-minded an individual as John R. Commons succumbed to the "poisonous demands of white supremacy" and accordingly failed to offer "the least that human courtesy can do" should serve as a reminder to us all how easy it is to fall prey to the pernicious influence of racism.

## ACKNOWLEDGMENTS

The first part of this paper was presented to the Western Social Science Association, Albuquerque, New Mexico, April 28, 1989. The authors would like to thank Charles Leathers, Robert Cherry, Warren Samuels and Jeff Biddle for insightful and helpful comments on earlier drafts.

## NOTES

1. We use the term "Negro" throughout this paper when referring to Americans of African descent to remain consistent with the usage of the writers whose work we summarize and cite.

2. A formal definition of racism is provided in Websters *Third New International Dictionary* (1986): the assumption that psychocultural traits and capacities are determined by biological race and that races differ decisively from one another which is usually coupled with a belief in the inherent superiority of a particular race and its right to domination over others.

3. See, for example, Lafayette G. Harter's biography of Commons (Harter, 1962). Although the fact that Commons wrote "Racial Composition" or *Races and Immigrants* is commented upon by Harter in three places, the word Negro is never introduced into the discussion. Neither is there even a hint regarding the nature of Commons's *expressed* views regarding the capacities of the Negro.

4. The racial views of Commons have been discussed by both Robert Cherry (1976) and Mark Aldrich (1985). For reasons to be spelled out below, we find each of these analyses deficient.

5. We will refer throughout to "Racial Composition" rather than *Races and Immigrants*.

6. The details in this brief overview are all taken from Commons's autobiography. See Commons (1934b, pp. 56-74). There may be reasons for questioning the adequacy with respect to particulars of the interpretation Commons therein forwards. DeBrizzi (1983, p. 92), for example, suggests that the real reason for Commons' dismissal may have been his unorthodox and somewhat "unprofessional" classroom performance. For hints that such "unorthodox" practices may indeed have undermined his status with his colleagues, see Commons (1934b, p. 54).

7. The nine articles were consecutively titled "Race and Democracy," "Colonial Race Elements," "The Negro," "Immigration During the Nineteenth Century" (two articles), "Industry," "Social and Industrial Problems," "City Life, Crime and Poverty," and "Amalgamation and Assimilation."

8. This is significant, for Commons later advocated the position that a truly valid understanding of a problem cannot be obtained without first-hand investigation (Ramstad, 1987b). See Commons (1934b, pp. 4, 130, 160). For evidence that Commons came to this conclusion early in his career, see Commons (1894, pp. 46, 75-76).

9. Commons connoted by the term "habitual assumption" a "predisposition inside ourselves" (Commons, 1934a, p. 121).

10. See DeBrizzi (1983, p. 114) for the judgment that Commons's outlook was firmly bound by the traditional world-view of the nineteenth century American middle class. This world-view seems to us clearly to undergird the following passage from "Racial Composition":

> It was not the peasant class of Europe that sought these shores in order to found a free government. It was the middle class, the merchants and yeomen, those who in religion and politics were literally 'protestants', and who possessed the intelligence, manliness and public spirit which urged them to assert for themselves those inalienable rights which the church or the state of their time had arrogated to itself. With such a social class democracy is the only acceptable form of government. They demand and secure equal opportunity because they are able to rise to those opportunities. By their own inherent nature they look forward to and aspire to the highest positions (Commons, 1903-1904:1, pp. 36-37).

We would further argue that when employed by Commons such terms as true independence and manliness embody precisely these values.

11. Commons was most likely influenced in this regard by his mentor, Richard T. Ely, who was himself a proponent of the Social Gospel (see Ely, 1889).

12. For extensive discussions of Commons's theory of Reasonable Value, see Wolfe (1936) and Ramstad (1991).

13. Also see Commons's later discussion in *Institutional Economics* regarding how efficiency gains *should* be shared (Commons, 1934a, pp. 789ff).

14. Commons attempted to analyze the role of force and commanded behavior in economic life in a series of essays published during the years 1899-1900. They have subsequently been assembled under the title, *A Sociological Theory of Sovereignty (1899-1900)*. For a systematic explication of Commons's conception of the State, see Chasse (1986).

15. See Ramstad (1987a) for an overview of Commons's position regarding the role of standards in maintaining a "fair and reasonable" plane of competition in the labor market. See Ramstad 1990 and 1991 for an overview of Commons's non-mechanistic "volitional" understanding of "the market" as a mechanism for effecting production and distribution.

16. Many of the themes developed in *Proportional Representation* were repeated by Commons in his discussion of A. H. Hadley's 1899 "Presidential Address" to the American Economic Association. See Commons (1913, Ch. 5).

17.    Commons later came to understand that it was actually the legal foundations of capitalism about which he was concerned. On this point, see Commons (1924, p. viii).

18.    Commons's favorable attitude toward unions actually dated back to his own experiences as a member of the typographical union while a college student (see Commons, 1934b, pp. 16-21. This predisposition was no doubt solidified by Commons's experience as a student of Ely, who was himself an early and vigorous advocate of trade unionism (see Ely, 1886); indeed, Ely was forced to leave Johns Hopkins in 1892 after forwarding an analysis unfavorable to the Pullman Company's role in fomenting the famous Pullman Strike and later, after joining the University of Wisconsin faculty, was investigated and absolved by the Board of Regents for justifying strikes and boycotts and upholding "socialism" (Stein and Taft, 1969, p.ii).

19.    Almost every analytical term Commons employed throughout his career was equally "loose and elastic." See Ramstad (1986).

20.    Commons was not altogether clear whether or not he placed the Malay in exactly the same category with respect to its origins as the Negro. However, it is clear Commons understood shared climatic conditions to have produced a character similar to the Negro's, as indicated in the passage cited above on p.: 1. Throughout this discussion, we ignore Commons's position with respect to the Malay, of whom the Phillipine was his principal exemplar.

21.    Born in 1862, Commons was already in his early forties when he wrote these articles.

22.    In the chapter of *Races and Immigrants* corresponding to this article, Commons did drop some specific charges levied in the article regarding the backward behavior of West Africans. Most of the insulting stereotypes presented in the original article were retained in unaltered form, however. Certainly there is no change in tone.

23.    Commons added a paragraph to *Races and Immigrants* to reinforce this point. See Commons (1907, p. 43).

24.    Commons was explicit regarding that disadvantage. "The prejudice of white workmen has undoubtedly played a part in excluding the Negro from mechanical trades, but the testimony of large employers, who have no race prejudice where profits can be made, also shows that low-priced Negro labor costs more than high-priced white labor. The iron and steel mills of Alabama have no advantage in the labor cost over the mills of Pennsylvania and Ohio" (Commons, 1903-1904:3, p. 227). Commons added a short section to *Races and Immigrants* to provide additional "evidence" in support of his generalization regarding the inferior performance in the labor market of Negro workers. See Commons (1907, p. 47).

25.    See the passage near the top of p. 2 above.

26.    The outlines of this interpretation were earlier presented in a series of articles Commons wrote in 1899- 1900 under the title "A Sociological View of Sovereignty." (In 1965, these articles were published in book form by Augustus M. Kelley, Publishers, as part of the Reprints of Economic Classics series.) As discussed above, Commons had in 1896 written a tract in which he called for a legislature based on proportional representation of various interest groups (Commons, 1896). Clearly, it is this framework that Commons had in the back of his mind here. The reader is again directed to Ramstad (1990) for an overview of Commons's interpretation of volitional social progress guided by public purposes.

27.    Regarding the latter, "preparing the Negro to profit by the suffrage," Commons added in *Races and Immigrants*:

> Neither should the negro be excluded from the higher education. Leadership is just as necessary in a democracy as in a tribe. Self-government is not suppression of leaders but cooperation with them. The true leader is one who knows his followers because he has suffered with them, but who can point the way out and inspire them with confidence. He feels what they feel, but can state what they cannot express. He is their spokesman, defender, and organizer. Not a social class nor a struggling race can reach equality with other classes

and races until its leaders can meet theirs on equal terms. It cannot depend on theirs, but must raise up leaders from its own ranks. This is the problem of higher education—not that scholastic education that ends in itself, but that broad education that equips for higher usefulness. If those individuals who are competent to become lawyers, physicians, teachers, preachers, organizers, guides, innovators, experimenters, are prevented from getting the right education, then there is little hope for progress among the race as a whole in the intelligence, manliness, and cooperation needed for self-government (Commons, 1907, pp. 52-53).

This passage illustrates in dramatic fashion the importance in Commons's mind of Negro leadership as a prerequisite to Negro progress. As we will establish below, however, it is clear that it was *mulatto* Negro leadership to which Commons was here referring.

28.   Commons added a lengthy discussion of the Magyars in *Races and Immigrants*, as well as a section titled "Asiatic Immigration." See Commons (1907, pp. 80-82, 84, 101-104).

29.   Commons here added two pages of material in *Races and Immigrants* in which he argued that a great deal of racial enmity is economic at its root:

The negro or immigrant strike breaker is befriended by the employer, but hated by the employee. . . . As the immigrant rises in the scale, the small farmer, contractor, or merchant feels his competition and begins to join in measures of race protection. This hostility is not primarily racial in character. It is the competitive struggle for standards of living. It appears to be racial because for the most part races have different standards. But where different races agree on their standards the racial struggle ceases, and the negro, Italian, Slav, and American join together in the class struggle of the trade-union" (Commons, 1907, pp. 114-115).

30.   The "Racial Composition" articles were actually written so as to make the conclusion implicit in the argument, with the reader apparently having the responsibility actually of stating it. Thus, when we say it was Commons's "conclusion," we mean in fact that there was only one reasonable conclusion consistent with the "facts" Commons presented. In that sense, it was Commons's actual recommendation that changes to the nation's immigration laws should be directed at "improvement" of immigration rather than "elimination" of immigration. In other words, "The object [is] to raise the average character of those admitted by excluding those who fall below certain standards on "an educational, or rather, literacy test." Cf. Commons (1903-1904:9, pp. 224-225). This issue is discussed at some length below.

31.   At this point in *Races and Immigrants*, Commons added two pages pertaining to his expectation that upon learning that "the right to quit work is the right to get higher wages," Negroes, as well as immigrant workers held in peonage, will be ushered into "a process of natural selection" in which industrious and steady Negro workmen will be produced (cf. Commons, 1907, pp. 138-141). The prerequisite of escape from "coerced labor," of course, was for the Negro to escape from the debt through which he was kept in peonage status. Commons had nothing constructive to say on that score.

32.   In *Races and Immigrants*, Commons at this juncture added some comments regarding the lack of ambition generally evident among Negroes. See Commons (1907, pp. 147-148).

33.   It is not our intention to elaborate on issues outside the scope of this paper. However, it is evident, given the rise of multinational corporations and the presently accelerating "internationalization" of labor competition, that Commons would have used analogous reasoning to protect present-day American workers from similar "race competition." For an analysis developing this implication, though formulated in somewhat different terms, see Ramstad (1987a).

34. In *Races and Immigrants*, Commons added a penultimate chapter titled "Politics" (Commons, 1907, pp. 179-197). Here he made explicit his theory of progress, spelled out earlier in *Proportional Representation*: "Men are not equal, neither as races or classes. True equality comes through equal opportunity. If individuals go forward, their race or class is elevated. They become spokesmen, defenders, examples. No race or class can rise without its own leaders" (Commons, 1907, p. 181). The discussion in this chapter is focused primarily on problems associated with the immigrant obtaining suffrage while still lacking the character traits through which he could benefit from that privilege. The analysis, accordingly, was not focused on the unique political problems of the Negro, although Commons did forward a judgment that suffrage was being unfairly taken from Negroes in "six Southern states." Cf. Commons (1907, p. 193).

35. The reader will recall that earlier Commons had referred to "the relations between the white and negro races" as "the most fundamental of all American political and social problems." See p. 11 above.

36. In the final chapter of *Races and Immigrants* Commons earlier inserted the following passage, which bears repeating in full:

> Our principal interest in amalgamation is its effect on the negro race. The census statisticians discontinued after 1890 the inquiry into the number of mulattoes, but the census of 1890 showed that mulattoes were 15 per cent of the total negro population. This was a slightly larger proportion than that of preceding years. The mulatto element of the negro race is almost a race of itself. Its members on the average differ but little if at all from those of the white race in their capacity for advancement, and it is the tragedy of race antagonism that they with their longings should suffer the fate of the more contented and thoughtless blacks. In their veins runs the blood of white aristocracy, and it is a curious psychology of the Anglo-Saxon that assigns to the inferior race those equally entitled to a place among the superior. But sociology offers compensation for the injustice to physiology. The mulatto is the natural leader, instructor, and spokesman of the black. Prevented from withdrawing himself above the fortunes of his fellows, he devotes himself to their elevation. This fact becomes clear in proportion as the need of practical education becomes clear. The effective work of the whites through missionary schools and colleges has not been the elevation of the black, but the elevation of mulattoes to teach the blacks. A new era for the blacks is beginning when the mulatto sees his own future in theirs (Commons, 1907, pp. 209-210).

In light of this addition, it is curious that further along in the chapter Commons chose to drop the final sentence of the lengthy passage quoted on page 2 above, namely, "Frederick Douglass, Booker Washington, Professor DuBois are an honor to any race, but they are mulattoes."

37. It will be recalled that Lodge was the source of Commons's information relating to the national origin of "prominent" Americans.

38. Indeed, at one time the leaders of the IRL considered changing the name of the group to the "Eugenic Immigration League" (Higham, 1988, p. 152).

39. It will be recalled that Commons made this same argument linking race and a supposed lack of "mechanical ingenuity." However, he limited its applicability to Negroes only.

40. We might add that it was Ely who first brought Commons to Wisconsin in 1904 to write a history of labor in the United States. See Commons (1934b, pp. 92, 128ff).

41. Bemis worked with Commons in 1900-1901 to produce the wholesale price index as recounted above. On this point, see Commons (1934b, p. 65).

42. The phrases are taken from Commons (1894, p. 20-21).

43. Commons actually categorized himself as a sociologist while at Syracuse University. See Commons (1934b, p. 53).

44.  Ely ultimately shifted to the view that the state itself must serve as the "uplift" agency. For an analysis of Ely's understanding of the role of the state, see DiBrizzi (1983, Ch. 4).

45.  In fact, Ross's public expression of pro-labor views resulted in his being dismissed from Stanford University. See DeBrizzi (1983, p. 132).

46.  It was apparently the racial arrogance of the "nordics" leading the immigration restriction movement at the turn of the century from which Ross was seeking to disassociate himself in this passage. Cf. Ross (1930, p. 203).

47.  Mayo-Smith, then at Columbia University, helped Commons secure a statistical assistant for his index number project. See Commons (1934b, p. 65).

48.  Given the fact that he not only chose to include "Economists and Class Partnership" but strategically placed it near the beginning of the volume, Commons evidently had not repudiated this position as of 1913 when he published a collection of his earlier essays under the title *Labor and Administration*. See Commons (1913, Ch. 5).

49.  Commons ultimately came to believe that the role of the economist should be limited to showing principals, in this case laborers themselves or their unions, how to achieve *ends of their own choosing*. Significantly, the economist was *not* to define for them what goals the principals should seek or try to define the "public interest" in terms independent of the goals actually articulated by principals. On this point, see Commons (1934a, pp. 852ff; 1934b, p. 88).

50.  Commons's remarks were subsequently published in 1908 in the *American Journal of Sociology* under the title "Class Conflict: Is it Growing in America, and is it Inevitable?" This essay also is incorporated into *Labor and Administration* (see Commons, 1913, Ch. 6).

51.  For an analysis of Commons's position regarding a protective tariff, see Ramstad (1987a). Commons' conception of "competition" is therein spelled out at greater length.

52.  We must emphasize that we are not suggesting that Cherry was unaware of Commons's antipodal stance toward immigrants as opposed to the Negro. Indeed, in his recent book Cherry uses Commons as a specific example of the tendency of many progressives to take a liberal attitude toward immigrants and a racist attitude toward the Negro (Cherry, 1989, pp. 28-29).

53.  The remainder of this summary is taken in its entirety from Faust (1986, pp. 119-123, 177).

54.  This characterization is attributed to Nathaniel Shaler in Haller (1971, pp. 184-185).

55.  We want to emphasize that we are not suggesting Commons advocated or acquiesced in the sexual exploitation of black women. Miscegenation was fairly widespread at the turn of the century; indeed, Ray Stannard Baker (1907a, p. 386) reported that it was not uncommon for white men openly to have two families, one white and one black, living in separate homes. Moreover, there seemed to be a double standard applied to miscegenation, as it was generally tolerated so long as it was confined to white men and black women. Clearly, there was no good reason for Commons to expect the practice to be discontinued. As a result, and as an objective matter, he could fully expect more potential mulatto leadership material to be produced.

56.  Jeff Biddle has wondered whether we might not have erred in concluding that by declaring amalgamation is their door to assimilation Commons had in mind the long process of infusing white blood into the veins of all Negroes. Instead, pointing to the strategic addition in *Races and Immigrants* of a crucial paragraph to the discussion leading up to this assertion (see note 36 above), Biddle proposes that Commons may have meant only that amalgamation was needed to provide the blacks with leaders (mulattoes) capable of directing Negroes as a group to a status of full participation in our democracy. Given Commons's strong commitment to the necessity of leadership emerging out of one's own class, we can understand how this conclusion might be reached on a reading of this portion of the manuscript alone. However, we find it implausible when taken in the context of the entire argument. As Commons makes clear at an earlier point in this same discussion, assimilation is an individual phenomenon—as he put it, assimilation is a process of *individual* training (Commons, 1903-1904:9, p. 221, emphasis added)—and hence one based on the precondition that the *individuals* constituting a race possess the capacity for

intelligence, manliness and cooperation. But it is Commons's argument, on the basis of geographical determinism coupled with artificial selection, that the blacks who constitute the preponderance of the Negro race inherently lack the capacity for developing these traits. This being the case, they are by Commons's own logic thus condemned to boss rule by the mulatto leaders that amalgamation of the type proposed by Biddle would produce. Indeed, in his condemnation of the disastrous granting of the voting franchise to Negroes, Commons averred: "[It] failed because it was based on the wrong theory of the ballot (sic). Self-government means intelligence, self-control, and capacity for cooperation. If these are lacking, the ballot only makes way for the 'boss', the corruptionist, and the oligarchy under the cloak of democracy" (Commons, 1903-1904:3, p. 224). Since Commons denounced this form of "democracy," it would constitute a major contradition in his argument if this is in fact what he had in mind by espousing amalgamation.

57. In the paragraphs immediately following this statement, Commons explored the issue of European peasants also being transformed into an enduring economic class, that is, into a caste. He concluded the discussion in the following manner, which we surmise to reinforce the interpretation we are here forwarding:

> Thus it is that the peasants of Catholic Europe, who constitute the bulk of our immigration of the past thirty years, have become almost a distinct race, drained of those superior qualities which are the foundation of democratic institutions. If in America our boasted freedom from the evils of social classes fails to be vindicated in the future, the reasons will be found in the immigration of races and classes incompetent to share in our democratic opportunities. Already in the case of the Negro this division has hardened *and seems destined to become more rigid.* Therein we must admit at least one exception to our claim of immunity from social classes (Commons, 1903-1904:1, p. 37, emphasis added).

58. Richmond Mayo-Smith, Commons's acquaintance and an authority he used extensively in "Racial Composition," was an advocate of amalgamation of "foreign elements" because it "renders the descendant of the immigrant practically identical with the native American in capacity, feeling and national characteristics" (Mayo-Smith, 1890, p. 66). He even went so far as to suggest the breaking up of concentrations of immigrant populations in America, arguing that such concentrations facilitate endogamous marriage and thereby retard amalgamation (Mayo-Smith, 1890, p. 77). But, according to Mayo-Smith, "Negroes are by birth and race and previous condition of servitude incapable of representing the American capacity for political and social life" (Mayo-Smith, 1890, pp. 64-65) and will never amalgamate successfuly with whites because of the "insuperable color obstacle" (Mayo-Smith, 1890, p. 75).

59. See Hoffman (1896) and Tillinghast (1902).

60. This work was cited several times by Commons in his selection on "The Negro."

61. We have suggested already that Commons's seeming advocacy of amalgamation was disingenuous. We might add at this point that of all his contempraries, Commons is the only one we have discovered to profess that this might be a solution to the "Negro Problem." Indeed, he is the only one who was not appalled by the prospect of miscegination and the resulting inferior "hybrid." In truth, we seriously question whether Commons was sincere in advocating miscegination. John Haller has argued that Jim Crow was just a holding action to quarantine the Negro until the laws of nature and the rigors of "competition" would generate the final solution of the Negro problem—extinction. In his view, the rationalizations concocted by the conservative were merely "a disguised anticipation for a more fundamental hope or belief" (Haller, 1971, p. 210).

62. Cherry has likewise noted the similarity between Commons's race views and the proslavery apologetics—what we refer to as the conservative standpoint—of the previous century. Cf. Cherry (1989, p. 28).

63.  Two of Semple's published works, one in 1901 and one in 1903, were cited by Commons in his list of references in *Races and Immigrants*, which was much more extensive than in "Racial Composition."

64.  The environmental hypothesis was prominent in at least two instances of social crisis prior to the period with which we are concerned. First, circa 1833 it was used by those in the West Indies wishing to institute coercive measures to control the emancipated slaves, who argued that, having evolved in the tropics, Negroes were basically lazy and would not work without coercion (Foner, 1983, p. 16). Second, in the United States, the environmental argument was used by those who supported Southern conservatives against radical Republicans during the debate over reconciliation following the Civil War; in particular, Carl Schurz, a senator from Missouri, argued in the U. S. Senate that people from tropical lands—that is, emancipated slaves—were not assimilable into American society (Camejo, 1976, p. 119).

65.  It might be added that the modern version of "environmentalism" is consistent with natural selection. Contemporary environmentalists argue that the environment determines the phenotypic expression of the genotype. The issue is to what extent phenotype can vary around genotype. See Lewontin, Rose and Kamin (1984, pp. 95-97).

66.  By "natural selection" we mean selection via the competitive struggle for survival from chance variations or, as Eiseley (1961, p. 53) put it, "biological variation combined with the pruning hook of selective struggle." This is the Darwin manifest in the first edition of the *Origin of the Species*. Darwin subsequently backed down from the strict natural selection view and, in his concept of *Pangenesis*, even retreated to Lamarckism (Eiseley, 1961, p. 217). When we use the term Darwinian we do *not* mean "genetic racialist," the term employed by Cherry. Darwin's concept of variation was not the same as the modern, genetic version. Darwin held at various times in his life either an archaic "blending" concept of heredity or his later "gemmule" theory which was essentially Lamarckian. The variation concept used by Darwin was based on observable, that is, phenotypic, differences in organisms, not genotypic differences. The latter were not understood until early in the twentieth century following the cytological work of German scientists and the rediscovery of the works of Gregor Mendel in 1900 (Eiseley, 1961, Ch. 8).

67.  Instinct is of course the term commonly used in reference to such an inherent behavioral propensity. The concept of instincts was widely accepted around the turn of the century by social theorists hostile to utilitariansim, who deemed various instincts to be the putative impetus for particular categories of action. Thorstein Veblen is undoubtedly the most famous of the instinct theorists, but many others similarly considered instincts to be fundamental determinants of economic and social behavior (see Cherry, 1980). Most of the instincts identified by social theorists of the period are tangential to the issues we raise, but some are germane, for example, the instinctive revulsion of one race for another proposed by the psychologist W.I. Thomas and E. G. Murphy's consciousness of kind (Newby, 1965, p. 47; Williamson, 1986, p. 211).

68.  Cope reasoned that if there were no "acquisitions from experience" passed on to the next generation there would be no progress as "inheritance without addition is mere repetition" (Haller, 1971, p. 197). Cope advocated the theory of recapitulation which led to the ranking of races according to how far each replicates the evolutionary stages through which the human race has passed. Cope asserted that climate determined how far each race progressed through this sequence and that races from the warmer climates ceased developing at earlier stages in the evolutionary process (Gould, 1981, p. 115). Cope appears to make the Negro a curious exception to this theory. In 1890 he argued that the Negro was unable to produce a civilization *even in the temperate zone*. For Cope, the *only* explanation for the failure of the Negro to develop a civilization was an unexplained "race peculiarity" (Cope, 1890, p. 2400).

69.  In truth, one would have difficulty finding any view upon which Ross and Commons explicitly disagreed.

70.  In the bibliographic references to his selection on "The Negro," Commons characterized Tillinghast's series of articles under the title "The Negro in Africa and America" (reprinted as

Tillinghast [1902]) as "The only systematic treatise based on a comparison of the Negro as a savage with the Negro as a slave and an American citizen" (Commons, 1903-1904:3, p. 234).

71.  As in the case of Semple, Shaler's work is included in the bibliography of neither "Racial Composition" nor *Races and Immigrants*. Nonetheless, a passage written by Shaler is used by Commons in the text of "Racial Composition" (see p. 59 below).

72.  Except where otherwise indicated, our summary of Shaler's views is derived from Haller (1971, pp. 167-176).

73.  Shaler also epitomizes the conservative view on race relations. For example, he believed that the Negro was a different species of man that was inherently inferior to the Aryan (Shaler, 1890, p. 36). Shaler also had a miscegenation phobia (Livingstone, 1987, p. 139) based on his belief that a blending of the blood of the Negro and whites would produce a third something that was as good as neither of the original stocks (Shaler, 1890, p. 37). Thus while Shaler advocated full political equality for the Negro, he also strongly urged segregation as a eugenic policy. Indeed, Shaler made clear his belief that a caste system is preferable to one where miscegenation occurs (Shaler, 1890, p. 37).

74.  At least one scholar, George Stocking, has argued that "implicit Lamarckianism played an important role in [Ross's] thinking" (cf. Stocking 1968, p. 251).

75.  Commons does not indicate on what grounds he had arrived at this generalization. However, in "Racial Composition" Commons explicitly calls attention to a 1904 article by H. W. Conn, "Social Heredity" (Conn, 1904) which contains essentially the same argument as made by Commons in "Natural Selection." Differentiating between "social evolution" and "organic evolution," Conn argued in this article that organic evolution, which is clearly his name for Darwinian evolution, accounts for very little of the evident differences between present-day human beings: "Doubltless man is born with certain innate tendencies, among which may be included moral sense. But it is certain that the method of expression of that moral sense is a matter of environment rather than heredity, one of social rather than organic heredity.... There is no reason to believe that the mental powers of the Chinaman are very different from those of the Englishman... . The mental powers of the adult are more dependent upon the kind of civilization under which he is reared than upon his innate capability" (Conn, 1904, pp. 144-145). Whether Commons had learned of Conn's views prior to 1897 is unknown to us; Stocking (1968, p. 241) asserts that one John Wesley Powell, founder of the Bureau of American Ethnology, "elaborated this point of view in 1888." Significantly, like Commons in "Natural Selection," Conn makes no mention of the Negro and hence does not indicate whether the general rule applies to him also.

76.  Commons had in fact made essentially this same argument, though in more abbreviated form, in *Social Reform & The Church*. See Commons (1894, p. 33).

77.  See p. 5 above. It might be added that the same term appears in *Social Reform & The Church*. See Commons (1894, p. 55).

78.  Weismann's theory of the "germ plasm," combined with the results of Mendel's experiments, devastated Lamarckism and laid the foundation for modern genetics (Eiseley, 1961, pp. 218-226). However, this victory was far from definitive in 1904 as the writings of Shaler and Cope clearly illustrate. Significantly, in his article, "Social Heredity" (see n. 75 above), Conn had emphasized that "as result of the discussion following Weismann's theories it has been pretty well acknowledged that acquired characteristics cannot ordinarily be inherited and cannot, therefore, be counted on as playing any very considerable part in evolution... Tho (sic) not yet admitted that acquired characteristics can never be inherited, it is practically agreed that their influence upon organic evolution must be slight" (Conn, 1904, p. 141).

79.  While, as noted already, Commons did not speak directly to the issue of the effects of amalgamation of Negroes and whites on the future fitness of the amalgamated race, he clearly believed that intra-*Caucasian* amalgamation generally produced a stronger race (cf. Commons, 1903-1904:1, p. 40). We have already recounted that he further suggested that all "non-tropical"

races are either an ancient amalgam or, going back even further, have "sprung from the same stock" (cf. Commons, 1903-1904:1, p. 39).

80.   See the bottom of p. 12.

81.   We expand on this point in the next section.

82.   It is worth repeating that Commons's failure to investigate the economic situation of the Negro personally and in a systematic manner violated one of the cardinal rules of discovering reliable knowledge emphasized in his later writings. There Commons made clear his belief that an investigator learning firsthand the details of a situation or problem is a key to acquiring knowledge that can be used to guide action. "(Cf. Commons, 1934b, pp. 4, 130, 160). Even more to the point are the remarks of Edwin E. Witte, made at a commemorative John R. Commons Birthday Dinner on October 10 ,1950: "Commons taught [his students] that they must thoroughly know the facts... He told them not only to study all that was written about a given subject and to reason logically about it, but to make their own observations... *and to learn from the people directly interested*" (quoted in Harter 1962, p. 77, emphasis added).

83.   This is a curious generalization in light of Commons having earlier referred to the report "of our most profound student of the American Indian," a Professor Brinton, that "several full-blood American Indians" given a proper education were, presumably aside from physical appearance, indistinguishable from the "usual type of the American gentleman" (Commons, 1903-1904:9, pp. 227-228).

84.   In the comprehensive bibliography of Commons's published writings provided in his final and posthumous work, *The Economics of Collective Action* (1950), the vast majority of the 45 items published during the years 1902 and 1903 pertain to the broad topic of labor organization.

85.   In the first article of the series, "Race and Democracy," Commons made the "extension" thusly: "Last of the immigrants to be mentioned but among the earliest in point of time, is the black race from the slave coast of Africa" (Commons, 1903-1904:1, p. 39).

86.   Obviously, there are questions left unresolved by our explanation. In his review of an earlier draft, Jeff Biddle opined that "Blacks were so powerless at this time, it seems hard to believe that Gompers or Commons would regard their displeasure with the labor movement as anything more than a nuisance." He then coyly added: "Can you imagine businessmen or congressmen of the time speaking to the white middle class against unionism on the grounds that the AFL was not integrated?" Biddle is undoubtedly correct in so far as the objective situation itself was concerned. Thus it should be understood that we are not contending Commons was directly or implicitly issued a directive by Gompers or other labor leaders to rationalize discrimination against Negro workers. However, we are unpersuaded that Commons would therefore not have bothered to develop an intellectual rationalization. Rather, it is our belief that it was Commons's own desire to provide coherent intellectual justification for AFL-style unions—and thereby to truly deserve the status of intellectual partner—that motivated him to develop the analysis regarding the inherent limitations of the Negro that he forwarded in "Racial Composition." For Commons, whose desire for recognition as a scholar and researcher is evident throughout his autobiography, placing intellectual closure on the issue was no doubt an important matter.

87.   See p. 1 above.

88.   It bears repeating that, judging by his writings, for Commons himself the Negro simply disappeared—became an invisible member of the American labor force—with the completion of "Racial Composition." Except in the reprint of *Races and Immigrants*, issued in 1920, Commons never again so much as mentioned the Negro worker as a distinct disadvantaged segment of the labor force posing unique problems for public policy This would appear to confirm that Commons's interest in facilitating progress for the Negro was not a deep one.

89.   In commenting on an earlier draft, Robert Cherry pointed out that in his strong support for the Chinese exclusion act, Commons in no way impugned the quality or character of the Chinese immigrant. Instead he simply argued that their presence would engender too much division within the working class. Cherry added that Commons's failure to employ the same argument in defending

the racist AFL policies provides additional evidence that, in contrast to his feelings about the Chinese, Commons harbored a deeply embedded racist view in regard to the Negro.

90. For more or less this type of characterization, see Barbash (1989).

# REFERENCES

Aldrich, Mark. 1979. "Progressive Economists and Scientific Racism: Walter Wilcox and Black Americans, 1895-1910." *Phylon* 40: 1-14.

_____ . 1985. "The Backward Races and the American Social Order: Race and Ethnicity in the Thought of John R. Commons." Mimeo.

Baker, Ray Stannard. [1907a 1973]. "The Tragedy of the Mulatto." Pp. 374-391 in *Racism at the Turn of the Century: Documentary Perspective, 1870-1910*, edited by Donald DeNevi and Doris R. Holmes, San Rafael, CA: Leswing Press.

_____ . (1907b), 1973. "What to do About the Negro Personal Conclusion." Pp. 392-399. in *Racism at the Turn of the Century: Documentary Perspective 1870-1910*, edited by Donald DeNevi and Doris R. Holmes. San Rafael, CA: Leswing Press.

Barbash, Jack. 1989. "John R. Commons: Pioneer of Labor Economics." *Monthly Labor Review* 112: 44-49.

Benedict, Ruth. 1940. *Race: Science and Politics*. New York: Modern Age Books.

Bloom, Jack M. 1987. *Class, Race and the Civil Rights Movement*. Bloomington: Indiana University Press.

Camejo, Peter. 1976. *Racism, Revolution, Reaction, 1861-1877: The Rise and Fall of Radical Reconstruction*. New York: Monad Press.

Chasse, John D. 1986. "John R. Commons and the Democratic State." *Journal of Economic Issues* 20: 759-784.

_____ . 1991. "The American Association for Labor Legislation: An Episode in Institutionalist Policy Analysis." *Journal of Economic Issues* 25: 799-828.

Cherry, Robert. 1976. "Racial Thought in the Early Economics Profession." *Review of Social Economy* 34: 147-162.

_____ . 1980. "Biology, Sociology and Economics—An Historical Analysis." *Review of Social Economy* 38: 141-154.

_____ . 1989. *Discrimination: Its Economic Impact on Blacks, Women, and Jews*. Lexington, MA: Lexington Books.

Comas, Juan. 1961. "Racial Myths." Pp. 13-55 in *The Race Question in Modern Science*. New York: Columbia University Press.

Commons, John R. [1894]. 1964. *Social Reform & The Church*. New York: Augustus M. Kelley.

_____ . (1896). 1967. *Proportional Representation*. New York: Augustus M. Kelley.

_____ . 1897. "Natural Selection, Social Selection, and Heredity." *The Arena* 18: 90-97.

_____ . [1899-1900]. 1967. *A Sociological View of Sovereignty*. New York: Augustus M. Kelley.

_____ . 1901. "Immigration and Its Economic Effects." Pp. 293-743 in *Reports of the U.S. Industrial Commission*, Vol. 15. Washington: Government Printing Office.

_____ . 1903-1904. "Racial Composition of the American People," a series of nine articles in *The Chautauquan*, Vols. 38 and 39: 1. "Race and Democracy," 38: 33-42; 2. "Colonial Race Elements," 38: 118-125; 3. "The Negro," 38: 223-234; 4. "Immigration During the Nineteenth Century," 38: 333-340; 5. "Immigration During the Nineteenth Century [Continued]" 38: 433-443; 6. "Industry," 38: 533-543; 7. "Social and Industrial Problems," 39: 13-22; 8. "City Life, Crime and Poverty," 39: 115-124; and 9. "Amalgamation and Assimilation," 39: 217-227.

_____ . [1905]. 1967. "Labor Conditions in Slaughtering and Meat Packing." Pp. 222-249 in *Trade Unionism and Labor Problems*, edited by John R. Commons. New York: Augustus M. Kelley.

_____ . 1907. *Races and Immigrants in America*. New York: The Chautaqua Press.

_____ . [1913]. 1964. *Labor and Administration*. New York: Augustus M. Kelley.

_____ . 1920. *Races and Immigrants in America*. New Edition. New York: The Macmillan Company.

_____ . 1924. *Legal Foundations of Capitalism*. New York: The Macmillan Company.

_____ . 1934a. *Institutional Economics: Its Place in Political Economy*. New York: Macmillan.

_____ . 1934b. *Myself*. New York: Macmillan.

_____ . 1950. *The Economics of Collective Action*, edited, with introductory essay, by Kenneth H. Parsons. New York: The Macmillan Company.

_____ , and John B. Andrews. [1919]. 1967. *Principles of Labor Legislation*. Augustus M. Kelley.

_____ , and associates. 1910. *A Documentary History of American Industrial Society*, 10 vol. Cleveland: The Arthur H. Clark Company.

_____ , and associates. 1918. *History of Labour in the United States*, 3 vol. New York: The Macmillan Company. (A fourth volume, under the editorship of Selig Perlman and Philip Taft, was published in 1935.)

Conn, H. W. 1904. "Social Heredity."*The Independent*, (January 21).

Cope, Edward D. 1890. "The African in America." Pp. 2299-2400 in *The Open Court*, 4.

Curtis, L. P. Jr. 1968. *Anglo-Saxons and Celts: A Study of Anti-Irish Prejudice in Victorian England*. Bridgeport: Conference on British Studies.

DeBrizzi, John A. 1983. *Ideology and the Rise of Labor Theory in America*. Westport, CN: Greenwood Press.

Degler, Carl N. 1974. *The Other South*. New York: Harper & Row.

Dillon, Merton L. 1985. *Ulrich Bonnell Phillips: Historian of the Old South*. Baton Rouge: Louisiana State University Press.

DuBois, W. E. B. 1901. "The Relation of the Negroes to the Whites in the South." *Annals of the American Academy of Political and Social Science* 18: 121-140.

_____ . [1903]. 1969. *The Souls of Black Folk*. Signet Classics Reprint Edition. New York: New American Library.

Eiseley, Loren. 1961. *Darwin's Century: Evolution and the Men Who Discovered It*. Garden City, NY: Anchor Books.

Elkins, Stanley. 1968. *Slavery: A Problem in American Institutional and Intellectual Life*, 2nd ed. Chicago: The University of Chicago Press.

Ely, Richard T. [1886]. 1969. *The Labor Movement in America*. Reprint edition. New York: Arno & The New York Times.

_____ . 1889. *Social Aspects of Christianity*. New York: T.Y. Crowell.

Faust, Drew G. 1986. *A Sacred Circle: The Dilemma of the Intellectual in the Old South*. Philadelphia: The University of Pennsylvania Press.

Foner, Eric. 1983. *Nothing But Freedom: Emancipation and Its Legacy*. Baton Rouge: Louisiana State University Press.

Fredrickson, George M. 1971. *The Black Image in the White Mind: The Debate on Afro-American Character and Destiny, 1817-1914*. New York: Harper & Row.

_____ . 1988. *The Arrogance of Race: Historical Perspectives on Slavery, Racism, and Social Inequality*. Middletown, CT: Wesleyan University Press.

Genovese, Eugene. 1969. Pp. vii-xxi, in "Foreword [to U. B. Phillips, *American Negro Slavery*]." Baton Rouge: Louisiana State University Press.

Gordon, Linda. 1977. *Woman's Body, Woman's Right: A Social History of Birth Control in America*. New York: Penguin Books.

Gossett, Thomas F. 1963. *Race: The History of an Idea in America.* Dallas: Southern Methodist University Press.

Gould, Steven J. 1981. *The Mismeasure of Man.* New York: W.W. Norton and Company.

Grantham, Dewey W., Jr. 1955. "The Progressive Movement and the Negro." *South Atlantic Quarterly* 54: 460-477.

Greene, John C. 1954. "Some Early Speculations on the Origins of Human Races." *American Anthropologist* 56: 31-41.

Haller, John S., Jr. 1971. *Outcasts from Evolution: Scientific Attitudes of Racial Inferiority, 1859-1900.* New York: McGraw-Hill.

Harris, Marvin. 1964. *Patterns of Race in the Americas.* New York: W. W. Norton & Co.

Harter, Lafayette G. 1962. *John R. Commons: His Assault on Laissez-Faire.* Corvallis, OR: Oregon State University Press.

Higham, John. 1975. *Send Them to Me: Jews and Other Immigrants in Urban America.* New York: Atheneum.

————. 1988. *Strangers in the Land: Patterns of American Nativism, 1860-1925.* 2nd ed. New Brunswick: Rutgers University Press.

Hoffman, Frederick L. 1896. "Race Traits and Tendencies of the American Negro." *Publications of the American Economic Association*, XI, Nos. 1, 2, 3.

Hofstadter, Richard. 1955. *The Age of Reform: From Bryant to Franklin Delano Roosevelt.* New York: Alfred A. Knopf.

Jones, Jacqueline. 1985. *Labor of Love, Labor of Sorrow: Black Women, Work and the Family from Slavery to the Present.* New York: Basic Books.

Lewontin, R.C., Steven Rose and Leon Kamin. 1984. *Not In Our Genes: Biology, Ideology, and Human Nature.* New York: Pantheon Books.

Livingstone, David. 1987. *Nathaniel Shaler and the Culture of American Science.* University, AL: University of Alabama Press.

Lubove, Roy. 1962. *The Progressives and the Slums: Tenement House Reform in New York City, 1890-1917.* Dallas: Southern Methodist University Press.

Mandel, Bernard. 1969. "Samuel Gompers and the Negro Workers, 1886-1914." Pp. 75-93 in *The Making of Black America*, Vol. III, edited by August Meier and Elliott Rudwick. New York: Atheneum.

Mayo-Smith, Richmond. 1890. *Emigration and Immigration: A Study in Social Science.* New York: Charles Scribner's Sons.

Meier, August and Elliot Rudwick. 1986. *Black History and the Historical Profession, 1915-1980.* Urbanna, IL: University of Illinois Press.

Miller, Kelley. 1908. *Race Adjustment: Essays on the Negro in America.* New York: Neale Publishing Co.

Newby, I. A. 1965. *Jim Crow's Defense: Anti-Negro Thought in America, 1900-1930.* Baton Rouge: Louisiana State University Press.

Phillips, U. B. 1904. "Conservatism and Progress in the Cotton Belt." *South Atlantic Quarterly* 3: 1-10.

————. 1928. "The Central Theme of Southen History." *The American Historical Review* 34: 30-43.

Poliakov, Leon. 1974. *The Aryan Myth.* New York: Basic Books.

Potter, David M. 1967. "The Work of Ulrich B. Phillips: A Comment." *Agriculture History* 41: 359-363.

Ramstad, Yngve. 1986. "A Pragmatist's Quest for Holistic Knowledge: The Scientific Methodology of John R. Commons." *Journal of Economic Issues* 20: 1067-1105.

————. 1987a. "Free Trade Versus Fair Trade: Import Barriers as a Problem of Reasonable Value." *Journal of Economic Issues* 21: 5-32.

_____ . 1987b. "Institutional Existentialism: More On Why John R. Commons Has So Few Followers." *Journal of Economic Issues* 21: 661-671.

_____ . 1990. "The Institutionalism of John R. Commons: Theoretical Foundations of a Volitional Economics." Pp. 53-104 in *Research in the History of Economic Thought and Methodology*, vol. 8, edited by Warren J. Samuels. Greenwich, CT: JAI Press Inc.

_____ . 1991. "Toward An Economics of the Just Price: John R. Commons and Reasonable Value." Paper presented to the Association for Institutional Thought, Reno, Nevada (April 25).

Roark, James L. 1977. *Masters Without Slaves: Southern Planters in the Civil War and Reconstruction*. New York: Norton.

Roosevelt, Theodore. 1912. "The Progressive and the Colored Man." Outlook 101: 909-912.

Roper, John Herbert. 1984. *U. B. Phillips: A Southern Mind*. Macon, GA: Mercer University Press.

Ross, Edward A. 1901. "The Causes of Race Superiority." *Annals of the American Academy of Political and Social Science* 18: 67-89.

_____ . 1930. *Principles of Sociology*. New York: D. Appleton-Century Company.

Shaler, Nathaniel. 1890. "Science and the African Problem." *Atlantic Monthly* 66: 36-45.

Solomon, Barbara M. 1956. *Ancestors and Immigrants: A Changing New England Tradition*. New York: John Wiley and Sons.

Snyder, Louis L. 1939. *Race: A History of Modern Ethnic Theories*. New York: Longmans, Green and Co.

Spero, Sterling D. and Abram L. Harris. 1968. *The Black Worker: The Negro and the Labor Movement*. New York: Atheneum.

Stein, Leon and Philip Taft. 1969. "Introduction." Pp. i-ii in *The Labor Movement in America*, edited by Richard T. Ely. New York: Arno & The New York Times.

Stocking, George. 1968. *Race, Culture and Evolution: Essays in the History of Anthropology*. New York: Free Press.

Storey, John W. 1986. *Texas Baptist Leadership and Social Christianity, 1900-1920*. College Station: Texas A & M Press.

Tillinghast, Joseph A. 1902. "The Negro in Africa and America." *Publications of the American Economic Association*. (2).

Turner, Arlin. 1956. *George Washington Cable: A Biography*. Durham, NC: Duke University Press.

Vidich, Arthur J. and Stanford M. Lyman. 1982. "Secular Evangelism at the University of Wisconsin." *Social Research* 49: 1047-1072.

Walker, Francis A. 1896. "Restriction of Immigration." *Atlantic Monthly* 77: 822-829.

Williamson, Joel. 1986. *A Rage for Order: Black-White Relations in the American South Since Emancipation*. New York: Oxford University Press.

Wolfe, A.B. 1936. "Institutional Reasonableness and Value." *Philosophical Review* 45: 192-206.

# GOD AND THE MARGINAL PRODUCT: COMPARATIVE PERSPECTIVE

## RELIGION AND THE DEVELOPMENT OF J. B. CLARK'S THEORY OF DISTRIBUTION

John F. Henry

The period following the Civil War was one of great social, political, and economic turbulence. In the South, Reconstruction elicited various upheavals before the planters regained control of the region; in the North, the modern labor movement was born, generating militant working class actions that resulted in significant strikes, including that of the "General Strike" of 1877; the populist movement, centered in the Midwest and South, produced a strenuous, if abortive, challenge to the growing economic and political rule of "the trusts." In Europe, while the specifics of the various conflicts differed, given different institutional arrangements and class forces, one observes the same general social stress.

**Research in the History of Economic Thought and Methodology,**
**Volume 13, pages 75-101.**
Copyright © 1995 by JAI Press Inc.
**All rights of reproduction in any form reserved.**
**ISBN: 1-55938-095-0**

Essentially, there was great flux in the world, symptomatic of the transition to large-scale, non-competitive forms of industrial organization. With the growing concentration of workers that was an outgrowth of this transition, labor organizing and actions designed to address the perceived onerous conditions of work were on the rise, and small-scale producers—the populists— organized their ill-fated attempt to stem the tide of industrial advance. With such developments, the old order of a largely rural, petty producing economy (in the non-slave areas) declined and a still to be specified new order started to emerge. Such developments had their effect on the ideological posture of the leading intellectuals of the period.[1]

In this paper the concerns are: the relationship among advances in science, in particular, the Darwinian theory of evolutionary change; religion, as representative of what was at this time one of the dominant—if not *the* dominant—form of ideological authority; the social distress as outlined above, and the development of John Bates Clark's theory of income distribution. It will be argued that Clark initially attempted to rationalize the economic order through a religious appeal: The economy was undergoing a constant progression under the direction of a deity in which "moral force" was the divine instrument through which the "Good Life," one of harmony and plenty, would eventually evolve. The economic success of this ongoing process was measured by the amount of distributional justice generated in the economy. The current turmoil, then, was symptomatic of a mere transitional step in God's long-run plan for humanity. By the mid-1880s, this type of argument had little currency within the modern intellectual community and was increasingly less successful in supporting existing authority. Clark then began to shed his overtly religious line of argumentation (in his writings for the profession only), and to develop a theory of distribution based on an apparent scientific foundation—his marginal productivity theory of distribution. God seemingly disappears from the argument and the economic system produces the desirable result based on its own "natural" workings. In reality, Clark's new theory of distribution was not motivated by a scientific intent to uncover the underlying laws of social phenomena, but, rather, designed to replace his older, religion-based statement with one that displayed the scientific virtues of the modern age—and one that served the same function of rationalizing the existing economic order. Indeed, Clark equated the two views: The new law of distribution was the equivalent expression of the older divinely ordered moral force.

# I.  SCIENCE, RELIGION, AND SOCIETY

By the second half of the nineteenth century, advances in knowledge had laid the basis for what now passes for modern science (Bernal [1954] 1971,Vol. 2). While these advances were not limited to biology—surely discoveries in chemistry and physics were just as important—it was the development of the Darwinian evolutionary theory of life that produced the greatest social impact (Ellegard, 1958; Glick, 1972; Hull, 1973; Randall, 1977).

This view of life as an ongoing, non-teleological, holistic organism took both the scientific and lay communities by storm. Great debates were held; the popular press was filled with reporting on the various issues; the educated lay population actually *read* serious popularized scientific accounts: Haeckel's *Riddle of the Universe* (though of a vulgar Darwinian nature) went through 10 editions, was translated into 25 languages, and sold millions of copies (Gasman, 1971, p. 14).[2]

One, I believe the most significant, effect of the Darwinian revolution was the undermining of established religion (Green, 1961, 1966). Prior to Darwin, religion and science could live a somewhat uneasy coexistence (Hovenkamp, 1978, pp. 10-18, passim). Pre-Darwinian science was of a mechanical nature, perhaps best illustrated by the Newtonian metaphor of the universe as a clock which when wound would work its inexorable way toward a deterministic conclusion: Given the underlying relations among gears, pulleys, belts, and so forth,—the natural bodies of the universe—a change at any point in this interconnected system would set in motion a series of changes throughout the rest of the system that would produce definite and knowable consequences of certain magnitudes. In the sphere of geology (where Darwin certainly made an enormous impact), this outlook is exemplified by the cosmogonies of Thomas Burnett, James Hutton, and Charles Lyell, among other noted representative of this discipline (Gould, 1987). These intellectuals either tried to fit the geological record into the biblical account (the "catastrophists") or, in the case of Lyell, developed a "uniformitarian" position in which change proceeds smoothly in a mechanically linear fashion where qualitative disruptions are removed from consideration. Such views could readily be accommodated within a religious framework. After all, something had to wind the clock; God could have created the world in all of its many features in one fell swoop (with periodic tinkering or repair, to be sure) and this world would then exhibit the harmonious and mechanical relations of the "grand design." Indeed, many notable scientists took exactly this position: The noted Harvard geologist Louis Agassiz once argued that a species is an "idea in the mind of God" (in Hovenkamp, 1978, p. 49).[3]

What is observed by historians of ideas who work in this area is that, while there has certainly been contention between science and religion throughout capitalism's life-history, a relationship existed where the demands of scientific truth did not intrude upon the non- or anti-scientific world of religion (Crimmins, 1989).

With the advent of the Darwinian theory of evolution (or that of natural selection from which Darwin's theory follows), the scientific world was not so accommodating. Now the mechanical, determinist view of the world was replaced with one of no necessary design, of constant motion within which all substance underwent change in quality as well as quantity. Permanence was a chimera; a divinely ordained universe, with a "first" or "final" cause, was an affront to scientific reality. And one could not fail to see the resemblance between the Darwinian picture of nature and Marx's view of society. Change was ongoing, and this change resulted from underlying causes based on the fundamental relations of matter or society—or, dialectical materialism (Gasman, 1971, pp. 106-125; Meek, 1953, pp. 193-212). Indeed, Marx, while critical of various aspects of Darwin's work and noting various differences, stated that the *Origin of the Species* "...contains the basis in natural history for our [Marx and Engels] view" (quoted in Meek, 1953, p. 193).[4]

While it is true that religion has been periodically utilized to offer a challenge to prevailing authority and a hope for the future, nevertheless, religious structures and ideas have been, and continue to be (though with considerably less authority) one of the major forms of ideological control in society. Through the inculcation of the notion that the existing world was divinely structured, it promotes the view that: (1) The world is purposive and harmonious (the "first" or "final" cause argument); (2) that nothing can be done to seriously affect or alter prevailing arrangements; and (3) as these arrangements *are* God imposed, they should be respected as so organized. That is, religion promotes the idea of a "natural" order within which people should submit to established authority.

Now, while religion did lose a great deal of its force as a result of the attacks on the feudal order and its monolithic Church that were promoted by capitalist development (see Hill, 1966, pp. 162-186; 1980, especially Ch. 10), this institution in general, whether in Catholic or Protestant form, remained a significant element in the ongoing attempt to maintain the social order.[5] Indeed, by the period in question, even the Catholic Church had ceased its attacks on capitalism (from the feudal point of view), and had accommodated itself to the dominant economic system, developing a position that spoke directly to the working class in promoting acceptance of capitalism and rejection of socialism and militant trade unionism (Leo XIII, *Rerum Novarum* [1891] 1963).

Further, religion was one part of the intellectual's arsenal of ideas which promoted acceptance of the prevailing system. It was, at this time, quite common for leading academics to invoke a deity in the course of developing ideology comforting to the dominant members of society.[6]

With the advent of the Darwinian theory (along with other advances in the natural sciences), religion was no longer capable of serving the same role as in previous periods. No longer did overtly religious appeals have "weight" within the intellectual community—or, at least, in that section that considered itself progressive and modern. Basically, religious dogma was losing ground:

The problem of intellectual authority developed during the 1860's and 1870's, as the harmony between science and religion declared by virtually all segments of Protestant Christianity proved increasingly difficult to maintain. By mid-century, the synthesis of physics and chemistry in the principle of the conservation of matter, new theories of thermodynamics, and advances in physiology and biology... all suggested that natural science had the power to provide a total worldview. At the same time, through technology, science was literally remaking the world.... American society was reaching the point of integration... when people became aware that human events were caused not by personal intentions and actions close at hand, but by impersonal, distant, and less apparent causes, and hence turned for authority and practical power to the impersonal explanations of natural science (Ross, 1991, p. 54).

In the seventeenth century, it was the new science that needed justification against the reigning religious and moral tradition.... But by 1860, the scientific faith had been reestablished, and no longer stood in need of philosophic support and defense. It was now, many came to feel, religious and moral values that needed defense against the "encroachments" of science (Randall, 1977, p. 4).

Or, succinctly, "Christianity is doomed to fail" (T. H. Huxley in Hayes, 1941, p. 124).

The main problem, from the standpoint of those intellectuals who represented prevailing authority, was this: Given the advances of science and the concomitant undermining of religion which was a most important prop in dominant ideology, how was it possible to maintain existing authority but not appear anti-scientific? How could one give the impression of accepting science while still holding on to the ideological framework that assisted in the maintenance of the existing social order? This is not to say that all intellectuals of the period who tried to find a middle ground were motivated by the attempt to maintain existing authority: Certainly one can be aloof from (or even ignorant of) such issues and develop honest expressions of ideas that still conform to the general thrust of the period. (See Turner, 1974 for examples of British intellectuals who, for the most part, seem to conform to this position.) Here, we are concerned only with American intellectuals who exemplify the issue from the point of view of dominant ideology.

This central problem was neatly summed up by Andrew Dickson White, author of the immensely influential *A History of The Warfare of Science with Theology in Christendom* (1896), and then President of Cornell University.[7] White, who *appeared* to welcome the advances of science, actually promoted a plan to contain science by pretending to accede to its authority, but in reality mold its conclusions to accommodate religious thought.

Comparing the ideological problem with that of the Russian peasants attempting to control the flow of a river when the winter ice dam begins to break up, White suggests that the rising waters represent "the flood of increased knowledge and new thought," that religion is the ice dam, and that his work is the peasants' channel by which the new knowledge may be let in gradually and in a controlled manner. What White hopes to prevent is "... a sudden breaking away, distressing and calamitous, sweeping before it not only outworn creeds and noxious dogmas, but cherished principles and ideals, and even wrenching our most precious religious and moral foundations of the whole social and political fabric" (A. White, 1896, p. vi).

While various responses were open to the intellectuals of the period, I am concerned with one only: Here, the intellectual *appears* to adopt the scientific point of view, but develops an argument that maintains the older religious doctrine in modified form. The result is the creation of theory that is non-scientific in substance but has a scientific veneer and produces the same general outlook as that of religion:

> The nineteenth century tried compromise.... Instead of accepting the inevitable, and seeking the Good Life in a naturalistic world... the nineteenth century searched frantically for a new Cosmic Companion, for an up-to-date and "scientific" God.... Men so much wanted to believe in God, they grasped at any straw: God was the "Unknowable," God was Evolution, God was Energy, God was the principle of "Concretion"—somewhere, in some scientific or pseudoscientific concept, lurked the Father of mankind, exercising his Divine Providence (Randall, 1977, p. 9).

This approach had any number of variations which can be illustrated by reference to specific notables of the period who adopted this line of argument.[8]

William James, arguing that the natural and the supernatural occupy two distinct realms of existence, and that scientific truth cannot impose itself on the world of religion, substituted a biologically determinist psychology that relied on unchanging instincts, habits, and emotions for the older religious "soul" theory (Wells [1954] 1971, pp. 63-76). Instinct replaces God but still fills the same role as final arbiter.

Some, like John William Draper, professor of chemistry and medicine, in his *History of the Conflict of Religion and Science* (1873), held that the conflict between science and religion was due to religion maintaining its power through the organized Church. In the quest for truth, then, "the conflict between science and religion implied the opposition of religion and faith" (in E. White, 1952, p. 2). The solution to this conflict was to demonstrate the irrationality of religious *institutions* while claiming that modern science demonstrated the truth of religious *ideas*—the existence of God, the soul, immortality, and the like. In Draper's view, God becomes a "rational, law-abiding, and single deity" (p. 19), one in seeming conformity to the modern scientific fashion.

Francis Johnson, an influential New England clergyman writing in the 1880s, represents that faction of church intellectuals who argued for the acceptance of evolution because this theory, rather than dispensing with the need for a deity, demonstrated exactly the opposite. "Fitting" the evolutionary approach to the familiar Judaic-Christian story, Johnson claimed that the basic causal factor in human evolution was that of the mind, and this mind was the handiwork of God, constantly striving to discover God's world that the deity had expressed through evolution (Noble, 1958, pp. 125-133).

This view is precisely the position set forth by the non-clerical academic intellectuals Edward Youmans and John Fiske. For Youmans, "Science is the revelation to reason of the policy by which God adminsters to the affairs of the world" (Youmans, 1867, p. 48). Fiske argued along the same line (see, Everett [1946] 1982, pp. 11-12).

Perhaps the most notable representative figure in this regard was Herbert Spencer. Through his *Social Statics* (1850), *Principles of Psychology* (1855), and *First Principles* (1862), Spencer influenced much of the history and sociology of the period under examination, and became one of the household names of European and United States intelligentsia. Exerting enormous influence on Fiske (of the Manifest Destiny of the Anglo-Saxon race [sic] theory of evolutionary progress) and William Graham Sumner (the founder of American sociology and originator of a non-theological teleological theory of "natural" human evolution), Spencer developed a seeming theory of evolution that while appearing non-theological, indeed even anti-religious, was most comforting to the *status quo ante*, and was (and continues to be) seized upon as a principal form of ideological support for prevailing authority.

Essentially:

> ... Spencerian doctrine, built around the current interest in evolution, postulated the other liberal thesis that evolution or progress was the product of extrahuman sources. Specifically, Spencer declared that evolution was the result of certain inexorable physical laws, and the individual, to find happiness, must conform to these laws by adjusting to their present expression in the immediate environment. Beyond the fact that it violated the value of individualism, reform was clearly impossible, because man had no power to adjust his social environment, which reflected the material process of inexorable evolution (Noble, 1958, p. 61).[9]

In Spencer's view, what existed was both natural and right. The class society of his period was the product of natural forces. Those at the top of the heap were simply demonstrating the "survival of the fittest" principle; those at the bottom were actually deserving of their position in society. Or, as Spencer's American disciple Sumner bluntly put it: "A drunkard in the gutter is just where he ought to be, according to the fitness and tendency of things" (Sumner, ([1883] 1952), p. 114).

To sum up this rather extended introduction to the issue at hand, an examination of United States social and intellectual history in the post-Civil War period shows great discord in the then-extant social relationships. Militant working class movements, the populist upsurge, Reconstruction, the transition from a competitive framework to one of an oligopolistic character all produced a disquieting effect on the leading intellectuals of the era. Further, the older, comfortable ideologies—in particular, religion—were no longer tenable as a defense of established authority. Intellectuals scrambled to develop theories that appeared to be in keeping with the new scientific age. In reality, what was produced was the old doctrine in modern guise—the substitution of "natural law" argumentation that demonstrated the same essential truths of the older divine law inherited from the past: a purposive, harmonious world in which everything and everyone has a proper place, and which, as it is ordained by nature, cannot be seriously challenged. Nature replaces God or serves alongside God as the arbiter of human fortunes.

With this, we now turn to an examination of the evolution of J. B. Clark's theory of distribution. It will be shown that Clark was a product of his times. In his early writings, he incorporated an overtly religious argument in his analysis of the economic issues of the period, an argument that, while recognizing the changes then underway and often calling for reform of the institutions of the day, in the final analysis places God in the position of final and supreme regulator working through *His* instrument of "moral force." By the 1890s, we no longer see a deity in his academic writings. Now, a "natural law" argument replaces the non-scientific religious-based theorizing of his earlier period. However, it will be demonstrated that the religious defense remains in Clark's mature period, and Clark himself sees the marginal productivity theory of distribution as correspondent with (not a negation of) divine law in upholding established authority. That is, Clark's writings evidence the same general thrust as that of Draper, James, Sumner et al.

## II.   CLARK OF THE "CHRISTIAN SOCIALIST" PERIOD (1877-1886)

That Clark was personally religious is without argument. He was raised in a devout and active Christian household, decided in his senior year at Amherst to enter the ministry, and throughout his professional career continued to practice religion and publish in religious or quasi-religious periodicals. Although Clark's personal beliefs are not irrelevant to the issue at hand, I contend that they are of secondary importance. The issue is not Clark's religious belief, but whether the ideological framework within which he based his theory of distribution was influenced by this belief.

The starting point for the examination of the *social* (rather than the personal) base for Clark's position is the outlook of Julius Seelye, president and professor of mental and moral philosophy at Amherst College, and Clark's instructor in economics there. It was at Seelye's urging that Clark abandoned his plans for a ministerial career and undertook the process of becoming an academic economist, and it was while a student under Seelye that Clark's ideas began to take shape (A. Clark, 1938, p. 8).

Seelye was representative of that wing of Christian intellectuals that sought to hold onto a religious defense of the established order by appearing to accommodate the new science. For Seelye, the Christian faith was to be accepted and followed because it was rational. Science dealt in generalizations concerning universal laws. These laws were established by God and humans had no power to break or amend them. The task of scientists in both the natural and social realms was to discover these immutable laws of activity that would then demonstrate the divine and rational wisdom which lay behind them (Everett [1946] 1982, pp. 29-31).

For his course on political economy, Seelye chose Amasa Walker's, *The Science of Wealth*, a work permeated by theological rationalizations, defense of capitalism, and the search for universals. The ideological thrust of Walker's tract can be seen in the following extract:

> That Political Economy is a science having nothing to do with morals or religion, nor in any way pertaining to human welfare... is a common opinion; but it may be fearlessly asserted, that no other science is so intimately connected with the destiny of the human race, in its highest and most enduring interests. Such has been the testimony of those in the clerical profession who have given special attention to its teachings.

Walker then elicits testimony from various clergymen/economists such as Chalmers and Whately as to the value of (sound) economics for religion, and continues:

> Agreeing fully with the opinions expressed by these eminent men, I have felt desirous, throughout the following work, to show how perfectly the laws of wealth accord with all those moral and social laws which appertain to the higher nature and aspirations of man (Walker [1874] 1969, pp. xvi-xvii).

And:

> Akin to it is the general belief that hatred and retaliation are the normal relations of capital and labor, and that mutual distrust and hurtfulness are inevitable in all the developments of industry. Such a belief blasphemes against the harmonies of Providence,—is sightless before the glorious order of man and nature (Walker, 1969, p. 22).[10]

Such was Clark's introduction to economics.

Clark's early training was not unique. It was true that, unlike the pre-Civil War programs in this discipline, economics could no longer be viewed as simply a "divinely ordained extension of Christian moral philosophy" (Barber, 1988, p. 7), but it was nevertheless the case that the major institutions within which economists were trained were cognizant of the necessity to maintain some semblance of religious indoctrination in their training of social science students. This instruction was seen as one aspect of a much larger program in which "faculty, administrators, trustees, and donors cooperated to establish social science...as part of a wider effort to nurture socially responsible ideas...." (Church, 1974, p. 574). Such ideas were those catering to the values of the "comfortable" classes (from which most faculty members were drawn in any case) in their attempt to withstand the challenges of the socialists and populists to property rights and relations. In addition, it was recognized that new conceptions were required to address the problems associated with the deterioration of "traditional" values, including those associated with religion (Church, pp. 571-577; Haskell, 1977).[11]

Upon his return from graduate training in Germany, Clark undertook his first academic position at Carleton and began his prolific outpouring of periodical literature. It has been argued that Clark developed his positions in response to Marxism (J. M. Clark, 1952). This is a partial truth. In reality, over the course of his development we can observe that Clark is reacting to *all* the major social changes around him. There are articles dealing with populism and Henry George ("The Ethics of Land Tenure," 1890c; "The Moral Basis of Property in Land," 1890d); labor unions and working class activity ("The Moral Outcome of Labor Troubles", 1886a; "The Labor Problem...", 1887a; "How to Prevent Strikes," 1889a); the change from a competitive to a non-competitive economic order ("Business Ethics...," 1879a); and, most importantly, socialism ("How to Deal with Communism," 1878; "The Nature and Progress of True Socialism", 1879b). It is under the rubric of the last item that I wish to detail the relationship between Clark's religious position, his defense of capitalism and established authority, and the unfolding arguments concerning distribution.

Clark's early period of "Christian Socialism" (Dorfman, 1949, p. 189) and its relationship to the issues specified above can be documented in a series of articles published in *The New Englander* (the forerunner of *The Yale Review*). Nine of these articles, in (sometimes drastically) modified form are reprinted as part of his 1886b *The Philosophy of Wealth*. (See the Appendix for a listing of *The New Englander* articles of this period and their relationship to the chapters comprising *The Philosophy of Wealth*.)

It should be noted that this journal was both one of the premier intellectual magazines of the post-Civil War period and a periodical largely given over to religious writers commenting on the state of society. Between 1877 and 1890, Clark wrote twelve articles and five book reviews for *The New Englander* as well as contributing several less important pieces to overtly religious magazines such as the *Christian Union*. Clark continued writing in such outlets well into his mature period, contributing articles and notes to *The Christian Observer, Congregationalist and Christian World,* and *The Christian Endeavor,* among others. (For an almost complete listing of Clark's writings, see the bibliography in Hollander, 1927.)

In summary form, *The New Englander* articles set forth the following argument: The world of the 1870s and 80s is no longer competitive in the Smithian sense. Although at one time competition carried a great moral force that allowed a just distribution of income to be produced, that is no longer the case. Given the increasingly non-competitive order of society, various problems, in particular the "labor problem," have been generated, and new theories, new codes of conduct are necessary to both understand and to direct the transition to the new order. This transitional period, if not properly understood and directed, could well lead to communism (or "political socialism"—Marxism). If this result is to be prevented, a "true" socialism based on religious morality and under God's direction must be effected to usher in a new, harmonious order.

Clark's first concern in these writings was to develop a theoretical argument in accord with the fact that the older, "crude" or "brute" competition was fast disappearing and was rapidly being replaced by a "modern" form based on large-scale, collectivized means of production along with an organized labor force.

In the older, Smithian form of capitalism, as long as there was rough equality between capitalists and workers, competition itself provided a just distribution that was morally defensible (Clark, [1886b] 1967, pp. 160-161):

> As it (competition) gradually came into existence it demonstrated its capacity for dividing products with a certain approach to justice. It commended itself to men's sense of right, and was established... on a moral basis (Clark, [1886a], p. 533).

With the organization of capital and the gradual elimination of the older, competitive forms, however, injustice became the rule given the inequality that resulted from an organized capitalist class facing an unorganized working class. With the more recent emergence of labor unions, however, capital and labor were now facing each other on a more equal footing (p. 534). The problem now becomes this: The old law of distribution, based upon competition and supply and demand, produced a just distribution of income. Given the disappearance of competition and its replacement by "co-operative", "non-competitive economics" (Clark, [1886b] 1967, Chs. 10,11), it is necessary to uncover a new law of distribution that will exhibit "moral force" as its overriding characteristic (Clark, [1886b] 1967, pp. 132-133).

In his "Christian Socialist" period, Clark had no theory of distribution as such. His argument could be reduced to the following: Under small-scale capitalist production, particularly where "free" land is available to workers (Clark, [1886b] 1967, p. 171), there is rough equality between the contending classes. The laws of supply and demand produce equal exchange (Clark, [1886b] 1967, Ch. 1), which results in a just distribution of income. Justice, then, is equated with competition. With the decline of competition, injustice becomes the norm as capitalists become better organized, hence stronger, than workers. With organization of workers, less inequality is produced and we now have the renewed possibility of a just distribution. To be morally sound, however, distribution can no longer be based on competitive supply and demand but must be founded on the new facts of industrial organization, and the new theory of distribution must reflect this change. For Clark, this new development initially meant distribution based on arbitration:

> ... that which favorably affects the terms of distribution is not merely the consolidation of labor, but that movement followed by the moral development for which it opens the way. The solidarity of labor calls imperatively for arbitration, in the adjustment of its claims, and accustoms the public mind to accept a standard of wages determined by justice rather than by force (Clark, [1886b] 1967, p. 171, see also Chapter 10 of *The Philosophy of Wealth*).

It is noteworthy that, at this stage of his development, Clark argues that until arbitration determines wage payments, coercion is the rule under the new, non-competitive forms of organization.

In this period, Clark often appears to take on an anti-capitalist stance, one sympathetic to the working class and socialism:

> We do not enslave men now-a-days. The emancipation proclamation ended all that, did it not? We offer a man a pittance, and tell him to take it and work for us from morning till night or starve; but we do not coerce him. It is at his option to choose whether he will work or not; he is free, you observe! We do not eat men—precisely. We consume the product of their labor, and they may have virtually worked body and soul into it; but we do it by such indirect and refined methods that it does not generally occur to us that we are cannibals. We kill men, it is true; but not with cudgels in open fight. We do it slowly, and frequently take the precaution to kill the soul first; and we do it in an orderly and systematic manner. Indeed we have any number of books and learned professors to tell us precisely in accordance with what laws we may kill them, and indeed must kill them, if we will not break with the system of which we are a part (Clark, 1878, p. 540).

Elsewhere, Clark compares the selling of labor under capitalism to the captain of a boat charging a drowning man for his rescue (Clark, 1879a, p. 165).

As I have argued elsewhere (Henry, 1982), this view is misleading.[12] Clark was always pro-capitalist and anti-socialist in any meaningful sense of these words. Essentially, what Clark exhibited during this early period was a populist outlook, a point of view that often appears anti-capitalist but is simply a response from a small producer's perspective during the transition from small-scale to large-scale production.

Clark distinguished "political socialism" (or Marxism) from "true" or "Christian" socialism. The former he consistently attacked, though recognizing that this ideology and political movement had great appeal given the changes in the economic organization of society (Clark, 1878, pp. 533-534). For Clark, political socialism, regardless of its causes or concerns, was a "wild, lawless protest against some real and some imaginary grievances" (Clark, 1878, p. 535).

While it is difficult to find in Clark a concrete statement of what he means by true socialism, we can uncover something of his meaning through somewhat casual statements scattered throughout his writings. The best statement of his position that I've found is the following:

> ... a practical movement, tending not to abolish the right of property, but to vest the ownership of it in social organization, rather than in individuals. The object of the movement is to secure a distribution of wealth founded on justice, instead of one determined by the actual results of the struggle of competition (Clark, 1879b, p. 567).

By vesting the ownership of property in social organization, Clark does not mean nationalization or socialization proper, but the establishment of small holdings for workers, cooperative societies and the like (Clark, 1878, p. 541). For Clark, private property is a necessary and sacrosanct institution (Clark, 1877, pp. 170,174). (For a more definitive statement, see Clark 1890c, 1890d.)

Further, and more importantly, this "true' socialism is God's handiwork, and it is God who is directing society toward this end:

> Unknown to social theorists, the way for true socialism has been preparing for a hundred years, and a consideration of these preliminary steps helps to give the true conception of it, as a general development, directed by the Providence which presides over all history.... Here is the dividing line between the false political socialism and the true; the one sees an ideal, and would force humanity to it through blood and fire; the other sees the ideal, and reverently studies and follows the course by which Providence is leading us toward it (Clark, 1879b, pp. 572, 577).

Indeed, for Clark, the social turmoil wrought by the transition from competitive to oligopolistic capitalism during the period is itself the product of divine guidance:

> ... there is a new economic system ...and...it stands in a special relation to Christian ethics.... The surface phenomena are misleading, and seem to be the superficial view, to mean rather the unchaining of demons rather than the ushering in of God's kingdom in the industrial world (Clark, 1887b, pp. 50, 53).

The problem for Clark at this stage of his intellectual development is to find a mechanism to replace that of competition in guiding the economic system toward a just distribution of income. For Clark, this is "moral force," the instrument through which God directs society and which he equated with Christianity:

> The final abolition of slavery is traceable to the same influence which abolished cannibalism in primitive times, and is another instance of moral force overcoming an

apparent economic necessity, and changing an established mode of industry.... The difference between present and former modes of competition may be credited to this moral force.... The sense of right is a silent and slow-acting force, but, when aroused, it is resistless. It makes a way where it cannot find one. It overcame obstacles in removing cannibalism and slavery, and it will overcome obstacles in removing the abuses of the present.... We need to recognize the moral force by which these earlier evils (slavery and cannibalism) have been removed, and to know that that force is still equally powerful (Clark, 1878, pp. 538, 39, 41,42).

For Clark, "true" socialism is God's kingdom on earth, the result of a long evolutionary process guided by the deity and eventually implemented as part of God's plan, but coming in God's time not man's (as per Marx) (Everett [1946] 1982, p. 50). Essentially, Clark's original argument can be seen as one possible version of the Newtonian clock in which a pre-determined path of development is established by "the winder" who then serves as periodic "tinkerer" in guiding society to a particular end.

At this time, Clark is not overtly anti-labor or anti-union. Labor is perfectly justified in organizing against organized capital. The basic issue is under what guidance labor will organize. For Clark, the great fear (and reality) was that labor would organize under the direction of socialists or anarchists (1878). To counter this leadership, it was necessary to bring the Church into a leadership position. (Clark, [1886b] 1967, Ch. 12). The problem, as Clark saw it, was that the organization of the Church had allied itself with wealth and had thus alienated itself from the working class. To remedy this situation, it was necessary for the Church—the *organization*—to return to its origins, its roots, its *faith*, and come to the assistance of the poor. That is, the problem was not that of religion, but of the organizational structure within which religion was housed. The structure required fundamental modification; the ideology remained a "moral force."

In the early, "Christian Socialist," period of his development, then, Clark represented the type of intellectual who, while arguing that the then-present form of capitalism was unjust and in need of significant reform, nevertheless defended the economic system in general. The form of defense, however, was that of a non-scientific appeal to a divinely ordered "progress" which, if allowed to reach fruition, would gradually produce a just, harmonious outcome: The current situation was one of temporary discord.

At this stage, Clark was content to set forth his over-arching theory largely on religious grounds. "Moral force," or a Providence-directed evolution, would provide the long-run solution. No appeal to scientific argument is made. In his mature period, the religious defense of prevailing authority is dropped from his argument (in his professional writings), and "science" replaces God.

## III. THE TRANSITION TO THE PRODUCTIVITY THEORY OF DISTRIBUTION

By the late 1880s, Clark had begun moving to a modified position on the distribution question. Up to 1887 (according to the official published record), Clark had argued that the then-extant distribution of income was unjust: With the disappearance of a competitive wage determined under conditions of equal exchange, wage-earners received less than they deserved, and arbitration had yet to establish a new standard by which wages should be determined. Now we see the beginning of a change in his outlook:

> Our predecessors divided the proceeds of industry by a free struggle of man with man; we divided them between classes rather than between individuals, and then by an appeal to some tribunal of equity. Economic science must take account of these changes.... We must master a new wage law...if we are able to predict at all confidently what the future has in store for the workingman. The mere discarding of the old law of wages frees us from an ugly cloud of scientific pessimism, and lets in upon the scene before us a flood of light (Clark, 1887a, p. 2).

It is important to note that at this stage of development Clark has no new theory of distribution, but calls for the creation of a theory which shows that the current distribution is just and equitable. The economic system will produce justice, though Clark has no theoretical basis from which to make such a claim: The theory *to be* produced is to support this claim. Further:

> We are drifting toward industrial war for lack of mental analysis. Classes in society are at variance over a ratio of division, and have no clear conception of the thing to be divided (Clark, 1887c, p. 35).

Note again the change in Clark's position from that of his earlier "Socialist" period. Previously, the basis of "industrial war" was the transition from a small-scale capitalist economy to one of large-scale plant and the attendant harsh conditions of work and *unjust* distribution of income. Now, the basis of conflict is one of "false consciousness." This, then, represents a fundamental shift in Clark's position. If the current distributional process is more or less just, then society must be so organized as to produce said justice: The basic economic structure is fundamentally sound (unlike his earlier position), but incorrect perceptions abound, which now become the root cause of conflict.

Indeed, in his 1888 "Capital and its Earnings," wherein he lays the foundation for the capital theory found in *Distribution*, Clark highlights the significance of the relationship between faulty ideas and the conflicts of the period:

> This practice (of confusing concepts of capital) has given a decided impulse to agrarianism and state socialism. Economic theory…is a main-spring of political action, and a faulty theory widely taught is sure to produce fruit in bad action (Clark, 1888, p. 92).

By 1889, we have the first recognizable statement of the forthcoming productivity- based theory of income distribution:

> Sound reasoning would seem to give us at once this formula: General wages tend to equal the actual product created by the last labor that is added to the social working force (Clark, 1889b, p. 49).

In this same article, Clark tells us that to satisfy the requirements for a truly "scientific" theory of wages (or distribution in general), it is necessary to uncover a principle that is based "on native impulses in men and in society" and that is universal in application (Clark, 1889 b, pp. 39-40). This, of course, takes us back to the admonitions of Clark's professor, J. H. Seelye, who instructed his students to search for natural, universal principles that regulated society, and which are above and independent of social forms themselves. Here, then, we find the first public indication that Clark has seemingly adopted the up-to-date scientific approach, and has apparently abandoned his previous religious line of argument. He now advances argumentation in which the laws of distribution are determined by non-social, non-providential forces.

In 1890, Clark produced the first treatment of distribution based specifically on the marginal productivity concept. "The Law of Wages and Interest" is indeed a hallmark study in the history of economic theory. (Contrary to the usual view, it was in this article and not in the 1891 "Distribution as Determined by a Law of Rent" that Clark first laid out more or less completely his theory of distribution, which was to be developed in finished form in his *The Distribution of Wealth* ([1899] 1965).) The thrust of the argument is directed toward settling the following issue:

> So great are the issues that depend on a solution of the wage problem, and so baffling has the problem proved, that the presenting of anything that claims to actually solve it involves no little boldness. Is present society rooted in inequity and does it give to a few men the earnings of many? Is robbery in which three quarters of the human family are victims perpetuated and legalized by the "capitalistic" system? These things we shall know if we can find the forces that govern the rate of pay for labor. We shall do more, for we shall discover in which direction the system is tending, and whether its very progress is baneful. We shall know whether the system that perfects society as a whole is merciless to the workers who chiefly compose it. This is little less than knowing whether in the long run human life is worth living. Yet we need, for the moment, to forget this issue in order to settle it; we must aim to study the Wage-and-Interest Law in as unbiased a way as if no practical contests were to be decided by it (Clark,.1890b, p. 43).

By now Clark has fully renounced his previous position on the relationship between then-modern capitalism and equity or justice; he is fully cognizant of the relationship between theories of distribution and political understanding and activity. Yet, once the new theory (which, of course, will eliminate the older—read Marxian—theory from contention) is written, the issue will be settled. Practice is to follow theory, and Clark's purpose is to provide a pacific theory, one that argues:

> To every man his product, his whole product and nothing but his product, is not merely the standard of wages; it is the standard that society tends to realize in fact, and that it would realize and forever retain if there were nothing to vitiate the action of a true competitive law (p. 44).

From this point, Clark goes on to develop the theory of distribution that is found in its fullest form in *The Distribution of Wealth.*[13] And, in the course of this development, he leaves little doubt that the marginal productivity theory of distribution is politically significant. In his 1894 Presidential address to the American Economics Association, published as "The Modern Appeal to Legal Forces in Economic Life," Clark informs his audience that there were two movements of discontent in the capitalist world, anarchism and socialism, of which the latter had the strongest theoretical foundation (that is, Marxism). The new theory of distribution, however, serves as a *scientific* repellant to such movements and their attendant theories, and it guides the modern economy into the *proper* channels of reform:

> The study that assures us of this [payment to factors based on the marginal product] incidentally shows how the work [of reform] is to be done. It reveals a line of public policy that is safe and efficient, and that offers an outlet for the reformatory energy that, with a zeal that is not according to knowledge, is now trying to undermine society (Clark, 1894b, p. 483).

The new theory is a guide to action: it constrains the possibilities of reform into "safe" channels, undermining the zealous but ignorant reformers (socialists and anarchists) who are undermining capitalism. What are the limits to reform? For Clark, the question is whether said reform would violate the law of distribution, that is, whether such programs would redistribute income away from capitalists toward workers (pp. 483-484) and thus upset the "natural" distribution that results from the universal laws of economics. To that end, for example, unions that attempt to raise wages above the "going" or "normal" rate (determined by competitive enterprises) are injurious to worker and capitalist alike, and states should maintain right to work laws (the open shop) (p. 494, See, Clark, 1902 for an extended treatment of this whole issue). Essentially, reform is to be limited to those actions designed to make the natural law of distribution work more efficaciously—the mitigation of monopoly power, and so forth—but should not seek to override this law.

Clark's new position is amply demonstrated in an article written for *The Christian Register* (Clark, 1891b), obviously a religious periodical and one indicative of Clark's continuing efforts to convince such readers of the need to adopt modern, "scientific" arguments in defense of established authority. Here, he asserts that Darwinian theory has conquered the field of social investigation; that it is time to understand wage (income) determination as one aspect of natural law; that said natural law specifies income shares as the measure of contribution to output; and that trade unions of the large, federated type, and, in particular, socialism, upset natural law and must, therefore, be resisted.[14]

We observe that, by this time, Clark has considerably modified his position on worker organizations. In his "Socialist" period, large federated unions were a necessary countervailing power to the organizations of businessmen—the non-competitive structures that were developing in the period: As late as 1886, the Knights of Labor, for instance, were viewed sympathetically (Clark [1886] 1967, pp. 136-137). Now, such large-scale unions violate the law of distribution and injure the very workers they are supposed to advantage. Further, we find Clark abandoning his previous position on oligopolistic structures. Now, competition is the norm and results in justice; non-competitive structures are an aberration that can be controlled through proper governmental regulations (Clark, 1901b).[15] Indeed, as early as 1890, we find Clark modifying his previous position and arguing that, now, trusts are doing a beneficent work in that they are better organizations for coordinating economic activity than the previous competitive structure (Clark, 1890a, p. 223).

The whole thrust of Clark's line of development can be demonstrated by reference to the opening sections of *The Distribution of Wealth*:

> It is the purpose of this work to show that the distribution of the income of society is controlled by a natural law, and that this law, if it worked without friction, would give to every agent of production the amount of wealth which that agent creates. However wages may be adjusted by bargains freely made between individual men, the rates of pay that result from such transactions tend, it is here claimed, to equal that part of the product of industry which is traceable to the labor itself; and however interest may be adjusted by similarly free bargaining, it naturally tends to equal the fractional product that is separately traceable to capital. At the point in the economic system where titles to property originate... the social procedure is true to the principle on which the right of property exists. So far as it is not obstructed, it assigns to every one what he had specifically produced (Clark, [1899] 1965, p. v).

> The indictment that hangs over society is that of "exploiting labor." "Workmen" it is said, "are regularly robbed of what they produce. This is done within the forms of law, and by the natural working of competition." If this charge were proved, every right-minded man should become a socialist; and his zeal in transforming the industrial system

would then measure and express his sense of justice. If we are to test the charge, however, we must enter the realm of production. We must resolve the product of social industry into its component elements, in order to see whether the natural effect of competition is or is not to give to each producer the amount of wealth that he specifically brings into existence (p. 4).

Clark now has found his subsitute for religion in supporting existing arrangements. A universal law of distribution exists that reaches fruition where "titles to property originate": By this Clark means capitalism (pp. 36-51).[16] Capitalism, then, is the natural, and final, product of a long evolutionary line of development. The universal law has always existed, but it's been concealed under pre-capitalist economic arrangements:

... so that, e.g., a gang of Aleutian Islanders slushing about in the wrack and surf with rakes and magical incantations for the capture of shell-fish are held, in point of taxonomic reality, to be engaged on a feat of hedonistic equilibration in rent, wages and interest. And that is all there is to it (Veblen [1908] 1961, p. 193).

With turn-of-the-century capitalism, however, the law can be seen in its full development, as non-capitalist social relations no longer serve to conceal it.

At this point, I want to deal with the underlying rationale for the development of Clark's productivity theory. The first issue is rationale of productivity theories in general.

Von Thünen is usually given credit for the invention of the marginal productivity theory of distribution (Spiegel, 1971, pp. 510-512), but productivity theories of a general nature pre date the argument contained in the volumes comprising *The Isolated State* (1826-1863). In the period between Smith and Ricardo, Say and Maitland (Lauderdale) both put forward crude productivity theories that argued, succinctly, that because "factors of production" were paid incomes, they had to be contributing to the generation of income as the payment itself was proof of said contribution (Maitland [1804] 1966, pp. 132-145; Say, [1804] 1827, pp. 269-270). In the period after Ricardo, such theoretical generalizations became something of a standard line of argument (see Henry 1990, Ch. 5).

The second issue regarding the development of productivity theories of distribution deals specifically with the topic at hand—the impact of scientific developments in the second half of the nineteenth century on ideological defenses of established authority. As Mirowski (1989) has demonstrated to a fare-thee-well, the neoclassicists of the period took a misspecified and somewhat outmoded physics as their methodological base. Since physics *is* scientific, this foundation provided the *apparently* scientific rather than religious defense of capitalism that became necessary following Darwin.

And, if the new economics was to be based on a mechanical physics metaphor, it could stand on a seemingly scientific foundation but *not* accede to the Darwinian demand for an evolutionary approach, which, of course, would call into question the standard position on capitalism as a "natural," "eternal," equitable economic system. Indeed, this is precisely one of the main complaints that Veblen had with neoclassicism ([1898] 1961).[17]

Last, it is fairly obvious that Clark abandoned his "socialist" (read critical, reformist) outlook as a reaction to actual developments within the United States labor movement. Until the mid-1880s, several fairly prominent academic social scientists (Adams and Ely among them) carried on a mild flirtation with socialism. With the formation of the Knights of Labor, then viewed as a dangerous, revolutionary organization, and the Haymarket affair of 1886, such a flirtation was no longer "respectable" within the institutional structure then-extant. In particular, academics were subjected to close scrutiny, a recantation of previously held views was demanded, and dismissals occurred in the case of recalcitrants. Clark, as a most respectable economist, quickly and vociferously abandoned all of his seemingly socialist posturing, separated himself from those who were suspect (Ely, for example), and framed his new position which demonstrated his loyalty to prevailing authority (Furner, 1975; Ross, 1977-1978, pp. 52-79).

And, while it is surely too tidy an accident that 1887 marks the dividing line between the "old" and the "new" Clark, it is not an accident that Clark did abandon his "socialist" dalliance and establish a new theoretical posture.

## IV.  CONCLUSION

In the early stages of his development, Clark had rejected the natural law argumentation of Smith, Ricardo, et al., which was based on a competitive framework (Clark, [1886b] 1967, ch. 3), and argued that a God-driven process was at work that would eventually produce justice under a capitalist form of economic organization, even though then-current arrangements generated injustice. By 1890, Clark had substituted a "natural law" argument for one based on divine law. This is not to say that he completely abandoned his religious rationalizations. Indeed, he continued to publish in overtly religious periodicals. But he now introduced his "scientific" defense of capitalism along with the religious rationalization (see Clark, 1909a, 1909b, 1909c): All his non-church sponsored publications were now based on his "scientific" line of argumentation.

However, it has been demonstrated that Clark's own natural law theory of distribution was developed with a particular end in mind—that of demonstrating that the existing system was itself just (barring "aberrations" such as monopoly). However, this theory did not evolve as the result of an objective investigation into the actual workings of the economy, but was an attempt to rationalize income shares against the charges of socialists, anarchists, and populists: The desired conclusion determined the necessary theory.

Moreover, it is readily seen that the new argument contains that same unifying theme as the now discredited religious defense: A set of laws exists which are just exists, over which humans have no control, and they produce equitable, harmonious results. For this reason, established (capitalist) society is just and its authority should not, must not, be challenged. In a large sense, then, there is a continuity between the young Clark and the mature Clark. The same general theme runs through both periods of his development, but the underlying rationalization changes from one dominated by a religious construction to one in which natural law emerges as primary.

The blending of the divine and natural law foundations of Clark's distribution theory can readily be observed in *Social Justice Without Socialism* (1914), Clark's last major work, and that which combines all the major themes argued over the course of his professional career in one argument:

> (There is a law that)...tends in the direction of a fair division of products between employer and employee, and if it could work entirely without hindrances, would actually give to every laborer substantially what he produces. In the midst of all prevalent abuses this basic law asserts itself like a law of gravitation, and so long as monopoly is excluded and competition is free...its actions cannot be stopped, while that of the forces that disturb it can be so. In this is the most inspiriting fact for the social reformer. If there are "inspirational points" on the mountain-tops of science...this is one of them, and it is reached whenever a man discovers that in a highly imperfect society, the fundamental law makes for justice, that it is impossible to prevent it from working and that it is entirely possible to remove the hindrances that it encounters.... Nature is behind the reformer.... To get a glimpse of what it can do and what man can help it do is to get a vision of the kingdoms of the earth, and the glory of them—a glory that may come from a moral redemption of the economic system.... A new Jerusalem may actually arise out of the fierce contentions of the modern market. The wrath of men may praise God and his Kingdom may come, not in spite of, but by means of the contests of the economic sphere (Clark, 1914, pp. 34-36, 47).

Clark, then, does not abandon his previous position concerning the relationship between capitalism, distribution, and justice. Now, however, the moral foundation for equity is not that of a God moving the economic system ever closer to "The Good Life," but the economic system itself, guided by the marginal productivity theory of distribution.

# APPENDIX

*The New Englander* Articles and *The Philosophy of Wealth*:
An Abbreviated Concordance

In the text, Clark's articles in *The New Englander* and *The Philosophy of Wealth* are cited. Where the point can be made by reference to *Philosophy*, that is the source cited as this publication is readily available. Sometimes, though, modifications made by Clark in revising the articles for this work significantly altered the tone, if not the substance, of the argument, making it less clear or overt. In such cases, I have cited the original article. Further, not all of the early *New Englander* pieces made their way into *Philosophy*: Obviously, these had to be cited independently.

Below is a listing of every article Clark wrote for *The New Englander* between 1877 and 1886. Given a publication date of 1886 for *Philosophy*, this represents the period from which chapters for that work could have been drawn. Following the title and date of the article, the relevant chapter number, title, and page numbers in *Philosophy* are given (when applicable). Where the article is not included in the later book, it is so specified. Finally, chapters in *Philosophy* that were written specifically for that work and are independent of *The New Englander* articles are specified.

1877 "The New Philosophy of Wealth." 36: pp. 170-186. (Chapter 1, "Wealth," pp. 1-9, and Chapter 2, "Labor and its Relation to Wealth," pp. 10-31). "Unrecognized Forces in Political Economy." 36(5) pp. 710-723. (Chapter 3, "The Basis of Economic Law," pp. 32-55).
1878 "How to Deal with Communism." 37(4): 533-542. (Not included).
1879 "Business Ethics, Past and Present." 38(2) pp. 157-168. (Chapter 9, "The Ethics of Trade," pp. 149-173).
"The Nature and Progress of True Socialism." 38(4): pp. 565-581. (Chapter 10, "The Principle of Cooperation," pp. 174-202).
1880 "Spiritual Economics." 39(3): pp. 305-318. (Chapter 12, "The Economic Function of the Church," pp. 221-236).
1881 "The Philosophy of Value." 40(4): pp. 457-469. (Chapter 4, "The Theory of Value," pp. 70-90).
1882 "Non-Competitive Economics." 41(6): pp. 837-46. (Chapter 11, "Non-Competitive Economics," pp. 203-220)
1883 "Recent Theories of Wages." 42(3): pp. 354-64. (Chapter 7, "The Law of Distribution," pp. 107-125, and Chapter 8, "Wages as Affected by Combinations," pp. 126-148 [though both chapters are radically modified]).
1886 "The Moral Outcome of Labor Troubles." 9(6): pp. 533-536. (Not included).
Chapters in *The Philosophy of Wealth* written independently of *The New Englander* articles:
"The Elements of Social Service." Chapter pp. 4, pp. 56-69.
"The Law of Supply and Demand." Chapter 6, pp. 91-106.

# ACKNOWLEGMENTS

A version of this paper was presented at a History of Economics Society session at the American Economics Association meetings in New Orleans, January, 1992. For helpful suggestions at that session, I thank William Barber, Juergen Backhaus, A. W. Coats, and Anne Mayhew. For most helpful criticism of an earlier draft of this paper, I thank William Dugger, Joseph Furey, Mason Gafney, Warren Samuels, Toshihiro Tanaka, A. M. C. Waterman, Paul Wendt, Nancy Wulwick, and two anonymous referees. For editorial assistance, I thank Charlene Heinen and Jeff Biddle; for technical assistance, I thank R. Scott McGowan. I am also grateful to the California State University for funding a Summer Fellowship that helped to support the research for this study. Lastly, I am grateful for support by the Economics Division of Staffordshire University where the final version of this paper was prepared while I was Visiting Senior Lecturer.

# NOTES

1.    For a general account of the relationship between political, economic, and social upheaval and ideological developments in the United States at this time, see Commager, 1952.

2.    And, lest one think that this reading was confined to the wealthy, or at least comfortable, section of the population, William Haywood, noted U. S. labor organizer, describes circulating libraries of miners in the West that included Darwin (Haywood, 1929, p. 23).

3.    It is telling that many academics of the period held joint appointments in their respective fields of natural science *and* theology. Indeed, prior to the Darwinian onslaught, the general view expressed was that "a good natural theologian is also a competent scientist" (Hovenkamp, 1978, p. 47).

4.    For discussions of the relationship between Darwin's views and other economic (and social science) theories, in particular those of the classical mode, see Schweber, 1980, 1985; and Young, 1985.

5.    When the youthful Haeckel first ventured to state the logical, scientific ramifications of Darwin's theory for religion at a conference in Stettin in 1863, he was cautioned by the more veteran biologist Rudolph Virchow not to push past a non-defined frontier that would intrude on the domains of both state and religion (Farrington, 1965, pp. 14-18).

6.    "Prior to the middle of the nineteenth century virtually all economics and politics had been taught by the professors of Mental and Moral philosophy. The philosophy of these classrooms usually consisted of an elaborate apologetic for Christianity and the inculcation of Christian moral ideas.... Secular social theory presented a direct challenge to both the authority and function of the church and its instruction" (Everett, [1946] 1982, p. 24).

7.    White was not the only major college president of the period who actively participated in the contest. James McCosh of Princeton was a leading proponent of the accommodation of science to faith. (Noble, 1958, p. 85)

8.    For general descriptions and analyses of these developments, see Ellegard, 1958; Glick, 1972; Hull, 1973; Noble, 1958; Randall, 1977, Ch. 3; Ross, 1991; Wells, [1954] 1971; E. White 1952.

9.    For a most trenchant, succinct account of Spencer's doctrine as teleological, see Randall 1977, pp. 42-49.

10.    It must be noted that Walker's text was not unusual for the period. Many of the most commonly used works in economics contained much the same, overtly religious, position. Texts by Perry and Bowen (to cite only two) are examples of such works. To quote Bowen: "But society is a complex and delicate machine, the real Author and Governor of which is divine. Men are often his agents.... Man cannot interfere with His work without marring it.... *Laissez faire...* means, of course, that God regulates them (prices, etc.) by his general laws...." (Bowen [1870] 1969, p. 18).

11.    While the institutional control of the training of economists and other academics is beyond the scope of this paper, it is imperative that one is constantly reminded of such control, and that the institutionalism of the profession was developed within the constraints established by individuals and bodies who were mindful of the scientific threat to religion and property.

The collection of articles in Barber (1988) should be read by all economists as a reminder of the social and political milieu from which modern economics sprang. Also, Bowles and Gintis (1976) and Furner (1975) are other important works in this regard.

12.  See, Jalladeau, 1975 and Tanaka, 1990 for the position that Clark did hold a socialist position and underwent a fundamental transformation to one of an anti-socialist or pro-capitalist perspective.

13.  "Distribution as Determined by a Law of Rent," 1891a; "The Genesis of Capital, 1893; "A Universal Law of Economic Variations," 1894a; "The Origin of Interest," 1895.

14.  This is a most remarkable article. Here, Clark commits three fundamental errors in arguing his case. He first equates the static marginal productivity principle with the evolutionary laws of Darwin. He then illustrates the marginal productivity principle without regard to property relations (the defense of which is the whole point of the exercise). And, finally, he concludes that the greatest improvement in workers' standard of living will come with workers owning capital: "The most favorable outlook, then, is that of a personal union of capital with labor, which means the ownership of capital, not the management of it, by the laboring class"(Clark, 1891b, p. 793). In other words, Clark ends with a communist solution to the wage question, a strange result indeed, and the only time we see such an argument in his mature period.

15.  Interestingly, Clark developed a rather ingenuous argument demonstrating that monopolies really had no monopoly power. In "Disarming the Trusts" (1900), "Monopolies and the Law" (1901b), and "The Real Dangers of the Trusts" (1904), he posited that while monopolies did have the power to raise prices arbitrarily and thus violate the natural law of distribution, they had little real power in this direction. If they were to raise prices above some limit, the monopoly profits generated would stimulate entry which would force prices down. Hence, monopolists have learned, through trial and error, to price their commodites more-or-less like a competitive firm in order to protect their monopoly position.

It is also notable that Clark was one of the team of academics that, under the guidance of the National Civic Foundation, assisted in laying out the structure that would eventually become the Federal Trade Commission. It has been argued that this commission with its attendant powers was created by "the trusts" to assist them in regulating the economy and preserving monopoly privilege. See, G. W. Domhoff (1970, pp. 201-206).

16.  As Clark is clearly expressing a point of view in which income is a reward for a contribution to output, he cannot but have in mind capitalist economic relationships. Surely property existed prior to capitalism, but such ownership could not be directly related to income shares. While slavery, for instance, was a property-holding organization, Clark never would have argued that the income of slaves was directly related to their productivity. Nor would private property in the form of non-productive assets—houses, women, and so forth—be of significance for Clark's position.

17.  Of course, Veblen also criticized classical political economy on the same issue. For Veblen, the *whole* of neoclassicism was wrong while only certain aspects of classical theory were.

# REFERENCES

Barber, W. J., ed. 1988. *Breaking the Academic Mold: Economics and American Learning in the Nineteenth Century*. Middletown, CT: Wesleyan University Press.

Bernal, J. D. [1954] 1971. *Science in History*, Vol. 2. Cambridge, MA: The MIT Press.

Bowen, F. [1870] 1969. *American Political Economy*. New York: Greenwood Press.

Bowles, S. and Gintis, H. 1976. *Schooling in Capitalist America*. New York: Basic Books.

Church, R. 1974. "Economists as Experts: The Rise of an Academic Profession in America 1870-1917." Pp. 571-610 in *The University in Society*, Vol. 2, edited by L. Stone, Princeton: Princeton University Press.

Clark, A. 1938. *John Bates Clark: A Memorial*. Privately Printed.

Clark, J. B. 1877. "The New Philosophy of Wealth." *The New Englander*. 36(1): 170-186.

———. 1878. "How to Deal with Communism." *The New Englander*. 37(4): 533-542.

———. 1879a. "Business Ethics, Past and Present." *The New Englander*. 38(2): 156-168.

———. 1879b. "The Nature and Progress of True Socialism." *The New Englander*. 38(4): 565-581.

———. 1883. "Recent Theories of Wages." *The New Englander*. 42(3): 354-364.

———. 1886a. "The Moral Outcomes of Labor Troubles." *The New Englander and Yale Review*. 9(6): 533-36.

———. (1886b) 1967. *The Philosophy of Wealth*. New York: Augustus M. Kelley.

———. 1887a. "The Labor Problem—Past and Present." *Work and Wages* 1(3): 1-2.

———. 1887b. "Christianity and Modern Economics." *The New Englander and Yale Review*. 11(1): 50-59.

———. 1887c. "Profits under Modern Conditions." *Political Science Quarterly* 2(4): 35-51.

———. 1888. "Capital and its Earnings." *Publications of the American Economic Association* 3(2): 81-149.

———. 1889a. "How to Prevent Strikes." *The Christian Union* 21: 231.

———. 1889b. "Posssibility of a Scientific Law of Wages." *Publications of the American Economic Association* 4(1): 37-64.

———. 1890a. "The 'Trust': A New Agent for Doing an Old Work" *The New Englander and Yale Review* 16(3): 223-230.

———. 1890b. "The Law of Wages and Interest." *Annals of the American Academy of Political and Social Sciences* 1(1): 43-65.

———. 1890c. "The Ethics of Land Tenure." *International Journal of Ethics*. 1: 62-79.

———. 1890d. "The Moral Basis of Property in Land." *Journal of Social Science* (27): 21-26.

———. 1891a. "Distribution as Determined by a Law of Rent." *Quarterly Journal of Economics*. 5: 289-318.

———. 1891b. "Natural Law in Political Economy." *The Christian Register* 3: 791-797.

———. 1893. "The Genesis of Capital." *Yale Review* 2: 302-315.

———. 1894a. "A Universal Law of Economic Variation." *Quarterly Journal of Economics*. 8: 261-279.

———. 1894b. "The Modern Appeal to Legal Forces in Economic Life." *Publications of the American Economic Association* 9(5): 481-502.

———. 1895. "The Origin of Interest." *Quarterly Journal of Economics* 9(3): 257-278.

———. [1899] 1965. *The Distribution of Wealth*. New York: Augustus M. Kelley.

———. 1900. "Disarming the Trusts." *The Atlantic Monthly* 85(5): 47-53.

———. 1901a. *The Control of Trusts*. New York: Macmillan Co.

———. 1901b. "Monopolies and the Law." *Political Science Quarterly* 16(3): 463-475.

———. 1902. "Is Authoritative Arbitration Inevitable." *Political Science Quartely* 17(4): 553-567.

———. 1904. "The Real Dangers of the Trusts." *The Century Magazine* 46(6): 954-959.

———. 1909a. "Present Day Socialism: What It Is." *Congregationalist and Christian World* April 24: 546.

———. 1909b. "Present Day Socialism: What It Would Do." May 1: 581.

———. 1909c. "Present Day Socialism: What We Should Do About It." May 15: 645.

———. 1914. *Social Justice Without Socialism*. Boston: Houghton Mifflin Co.

Clark, J. M. 1952. "J. M. Clark on J. B. Clark." Pp. 592-612 in *The Development of Economic Thought*, edited by H. Spiegel. New York: J. Wiley.

Commager, H. 1952. *The American Mind*. New Haven: Yale University Press.

Crimmins, J. 1989. *Religion, Secularization and Political Thought*. London: Routledge.

Domhoff, G. W. 1970. *The Higher Circles*. New York: Random House.

Dorfman, J. 1949. *The Economic Mind in American Civilization*, Vol. 3. New York: The Viking Press.

Ellegard, A. 1958. *Darwin and the General Reader*. Goteberg, Sweden: Elanders Boktryckeri Aktiebolag.

Everett, J. [1946] 1982. *Religion in Economics*. Philadelphia: Porcupine Press.

Farrington, B. 1965. *Science and Politics in the Ancient World*, 2d ed. New York: Barnes and Noble, Inc.

Furner, M. 1975. *Advocacy and Objectivity: A Crisis in the Professionalization of American Social Science*. Lexington, KY: University Press of Kentucky.

Gasman, D. 1971. *The Scientific Origins of National Socialism*. New York: American Elsevier.

Glick, T., ed. 1972. *The Comparative Reception of Darwin*. Austin: University of Texas Press.

Gould, S. 1987. *Time's Arrow, Time's Cycle*. Cambridge, MA: Harvard University Press.

Green, J. 1961. *Darwin and the Modern World View*. Baton Rouge: Louisiana State University Press.

_____. 1966. "Darwin and Religion." Pp. 12-34 in *European Intellectual History Since Darwin and Marx*, edited by W. Wagar. New York: Harper and Row.

Haskell, T. 1977. *The Emergence of a Professional Social Science*. Urbana IL: University of Illinois Press.

Hayes, C. 1941. *A Generation of Materialism*. New York: Harper and Brothers.

Haywood, W. 1929. *The Autobiography of Big Bill Haywood*. New York: International Publishers.

Henry, J. 1982. "The Transformation of John Bates Clark: An Essay in Interpretation." *History of Political Economy* 14(2): 166-177.

_____. 1990. *The Making of Neoclassical Economics*. London: Unwin-Hyman.

Hill, C. 1966. *The Century of Revolution, 1603-1714*. New York: W. W. Norton.

_____. 1980. *Some Intellectual Consequences of the English Revolution*. Madison: University of Wisconsin Press.

Hollander, J. H., ed. 1927. *Economic Essays Contributed in Honor of J. B. Clark*. New York: Macmillan and Co.

Hooykaas, R. 1972. *Religion and the Rise of Modern Science*. Grand Rapids, MI: William B. Eerdmans.

Hovenkamp, H. 1978. *Science and Religion in America 1800-1860*. Philadelphia: University of Pennsylvania Press.

Hull, D. 1973. *Darwin and His Critics*. Cambridge MA: Harvard University Press.

Jalladeau, J. 1975. "The Methodological Conversion of John Bates Clark." *History of Political Economy* 7(2): 209-26.

Kohn, D., ed. 1985. *The Darwinian Heritage*. Princeton: Princeton University Press.

Leo XIII (Pope). [1891] 1963. *Rerum Novarum*. In *Great Encyclicals*, edited by James Sweeney. New York: Paulist Press.

Maitland, J. [1804] 1966. *An Inquiry into the Nature and Origins of Public Wealth*. New York: Augustus M. Kelley.

Meek, R. 1953. *Marx and Engels on Malthus*. London: Lawrence and Wishart.

Mirowski, P. 1989. *More Heat Than Light: Economics as Social Physics; Physics as Nature's Economics*. Cambridge, MA: Cambridge University Press.

Noble, D. 1958. *The Paradox of Progressive Thought*. Minneapolis: University of Minnesota Press.

Perry, A. 1875. *Elements of Political Economy*. New York: Scribner, Armstrong, and Co.

Randall, J. 1977. *Philosophy after Darwin*. New York: Columbia University Press.

Ross, D. 1977-1978. "Socialism and American Liberalism: Academic Social Thought in the 1880's." *Perspectives in American History* 11(1) 5-79.

_____ 1991. *The Origins of American Social Science*. Cambridge, MA: Cambridge University Press.

Say, J. B. [1804] 1827. *A Treatise on Political Economy*, 3d U.S. ed. Philadelphia: John Grigg.

Schweber, S. 1980. "Darwin and the Political Economists: Divergence of Character." *Journal of the History of Biology* 13(2): 195-289.

————. 1985. "The Wider British Context." Pp. 35-69 in *Darwin's Theorizing*, edited by E. Kohn.

Spiegel, H. 1971. *The Growth of Economic Thought*. Englewood Cliffs, NJ: Prentice-Hall.

Sumner, W. [1883] 1952. *What Social Classes Owe Each Other*. Caldwell, ID: The Caxton Printers.

Tanaka, T. 1990. "The Economic Thought of J. B. Clark: An Interpretation of 'The Clark Problem'". Pp. 147-156 in *Perspectives on the History of Economic Thought*, Vol. III.

Turner, F. 1974. *Between Science and Religion*. New Haven: Yale University Press.

Veblen, T. [1898] 1961. "Why is Economics Not an Evolutionary Science." Pp. 56-82 in *The Place of Science in Modern Civilization*. New York: Russell and Russell.

————. [1908] 1961. "Professor Clark's Economics." Pp. 180-230 in *The Place of Science in Modern Civilization*. New York: Russell and Russell.

Walker, A. [1874] 1969. *The Science of Wealth*. New York: Kraus Reprint Co.

Wells, H. [1954] 1971. *Pragmatism*. Freeport, NY: Books for Libraries Press.

White, A. 1896. *A History of the Warfare of Science with Theology in Christendom*. New York: D. Appleton.

White, E. 1952. *Science and Religion in American Thought*. Stanford, CA: Stanford University Press.

Youmans, E. 1867. *The Culture Demanded by Human Life*. New York: D. Appleton.

Young, R. 1985. Darwinism *Is* Social.

# CHANGING PATTERNS OF SUBFIELD SPECIALIZATION AMONG COHORTS OF ECONOMISTS FROM 1927-1988

Arthur M. Diamond, Jr. and Donald R. Haurin

## I. INTRODUCTION

Historians of economic thought have focused relatively little energy on tracing the histories of the subfields of economics. Cochrane's remark in 1979 (p. 6) remains true that "the general lack of detailed histories of sub-disciplines seems to be one of the major weaknesses in the history of economics as it stands today." Nevertheless, some important first steps have been taken. The prestige ranking of subfields has been described satirically by Leijonhufvud (1973) and has been frequently discussed by those making methodological points. McCloskey, for instance, criticizes "theory-spinners" for believing that their hypotheses should be tested by the "... dolts who work the libraries instead of the bright lads at the blackboards" (1980, p. 213).

**Research in the History of Economic Thought and Methodology,**
**Volume 13, pages 103-123.**
Copyright © 1995 by JAI Press Inc.
All rights of reproduction in any form reserved.
ISBN: 1-55938-095-0

The ranking of subfields within economics according to prestige, quality of output, quantity of output, and number of practitioners varies over time. Although such variations are a frequent topic of casual conversation among economists, little analysis of a systematic nature has been written to document and explain them.

Some have casually emphasized demand forces in their explanations. One example would be Stigler's emphasis on U.S. antitrust policy in explaining the greater importance of industrial organization in the United States than in Britain. Others have casually emphasized supply forces. A subfield becomes important because the development of tools of analysis or data has reached the point where the time is ripe for advance in the subfield. Medawar, for instance, has emphasized that the good scientist will be attracted to the field where important problems are currently soluble.

Systematic analysis of the market for economists has so far mainly been limited to the supply and demand for economists without regard to subfields of specialization (see, e.g, Brook and Marshall, 1974; Johnson and Stafford, 1974; Reagan, 1979; Scott, 1979). We seek here first to provide additional evidence on how the importance of subfields has fluctuated and then to give a preliminary analysis of the fluctuations in terms of the supply and demand for knowledge in the subfields. We begin by reviewing some of the relevant literature.

Stigler (1965, pp. 49-50), for instance, may have been the first to document the changes in importance of subfields within economics. Using articles listed in the *Index of Economic Journals* from the 1880s through the 1950s, he found a doubling of the articles on theory from 8 percent in the first period to 16 percent in the late 1950's.[1] He also documented the increasing importance of mathematical and statistical tools of analysis. The only other trend emphasized by Stigler was "the virtual disappearance" of monetary economics from the 1930s through the 1950s.

Following Stigler's lead in exploiting the data of the AEA's *Index of Economic Journals*, Bronfenbrenner (1966) and Coats (1971) examined how the distribution of articles by subfield changed over time. Bronfenbrenner looks at changes over six time periods in the percentage of articles that appeared in the 23 subject categories used in the *Index*. Coats focuses more narrowly on the percentage of articles over six periods that appeared in five general economics journals in seven of the subject categories used in the *Index*. The periods used in the two studies differ slightly in that Bronfenbrenner includes the period 1960-63, while Coats does not. Also, Coats subdivides the *Index's* long first period into a pre-*AER* period and a post-*AER* period. A disadvantage of both studies is that the *Index's* time periods are arbitrary and vastly different in length—the first period covered 1886-1924, while the last period (as of the time of Bronfenbrenner's study) was 1960-1963.

In a more recent article, Stigler and Friedland (1982, p. 181) compared the subfields of AEA presidents with a random sample of other economists. The most important difference is that the presidents have a higher percentage of articles in theory and methodology than the other economists who have higher percentages in industrial organization, agriculture, and labor economics.

In an unpublished work, McDowell (1984) notes the differences in the durability of knowledge in eight subfields of economics. Specifically, he looks at the year of publication of articles being referenced in various subfields. The higher the percentage of cited articles that were written in the last five years, the less durable the knowledge in that subfield.

Elsewhere (Diamond and Haurin, 1993) we test the hypothesis that changes in subfield popularity among the elite lead changes in subfield popularity among the rank-and-file. Although the results differ among subfields, in general we find that subfield changes occur simultaneously in the elite and the rank-and-file.

Using the 1942, 1956, 1969, 1981, and 1989 directories of the American Economics Association (AEA), we document changes in the distribution of economists among subfields. Two populations are compared: the "elite," which includes all of those who received their Ph.Ds at Harvard, Yale, or Chicago, and the "rank-and-file," which includes all those who received their Ph.Ds at universities ranked below the top 16. Both series show changes over time that are broadly consistent with the casual impressions of historians of economic thought.

## II. THE DETERMINANTS OF SUPPLY AND DEMAND FOR ECONOMIC SUBFIELDS

We assume that economics Ph.D students maximize the present value of their lifetime income. Then the subfield of specialization chosen would depend on the subfield's impact on: the probability of getting a good job, the probability of writing a good dissertation, the probability of getting the dissertation published, current funding in an area, the technical difficulty of an area, the student's technical human capital, the student's knowledge of the reward structure of the profession (dependent, in part, on how well-informed the student's advisors are on which subfields are prospering).

Salary differences across subfields might persist in the long run if the subfields differ in their psychic costs and returns, or if economists differ in their ability to succeed at differing subfields. Psychic costs might exist, for instance, if a subfield required contemplation of the unpleasant (poverty or war?) or involved drudgery (data collection). Psychic benefits might exist, for instance, if a subfield produced positive utility for the economist. Such utility might take the form of a feeling of having contributed to a better world or

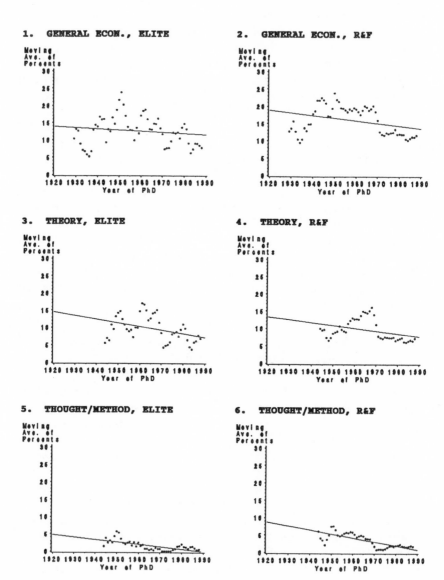

*Figure 1.*

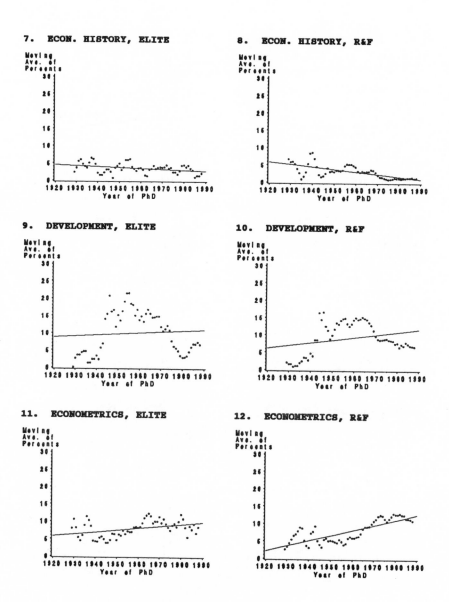

*Figure 1.* (*Continued*)

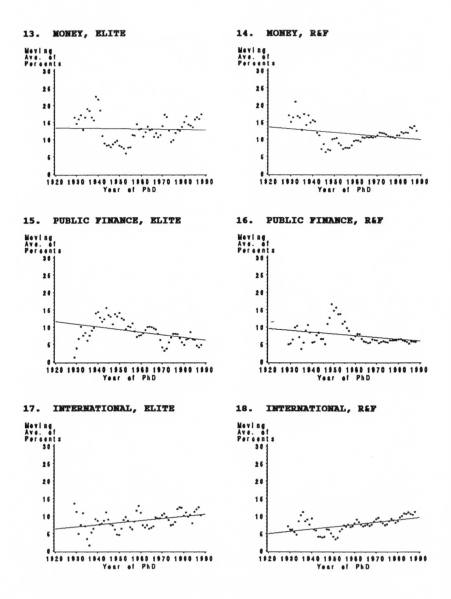

*Figure 1.*   (*Continued*)

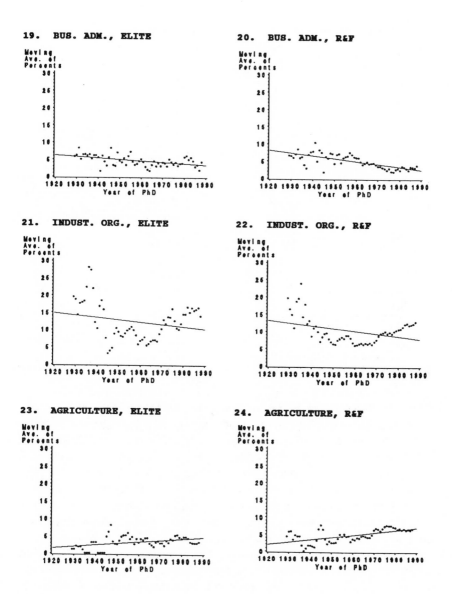

*Figure 1.* (*Continued*)

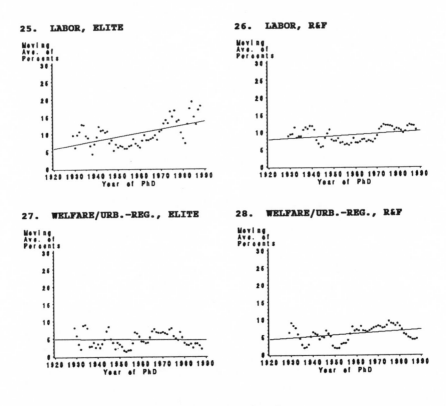

*Figure 1.* (*Continued*)

of the intellectual satisfaction of having advanced knowledge. Also, salaries might differ across subfields if economists differ in their ability to succeed in a given subfield. Those with abilities that were scarcer or more in demand might command economic rents. Unfortunately, little data is available on salary differences across subfields. The only exceptions are two reports sponsored by the NSF and published by the AEA (Tolles, Jones, and Clague, 1965; Tolles, and Melichar, 1968). We reproduce as Table 1 the results of those studies on salary differences among economists by subfield. It is interesting to note that the combined economic history and history of economic thought subfields were the worst paid in each year. More surprising may be the relatively low salary for the economic statistics subfield. The explanation may be that this subfield has changed substantially in the last 30 years. In the 1960s "economic statistics" involved more collection and presentation of data and less sophisticated econometric analysis than it does today. Although the salary data are intriguing, we would need more than two observations before such data would be of much use in the study of the longer time series movements among subfields.

*Table 1.*    Salaries by Subfield in 1964 and 1966

| Subfield | Median Salary ($000's) | |
|---|---|---|
| | *1964* | *1966* |
| Economic history; history of thought | 9.8 | 10.5 |
| General economic theory | 10.6 | 11.5 |
| Economic statistics | 11.0 | 12.2 |
| Land economics | 11.3 | 12.5 |
| Monetary | 11.4 | 12.3 |
| Labor economics | 12.0 | 13.8 |
| Welfare, population, etc. | 12.0 | 13.8 |
| Economic systems, development and planning | 12.1 | 12.8 |
| International economics | 12.5 | 12.9 |
| Business finance and administration; marketing; accounting | 13.0 | 14.5 |
| Industrial organization, government and business; industry studies | 13.0 | 14.0 |
| Economics, other | 13.0 | 14.0 |
| Total | 12.0 | 13.1 |

*Source:*  Tolles et al, 1965, p. 58; Tolles and Melichar, 1968, p. 121

*Note:*  The salary figures are in nominal dollars.

The major demanders of Ph.D economists are institutions of higher education. Business and government also employ significant numbers of Ph.D economists. Because academic economists often supplement their income with foundation grants and professional consulting fees, the demands of philanthropists (Stigler, 1967; Craver, 1986), business, and government (Friedman, 1981; Lucas, 1981) may be more important determinants of economists' subfield choice than might be inferred from the percentage of economists working directly for business and government. Doti (1976, 1978, p. 623), for instance, found a close relationship between the rate of increase in military spending and the number of articles on defense economics. Although data on funding by agency is available 1967-1990, it is nearly impossible to map that data to subfields.[2]

One measure of changes in demand for subfields might be the listings of *Job Openings for Economists* published several times a year by the American Economic Association. Unfortunately, the publication only goes back to 1975. Our review of the data suggests that over the last 15 years, demand for econometricians and macroeconomists has remained strong while the demand for welfare and urban economists has declined.[3] Demand for economists in the business and finance subfield has fallen, perhaps due to an increase in the production of bona fide finance Ph.Ds. Demand in most other subfields seems to have shown no dramatic long-run trend.

# III.  THE DATA: VARIATIONS IN THE NUMBER OF NEW ECONOMISTS IN THE SUBFIELDS OF ECONOMICS

Some information on the areas of specialization of economists can be found in the American Economic Association directories of members published in the years 1905, 1938, 1942, 1948, 1956, 1964, 1969, 1974, 1978, 1981, 1985 and 1989 as part of the Association's *Handbook* series.[4] Data on the size and the response rate for the various directories are reported in Table 2. For the current research we have categorized into three groups all Ph.D economists listed in the AEA directories for 1942, 1956, 1969, 1981, and 1989. A cohort consists of all economists who received their Ph.Ds in a particular year. In the 1942 directory we collected subfield codes for all Ph.D economists who received their Ph.Ds from 1927-1941. In the 1956 directory we collected subfield codes for all Ph.D economists who received their Ph.Ds from 1942-1955. In the 1969 directory we collected subfield codes for all Ph.D economists who received their Ph.Ds from 1956-1968. From the data tape for the 1981 directory, we extracted subfield codes for all Ph.D economists who received their Ph.Ds from 1969-1980. Finally, from the data tape for the 1989 directory, we extracted subfield codes for all Ph.D economists who received their Ph.Ds from 1981-1988.

Operationally, we define "elite" economists as those who received their Ph.Ds from three of the most distinguished economics departments in the country.[5] Chicago, Harvard, and Yale were chosen because they, alone among distinguished economics departments, were consistently ranked among the top five departments for the entire period covered in our study (1927-1988). The first sample consists of economists who graduated from institutions that were highly ranked throughout the period of study; the second sample consists of new Ph.D economists who graduated from schools ranked below the top sixteen.[6]

One issue that must be addressed is the extent to which the directories are representative of the economics profession. One positive note is the high response rate for the AEA surveys, as reported in Table 2. Also, AEA membership is more valuable to those who are likely to reenter the job market, this group including young economists. Membership is also a way for young economists to advertise their location and areas of interest. On the other hand, some economists never join the association and some allow their AEA membership to lapse.[7] One could hypothesize that non-AEA economists will be more common among some groups than others. Stigler, for instance, suggested that "as specialist journals emerged, perhaps more and more specialists have dropped out of the AEA" (letter dated November 1, 1985).

*Table 2.* Size and Response Rates for Editions of the AEA Directory

| Year | Pages | Members | Returns | Percentage |
|------|-------|---------|---------|------------|
| 1938 | 112 | 2,800 | 2,400 | 85 |
| 1942 | 208 | 3,645 | 2,557 | 73 |
| 1948 | 345 | 5,700 | 3,232 | 57 |
| 1956 | 650 | 8,387 | 6,227 | 73 |
| 1964 | 480 | 11,285 | 9,308 | 83 |
| 1969 | 620 | 18,576 | 12,744 | 69 |
| 1981 | 566 | 19,310 | 15,310 | 79 |
| 1985 | 688 | 20,935 | 15,299 | 73 |
| 1989 | 680 | 21,692 | 15,130 | 70 |

*Notes:* The source for the years 1938-1969 was the *1969 Handbook*, p. iii. Conversations with Mary Winer, Administrative Director, American Economic Association, on July 29, 1985; March 12, 1987; and February 25, 1991 were the sources, respectively, for the information on the 1981, 1985, and 1989 directories.

The coding of subfields changed in a major way between 1942 and 1956, in a minor way between 1956 and 1969, and again in a major way between 1969 and 1981. No change occurred in the coding between 1981 and 1989. In order to make comparisons over time we first aggregated the 48 codes that were used in the 1981 (and 1989) directories into 14 combined codes. We then recoded the subfield codes for 1942, 1956, and 1969 so that they corresponded to the codes used in 1981 and 1989. The details of the aggregation and recoding may be found in an appendix available from the authors.

In 1981 (and again in 1989) the American Economic Association surveyed its members for information to be included in the "Biographical Listing of Members" that was published in the December issue of the *American Economic Review*. The survey asked members to "... list fields with which you currently identify." Members were to choose two subfield codes from among a list provided. In the 1956 and 1969 directories the members had been asked to "indicate, in order of interest, your three general fields ... and check subdivisions representing your specialized fields ..." (1956, p. xiv; 1970, p. vii). In the 1942 directory the members had been asked for their "fields of major interest" which were printed "in order of expressed preference" (1942, p. 1). For each member, we made use of the first two subfield codes (but not the third) in the 1956 and 1969 directories, in order to assure comparability with the 1942, 1981, and 1989 directories (in which only two codes had been listed). The 1956 and 1969 coding did not always map uniquely into the 1981/1989 coding; thus, the two retained subfield codes for economists in the 1956 or 1969 directories might be recoded into more than two codes expressed in the 1981/1989 coding.

Because we make use of two subfield codes for each economist, the percentages that we report would not sum to 100 percent if they represented percentages of economists reporting a given code. Instead, the percentages reported in the rest of the paper are the percentages of the reported codes for each cohort that belong to each of the aggregated subfields.

Because we measure several years' cohorts from a given directory, some noise would enter our data if a young economist changed her subfields from the year of completion of her Ph.D to the year of publication of the directory we use as a source to locate her. For example, the greatest potential for a problem would seem to be an economist who received her Ph.D in 1927, but for whom we obtained subfield data in the 1942 directory. In order to gauge the potential magnitude of this problem, we compared the subfields of the cohort of economists who received their Ph.Ds in 1978-1980 as reported in the 1981 directory with the subfields reported by those same economists in the 1989 directory. We found that 67.8 percent of the economists reported the same two subfields in both years, 28.8 percent reported one subfield the same, and 3.4 percent reported neither subfield the same. Thus, subfield choice is relatively stable, but some measurement error is likely for data between the dates of issue of the directories. Clearly, a promising topic for future research would be to examine life-cycle changes in subfield choice among economists.[8]

In order to reduce the noise, we calculated three-year moving averages for the percentages. Plots of the moving averages of the percentage of reported codes in each subfield are presented in graphs 1-28. The odd-numbered graphs (on the left-hand side of each page) are for subfield codes of economists who received their Ph.D's from rank-and-file schools. Similarly, the even numbered graphs (on the right-hand side of each page) are for subfield codes of economists who received their Ph.D's from elite schools. Most of the graphs span the years 1922-1988. Graphs 3 through 6, however, only span the years 1940-1988. The reason is that in the 1942 handbook, which is the source for the early cohorts, the theory subfield and the history of thought/methodology subfield were not differentiated from the general economics subfield. In order to consistently represent the general economics subfield in graphs 1 and 2, the percentages for the theory subfield and the history of thought subfield were added to the percentages for the general economics subfield.

The fluctuations in the data are also revealed in a table of multiple-year averages (Table 3). We present the subfield distribution percentages for the graduates of both the rank-and-file and the elite schools. Most of the subfields span the years 1927-1988; however, theory and history of thought/ methodology only span the years 1942-1988, for the reason described above.

In order to detect important broader trends, Table 4 reports the raw subfield percentages (*not* the multiple-year averages) regressed on time, and sometimes time-squared. We report the quadratic specification when both the coefficients on time and on time-squared are statistically significant. We report the linear specification in all other cases. The "year at extreme" columns report the year

*Table 3A.* Percentage New Economists in Each Subfield from 1927-1988*

| Subfield | 1 27-33 | 2 34-41 | 3 42-47 | 4 48-55 | 5 56-62 | 6 63-68 | 7 69-74 | 8 75-80 | 9 81-84 | 10 85-88 |
|---|---|---|---|---|---|---|---|---|---|---|
| General | 11.6 | 15.6 | 19.8 | 20.7 | 18.6 | 19.8 | 12.4 | 12.1 | 10.8 | 11.3 |
| Economics | (9.6) | (11.9) | (12.8) | (16.9) | (15.6) | (14.4) | (8.3) | (13.4) | (7.0) | (8.3) |
| Theory** | — | — | 8.6 | 9.0 | 12.6 | 15.3 | 7.6 | 7.0 | 6.5 | 6.9 |
| | — | — | (8.1) | (11.1) | (13.2) | (13.7) | (4.9) | (9.8) | (4.1) | (7.3) |
| Thought & | — | — | 4.0 | 5.9 | 5.2 | 4.2 | 0.8 | 1.8 | 1.7 | 1.7 |
| Methodol.** | — | — | (2.2) | (3.6) | (1.8) | (0.6) | (0.0) | (1.3) | (1.0) | (0.7) |
| Economic | 5.0 | 4.7 | 2.8 | 3.6 | 4.0 | 3.2 | 1.2 | 1.0 | 1.2 | 1.2 |
| History | (3.5) | (4.2) | (1.8) | (4.9) | (2.6) | (3.4) | (3.7) | (3.0) | (3.0) | (1.8) |
| Development | 1.5 | 3.0 | 14.3 | 12.4 | 13.8 | 13.7 | 8.7 | 7.9 | 7.0 | 6.5 |
| | (2.9) | (2.2) | (14.9) | (17.5) | (15.2) | (15.1) | (10.6) | (4.2) | (4.9) | (6.6) |
| E-metrics | 4.2 | 6.8 | 5.1 | 4.6 | 5.7 | 8.8 | 11.7 | 11.9 | 12.3 | 10.9 |
| | (6.4) | (7.4) | (4.8) | (6.0) | (8.8) | (11.0) | (8.8) | (10.6) | (7.2) | (7.4) |
| Money | 17.4 | 15.7 | 6.9 | 8.7 | 8.9 | 10.4 | 11.5 | 10.7 | 11.8 | 13.2 |
| | (15.7) | (18.4) | (8.3) | (7.9) | (12.3) | (11.6) | (13.1) | (13.8) | (14.3) | (17.1) |

*Table 3B.* Percentage New Economists in Each Subfield from 1927-1988

| Subfield | 1 27-33 | 2 34-41 | 3 42-47 | 4 48-55 | 5 56-62 | 6 63-68 | 7 69-74 | 8 75-80 | 9 81-84 | 10 85-88 |
|---|---|---|---|---|---|---|---|---|---|---|
| Public | 7.1 | 6.6 | 8.6 | 13.4 | 7.0 | 5.9 | 5.4 | 6.2 | 5.7 | 5.4 |
| Finance | (4.8) | (10.6) | (13.1) | (12.1) | (7.9) | (9.0) | (4.9) | (6.3) | (7.2) | (4.6) |
| Int'l. | 6.5 | 8.4 | 5.1 | 5.2 | 7.6 | 7.3 | 8.4 | 8.8 | 10.4 | 10.9 |
| | (10.4) | (5.2) | (9.1) | (6.8) | (9.2) | (7.9) | (9.0) | (10.9) | (8.8) | (12.1) |
| Business | 9.1 | 10.1 | 11.6 | 11.7 | 9.4 | 6.4 | 5.7 | 5.2 | 6.7 | 7.2 |
| Admin. | (9.6) | (7.8) | (10.5) | (6.1) | (5.2) | (3.2) | (3.8) | (5.9) | (7.8) | (6.7) |
| Industrial | 17.8 | 13.4 | 8.2 | 7.4 | 6.8 | 6.3 | 9.2 | 9.8 | 12.1 | 12.3 |
| Organ. | (18.7) | (20.2) | (6.1) | (9.4) | (7.3) | (6.5) | (13.2) | (12.4) | (15.9) | (14.7) |
| Agriculture | 4.5 | 1.4 | 5.0 | 3.3 | 3.9 | 4.3 | 6.7 | 7.2 | 6.5 | 6.4 |
| | (1.3) | (1.2) | (4.1) | (4.3) | (3.6) | (2.9) | (3.0) | (4.7) | (4.0) | (3.0) |

*Notes:* * The top numbers are means for the rank-and-file sample; bottom numbers (in parentheses) are means for the elite sample.

Columns 1 and 2 are based on the 1942 Directory, columns 3 and 4 are based on the 1956 Directory, columns 5 and 6 are based on the 1969 Directory, columns 7 and 8 are based on the 1981 Directory, and columns 9 and 10 base on the 1989 Directory. We believe comparisons between columns 1 and 2 are valid as are comparisons among columns 3 through 10; however, conclusions based on comparing columns 2 and 3 should be drawn with caution.

** Theory and thought were not distinguished from general economics until after the 1942 cohort. The general economics data consistently includes these subfields, thus begining in 1942 column totals sum to 100% only if the values for theory and thought/methodology are excluded.

*Table 3.B   (Continued)*

| Labor | 9.4 | 10.5 | 7.4 | 7.0 | 7.2 | 6.9 | 11.2 | 11.0 | 10.6 | 10.7 |
|---|---|---|---|---|---|---|---|---|---|---|
|  | (10.0) | (8.2) | (9.1) | (6.0) | (7.7) | (8.2) | (14.5) | (10.9) | (16.7) | (15.4) |
| Welfare | 6.1 | 3.8 | 5.3 | 2.2 | 7.2 | 6.8 | 7.9 | 8.2 | 5.2 | 4.2 |
| Urb-Region | (7.1) | (2.7) | (5.3) | (2.0) | (4.8) | (6.6) | (7.0) | (3.9) | (3.2) | (2.5) |

of highest percentage when the squared term is negative and the year of lowest percentage when the squared term is positive. Most of the subfields span the years 1927-1988; however, theory and history of thought/methodology only span the years 1942-1988, for the reason described above.

Our evidence generally supports Stigler's (1965) claim that monetary economics declined in the 1930s and remained at a low level through the 1950s (although it may be an exaggeration to write of a "virtual disappearance").

The comparability of our results with those of Bronfenbrenner (1966) and Coats (1977) is limited because our subfields are defined differently and are more highly aggregated. Also, the time coverage only partially overlaps and the subperiods differ. Some rough comparisons can be made, however. Like Bronfenbrenner and Coats, we find an increase in economic theory up to the early 1960s, although we record a decline in more recent years. Also, like Bronfenbrenner and Coats, we find a decrease in money and banking from the late 1920s through the early 1960s, although we record a slight rebound in the years that follow. For the years and subfields of overlap, the other evidence in the Bronfenbrenner and Coats papers appears to be broadly consistent with our findings here.

We can compare the elite to the rank-and-file samples for the industrial organization, agriculture and labor economics subfields in order to see whether Stigler and Friedland's findings carry over to a more inclusive definition of the top members of the profession. A comparison of the means of the ten subperiods yields the following conclusions. In each period, the percentage of new economists identifying with the theory subfield has been roughly the same in the elite and rank-and-file samples. In contrast with Stigler and Friedland, we find that in all periods the percentage selecting history of thought/ methodology was higher for the rank-and-file sample than for the elite sample. Also, the percentage has been higher in the elite sample than in the rank-and-file sample in industrial organization in all but the 1942-1947 period. In labor, the percentages have been quite similar between groups, except that in the last two subperiods (1981-1988) the percentage has been higher in the elite sample than in the rank-and-file sample. The percentage of new economists

*Table 4.* Descriptive Regressions of Percentages on Time[a]

| Subfield | Elite Regressions | | | | Rank-and-File Regressions | | | |
|---|---|---|---|---|---|---|---|---|
| | Constant | Time | Time-Squared | Year at Extreme | Constant | Time | Time-Squared | Year at Extreme |
| General Economics | 8.025* | 0.492* | -0.009* | 1954 | 11.100* | 0.590* | -0.011* | 1954 |
| Theory** | 1.683 | 0.596* | -0.009* | 1960 | -0.098 | 0.673* | -0.010* | 1961 |
| Thought/ Methodology** | 3.854* | -0.061 | — | — | 7.616* | -0.110* | — | — |
| Economic History | 3.898* | -0.019 | — | — | 5.194* | -0.071* | — | — |
| Development | -1.896 | 1.085* | -0.017* | 1959 | -1.313 | 0.866* | -0.013* | 1960 |
| Econometrics | 6.059* | 0.055* | — | — | 3.731* | 0.147* | — | — |
| Money | 18.924* | -0.555* | 0.009* | 1958 | 18.873* | -0.598* | 0.009* | 1960 |
| Public Finance | 6.426* | 0.322* | -0.006* | 1954 | 8.900* | -0.049 | — | — |
| International | 7.246* | 0.047 | — | — | 7.833* | -0.153* | 0.004* | 1965 |
| Business Admin. | 11.571* | -0.339* | 0.004* | 1969 | 11.481* | -0.095* | — | — |
| Industrial Organ. | 23.166* | -0.913* | 0.014* | 1960 | 19.349* | -0.740* | 0.011* | 1961 |
| Agriculture | 1.804* | 0.043* | — | — | 2.418* | 0.072* | — | — |
| Labor | 10.451* | -0.276* | 0.006* | 1950 | 10.566* | -0.214* | 0.004* | 1954 |
| Welfare/ Urban- Regional | 4.990* | -0.015 | — | — | 4.425* | 0.039* | — | — |

*Notes:* [a] Time was defined as the year of the cohort minus 1927. (1927 was the year of the first cohort in the study.)

* Statistically significant at the .05 level.

** Theory and thought-methology were not distinguished from general economics until after the 1942 cohort. The general economics data consistently includes these subfields, thus beginning in 1942 the column totals sum to 100% only if the values for theory and thought are excluded.

entering agriculture has been larger among the rank-and-file (except for 1948-1955). Our results differ substantially from Stigler and Friedland's, suggesting that our sample of the population of elite economists differs significantly from the more distinguished sample of elite economists that consists of AEA presidents. A few other comparisons between the elite and the rank-and-file are noteworthy. The number of new Ph.Ds who selected money as a subfield has generally been higher among the elite sample, this observation also holding for development (except for 1934-1941 and 1975-1984) and international. The rank-and-file have selected both the business category (except for 1981-1984) and welfare/urban-regional with greater frequency than the elite. The percentages for the rank-and-file and elite are similar for public finance. The pattern in econometrics changed over time. From 1927-1955 the percentages were similar; from 1956-1968 the elite percentages were greater; from 1969-1988 the rank-and-file percentages were greater.

Table 4 permits broader comparisons between the elite and the rank-and-file percentages. In cases where change is monotonic, it is usually monotonic in the same direction for both elite and rank-and-file. For the subfields where the field has gained in popularity, then peaked, and then lost in popularity, this too is usually similar for both the elite and the rank-and-file. There is also usually a similarity when a subfield has lost popularity, bottomed out, and then gained. One interesting "stylized fact" is that for the consistently non-monotonic subfields the year of the elite's turning point precedes (or in one case, is equal to) the year of the rank-and-file's turning point.

In terms of overall fluctuations in the interest among subfields, we note an increased selection of theory in 1956-1968, but a subsequent decline (except interest picked up among the elite in 1975-1980). Interest in the history of thought declines fairly continuously from 1955 through the 1969-1974 period, but has made a minuscule rebound to stagnate at a low level for the remaining periods. This verifies the decline discussed in de Marchi and Lodewyks (1983) and in Anderson and Tollison (1986). The development subfield declined overall in the period from 1968 to 1985, verifying Lewis' 1983 observation (p. 1) that after prospering in the 1950s and 1960s "... the subject has been deserted by American Ph.D. students." However, interest in development picked up slightly in the elite schools after 1980, and more substantially after 1984. Among the rank-and-file, economic history suffered a decline in interest by new Ph.Ds after 1962; among the elite interest in the subfield declined less and more slowly. The percentage of new Ph.Ds selecting money, econometrics, international, and industrial organization generally increased in both groups after 1942.

We should emphasize that not all important secular trends in the economics profession will be captured by the changes in the distribution of economists among subfields. Grubel and Boland (1986), as well as others, have noted an increasing mathematization of the discipline. Because the phenomenon is occurring in all subfields to some extent, we would not expect to see it fully reflected in changes in the percentage of economists choosing mathematical economics as a subfield.

## IV.  EXPLAINING THE CHANGES

Earlier in the paper, we suggested that changes in the popularity of subfields were due partly to demand factors and partly to supply factors. The prospect of measuring the importance of various factors is daunting mainly because of the difficulty of measuring changes in the demand for a subfield from outside of academe and in the psychic appeal of a subfield to economists. Most of this effort we leave to future work. As a first attempt to consider these issues, we make use of data on job openings in economics from 1974-1988 from *Job Openings for Economists* (*JOE*). Starting in 1975, data on jobs by subfield have been reported in the proceedings issue of the *AER*. For the purposes of the analysis, we used our data on elite and rank-and-file subfield distributions for the 10 subfields that are listed in the *JOE* reports.[9] We have 14 years of data from the *JOE*, implying that we have 140 observations for each regression. The dependent variables are the raw percentages, not the three-year moving averages used in some of the analysis. The regression for the elite percentages regressed on the *JOE* percentages (*t*-statistics in parentheses) is:

$$\text{elite}\% = 6.79 + 0.33*\text{job}\% \text{ adjusted } R^2 = 0.08.$$
$$\quad (6.9) \quad (3.8)$$

The regression for the rank-and-file percentages regressed on the *JOE* percentages is:

$$\text{r\&f}\% = 7.14 + 0.29*\text{job}\% \text{ adjusted } R^2 = 0.20.$$
$$\quad (13.4) \quad (6.2)$$

We interpret these results as indicating that choice of subfields is influenced by the availability of jobs in the subfield.[10] The higher t-statistics and $R^2$ for the rank-and-file regression indicate that the relationship appears to be stronger for those who received their Ph.Ds at rank-and-file schools than for those who received their Ph.Ds at elite schools. This finding is consistent with the hypothesis that supply side considerations (such as the intellectual promise of a subfield) matter more for those from the elite schools. Conversely, subfield choice in the rank-and-file appears to be determined more by the number of jobs in the respective subfields.

# V.   CONCLUSIONS AND FUTURE WORK

We have used the 1942, 1956, 1969, 1981, and 1989 directories of the AEA to document changes in the distribution of economists among subfields. Two samples were compared: a sample including all of those who received their Ph.Ds at Harvard, Yale or Chicago and a sample including all those who received their Ph.Ds at universities ranked below the top 16. The popularity of most subfields of economics has varied substantially in the last 61 years in both samples. The characteristics of the variation are often consistent with the casual observations of historians of economic thought. Over the last couple of decades of our analysis (1969-1988) we find increased popularity compared with the previous 20 years for: international, industrial organization, labor, and money. Over the same period, we find a decreased popularity for: theory, methodology/history of economic thought, development, and public finance. For new Ph.Ds graduating from schools ranked below the top 16, an increase in popularity occurred in agricultural economics and econometrics, while economic history declined.

In the future, we hope that the robustness of the results reported here will be tested in various ways. One test would be to trace the relative popularity of subfields by looking at the changing subfield distribution of published articles. Such a test would provide evidence on one referee's speculation that monetary economics continued to be marked down as a subfield in the directories out of "inertia" rather than an active interest in the subfield. Another test of the robustness of our results would be to see if similar trends were reflected in the subfield distribution of dissertations listed annually by the American Economic Association (originally in the *AER*, now in the *Journal of Economic Perspectives*). In the future, we also hope to continue to seek good measures of the supply and demand for particular subfields. If sufficient good measures can be obtained, we might hope eventually to be able to estimate a general equilibrium model of market for subfields.

A promising path for further study might also be to study the supply and demand for particular subfields in greater detail. One might ask, for instance, whether the rise and fall of the development subfield is due to rising, and then falling, funding levels from government agencies. Or, one might investigate whether part of the decline in the general economics subfield has been due to the increasing specialization of the profession.

# ACKNOWLEDGMENTS

We are grateful to the late George J. Stigler and A. W. Coats for several useful comments. We also appreciate comments from Aloysius Siow, Pok-Sang Lam, John M. McDowell, Stephen Pressman, David C. Colander, R. Jean Haurin, William J. Barber and Warren Samuels. Mary Winer, Violet Sikes and C. Elton Hinshaw of the AEA were helpful in providing AEA publication information. We have received able research assistance from Peter Gatsch, Darren Johnson, Kathryn Williams, Joseph Buckley,/James Thomas, Di Cao, Monica Densmore, and Fran Mallory. An earlier draft of this paper was presented at the meetings of the History of Economics Society. Funding for the 1981 AEA directory data tape was provided by the Department of Economics at the Ohio State University. The 1981 and 1989 data tapes from the AEA were made available on the condition that confidentiality be maintained for individuals' answers on the unpublished race, sex, ethnicity, and nationality responses. Neither the AEA nor any official of the AEA is in any way responsible for the data analysis reported in this paper. Diamond is grateful for support from the University Committee on Research at the University of Nebraska at Omaha.

# NOTES

1.  After 1965 it has been called the *Index Economic Articles*.
2.  Data on federal funding by agency for the years 1967 through 1990 (which were extracted from National Science Foundation publications) are available from the authors.
3.  A table summarizing the *Job Openings for Economists* data is available from the authors upon request.
4.  The 1905 edition contains a sample of the economic writings to the respondents from which subfields of specialization might be inferred. Frank A. Fetter, the editor, noted that the "... uneven execution of this first attempt is due, for the most part, to the failure of the members to return answers to the schedules of inquiry" (as quoted in 1956 *Handbook*, p. iii). In 1938, members of the association were asked to report their fields, but the fields were not coded. In the 1942 edition, fields were coded for the first time. Skeels and Fairbanks, in their study of mobility (1968-1969), may have been the first to make use of the AEA directories to answer a research question about the economics profession.
5.  Harry Johnson (1975, p. 131) defined "... the elite of the profession ..." in two ways. One was "those who have been to a top-notch graduate school in the United States, or a school there or elsewhere good enough for them to have acquired the research techniques and orientation, and who have stuck with them in a research-and-publication-oriented career, wherever they may be teaching." The other definition was "those who communicate with each other by exchanging papers before publication and by attending international conferences, rather than by reading each other's work with a long lag in journals and still longer lag in books." Our definition is close to the first although not coextensive with it. Most notably, we haven't excluded those graduates of a top university who later abandoned a "research-and-publication-oriented career." The term "rank-and-file" was also used by Crane to indicate the members of a research group who are not "the most active and influential members of the area" (see Crane, 1970, p. 314).
6.  The sources for the various year's ratings were: Cartter for 1925, 1957, and 1966; Roose and Andersen (sic) for 1970; *The Chronicle of Higher Education* for 1979; unpublished survey by F.M. Boddy of University of Minnesota for 1981. The 1925-1981 rankings are based on survey results. The 1989 report is by Tremblay, Tremblay, and Lee (1989) for total publications in the period 1980-1986. Besides the top three schools, the top 16 include: MIT, Berkeley, Stanford, Princeton, Michigan, Columbia, Wisconsin, Minnesota, Northwestern, Carnegie Tech (a.k.a Carnegie Mellon), Pennsylvania, Johns Hopkins, and UCLA. Only two rankings of institutions by economic subfields have been performed, both recently (Baumann et al., 1987; Tremblay, et al., 1990). Since rankings for earlier periods were not disaggregated by subfield, we are constrained to assume that departments identified as elite are elite in all subfields. The appropriateness of this assumption when applied to particular subfields will be discussed later.
7.  Preliminary tests indicated that we could not reliably use solely the 1981 survey to obtain data on subfield choices for the 1940s or 1950s. The problems resulted from non-random attrition and individuals changing subfields over long time periods.
8.  We also examined the distribution of subfields among all economists who received their Ph.D in 1978-1980 as reported in the 1981 directory and the distribution of all economists who received their Ph.D in 1978-1980 as reported in the 1989 directory. (In this examination, we thus include those who appeared in either the 1981 directory, the 1989 directory, or both.) Although a casual visual inspection reveals a similar distribution in both years, a systematic chi-squared test (5 percent level) rejects the null hypothesis that both distributions were drawn from the same underlying population.

9.  If the category "related disciplines" is counted as a subfield, then the *JOE* lists 11 subfields.

10.  We also estimated regressions that substituted for the current *JOE* percents either one-year lagged values or two-year lagged values. Such specifications result in lower $R^2$'s and t-statistics, but similar (and still significant) values for the coefficients. We conclude that even in this framework, the choice of subfields is influenced by the availability of jobs in the subfield.

# REFERENCES

American Economic Association. 1961. *Index of Economic Journals*, Vol. 1, Homewood, IL: Richard D. Irwin, Inc.

American Economic Association. 1942. "The 1942 Directory of the American Economic Association." *The American Economic Review* 32(3).

————. 1957. "Handbook of the American Economic Association." *The American Economic Review* 47(4).

————. 1970. "1969 Handbook of the American Economic Association." *The American Economic Review* 59(6).

————. 1981. "Biographical Listing of Members." *The American Economic Review* 71(6).

————. 1989. "Biographical Listing of Members." *The American Economic Review* 79(6).

Anderson, Gary M. and Robert D. Tollison. 1986. "Dead Men Tell No Tales." *The History of Economics Society Bulletin* 8: 59-68.

Baumann, Michael G., Gregory J. Werden, and Michael A. Williams. 1987. "Rankings of Economics Departments by Field." *The American Economist* 31: 56-61.

Brook, Kathleen and F. Ray Marshall. 1974. "Report of the Committee on Hiring Practices, The Labor Market for Economists." *American Economic Review* 64: 488-511.

Bronfenbrenner, Martin. 1966. "Trends, Cycles, and Fads in Economic Writing." *American Economic Review* 56: 538-558.

Cartter, Allan M. 1966. *An Assessment of Quality in Graduate Education*. Washington, D.C: American Council on Education.

Coats, A. W. 1971. "The Role of Scholarly Journals in the History of Economics: An Essay." *Journal of Economic Literature* 9: 29-44.

Cochrane, James L. 1979. *Industrialism and Industrial Man in Retrospect: A Critical Review of the Ford Foundation's Support for the Inter-University Study of Labor*. New York: The Ford Foundation, (produced and distributed by University Microfilms International, Ann Arbor Michigan).

Crane, Diana. 1970. "Social Structure in a Group of Scientists: A Test of the 'Invisible College' Hypothesis." Pp. 295-323, in *The Sociology of Sociology*, edited by L. Reynolds and J. Reynolds. New York: David McKay Co.

Craver, Earlene. 1986. "Patronage and the Directions of Research in Economics: The Rockefeller Foundation in Europe, 1924-1938." *Minerva* 24: 205-222.

de Marchi, Neil and John Lodewyks. 1983. "HOPE and the Journal Literature in the History of Economic Thought." *History of Political Economy* 15: 321-343.

Diamond, Arthur M., Jr. and Donald R. Haurin. 1993. "The Dissemination of Research Agendas Among Young Economists." *Journal of Economic Education* 24(1): 53-61.

Doti, James. 1978. "The Response of Economic Literature to Wars." *Economic Inquiry* 16: 616-626.

Doti, James. 1976. *The Response of Economics to Environmental Influences*. University of Chicago, Department of Economics, Ph.D Thesis.

Friedman, Milton. 1981. "An Open Letter on Grants." *Newsweek* (May 18, p. 99).

Grubel, Herbert G. and Lawrence A. Boland. 1986. "On the Efficient Use of Mathematics in Economics." *Kyklos* 39: 419-442.

Hinshaw, C. Elton. 1975-1990. "Report of the Director, *Job Openings for Economists.*" *American Economic Review* Vols. 65-80, various pages depending on year.

"How Professors Rated Faculties in 19 Fields." 1979. *The Chronicle of Higher Education* (January 15, p. 6).

Johnson, George E. and Frank P. Stafford. 1974. "Lifetime Earnings in a Professional Labor Market: Academic Economists." *Journal of Political Economy* 82: 549-569.

Johnson, Harry G. 1975. "National Styles in Economic Research: The United States, the United Kingdom, and Various European Countries." Pp. 129-139 in *On Economics and Society.* Chicago: The University of Chicago Press.

Leijonhufvud, Axel. 1973. "Life Among the Econ." *Western Economic Journal* 11(3): 327-337.

Lewis, W. Arthur. 1984. "The State of Development Theory." *American Economic Review* 74: 1-10.

Lucas, Robert E., Jr. 1981. "Incentives for Ideas" p. 23 in *New York Times* (April 13).

McCloskey, Donald N. 1980. "Scattering in Open Fields: A Comment." *The Journal of European Economic History* 9: 209-213.

McDowell, John M. 1984. "An Analysis of the Durability of Economic Knowledge" (unpublished). Arizona State University.

Reagan, Barbara B. 1979. "Stocks and Flows of Academic Economists." *American Economic Review* 69: 143-147.

Roose, Kenneth D. and Charles J. Andersen. 1970. *A Rating of Graduate Programs.* Washington, D.C.: American Council on Education.

Scott, Charles E. 1979. "The Market for Ph.D. Economists: The Academic Sector." *American Economic Review* 69: 137-142.

Skeels, Jack W. and Robert P. Fairbanks. 1968. "Publish or Perish: An Analysis of the Mobility of Publishing and Nonpublishing Economists." *The Southern Economic Journal* 35(1-4): 17-25.

Stigler, George J. 1967. "Economics." In *U.S. Philanthropic Foundations,* edited by Warren W. Faver. New York: Harper and Row.

Stigler, George J. 1965. "Statistical Studies in the History of Economic Thought." Pp. 31-50 in *Essays in the History of Economics* Chicago: The University of Chicago Press.

Stingler, George J. and Claire Friedland. 1982. "The Pattern of Citation Practices in Economics." P. 173-192, in *The Economist as Preacher and Other Essays.* Chicago: University of Chicago Press.

Tolles, N. Arnold, Alice Hanson Jones and Ewan Clague. 1965. "The Structure of Economists' Employment and Salaries, 1964." *American Economic Review* 55: 1-98.

Tolles, N. Arnold, and Emanuel Melichar. 1968. "Studies of the Structure of Economists' Salaries and Income." *American Economic Review* 58(2): i-xxxv and 1-153.

Tremblay, Carol Horton, Victor J. Tremblay, and Byunglak Lee. 1990. "Field Publishing Performance of U.S. Economics Departments." *Atlantic Economic Journal* 18: 37-48.

# THE MONEY DOCTOR IN CHINA:
## EDWIN KEMMERER'S COMMISSION OF FINANCIAL EXPERTS, 1929

Paul B. Trescott

*In thinking of progress here one must think in time units of generations rather than years.*

–Kemmerer's Diary, November 20, 1929.

Edwin Walter Kemmerer (1875-1945) was a major figure in the American economics profession and was elected President of the American Economic Association in 1926. During the 1920s he organized a series of "commissions of financial experts" primarily to advise Latin American govenments, an activity which earned him the nickname "The Money Doctor."

Late in 1923, Kemmerer agreed to head a commission to advise the newly formed Kuomintang (Nationalist) government of China. Besides Kemmerer, 16 other Americans went to China as members—the largest of his consulting groups ever assembled. They lived and worked in China for most of 1920—the longest period of residence for any of his missions. Seven of the commission members remained in China as advisers—a holdover far greater than for his other missions.

Research in the History of Economic Thought and Methodology,
Volume 13, pages 125-158.
Copyright © 1995 by JAI Press Inc.
All rights of reproduction in any form reserved.
ISBN: 1-55938-095-0

In this paper, Kemmerer's China mission is examined with particular emphasis on its role as a transmitter of western economic ideas into China. We begin by looking at Kemmerer's own ideas, then identify the other principal members of his group. Next we examine the Chinese environment into which they came. The reports themselves are next analyzed and compared with Kemmerer proposals for other countries. We describe the effects of these proposals on Chinese policy and the post-Commision work of those participants who remained in China.

# I. KEMMERER'S BACKGROUND AND IDEAS

Kemmerer was a contemporary of Irving Fisher and John Maynard Keynes, and his work may properly be compared with theirs. His early work displayed the attention to empirical evidence and institutional detail which he consistently maintained. Kemmerer was satisfied that the basic principles of economics were clearcut and wellknown. What was needed was to express them clearly and to relate them to the ever changing complexities of real life.[1]

At Cornel, Kemmerer was a protege of Jeremiah Whipple Jenks, who headed an early advisory groups dealing with Chinese finance (1904). In 1903, Jenks helped Kemmerer to secure a position in the newly formed U.S.-colonial government of the Philippines (Hanna 1904). Kemmerer helped to develop a gold-exchange standard monetary system. The system was intended to permit a small open economy to gain the benefits of stable exchange rates and currency convertibility without the need to coin gold or maintain a significant gold reserve. Kemmerer often referred back to his Philippine program, and it was the model for his China recommendations (Kemmerer, 1916).

Kemmerer taught at Cornell 1906-1912 and then moved to Princeton. In 1918, he published the first edition of *The ABC of the Federal Reserve System*. The book was widely used in college classes and by 1938 was in its eleventh edition. Kemmerer believed strongly in the principles embodied in the original Federal Reserve act, and they were reflected in many of his advisory reports. In particular, he urged that an inflow of gold or foreign exchange should generate an increase in the money supply; an outflow should bring about a decrease. Further, the central bank should keep its earning assets in liquid form, preferably in short-term bills of exchange or similar paper. It should be a "lender of last resort."

An advisory visit to Mexico in 1917 set off a whirlwind series of Latin American consultancies. These included Guatemala (1919, 1924), Colombia (1923), Chile (1925), Ecuador (1926-1927) and Bolivia (1927). In between these Kemmerer found time for work involving South Africa (1924-1925), Germany (with the Dawes Committee in 1924) and Poland (1926).[2]

In his presidential address to the American Economic Association in December, 1926, Kemmerer reflected on his international advisory work. He noted that his host countries were eager to attract American capital. His advisory work for 10 governments had focused on the gold standard, central and commercial banking, government budgeting, accounting, and audit, tax and tariff systems, and foreign indebtedness. He argued that "their solution requires scientific imagination in the application of sound economic theory to unsound and often very strange economic practices" (Kemmerer, 1927, pp. 5-6). However, Kemmerer did not undertake in this talk to sketch the elements of the "sound economic theory" involved.[3]

While Kemmerer's economic views would now be characterized by many economists as conservative, Seidel appropriately characterized him as a Progressive, devoted to efficiency and economy in government and lacking much patience for "politics." (1972, pp. 520-521). He was confident that his economic principles were not merely analytically defensible but also morally sound. By implication, he favored private enterprise, private property, and a limited role for government (Dalgaard, 1982, pp. 40-42; Drake, 1989, pp. 10, 250-256). However, in his advisory work he generally avoided passing judgment on existing government programs and concentrated on ways to manage them efficiently. Ironically, the Kemmerer mission to China was a response to the ideas of Sun Yat-Sen, who envisioned a comprehensive socialist economic program, supplemented by foreign capital and foreign expertise.

## II.  THE MISSION TO CHINA

When the Commission of Financial Experts set up their operation in Shanghai in February, 1929, the group included 16 Americans besides Kemmerer. The *New York Herald Tribune* called it "the largest corps of economic experts ever assembled for such service ..." (February 15, 1929) The five "Experts" were as follows:[4]

1.  Arthur N. Young, age 38, had studied with Kemmerer, had worked in Mexico and Honduras, and been an economic adviser to the U.S. State Department. Besides his Ph.D. in economics from Princeton, Young had earned a law degree from George Washington University.
2.  Frederick A. Cleveland, 63, had studied and practiced law, then received a Ph.D. from the University of Pennsylvania in Finance in 1900. He served as Director of the Bureau of Municipal Research in New York City and chaired President Taft's Commission on Economy and Efficiency in 1911-1913. In 1919, he was appointed Professor of United States Citizenship at Boston University. His books included two very widely acclaimed studies dealing with railroad finance.
3.  Oliver Lockhart, 48, had received his Ph.D. from Cornell in 1908. He taught at Ohio State 1908-1918, worked as an economist with the

National Bank of Commerce in New York 1918-1924, then became chair of the economics department at the University of Buffalo. He had been a member of Kemmerer's missions to Ecuador and Bolivia in 1926-1927.

4. Benjamin B. Wallace, 46, had received a Ph.D. in Political Science from Wisconsin in 1912. In 1918, he joined the U.S. Tariff Commission, becoming in 1921 chief of the division of preferential tariffs and commercial treaties. His brother DeWitt Wallace was founder and editor of the *Readers Digest*.

5. William B. Poland arrived March 12 from Persia where he had been serving as Director General of Railways. Poland had graduated from MIT and served during World War I as director of relief in France and Belgium. During the early 1920s he investigated the possible savings from consolidating U.S. railways into seven major systems.

Four other members of the group were designated Assistant Experts. They were:

6. John Parke Young, 33, like his brother, Arthur, had received a Ph.D. from Princeton. He served as staff director for the foreign currency and exchange investigation of the U.S. Senate in 1923-1925. In 1926, he became professor and chair of the economics department at Occidental College, a position to which he returned after serving in China.

7. William Watson, 47, had been associated with the New York Bureau of Municipal Research and the National Institute of Public Administration from 1917 on. He specialized in studies of financial administration in units of state and local government.

8. Fenimore B. Lynch, 37, had lived and worked in China in various positions with the International Banking Corporation, beginning in 1913.

9. Richard Bonnevalle, 34, had served in 1922 as a member of the American Relief Administration in Russia, working under Herbert Hoover. He worked for the U.S. Department of Commerce until 1926, when he went to Persia with the same mission of which Poland was a member.

The other members of Kemmerer's group were denoted secretaries, assistant secretaries, and assistants. Three of these are of particular interest to economists, namely:

10. Frank Whitson Fetter, 29, was the son of Kemmerer's distinguished colleague Frank A. Fetter. Whitson Fetter had completed his Ph.D. under Kemmerer at Princeton and accompanied him on the missions to Guatemala, Chile, Poland, Ecuador, and Bolivia, interspersed with teaching at Princeton.

11. Donald L. Kemmerer, 23, was Edwin Kemmerer's son. He had assisted in his father's missions to Guatemala, Chile, and Poland. He graduated from Princeton in 1927 and did post-graduate study in economics at Harvard and abroad.
12. Harry B. Price, 23, had been born in China to missionary parents and lived there most of his first 15 years. He had entered the graduate program in economics at Princeton in 1928.

The other four members were Edward Feely (subsequently U.S. ambassador to Bolivia), John McGregor Gibb, former chemist and administrator at Yenching University in Peking, and two recent Princeton graduates, Wetmore Dawes and George M. Thompson.

Compared to the other Kemmerer missions, the China group contained a strong representation of economists. Six (counting Kemmerer) held Ph.D. degrees in economics and finance and four others had substantial academic training in economics. John Parke Young, Whitson Fetter, and Donald Kemmerer all went on to distinguished academic careers in economics.

## III. THE CHINESE ENVIRONMENT

The China into which Kemmerer and his colleagues came in 1929 was one of the poorest countries in the world. Its arable areas were densely populated by peasants eking out bare subsistence with traditional farming techniques on pitifully small tracts of land. Industry, transport and communication were poorly developed.

China's political system had been turbulent and unstable ever since the overthrow of the monarchy in 1911-1912. In the early 1920s, the weak central government in Peking was challenged by numerous regional warlords. China's sovereignty was impaired by the presence of foreign troops and by "unequal" treaties which restricted customs duties to 5 percent or less of import value. The Chinese customs service and the salt administration, both major sources of government revenue, were under international (chiefly British) control.

The Chinese political situation changed dramatically in 1926-27. Before his death in 1925, Sun Yat-Sen had been influential in forming the Kuomintang, a political party which stressed themes of national self-determination, political reform, and social justice. Following Sun's death, Chiang Kai-Shek emerged as the leader of Kuomintang military forces and was able to overthrow the weak national government in 1927-1928. He continued military campaigns against Communist insurgents.

The Kuomintang avowed its loyalty to the ideas of Sun Yat-Sen. In 1919, Sun had argued that, "in order to facilitate the industrial development by private enterprise in China, the hitherto existing internal taxes must be abolished, the cumbersome currency must be reformed, the various kinds of official obstacles must be removed, and transportation facilities must be provided" (Sun, 1928, p. 14). This statement came close to being an agenda for the Kemmerer Commission.

His son, Sun Fo, was appointed in 1927 as the first Minister of Railways under the new government, and presented ambitious plans for railway and highway development.[5] Consequently, the government endorsed another of Sun Yat-Sen's themes: heavy reliance on foreign capital and foreign technical expertise. The Kemmerer Commission was to bring some of the expertise directly and help bring in foreign capital. Appropriately, it was Sun Fo himself who invited Kemmerer in 1928.

Many of the policies on which the Commission was called to advise had weighty international ramifications. Governments and business interests in Japan, the United States and Europe had direct concern for the payment of individual debt issues owed to overseas creditors, for instance.[6] Debt service was in turn dependent on revenue enhancement. Foreign companies trading in China were directly concerned with probable changes in internal taxes and the duties on imports, some of which were pledged for service of existing debts (Young, 1971, pp. 115- 6, 119-127). Foreign banks constituted a major element in China's banking system. Foreign interests were directly involved in decision making regarding railways, customs service, and the salt revenue.

International competition extended to advisory activities. The invitation of the Kemmerer Commission represented, among other things, a Chinese effort to counter the existing influence of Britain, France, and Japan. A similar motive led China to turn to the League of Nations. In early 1929, Dr. Ludvik Rajchman, Director of the Health Section of the League Secretariat, headed a China mission dealing with public health issues (Hoe, 1933). Another important League adviser was Sir Arthur Salter who visited China in 1931 and 1933-1934 (below).

## IV.  THE COMMISSION AT WORK IN 1929

Most of the commission members began work in February in offices within the Central Bank building in Shanghai, close to the Ministry of Finance. The Commission's chief contact person was Finance Minister T.V. Soong, Chiang Kai-Shek's brother-in-law. Soong had studied at Harvard and had a very "western" style which impressed most of the Americans who dealt with him.

Kemmerer organized the Commission into six subcommittees, dealing with currency and banking, public credit, railroad finance, taxation, tariff and budget, accounting and fiscal control. Each was to prepare a report which would be endorsed by the entire Commission and which would include "definite projects of law."

The committees were soon hard at work, assembling documents, conducting interviews and conferences.[7] A major task was an ambitious questionnaire to learn details of the country's currency situation. This was primarily managed by Whitson Fetter, aided by the offices of Standard Oil and British-American Tobacco companies (see EWK Diary, 1929, March 12 and 21; Tsai, 1979, pp. 55-71).

Although Kemmerer had hoped to keep the Commission somewhat aloof from the day-to-day problems of the Chinese government, this proved impossible. Within a week of their arrival in Shanghai, Soong was seeking advice about immediate measures to raise revenue. (EWK Diary, Feb. 15) Kemmerer also quickly observed conditions which threatened to make the Commission's task more difficult. On March 27, they sent forward a memo urging the government to discontinue minting of copper and fractional silver coins, all of which were currently circulating below their nominal value. Issues of paper money by banks and by political units should be curtailed.[8]

In May, at the urging of Arthur Young, the Commission recommended to the government a plan for putting the customs revenue "on a gold basis." The proposal was aimed at protecting the customs revenue from decline in the market value of silver. The proposal, adopted in 1930, is discussed below.[9]

Within the new government, several study groups and agencies were involved with the policy areas which concerned the Commission. A National Economic Conference in June, 1928, and a National Financial Conference the following month had adopted resolutions on taxation, money and banking policies, and public debt policies similar to those later supported by the commission. Kemmerer was able to read their reports (Diary, March 13, 25) but complained of problems of coordinating with government agencies dealing with accounting, tariff policy, budget and fiscal control. (Diary, Feb. 13, 14, 15, 16; March 5; July 30; August 8, 9, 10).

By the middle of the year the Commission members had begun drafting their major reports.[10] After a hectic last month, all but Poland's railway report were handed in by the official end of the Commission's existence (Dec. 10). The government had already shown its appreciation by engaging seven members to stay on in China. (Diary, Sept. 23; Nov. 4, 6, 13; Dec. 2, 4). Soong urged Kemmerer to return after a few months to help with the implementation, but Kemmerer made no commitment. (Diary, Dec. 16). He sailed for Manila December 17, never to return.

Kemmerer's assessment of China's prospects was not optimistic. His diary for December 7, 1929, recorded:

Serious new revolutionary outbreak. These people have no capacity for enduring group action and cannot cooperate for any length of time. Individual and family selfishness too strong and bitter and no national patriotism or sense of obligation above family obligation.

# V.  THE REPORTS

For our purposes, the Commission's reports and proposals can be divided into two groups. First we consider those dealing with money and banking, Kemmerer's area of special expertise. Second we consider the others, many of which were primarily concerned with issues of government structure and organization rather than economics.

## A.  The Monetary Standard

Not surprisingly, the Commission proposed the adoption of a gold-exchange monetary standard for China.[11] China was on a silver standard—or, more accurately, a combination of silver standards. Dickson Leavens, who lived in China from 1909 to 1928, described the situation as follows:

> to say that China is on a silver standard simply means that for large transactions, silver is the medium of exchange, or at least the basis of the money of account. Silver is more and more taking the form of dollars coined by Government mints, but large quantities of it still circulate in other forms, and the relationship between various kinds of currency is determined by supply and demand, not by Government support. Moreover, for small transactions the standard is copper, and it fluctuates relatively to silver. In addition, more or less unregulated paper currency is issued by various banks and by governmental bodies, and this circulates at a rate determined by the current degree of confidence in the issuers (Leavens, 1930, p. 206).

The Commission's goals were to unify and simplify the currency and to place it on the gold-equivalent basis. The basic monetary unit was to be designated as the "Sun" (after Sun Yat-Sen) with a gold value equal to existing Chinese silver dollars (about $.40 U.S.). No gold was to be coined, however, and the new "Sun" was to be a silver coin with silver content substantially below its nominal value. Its nominal value would be maintained by convertibility into gold bars or gold-denominated foreign exchange.[12] Fully convertible paper currency would be issued by the Central Bank. A reserve of gold and foreign exchange equal to 35 percent of coins and notes would be required.

A major advantage of the proposal would be to stabilize China's foreign-exchange rate relative to the major (gold-standard) countries, facilitating foreign loans (pp. 65-72). The proposed system would cause China's money supply to rise or fall in response to the "needs of trade." If China's international accounts were in deficit, foreign-exchange drafts (or possibly gold bars) would be sold out of the currency reserve. The Chinese money used to purchase these assets would be withdrawn from circulation, and China would experience a deflating monetary adjustment presumably appropriate to remedy the international deficit. If China's international balance was in surplus, additional Chinese money would be created.

Much of the Commission's report dealt with procedures for simplifying the types of circulating money and insuring that all would be maintained at their nominal values in relation to the standard. These goals had already been endorsed by the economic and financial conferences in 1928 (Kwei, 1931, pp. 334-335).

The currency report was released to the public in mimeographed form in March, 1930, and appeared in book form (both English and Chinese) that summer.[13] The report was widely circulated and widely criticized. One influential critic was Ma Yin-chu, a Columbia Ph.D. and one of China's most prolific writers on economic topics. (Hsia, 1961). In a 1929 book, he had already expressed reservations about moving to a gold standard, though he strongly supported unification of the currency and suppression of provincial and private money issue (Ma, 1929). In a 1930 article, Ma opposed the Kemmerer plan, citing the instability of the political situation and the difficulty of borrowing sufficient funds to set up the reserve. He also feared the effects of a decline in the value of silver if China demonetized it (Ma, 1930; Shen, 1992).

Many people were skeptical about the reception of the new Sun and compared it adversely to the existing full-bodied silver dollars. Chu Ching-Lai feared there would be no convertibility except into foreign-exchange drafts and that this was "absolutely not in practice" elsewhere in the world. He questioned the feasibility of accumulating the needed large reserve and claimed it might be looted (Chu, 1931).

Sir Arthur Salter, who visited China several times as a League adviser, prepared a lengthy commentary in March, 1931. He endorsed the Kemmerer conviction that China should move to gold, but urged that it be done gradually and only after more nearly "normal" conditions had been restored. He feared Kemmerer had underestimated the size of the needed gold reserve, and urged that both the silver content of the proposed Sun coin and its gold equivalent be reduced (Salter, 1934, pp. 90-116).

Writing after the British departure from gold in September, 1931, J.B. Condliffe (1932) questioned whether the Chinese government was strong enough to carry through a systematic reform and urged the more feasible clean-up of the existing silver standard (pp. 166-170). In 1929, the Ministry of Finance indicated they felt the commission's proposal could not be carried through in the near future (EWK Diary, Nov. 13, 1929). And it was not.

With the onset of the world depression in 1929, the international value of silver was declining rapidly. Since the Chinese dollar depreciated relative to gold, prices in China were not forced down as in gold standard countries. Adoption of the Kemmerer proposals at such a time would undoubtedly have imposed greater deflation on China.[14]

However, China's government owed substantial overseas debts payable in gold, and the burdens of these debts were increasing. At Arthur Young's initiative, the Commission recommended that the valuation of Chinese currency for customs duties (the chief source of central government revenue) be fixed in terms of gold (Young, 1971, p. 46). In February, 1930, the Chinese government put the proposal into effect. The Chinese customs gold unit (CGU) was given a gold valuation equivalent to $.40 U.S.[15]

The government then arranged for the creation of CGU paper currency and bank deposits. The Central Bank and the Bank of China encouraged CGU accounts for firms involved in international trade. These banks in turn developed correspondent banking relationships overseas in order to maintain the CGU effectively at its gold parity. So in this limited domain, at least, China did create a sort of gold-exchange standard. In 1931, Salter suggested that the government could move gradually to a gold-exchange standard by widening the CGU system (1934, pp. 109-111). But in 1933, Lockhart complained that "efforts to get the Minister [Soong] to further the use of that currency by making other taxes payable in it and by other means have not been effective."[16] Lockhart went on to observe that "The Minister's present attitude toward adoption of a gold standard seems to be unfavorable. Sir Arthur Salter seems to have influenced him in that regard ..." Adoption of the CGU helped raise customs revenue from $244 million in 1929 to $388 million (Chinese) in 1931 (Young, "Cycle" V, p. 5). Insofar as the improvement of China's international credit rating was a goal for inviting the Kemmerer commission, the adoption of the customs gold unit clearly contributed to that goal (Salter, 1934, p. 60).

China's relative insulation from the world deflation ended in 1931 with Britain's departure from gold. In November, 1935, the Chinese government took the country off the silver standard entirely. We examine these developments below.

## B.  Central Banking

The Commission recommended that the existing Central Bank (which was simply a government-dominated commercial bank) should be modified to resemble the U.S. Federal Reserve and the Kemmerer-sponsored central banks in Latin America. The proposed Central Reserve Bank (CRB) would hold reserve deposits and rediscount for "affiliated" banks. The CRB would be virtually the only issuer of banknote currency and would be the major holder of government deposits. The Commission tried to design an organizational structure which would preserve the independence of the CRB. The proposal "contemplated" (over-optimistically) that the government would sell its stock in the existing Central Bank and use the proceeds to build up the currency redemption fund provided in the gold-standard proposal.

A major departure from Federal Reserve precedent was the proposal that the Bank conduct loan and deposit business with the general public as well as with banks and government. However, lending to any one borrower was to be limited, and the CRB was to confine most of its lending to short-term commercial credits very similar to the "eligible" paper required by Federal Reserve policy. Dealing with the general public would enable the CRB to conduct open-market operations, selling assets to force the money supply down, or buying assets to enlarge it to keep pace with the "needs of trade."[17]

The central bank proposal, among all the Commission proposals, was the one most completely adopted, though with considerable delay. In May, 1935, some of the recommendations were embodied in a law rechartering the existing Central Bank. Specifically, the law limited its lending to short-term items, primarily those relating to production and trade. It also restricted its ownership of real estate and the amount of loans to one borrower. Credit instruments for financing fixed capital, luxury goods, or speculation were not to be purchased or to serve as ordinary collateral, nor was the bank to engage directly in commercial or industrial enterprises. The provisions relating to these topics appear to follow the Kemmerer proposals almost word for word.[18]

However, the recharter of 1935 did not enable the Central Bank to function as a central bank. The Kemmerer report had glossed over two important characteristics of the Chinese banking system. The first was that three other large banks had semi-official status, being primarily government owned and participating in correspondent banking, note issue, and government deposit business. Second, branches of foreign banks played a major role in Shanghai and the other treaty ports (Tamagna, 1942, pp. 218-219).

In November, 1935, the government indicated its intention to develop the Central Bank into a true central bank and appointed a committee (including Young and Lynch) to draft details (Young, 1971, pp. 273-276). The Committee's report was approved with a few modifications in June, 1937, and contained more of the Kemmerer proposals. It followed the Kemmerer recommendation that stock in the Central Reserve Bank be divided into several categories, with each category to choose some of the board of directors (Tamagna, 1942, pp. 219-221). The 1937 plan also provided for centralization of bank reserves and for monetary "elasticity" suitable to stabilize the foreign exchange value of the Chinese currency (p. 220). The CRB itself was to have a reserve requirement of 40 percent against notes plus deposits. However, because of the outbreak of war with Japan, the 1937 provisions were never put into effect.

Despite the shelving of the detailed program for a more centralized central bank, the existing Central Bank moved in that direction, taking an expanded role in fiscal agency, foreign exchange and note issue.

## C. Commercial Banking

Before 1929, China's commercial banks were virtually unregulated. The Kemmerer Commission recommended many principles embodied in American banking practice and regulation.[19] Some of these were put into practice by legislation in 1931. Major areas covered by the Commission included the following:

1.  An office of Superintendent of Banking should be established within the Ministry of Finance. No bank was permitted to operate without a license from the Superintendent, who was to require periodic reports of condition and conduct bank examinations. The 1931 law gave similar jurisdiction to the Ministry of Finance, but without the suggested safeguards of independence. According to Tamagna, the 1931 law reflected "the political-social program of the Kuomintang which called for a controlled economy and an essentially public banking structure" (p. 159).

2.  The Commission recommended that banks be classified as either copartnerships of unlimited liability or corporations. The 1931 law required all to be corporations, but provided for a category of unlimited corporations which seems to be similar to the Commission's copartnership. The 1931 law followed the Commission's recommendations for double liability of stockholders and for minimum capital (Lee, 1932).

3.  The Commission recommended a very high reserve requirement, namely 30 percent for demand deposits and 15 percent for time deposits. Capital accounts were to be at least 25 percent of liabilities. These recommendations were not adopted. As further protection, the Commission recommended each bank be required to deposit with the Superintendent high-grade securities worth C$5,000 or more (depending on size). The law of 1931 adopted a required guarantee fund for only the unlimited corporations, to be 20 percent of their capital—a level probably substantially higher than that contemplated by the Commission.

4.  The Commission recommended a large number of restrictions to limit risk exposure and preserve liquidity. These included prohibiting bank lending to one borrower in excess of 10 percent of the bank's capital and surplus. This was adopted in 1931. The 1931 law also followed the Commission in forbidding banks to own shares in commercial and industrial concerns, but diverged from the Commission in permitting banks to engage in warehousing operations as they traditionally had done.

The 1931 law contained many provisions paralleling the Kemmerer recommendations. However, the Commission stressed impersonal rules and controls designed to maintain the bounds of propriety. The law of 1931 permitted the individual banks greater freedom of action, on the one hand, but also gave the Ministry of Finance much greater discretionary authority. Arthur Young concluded that:

> The Kemmerer project ... which provided for extensive regulation, was shelved because of banking opposition ... There was little effective regulation of banking, and a number of modern-style banks and many native banks got into serious difficulties during the depression.[20]

## D.  Revenue Policies, Public-Debt Management, and Financial Controls

Much of the Commission's effort was devoted to fiscal concerns. These were essential to the creation of a system of financial law and order within which economic development could proceed. Many of the reports were primarily administrative in nature, and did not raise interesting issues of economic analysis. Thus, Poland's report on railway finance focused on generating sufficient revenues to service the sizeable indebtedness linked to rail revenues and expenditures.[21] The report examined each major rail line with regard to revenue yields and the financial requirements of rehabilitation.

Similarly, the monumental study of China's national debt, directed by Arthur Young, laid out the details of all the valid debt claims against the Chinese government and recommended procedures to reassure the public creditors, thus aiding China to attract foreign capital "for rehabilitation and the promotion of economic progress."[22] Much of the existing debt was in arrears. Debt management responsibilities were dispersed among several agencies. Young's work with the Commission initiated the monumental task of debt administration which continued to be his major concern for the next 18 years.

However, in their "Report on Revenue Policy," the Commission presented a concise statement of some fundamental issues in public finance. The crucial first principle was this: "The realization that taxes are in fact a contribution to collective purposes, not a mere "one-sided" compulsory exaction of wealth by the Government (or, ... by officials, largely for their private and personal benefit) must be gradually built up through the devotion of public funds to useful public purposes ... "[23]

The Commission urged improving existing revenue sources in order to take advantage of existing administrative capabilities. Further, they urged that policy should tax more heavily a limited group of commodities and try to reduce the number of taxed items, in order to reduce burdens on trade. They recommended commodity taxes on matches and on Portland cement, and modifications of an existing documentary stamps tax.[24]

The Commission did not feel that China's economy was ready for taxation of incomes and inheritance. Land taxation should remain primarily a resource for local governments. The Commission noted the possibility of taxing "unearned increment" of land in major cities:

> In the many cities of China, notably in the National capital, extensive public improvements are being made which will add materially to property values. It is entirely just that a considerable portion of these increases in the value of private property should be taken by government to defray the cost, or part of the cost, of the improvements which caused the increases ("Revenue Policy," p. 7).

On this point, the interests of Arthur Young (who had written his dissertation on Henry George's single-tax proposal) joined those of Sun Yat-sen, who had been influenced by Henry George.[25]

The Commission anticipated that most revenue increase would come from import duties and domestic excises, but feared a regressive impact on the poor. However, this could be alleviated by simplification and improved administration. Further, they identified a number of imported commodities which were particularly purchased by low-income consumers, and urged that import duties not be increased on these items (p. 8). They urged abolition of the notorious *likin*, under which taxes were repeatedly imposed on the same goods moving through internal trade channels. In a similar vein, removing native customs duties and duties on coastwise vessels and trade would help to raise productivity and increase taxable capacity (pp. 3-4).

The Commission came out forthrightly against protectionism: "Customs import duties should not be increased to such a point as to attract capital and labor from industries that are naturally profitable to those that are made profitable only as a result of higher prices induced by the shutting out of foreign produce" (p. 10). Protectionism would impair revenue in the short run and harm productivity in the long run.[26] The use of countervailing duties (taxing domestic and imported items equally) was urged as one way to prevent harmful reallocation of domestic resources.

The tariff issue was a very emotional one in China at the time, for the "unequal treaties" of the nineteenth century had imposed on China a customs administration directed by foreigners (chiefly British) and a requirement that import duties not exceed five percent (Young, 1971, pp. 17-20, 37-45; Wright, 1938). The Commission recommended a modest but general increase in rates to achieve specific revenue goals related to public debt service. The Commission went on to suggest that "If the need for revenue makes it impossible to avoid imposing duties which artificially stimulate domestic industries, such stimulus should be given first of all to basic industries, such as the metal and chemical industries ... development [of which] would facilitate the general industrial development of the country" (p. 8).

During 1929, China was rapidly regaining tariff autonomy (Wright, 1938, pp. 601-651). Not surprisingly, rates were generally increased (effective January, 1931), since this initially served both revenue and protection motives. Frequent tariff rate increases were added during the 1930s, often over the objections of Lockhart and Young.[27] Tariff rates, which averaged only about 4 percent before 1929, went above 25 percent after 1934. Putting the customs revenue on a gold basis helped to increase revenues as the value of silver slumped. The National government did abolish the *likin*, although in some regions, local authorities continued to collect it. Other nuisance duties, such as those on coastal trade, were removed and reduced.

The Commission's recommended tax increases for matches and cement were imposed, but increases were applied to more other items than the Commission had recommended. Commission recommendations for administrative unification and coordination within the tax system were also adopted, aided by the continued presence of Lockhart and Cleveland as advisers (Young, 1971, pp. 63-67; Fong, 1936, pp. 47-49).

Cleveland's ambitious but much maligned reports dealing with the organization and management of the Government's financial affairs were addressed to a new government which had "no real system of budgets, accounts, and fiscal control" (Young, 1970, p. 103). Fiscal management in China encountered an age-old problem—the difficulty of separating public and private spheres.[28] In January, 1931, the Ministry of Finance adopted a comprehensive accounting system based on the Kemmerer recommendations. An independent office, the Directorate General of Budgets, Accounts and Statistics, was created in that year. Improvement was aided by the continued presence of Commission members William Watson (who left in late 1931) and Frederick Cleveland (who remained until 1935). However, Arthur Young concluded that actual administrative improvements in China's financial management were disappointing in the 1930s. "Lack of fiscal control of the military was a continuing weakness" (Young, 1970, p. 104).

## VI.  SOME COMPARISONS WITH OTHER MISSIONS

Comparing Kemmerer's mission to China with his similar projects in other countries, is facilitated by Paul Drake's excellent survey (1989). Appendix A surveys the personnel of all of Kemmerer's missions. The mission to China was the largest and spent the most time in the host country. It was also unusual in the large number of mission experts who remained behind and in the duration of the stay. The China mission had a much higher representation of economists.

A huge difference is evident, however, in the adoption of Kemmerer's proposals. In his pre-1929 missions, rapid uncritical adoption of virtually his entire package of proposals was achieved in Colombia, Chile, Ecuador, and Bolivia (Drake, pp. 39-40, 92, 148, 158, 191). A major motive was the conviction that the governments would be able to obtain loans in the United States once the Kemmerer recommendations were followed and they were. In each of the four countries, a central bank was created (or adapted) along similar lines to those proposed for China (Drake, pp. 45-47, 97-98, 152-155, 194). Each of the four countries (and Peru in 1931) accepted the implied role of a "small open economy," in which the domestic money supply, price level, and interest rates were all left to free-market adjustments while the central bank concentrated on exchange rate stabilization. In each of the five countries, the deflationary process which began in 1929 hit with great force, causing gold outflow, monetary contraction, deflation of prices, depression and unemployment (Drake, pp. 60-61, 115-121, 169-174, 205- 210, 234, 246-247; Triffin, 1944, pp. 96-99). Ultimately each country severed its ties to gold, devalued its currency, and permitted much foreign debt to go into default.

In China, however, the recommended gold-exchange standard was not adopted. Consequently, China's monetary system adjusted better to the deflation, especially in 1929-1931, than the other Kemmerer countries. China also did not create a Kemmerer-style central bank. China did gain credit-worthiness, however, by putting its customs system on a gold basis and by improving public-debt service.

The programs for the monetary standard, central bank, and commercial banking were those most closely linked to Kemmerer himself. The central features of the China proposals did not differ substantially from those previously presented in Latin America. The monetary standard proposal was unique in that there was to be no full-bodied gold coinage at all. And conditions specific to China were effectively addressed in the special reports relating to monetary unification and to putting the customs on a gold basis. In most other topics, it is evident that the Kemmerer reports were very specific to China. This was particularly true in the areas of public debt, railway finance, tax and tariff policy.[29]

China's budgets and indebtedness were in such disarray and default in 1929 that no significant new international credits were in prospect unless revenues and administration improved substantially (Fong, 1936, pp. 80-81). The influence of the Commission on China's credit standing came chiefly in the extended involvement of Arthur Young, Frederick Cleveland, and Oliver Lockhart in the management of revenue and public debt policies, rather than simply through paper proposals. We can also infer that, where the Kemmerer China proposals were adopted, they were judged more on their individual merits than had been the case in Latin America. Curti and Birr introduced their discussion of the Kemmerer Commission in China with the comment that "American technical and advisory work proved to be of far greater importance in China than in many smaller countries" (1954, p. 176).

## VII. WHAT HAPPENED AFTER 1929?

After Kemmerer left China in December, 1929, he had virtually no continuing relation with China. He never published any scholarly studies directly related to China or his work there. With the collapse of the gold-exchange standard and the drying up of U.S. lending overseas, Kemmerer's off-shore advisory work ended with a mission to Turkey in 1934-1935. He remained a staunch defender of the gold standard, advocating its restoration after 1933 and criticizing the interventionist measures of the New Deal.

Much of the influence of the Commission came through the unusual number of its members who continued to play important roles in China. All five of the "Experts" remained. Tariff expert Benjamin Wallace remained for another year, helping the government navigate through the complexities of diplomacy involved in securing tariff autonomy.[30] William Watson remained until later in 1931. According to Lockhart, "Watson had begun an organization of the reports reaching the Ministry in a fashion which I thought promised to give the Minister of Finance a much better picture of the financial situation than he had ever had before."[31] Poland stayed on for more than a year to advise on railroad management and finance (Tyau, 1930, pp. 246, 260).

Frederick Cleveland, despite his advanced age, remained in China until 1935. Officially, he became one of the administrative heads of the Salt Revenue, a government monopoly of salt production and sale, organized to collect a heavy tax on this necessity (Young, 1971, pp. 20-21; Fong,-1936, pp. 45-47). In his first report in 1930, Cleveland found ample scope for his demonstrated reforming zeal: "it is necessary to eradicate the ancient practices that now cumber it [the salt service], such as farming the revenues, selling offices ..., the whole system of squeeze, tribute, and personal, political and military appointments ... When ... administered with economy and efficiency the salt revenue would go far toward providing the means necessary for carrying out a well coordinated program of public education, public health, famine relief, sanitation, conservation and public improvements ..."[32] The amount of salt revenues actually available for general government increased several-fold in the 1930s, compared with pre-1929 (Young, 1971, pp. 54-63). Cleveland also continued to provide advice on issues of budgeting and financial control, such as the Budget Law of August, 1932.

Oliver Lockhart remained in China until 1941. His chief work was advising on tax matters. His lengthy 1933 review of the fate of the Kemmerer recommendations has been noted at several points. Regarding tax policies, he commented that "the taxes on matches and cement were instituted substantially as proposed [by the Commission] and the reorganization of tax administration along the lines laid down in the Report on Revenue Policy has been effected ... Some of the Commission's recommendations with respect to the schedule of taxable documents have been adopted ... "[33] Young credits Lockhart with "the development of a respected service to operate the consolidated taxes on factory products" (1971, p. 339). In June, 1931, Young and Lockhart aided in drafting material for the constitutional convention.[34] In 1936 Lockhart replaced Cleveland in the Salt Revenue.

Fenimore Lynch, who had spent most of his adult life in China, remained until his tragic death in a plane crash in 1942, working primarily as an adviser to the Central Bank. He helped the Bank to develop correspondent banking connections in London and New York for foreign-exchange operations (Young, 1971, pp. 41, 48, 158-159, 341).

Arthur Young continued as an adviser to the Ministry of Finance until 1947. The central focus of his responsibilities was on public debt administration. During 1929, much of his task was simply assembling information on the vast melange of debts incurred by various units of government under very diverse types of security and guarantee. Many of the issues were in default. He persuaded the Government to keep interest payments current and to make some payments, however small, toward the repayment of principal. These efforts continued into the mid-1930s (Young, 1971, pp. 118-141).

Much of Arthur Young's value to the Chinese government came because of his good relations with the U.S. government, particularly the State Department, where he had worked from 1922 until 1928. He was intimately involved in loan negotiations arising out of emergency conditions in both China and the United States. In 1931, China experienced one of the most devastating Yangtze River floods in history. Young helped negotiate a loan in the United States to buy wheat, a measure which would feed China's disaster areas and provide financial aid to distressed American farmers (Cycle, IV, pp. 7-11).

In 1933, Young accompanied T.V. Soong to Washington. President Roosevelt was eager to lend China $50 million to purchase U.S. cotton and wheat. The Chinese expected to sell the products at home as a revenue raising measure. Young spent several weeks in the United States managing the details of purchase and shipment (Cycle, IV, pp. 17-20). Ultimately, China took U.S. $17 million under this loan, most of it being expended for infrastructure and social welfare under the newly formed National Economic Council.[35]

Attention to debt management brought a steady improvement in China's international credit standing during the 1930s. By 1937, existing Chinese international loan securities were selling at prices in London yielding about 5 percent, better than comparable Japanese securities (Young, 1971, p. 154). Although Chinese government deficits brought sizeable increase in the domestic debt, these issues yielded only about 8 percent in 1937 (Young, 1971, p. 154; Brandt and Sargent, 1989, pp. 41-43; Fong, 1936, pp. 49-51). In contrast with the Kemmerer clients in Latin America, the Chinese government made no major foreign borrowing during 1929-1937. China did benefit from its improved international credit standing by attracting an increased flow of private capital after 1934, particularly for railway investment (Young, 1971, p. 367).

Lynch, Lockhart, and Arthur Young were all involved in the turbulent changes in China's monetary policy. Britain's departure from gold in September, 1931, put an end to any prospect of putting China on a gold standard. Instead, preparations were under way to open the new mint and to unify the currency on a silver basis (Young, 1971, pp. 164, 186; Fetter, 1936; J.P. Young, 1931).

When the United States in 1933 adopted a policy of trying to purchase silver and drive up its price, China experienced serious deflationary effects. Young "kept busy drafting cables" trying to restrain the U.S. pressures raising the world price (Young, 1971, pp. 212-214). In December, 1934, President Roosevelt sent a memorandum to Treasury Secretary Morgenthau which used some very strong language presumably aimed at the Kemmerer remnants:

> Please remember that I have a background of a little over a century in Chinese affairs ... The government of China, because it must use or deal with foreign capital, is obliged to conform with international standards. These standards expressed by the foreign advisers of the Chinese Government ... represent ... what the banking interests of the world call "orthodox." ...
>
> China has been the Mecca of the people whom I have called the "money changers in the Temple." They are still in absolute control. It will take many years and possibly several revolutions to eliminate them ... I am inclined to believe that the "money changers" are wrong and that it is better to hasten the crisis in China ...[36]

In 1935 it became evident that trying to operate a silver-based domestic system at a different value from that in world markets was not viable. The Government prepared for a monetary reconstruction by purchasing majority control of the Bank of China and the Bank of Communications, both of which held large silver reserves.[37] In November, 1935 China went off the silver standard.[38] China required that silver be sold to the Government at the relatively unfavorable official price.[39] Banknote currency was declared to be legal tender. The international value of the currency was to be stabilized in relation to a combination of U.S. and British currencies (Young, 1971, pp. 231-245; J.P. Young, 1936; Lewis, 1935). The new program, with its emphasis on "managed currency," was a far cry from the simple automatic monetary system envisioned in the Commission's gold standard report.[40] However, the new system committed China to keep the yuan more or less pegged to the U.S. dollar and the pound sterling, so it did involve a relatively fixed exchange rate (which the silver standard had not provided).

We make no attempt to survey the activities of Young, Lockhart, and Lynch after 1935. Our summary has been sufficient to show that they were an important element in important developments in monetary and fiscal policy.[41]

That they could play such a role is a testimonial to the fact that a significant component in the Chinese government was sincerely committed to modernization.

After returning to the United States for graduate study at Columbia and Yale, Harry Price returned to China in 1932 as an economics instructor and sometime dean at Yenching University, one of China's leading Christian colleges. After China-related work in the United States 1937-1944, he returned to China to spend four years as Deputy Director of the Chinese operations of the United National Relief and Rehabilitation Administration.[42] McGregor Gibb returned to China, though we do not know the details. Richard Bonnevalle joined Harry Price in working for China Defense Supplies during the war.[43]

# VIII. CONCLUSIONS

Edwin Kemmerer's 1929 mission to China was the largest of his international advisory teams of the 1920s and 1930s. It was the longest in the duration of its overseas activity and contained a much larger component of professional economists than did the others.

The China commission recommended programs to establish the gold-exchange standard, to create a genuine central bank, and to regulate commercial banking. China did not adopt the gold-exchange standard, but did follow Commission recommendations to put customs collections on a gold basis (thus preserving revenues in the early 1930s), and to unify and simplify the currency system. The managed-currency foreign-exchange standard adopted in 1935 was remote from the Kemmerer recommendation. China did not establish a central bank along Kemmerer's lines. However, elements of his proposals for central and commercial banking were adopted piecemeal during the 1930s.

The Commission achieved more in the areas of public finance and financial administration. Besides putting customs revenue on a gold basis, Arthur Young helped improve the condition of China's external debts. Evidence that China's debts would be honored helped in the broader diplomatic negotiations relating to tariff autonomy.

What determined whether particular Commission proposals were adopted or not? The government did hope to improve China's international credit rating. Adoption of the CGU, revenue enhancement, improved public debt management, and the continuing appointment of Arthur Young all reflected this motivation. A second criterion was whether proposed measures would strengthen the power of the new central government. The banking reforms definitely inclined in this direction (Tamagna, 1942, p. 159). Tax reform measures were designed both to increase central-government revenue and also to weaken the power of regional warlords. Athwart these ran considerations of factional politics within the Kuomintang. The Commission and its on-staying members worked chiefly with Finance Minister T.V. Soong, whose influence waxed and waned. His role weakened after 1931 as Japanese incursions became a major problem, and as Chiang Kai-shek gave increasing priority to military attack on the Communists. Loss of Manchuria to Japan in 1931 entailed heavy revenue losses from customs and railroads, undermining the whole commitment to orderly budgeting and financial management. Some Commission proposals were simply not very feasible. The gold standard proposal involved a costly and risky reserve. And the Commission's oft-reiterated goal of creating "non-political" (and uncorrupt) bodies for tax administration, budgeting and accounting, and management of the central bank ran very contrary to Chinese tradition and the perceived political interests of the leaders of the Kuomintang.

Compared to the virtually overnight adoption of Kemmerer proposals in Latin America, the short-run adoption in China was meager. Oliver Lockhart's review in 1933 could point to only a few instances of direct impact, notably the gold-based customs. Lockhart noted with regret that the government did not publish most of the Commission's reports.[44]

In the long run, however, the impact of China Mission was probably as great, if not greater, than those in Latin America. This was a reflection of the large number of mission members who remained in China. In this respect the China Mission was unique. Of the 10 members of Kemmerer's pre-1929 missions, only five (one economist) stayed on in the host countries, their combined added time amounting to at most 9 or 10 man-years (Drake, 1989, pp. 54, 92, 142, 199, 227). As we have seen, seven members (three economists) of Kemmerer's China Mission remained in China, and the total duration of their added service was at least 47 man years.

The Commission's mandate did not extend into specific programs for economic development in the modern sense. However, their work addressed crucial prerequisites for effective development in both private and public sectors.[45] Indeed, the Kemmerer reports can be seen as having significant parallels with the work of Alexander Hamilton, the first U.S. Treasury Secretary, in 1790-1792 (noted by Brandt and Sargent, 1989, p. 41). Financial stability and public order were essential for private development.

Further, the Kemmerer Commission's work was simply one of several elements in the Nationalist government's program for economic development. China began in 1929 to solicit programmatic support from the League of Nations. In 1930-1931, the League sponsored visits by Ludvik Rajchman, by Sir Arthur Salter, and by Robert Haas, Director of the Transit and Communications Organization. The Chinese government formed in April, 1931, a National Economic Council, mainly oriented toward cooperation with advisers from the League. In 1931-1932, League advisers also came to deal with education, with public works construction, with agriculture, the postal savings system, Yangtze flood relief, telephone and telegraph service and civil service organization. In June, 1933, T.V. Soong requested that the League appoint a "technical delegate" to be a link with the various League-sponsored programs. Ludvik Rajchman was appointed to this position, and from this point on became an influential adviser and confidant to T.V. Soong (Hoe, 1933; Rajchman, 1934).

In 1937, the U.S. commercial attache in China reported to Washington that "At the beginning of 1937, China faced a more favorable outlook in internal political unity, currency stabilization, economic reconstruction, agricultural betterment and improved social and cultural conditions than for many years past" (Quoted Young, 1971, p. 419; see also Wye, 1935). A similar tone dominated a report by the British Acting Commercial Counsellor at Shanghai. The report noted "striking" progress in tax policy, and substantial revenue improvement while observing that "over 3,000 items of miscellaneous taxes ... have already been abolished by the provincial and municipal authorities." The author concluded that the ambitious development programs based on Sun Yat-Sen's ideas were "being tackled by the Government with energy and sincerity in the face of numerous difficulties" (George, 1935, pp. 68-69; see also Salter, 1934, p. 13). Affirmative evaluations of China's financial developments in the mid-1930s were also given by important Chinese economists (Chen, 1934, pp. 363-364; Fong, 1936, pp. 40-57).

Scholarly evaluation of the Nationalist regime in 1927-1937 remains controversial. Traditionally, western assessments have been negative in tone, noting militarist and fascistic excesses, corruption, and failure to follow through effectively in government programs, particularly regarding rural conditions (Shewmaker, 1971; Eastman, 1974). A substantial revisionist literature has noted that industrial output was growing during this period and that, in the words of John K. Chang, "a firm economic, social, and political foundation for modern economic transformation was being built ... " (Chang, 1969, p. 113; see also Brandt and Sargent, 1989; Gray, 1990, pp. 152-161). The revisionist case is supplemented by the subsequent success of Taiwan's economic development under the same leadership.[46]

Since 1976, the People's Republic of China has shown more receptiveness to a program which welcomes the inflow of foreign capital and technical assistance. In its efforts to achieve political and economic reforms, many of the same considerations have arisen as were confronted by the Kemmerer Commission in 1929.[47] The Commission's efforts were part of a wide-scale government concern for and commitment to China's economic development. It is not easy to determine whether that commitment foundered chiefly because of the internal shortcomings of the Kuomintang. But that commitment did exist and the story of the Kemmerer Commission helps to fill out many of the missing details.

*Appendix A.* Membership of Principal Kemmerer Missions, 1923-1931

| Economists | Name | Identification | Colombia March 10-Aug. 20, 1923 | Guatemala July 8-Sept. 13, 1924 | Chile July-Oct. 1925 | Poland [EWK Dec. 1925-Jan. 1926] July 3-Sept. 1926 | Ecuador Oct. 18, 1926-March 1927 | Bolivia March 29-early July, 1927 | China Feb 9-Dec 10, 1929 | Colombia Aug. 4-Nov. 20, 1930 | Peru [EWK, Jan. 12, 1931] Late April, 1931 | Turkey (1934) |
|---|---|---|---|---|---|---|---|---|---|---|---|---|
| E | Fairchild, Fred | Yale, economics prof. | X | | | | | | | | | |
| | Jefferson, Howard | New York banker | X | | * | | X | X | | | | |
| | Lill, Thomas | Accounting firm | * | | | | | | | | | |
| | Luqiens, Frederick | Yale Spanish prof. | X | | | | | | | | | |
| | Byrne, Joseph | Public accountant | | | * | X | X | * | | X | | |
| E | Lutz, Harley | Stanford economics prof. | | | X | X· | | | | | | |
| | Renwick, Wm. W. | New York banker | | | X | | | | | X | | |
| | West, Henry H. | Financial adviser in Latin Am. | | | X | | | | | X | | |
| E | Fetter, Frank Whitson | Princeton economics prof. | | X | * | X | X | X | X | | | |

147

# Appendix A. (Continued)

| | Name | Description | | | | | |
|---|---|---|---|---|---|---|---|
| | Van Zandt, G. | Engineering prof railway expert | X | | | | |
| E | Vorfeld, Robert | U.S. Tariff Commission | | | X | X | |
| E | Lockhart, Oliver | Buffalo economics prof. | | | X | X | * |
| | Feely, Edward | U.S. commercial attache in L. Am. | | | X | X | X |
| | Milner, B.B. | Railway expert | | | * | | |
| | Broderick, Joseph A. | New York banker | | X | | | |
| | Clark, Wallace | Industrial Consultant | | X | | | |
| | Eble, Frank A. | U.S. customs agent in Europe | | X | | | |
| E | Graham, Frank D. | Princeton economics prof. | | X | | | |
| E | Kemmerer, Donald | Economics student | X | X | X | | X |

(continued)

Appendix A. (Continued)

| Economists | Name | Identification | Colombia March 10-Aug. 20, 1923 | Guatemala July 8-Sept. 13, 1924 | Chile July-Oct. 1925 | Poland [EWK Dec. 1925-Jan 1926] July 3-Sept. 1926 | Ecuador Oct. 18, 1926-March 1927 | Bolivia March 29-early July, 1927 | China Feb 9-Dec 10, 1929 | Colombia Aug. 4-Nov. 20, 1930 | Peru [EWK, 12, 1931] Jan. 12-Late April, 1931 | Turkey (1934) |
|---|---|---|---|---|---|---|---|---|---|---|---|---|
| | Detlefsen, E.O. | Tax expert | | | | | | X | | | | |
| E | Young, Arthur | Economist, U.S. State Dept. | | | | | | | * | | | |
| E | Cleveland, Frederick | Prof. Citizenship Boston Un. | | | | | | | * | | | |
| | Bonnevalle, Richard | Govt. and business admin. | | | | | | | X | | | |
| | Watson, William | Govt. Acc. Advisor | | | | | | | .. | | | |
| | Wallace, Benjamin | U.S. Tariff Comm. | | | | | | | * | | | |
| E | Young, John P. | Occidental economics prof. | | | | | | | X | | | |
| | Lynch, Fenimore | Banker in China | | | | | | | * | | | |
| | Gibb, John McGregor | Univ. Adm. in China | | | | | | | X | | | |
| E | Price, Harry | Economics grad. st | | | | | | | X | | | |

(continued)

149

Appendix A. (Continued)

| | Name | Description | | | |
|---|---|---|---|---|---|
| | Dawes, Wetmore | NY financial firm | X | | |
| | Thompson, George | NY financial firm | X | | |
| | Poland, Wm. B. | Railway Mgt. expert | * | | |
| | Lagerquist, Walter | | | X | |
| E | Williamson, Kossuth | Wesleyan economics prof. | | X | |
| | Dunn, W.E. | | | X | |
| | Schaefer, J.C. | | | X | |
| E | Wernette, John Phillip | Economics graduate student | X | | X |
| | Van Deusen, Walter | | | | X |
| | Atkins, Paul Moody | Investment advisor | | | X |
| | Roddy, Wm. F. | Customs advisor | | | X |
| | Morgan, Stokely W. | State Dept. Lehman Bros. | | | X |

(continued)

150

Appendix A. (Continued)

| Economists | Name | Identification | Colombia March 10-Aug. 20, 1923 | Guatemala July 8-Sept. 13, 1924 | Chile July-Oct. 1925 | Poland [EWK Dec. 1925-Jan 1926] July 3-Sept. 1926 | Ecuador Oct. 18, 1926-March 1927 | Bolivia March 29-early July, 1927 | China Feb 9-Dec 10, 1929 | Colombia Aug. 4-Nov. 20, 1930 | Peru [EWK, 12, 1931] Jan. 12-Late April, 1931 | Turkey (1934) |
|---|---|---|---|---|---|---|---|---|---|---|---|---|
| | Dodd, Philip Lindsley | Diplomat and Advisor | | | | | | | | | X | |
| | Wright, Walter L. | | | | | | | | | | | X |
| E | Whittlessey, C.R. | Princeton economics prof | | | | | | | | | | X |

Note: * Indicates members who remained in host country after mission left.

Sources: Colombia, Drake, *The Money Doctor in the Andes* (1989, pp. 38, 40, 54, 68-69, 227).
Guatemala, D. Kemmerer and Dalgaard, "Inflation, Intrigue, and Monetary Reform in Guatemala, 1919-1926," *The Historian*.
Chile, Drake, pp. 89, 92.
Poland, Republic of Poland, *Reports submitted by the Commission of the American Financial Experts Headed by Dr. E.W. Kemmerer*, Warsaw, 1926, pp. V-VI.
Ecuador, Drake, pp. 142, 166.
Bolivia, Drake, pp. 189-191, 196, 199, 201.
Peru, Drake, pp. 226-227.
Turkey, Curti and Birr, pp. 184-185. Kemmerer, aided by Wright and Whittlesey, completed a project begun by Walker D. Hines aided by Goldthwaite H. Dorr, Brehon Somervell, and O.F. Gardner. None of these were economists.

151

# ACKNOWLEDGMENTS

An earlier vesion of this paper was presented at the annual meeting of the History of Economics Society, Lexington, VA, June, 1990. The author would like to thank the three surviving members of the Kemmerer Commission, Donald Kemmerer, the late Whitson Fetter, and Harry Price, for helpful discussions and source materials. Arthur Young's children, Allen Young and Elizabeth Young Roulac provided much helpful material, particularly in permitting me to read Arthur Young's autobiographical manuscript "A Cycle of Cathay." Mrs. John Parke Young shared recollections of her husband and Arthur Young. Most of the primary source work was done in the Kemmerer Collection, Seeley Mudd Manuscript Library, Princeton University, for which my thanks go to Ms. Nancy Bressler. Quotations from these sources are published with permission of Princeton University libraries. I found much useful material in the Arthur Young papers, Hoover Institution, at Stanford University, and in the Occidental College Library. Helpful materials on McGregor Gibb and Harry Price came from the files of the United Board for Christian Missions at Yale Divinity School and from Maryville College. Edward Rada kindly provided his paper and helpful comments. Xiao Zhijie and Shen Yu-jing helped with my Beijing research during Spring, 1992.

# NOTES

1.  Kemmerer's life and work are reviewed in Dalgaard (1982); see also the very laudatory references in Schumpeter, 1954, pp. 1076, 1089, 1096, Kemmerer's papers constitute a 500-box collection in the Seeley Mudd Manuscript Library at Princeton University. This contains his diary, to which we refer frequently. D. Kemmerer (1993) is a brief biography.

2.  The Latin American missions are extensively examined in Drake, 1989. See also Seidel (1972); Dalgaard (1980); Kemmerer and Dalgaard (1983); Eichengreen (1989); Triffin (1944). On South Africa, see Dalgaard (1981); on Poland, see Meyer (1970, pp. 65-75, 111). The Kemmerer missions are put into broader context in Curti and Birr (1954, pp. 161-166, 176, 182-188) and Rosenberg and Rosenberg (1987).

3.  Kemmerer told a large luncheon audience in Peiping, October, 1929, that "experience showed him that economic laws were the same the world over, like all other natural laws." *The Leader*, Peiping, Oct. 23, 1929, clipping in Kemmerer's Diary, 1929, box 478, Kemmerer Collection, Princeton.

4.  The following biographical sketches are based primarily on the vitae in Kemmerer's files, Box 74, Folder 2-16, Kemmerer Collection, Princeton. These are supplemented by Sokolsky, 1929, by *New York Times* obituaries, biographical sources such as *Who's Who, Who Was Who*, and the directories of the American Economic Association.

5.  Sun Fo, 1930, pp. 357-361; Chen, 1934, pp. 355-356. Sun Fo had received a master's degree in economics from Columbia University in 1917. Boorman, 1967-1971, p. 163.

6.  China's foreign debt was intricately involved with the International Banking Consortium for China, a cartel which included American, Japanese, and European interests (Field, 1931; Cohen, 1978).

7.  The scope of their work is apparent in the magnitude (43 boxes) of the China mission papers within the Kemmerer Collection at Princeton. The inventory of the collection is itself a valuable guide to the Commission's work: Tsai, (1979, 119 pages).

8.　"Memorandum on Certain Matters Relating to the Currency," March 27, 1929, in Vol. 1, *Currency and Banking*, Box 75, Kemmerer papers, Princeton; EWK Diary, March 15-27, 1929.

9.　Arthur Young, "Cycle of Cathay" (unpublished manuscript), Ch. III, p. 7; EWK Diary, May 28, June 3, Sept. 26, Oct. 7, 1929. Young based his proposal on policies he had observed in France in the 1920s.

10.　Kemmerer complained that Cleveland interpreted his topic so broadly that it covered the "whole organization of the Government. The only kind of control he seems to have overlooked is 'birth control'." EWK Diary, Aug. 6; see also entries for July 16, 19; Aug. 20; Dec. 3, 4, 6, 9-13, 1929.

11.　The National Finance Conference of July 1928 had already endorsed moving toward a gold standard (Kwei, 1931, pp. 334-345). The Commission report summarized this and numerous other pre-1929 proposals for Chinese monetary reform. "Project of Law for the Gradual Introduction of a Gold-Standard Currency System into China ...," Nov. 11, 1929, pp. 198-206. I have used the copy in the University of Illinois Library.

12.　The plan evidently underwent considerable evolution within the Commission. EWK Diary, Feb. 20, March 7, March 28. Some members of the Commission favored remaining on a silver-based system (Young, 1971, p. 184).

13.　Young, 1971, p. 181. Besides the text of the report itself (published by the Ministry of Industry, Commerce, and Labor, Shanghai, 1930; summaries were published in the *China Year Book* and in the *Chinese Economic Journal* (Kwei, 1931, p. 1181; "Kemmerer Currency Reform Project ..." 1930, pp. 470-486). A French edition appeared in 1931, and another (with parallel Chinese text) in 1934 (Kemmerer, 1931, 1934). Augusta Wagner, an economics professor at Peking's Yenching University, reprinted part of the Kemmerer report for her students (Wagner, 1936, pp. 166-177).

14.　These issues may have been involved in Kemmerer's discussion with Fetter, of which he wrote, "Shocked to find that Whitson's ideas of the function of a reserve ... /are/ primarily ... of a 'banker fund' to prevent depreciation rather than a regulator fund, as I have long maintained, to adjust and regulate the supply of money ... For years and in every country in which he has been with me in currency reform I have maintained this doctrine ... and he has apparently accepted it and signed the reports. I can't understand his new position" (EWK Diary, Nov. 1, 1929).

15.　Leavens, 1939, p. 202; Young, "Cycle," III, pp. 10-11; "Project of Law for Placing Customs Duties on Imports from Abroad upon a Gold Basis," Dec. 10, 1929, in Vol. 1, *Currency and Banking*, Box 75, Kemmerer Papers, Princeton. The use of a gold basis would not apply to export duties, tonnage dues, coast trade, transit dues, or native customs duties, but only to duties on imported goods. The Commission estimated this would be sufficient to cover China's international obligations payable in gold (p. 3).

16.　Lockhart to Kemmerer, January 29, 1933, Box 89, Kemmerer papers.

17.　"Project of Law for the Creation of the Central Reserve Bank of China, ...," Dec. 10, 1929, in Vol. 1, *Currency and Banking*, Box 75, Kemmerer papers. Both the economic and financial conferences of 1928 had endorsed creation of a central bank with monopoly of note issue (Kwei, 1931, pp. 334-345). Ma Yin-chu's 1929 book on Chinese banking had urged that the country develop a stronger central bank holding the reserves of the commercial banks and utilizing open-market operations (Ma, 1929, Ch. 3, Section 11).

18.　Compare "Project ... Central Reserve Bank ...," with Tamagna, 1942, pp. 123-125.

19.　"Project of a General Banking Law, ...," Dec. 10, 1929, in Vol. 1, *Currency and Banking*, Box 75, Kemmerer Papers.

20.　Young, 1971, p. 266. More favorable assessments are given by Tamagna, 1942, p. 199, Chang Kia-Ngau, 1970, pp. 163-164; Brandt and Sargent, 1990, pp. 34-35, 38.

21.　However, Poland's involvement in the U.S. rail-consolidation planning of the early 1920s was reflected in the Commission's detailed proposals for consolidation of China's very decentralized railway administrative system. "Report: Railway Finance," Dec. 10, 1929 (actually completed in January, 1930), in Vol. 4, *Taxation, Railway Finance*, Box 76, Kemmerer Papers; Young, 1971, p. 319.

22. "Project of a Public Credit Rehabilitation Law, Together with a Report on the National Debt of China ...," Dec. 10, 1929, in Vol. 3, *Public Credit*, Box 76, Kemmerer Papers, p. xlii; Young, 1971, pp. 110-141.

23. "Report on Revenue Policy," Dec. 10, 1929, in Vol. 4, *Taxation, Tariff, and Railway Finance*, Box 76, Kemmerer Papers, p. 1.

24. "Project of Law for a Special Consumption Tax on Matches ..." Sept. 6, 1929; "Project of Law for a Special Consumption Tax on Portland Cement ..." Dec. 10, 1929; "Project of Law for a Documentary Stamp Tax ..." Nov. 18, 1929. All are bound in Vol. 4, *Taxation, Tariff and Railway Finance*, Box 76, Kemmerer papers.

25. In 1917, Young supported "special assessments ... to absorb as large a share as possible of increases in the value of land that result directly from public or quasi-public expenditures" (1917, p. 8). Sun Yat-sen's *International Development* contained many references to the rise in land values expected from his proposed development program, and the opportunities for government to capture these (1928, pp. 36, 40-41, 44, 49, 56- 57, 75, 81; Schiffren, 1957).

26. "Project of Law for Increasing the Customs Revenue from Import Duties, ...," Dec. 10, 1929, in Vol. 4, *Taxation, Tariff, and Railway Finance*, Box 76, Kemmerer Papers.
Another tariff report dealt extensively with tariff diplomacy, reflecting Wallace's long experience with the U.S. Tariff Commission. "Project of Tariff Law, ...," Dec. 10, 1929, in Vol. 4, *Taxation, Tariff, and Railway Finance*, Box 76, Kemmerer Papers.

27. Young, 1971, pp. 48-54. Lockhart wrote to Kemmerer in 1933, "Not much can be claimed for the results of the recommendations on Tariff and Tariff policies. An influential section of Chinese officialdom is strongly and crudely mercantilistic ..." Jan. 29, 1933, Box 89, Kemmerer papers (see also Wright, 1938, pp. 676-680).

28. "The older assumption was that the revenue and monies in hand or in the Treasury belonged to the Emperor, to the Viceroy ... or to some other person ...; and that the disposition or use of [these funds] was a matter of personal arrangement." "Projects of Law Dealing with Financial Planning, Budget Preparation, Budget Enforcement, Accounting, Fiscal Control, Supervisory Inspection and Audit; ...," Dec. 10, 1929, p. 115, in Vol. 2, *Financial Planning, Budget and Accounting* (University of Illinois Library).

29. Thus, China, at least, does not seem to support Drake's jibe, "Hardly a word in his [Kemmerer's] reports varied from Poland to Bolivia ... He could have delivered most of his reports by mail" (Drake, 1989, p. 250).

30. Wallace left China June 13, 1931—Arthur Young's Diary, June 13, 1931, Box 113, Arthur Young Papers, Hoover Institution. Wallace's article (1931) on "China's Imports and Exports of Foodstuffs" displays familiarity with neoclassical trade theory and the link between trade and development.

31. Lockhart to Kemmerer, Jan. 29, 1933, p. 4; Box 89, Kemmerer Papers.

32. "Estimates and Budget of the Inspectorate of Salt Revenue for the 19th Fiscal Year ...," Sept. 19, 1930, pp. 9-10, Box 115, Arthur Young Papers, Hoover Institute.

33. Lockhart to Kemmerer, Jan. 29, 1933, Box 89, Kemmerer Papers.

34. Young Diary, June 1-9, 1931; Box 113, Arthur Young Papers, Hoover Institute.

35. Young, 1971, pp. 293-298; "Activities of the National Economic Council." *China Quarterly* (Shanghai) I(1): 157-166; Chen, 1934.

36. Quoted in Young, 1971, p. 206. That Roosevelt was aware of Kemmerer's positions and disliked them was made very clear in discussions at Princeton with Roosevelt's confidant Louis Howe in 1933 (Dalgaard, 1982, pp. 39-40).

37. "For a long time, plans for comprehensive reform had been ready, on which my colleagues Lockhart and Lynch and I had been working in close collaboration with Kung and Soong" (Young, 1971, pp. 229-230).

38.   John Lossing Buck, Nanking University's pioneering agricultural economist, asserted that he and his colleague Ardron Lewis were influential in bringing about the break from silver (Buck, 1973, pp. 36-37). They were signatories to a 1934 report which implied that China's farm prices were being dragged down by adhering to silver. The report was strongly influenced by Lewis, who put into it many of the ideas of his Cornell professors George Warren and Frank Pearson (Committee ... 1935). Another participant in the decision to leave silver was Sir Frederick Leith-Ross, who came to China in September, 1935, representing the British government (Young, 1971, pp. 228-235).

39.   Brandt and Sargent, 1989, argued that a major goal of these actions was to secure for the government the capital gain obtainable by buying the silver at an enforced low price and then reselling it at market value (pp. 48-49). Eastman, 1974, stressed the shift in political power involved in the banking "coup" (pp. 232-3). Both noted that cutting the ties to silver opened the way for government to use monetary creation to cover its deficits, leading to accelerating inflation.

40.   The new "managed currency" also went contrary to Sir Arthur Salter's strong warning in 1934 that: "The substitution of a paper currency for the silver dollar" would be "disastrous," because of "the impossibility of limiting depreciation" (Salter, 1934, p. 40).

41.   One can obtain some idea of the contributions of Young, Cleveland, Lockhart, and Lynch from Young's 1963, 1965 and 1971 books. His unpublished "Cycle of Cathay" brings out his personal activities more fully, as does his long letter to Merle Curti, Sept. 10, 1951, Box G, Arthur Young Papers, Occidental College. Testimonials to the quality of Young's work appear in S.C. Tsiang, 1970; Curti and Birr, 1954, pp. 161-162, 176-178; and Rada, 1980. The prevailing tone of Western writing on the Nationalist Government, 1927-1937 is negative. See Pauuw, 1957, and Eastman, 1974, for examples which Young himself discussed in his writings. For more affirmative views, see Wye, 1935; Harry Price, 1937; Sih, 1970. Arthur Young's credibility is well affirmed in the reviews of his books: Michael, 1963; Liu, 1972; Feuerwerker, 1966, 1972; Chang, 1966; Gurley, 1966. It is noteworthy that both Arthur and John Parke Young participated in the Bretton Woods Conference in 1944.

42.   Biographical information from interviews with Dr. Price and from Maryville College.

43.   American University Club of Shanghai, 1935, p. 191, lists Gibb as a member. For Bonnevale, see Arthur Young letter to T.V. Soong, Aug. 10, 1942, Box 10, Arthur Young folder, T.V. Soong papers, Hoover Institution.

44.   "I believe only the Currency Project, the Report on Revenue Policy, and a summary of the budget and accounting projects have been really released ..." To Kemmerer, Jan. 29, 1933; Box 89, Kemmerer Papers. Summaries of the report on currency and on fiscal control are in Kwei, 1931, pp. 346, 392-394. Besides the widely publicized gold-standard report, the Yenching University library held copies of the Report on Revenue Policy and the Report on Financial Planning ... and Audit; these are now in the Peking University Library with the original Yenching bookplates still affixed. Citations to Kemmerer reports on taxation can be found in Li, 1937, pp. 58-59; Su, 1939, p. 22; and Chu Chi, 1936 (see Tin, 1937, pp. 1098-1099).

45.   Young to Soong, July 6, 1931, Box 113, Arthur Young Papers, Hoover Institute; Hsu, 1927, p. 113; Baker, 1935; Perkins, 1975, pp. 15-16.

46.   Rada, 1981 notes that Arthur Young visited Taiwan in 1958 and offered recommendations consistent with the policies toward export growth and free markets which subsequently proved so successful (pp. 18-19). In 1980, Soochow University in Taiwan established an Arthur N. Young Chair of Finance.

47.   Recent Chinese publications have dealt more objectively with China's pre-1949 developments. A documentary collection in China's monetary history devoted several pages to the personnel of the Kemmerer mission and their gold-standard recommendations (People's Bank of China, 1991, pp. 66-74). A biographical dictionary of foreigners important to China includes entries for Kemmerer, Cleveland, and Arthur Young (Huang and Gu, 1981, pp. 85, 250, 532).

# REFERENCES

"Activities of the National Economic Council." 1935. *China Quarterly* (Shanghai) I(1), pp. 157-166.

American University Club of Shanghai. 1935. *25th Anniversary Memorial Volume*, Shanghai: Peking University Library.

Baker, John Earl. 1935. "Outline for Rural Reconstruction," *China Quarterly* (Shanghai), I(1):

Boorman, Howard L., ed. 1970. *Biographical Dictionary of Republican China* (vol. 3), New York: Columbia University Press.

Brandt, Loren and Thomas J. Sargent. 1989. "Interpreting New Evidence About China and U.S. Silver Purchases." *Journal of Monetary Economics* 23(1): 31-51.

Buck, John Lossing. 1973. *Development of Agricultural Economics at the University of Nanking, 1926-1946*. Ithaca, NY: Cornell International Agricultural Development Bulletin 25.

Chang, Kia-Ngau. 1970. "Toward Modernization of China's Currency and Banking, 1927-1937." Pp. 129-165 in *The Strenuous Decade*, edited by Paul Sih. New York: St. John's University Press.

————— . 1965. Review of Young. *Journal of Political Economy*, 74(3): 304-305.

Chang, John K. 1934. *Industrial Development in Pre-Communist China*. Chicago: Aldine.

Chen, Gideon. 1934. "Chinese Government Economic Planning and Reconstruction." Pp. 352-382 in *Problems of the Pacific, 1933*, edited by Bruno Lasker and W.L. Holland. Chicago: Institute of Pacific Relations.

Cohen, Warren. 1978. *The Chinese Connection*. New York: Columbia University.

Committee for the Study of Silver Values and Commodity Prices. 1935. *Silver and Prices in China*. Shanghai: Commercial Press. I am indebted to Prof. A.B. Lewis for giving me his copy.

Condliffe, J.B. 1932. *China Today: Economic*, Boston: World Peace Federation.

Chu, Ching-lai. 1931. "A Critical Study of the Kemmerer Report," *Pacific Affairs*, 4(1): 210-224.

Curti, Merle and Kendal Birr 1954. *Prelude to Point Four: American Technical Missions Overseas 1838-1938*. Madison: University of Wisconsin.

Dalgaard, Bruce R. 1982. "E.W. Kemmerer: The Origins and Impact of the 'Money Doctor's' Monetary Economics." Pp. 31-44 in *Variations in Business and Economic History: Essays in Honor of Donald L. Kemmerer*. Greenwich, CT: JAI Press.

————— . 1981. *South Africa's Impact on Britain's Return to Gold*. New York: Arno Press.

Drake, Paul W. 1989. *The Money Doctor in the Andes: The Kemmerer Missions, 1923-1933*. Durham: Duke University Press.

Eastman, Lloyd. 1974. *The Abortive Revolution: China under Nationalist Rule, 1927-1937*. Cambridge, MA: Harvard.

Eichengreen, Barry. 1989. "House Calls of the Money Doctor: The Kemmerer Missions to Latin America, 1917-1931." In *Debt, Stabilization and Development: Essays in Memory of Carlos Diaz-Alejandro*, edited by Guillermo Calvo et al. Cambridge, MA: Harvard University Press.

Fetter, Frank Whitson. "China and the Flow of Silver." *Geographical Review* 26(1): 32-45.

Feuerwerker, Albert. 1965. Review of Young. *American Historical Review*, 71(4): 304-305.

————— . 1971. Review of Young. *American Historical Review*. 77(5): 1494-1495.

Field, Frederick V. 1931. *American Participation in the China Consortiums*. Chicago: University of Chicago.

Fong, H.D. 1936. "Economic Control in China." (pamphlet). Shanghai: China Institute of Pacific Relations.

George, A.G.H. 1935. "Trade and Economic Conditions in China, 1933-1935." (British) Department of Overseas Trade.

Gray, Jack. 1980. *Rebellions and Revolutions: China from the 1800s to the 1980s.* New York: Oxford University Press.

Gurley, John G. 1965. Review of Young. *American Economic Review,* 56(5): 1266-1268.

Hanna, Hugh H., Charles A. Conant, and Jeremiah W. Jenks. 1904. *Report on the Introduction of the Gold-Exchange Standard into China, the Philippine Islands, Panama, and other Silver- Using Countries and on the Stability of Exchange.* Washington, DC: Government Printing Office.

Hoe, Y.C. 1933. "The Programme of Technical Cooperation between China and the League of Nations." Paper presented to Institute of Pacific Relations, Aug., 1933; copy in Peking University Library.

Hsia, Ronald. 1961. "The Intellectual and Public Life of Ma Yin-chu." *China Quarterly,* No. 6: 53-63.

Hsu, C.Y. 1927. "Present-Day Social Thinking in China and Christian Ethics." *Report of the Conference on Christianizing Economic Relations.* Shanghai:

Huang, Guanyu and Gu Ya. 1981. *Biographical Dictionary of Foreign Visitors in Modern Times.* Beijing: China Social Science Press. (Chinese language).

"Kemmerer Currency Reform Project: A Summary." 1930. *Chinese Economic Journal,* 6(4): 470-486.

Kemmerer, Donald L. 1933. *The Life and Times of Professor Edwin Walter Kemmerer, 1875-1945,* privately printed.

Kemmerer, Donald and Bruce Dalgaard. 1983. "Inflation, Intrigue, and Monetary Reform in Guatemala, 1919-1926." *The Historian,* 46(1): 21-38.

Kemmerer, Edwin W. 1916. *Modern Currency Reforms.* New York: Macmillan.

————. 1918. *The ABCs of the Federal Reserve System.* New York: McGraw-Hill.

————. 1927. "Economic Advisory Work for Governments." *American Economic Review,* 17(1): 1-12.

————. 1931. "L'Etalon Or en Chine." Peking: Editions Albert Nachbaur.

————. 1934. "Le'Etalon Or en Chine." Tientsin: Hautes Etudes Industrielles et Commercieles.

Kwei, Chungshu, ed. 1931-1934. *The Chinese Yearbook.* Shanghai: Commercial Press.

Lee, Frederick Edward. 1932. "New Banking Laws for China." *Barron's* (20), p. 20.

Leavens, Dickson. 1930. "Chinese Money and Banking." *Annals.* 152, 206-213.

————. 1939. *Silver Money.* Bloomington, IN: Principia Press.

Lewis, A.B. 1937. "Silver and Chinese Economic Problems." *Pacific Affairs* 8(1): 48-55.

Li, Pao Chen. 1937. "Income Tax in China." Economic Studies Series (pamphlets). Tientsin: Hautes Etudes Industrielles et Commerciales, (Peking University Library).

Liu, Alan P.L. 1971. Review of Young. *Annals,* 402: 151-152.

Ma, Yin-chu. 1929. *On Chinese Banking* (Chinese language). Shanghai: Commercial Press.

————. 1930. "The Plan for Reforming the Monetary System Written by Kemmerer's Group for the Ministry of Finance." In *Collected Works ...* (Chinese language).

Meyer, Richard Hemmig. 1970. *Bankers Diplomacy: Monetary Stabilization in the Twenties.* New York: Columbia University.

Michael, Franz. 1964. Review of Young. *Annals* 356: 229-230.

Paauw, Douglas. 1957. "The Kuomintang and Economic Stagnation, 1928-1937." *Journal of Asian Studies,* 16(1): 213-220.

People's Bank of China. 1991. *Files on Monetary History of Republic of China.* Shanghai: People's Publishing House.

Perkins, Dwight. 1975. "Introduction." In *China's Modern Economy in Historical Perspective.* Stanford: Stanford University Press.

Price, Harry B. 1937. "Can China Rule Herself—The Ten Year Record," *New York Times Magazine,* (Dec. 12), pp. 12, 18.

Rada, Edward L. 1981. "Arthur N. Young and Nationalist China's Finances." (pamphlet). Taiwan: Soochow University.

Rajchman, Ludvik. 1934. "Report to the Council ... on his Mission to China from Date of Appointment until April 1, 1934." Geneva: League of Nations.

Rosenberg, Emily S. and Norman L. 1987. "From Colonialism to Professionalism: The Public-Private Dynamic in United States Foreign Financial Advising, 1898-1929." *Journal of American History* 74(1): 59-82.

Salter, Sir Arthur. 1934. *China and the Depression: Impressions of a Three Month Visit.* Nanjing: National Economic Council.

Schiffrin, Harold. 1957. "Sun Yat-Sen's Early Land Policy: The Origin and Meaning of Equalization of Land Rights." *Journal of Asian Studies* 16(4): 549-564.

Schumpeter, Joseph A. 1954. *History of Economic Analysis.* New York: Oxford University Press.

Seidel, Robert N. 1972. "American Reformers Abroad: The Kemmerer Missions in South America, 1923-1931." *Journal of Economic History*, 32(2): 520-545.

Shen, Yu-jing. 1992. "Ma Yin-chu's Ideas on Money," unpublished paper. Beijing: People's University.

Shewmaker, Kenneth E. 1971. *Americans and Chinese Communists: A Persuading Encounter.* Ithaca: Cornell University Press.

Sih, Paul, ed. 1970. *The Strenuous Decade: China's Nation-Building Efforts, 1927-1937.* New York:

Sokolsky, George. 1929. "The Kemmerer Commission in China." *Far Eastern Review* (Dec.): 539-540.

Su, Shou-ch'ang. 1939. "Collection of Death Duties in China." *Economic Studies Series* (pamphlets). Tientsin: Hautes Etudes Industrielles et Commerciales.

Sun, Fo. 1929-1930. "National Scheme of Railway Construction." *China Year Book*, pp. 357-379.

Sun, Yat-Sen. 1928. [1919]. *The International Development of China.* London:

Tamagna, Frank. 1942. *Banking and Finance in China.* New York: Institute of Pacific Relations

Tin, H.V. 1936. Review of Chu Chi. 1937. *"The Problem of Taxation in China."* *Nankai Social and Economic Quarterly*: 1097-1099.

Triffin, Robert. 1944. "Central Banking and Monetary Management in Latin America." Pp. 93-116 in *Economic Problems of Latin America*, edited by Seymour Harris. New York: McGraw-Hill.

Tsai, David. 1979. "Guide to the Edwin W. Kemmerer Papers." Princeton: Seeley Mudd Manuscript Library.

Tyau, Min-chien T.Z. 1930. *Two Years of Nationalist China.* Shanghai: Kelley and Walsh.

Wagner, Augusta, ed. 1936. *Yenching Readings in Economics.* Peiping: Peking University Library.

Wye, C. Kay. 1935. "Chinese Unification and Foreign Penetration." *Pacific Affairs* 8(4): 473-474.

Wright, Stanley F. 1938. *China's Struggle for Tariff Autonomy.* Shanghai: Kelley and Walsh.

Young, Arthur N. 1917. "The Possibilities and Limitations of Special Taxation of Land." *National Conference of Social Work Reprint*, No. 101.

_____ . 1963. *China and the Helping Hand.* Cambridge, MA: Harvard University Press.

_____ . 1965. *China's Wartime Finance and Inflation, 1937-1945.* Cambridge, MA: Harvard University Press.

_____ . 1970. "China's Fiscal Transformation, 1927-1937."

_____ . 1971. *China's Nation-Building Effort, 1927-1937.* Stanford, CA: Hoover Institute.

Young, John Parke. 1931. "The Shanghai Tael." *American Economic Review.* 21(4): 682-684.

_____ . 1936. "The United States Silver Policy." *Foreign Policy Reports* (pamphlet), July 1.

# Reflections on Reflections

# How Does Social Science Work?

by Paul Diesing
(Pittsburgh: University of Pittsburgh, 1991; 414 pp.)

Review Essay by **Nahid Aslanbeigui**

## I.

If T.W. Hutchison's *The Significance and Basic Postulates of Economic Theory* (1938) was the embodiment of the positivist philosophy of the 1920s and 1930s, Paul Diesing's *How Does Social Science Work? Reflections on Practice* (1991) is the epitome of the post-positivist tides that are gradually sweeping economics (and other social sciences) in recent years. It is not too uncommon now to see positivism denounced for imposing on science a set of normative rules designed to "affect practice by criticizing practice from a position apart from practice" (Weintraub, 1990, p. 263). Neither is the argument that knowledge is socially produced within the context of scientific communities (Pheby, 1988). Consequently, methodologists of economics have ventured into many different territories. Some have been borrowing from Kuhn and Lakatos to identify paradigms or research programs in the discipline (De Vroey, 1980). Others have focused on language and discourse (Samuels, 1990), applying to economics ideas from hermeneutics (Lavoie, 1990), classical rhetoric (McClosky, 1986), or literary theory (Brown, 1992). Concurrently, due to a growing appreciation of the historical nature of knowledge, some methodologists have called upon practitioners to pay serious attention to the history of their own discipline (Blaug, 1990; Weintraub, 1990).[1]

**Research in the History of Economic Thought and Methodology,**
Volume 13, pages 159-167.
Copyright © 1995 by JAI Press Inc.
All rights of reproduction in any form reserved.
ISBN: 1-55938-095-0

Diesing's *How Does Social Science Work?* should be viewed as an attempt to synthesize the above currents. The philosophical positions that Diesing relies on are various: Kuhn, Lakatos, and Feyerabend teach him to look at social science in the context of communities. The pragmatists such as Dewey inform him that truth or knowledge is everchanging and time specific. Structuralists such as Stegmüller advise Diesing that knowledge is holistic, it comes within a structure or network of concepts that develop over time and that therefore "scientific theories have a history" (Diesing, 1991, p. 68). Finally, Diesing learns from Gadamer and others that since science is a social activity, it has to be armed with hermeneutics to be able to interpret and communicate (p. 138).

The most original part of Diesing's work is his data bank. It is refreshing to see him rely on social sciences—not just economics but also sociology, psychology, anthropology and political science. Diesing's use of social science is double edged: he employs the theories to support his philosophical position (e.g., sociology explains scientific communities and psychology shows the transient nature of truth) as well as providing case studies of scientific developments or episodes. In this book, you can take the statement "social science studies itself" literally.

Diesing's reflections on practice are designed to specifically answer questions that have preoccupied many a methodologist in the past:

> (1) What sort of truth or knowledge does social science provide? (2) How does or should it do this? (3) What weaknesses and dangers appear, and how can they be avoided or corrected (p. 303).

But his main intent is to use his impressive knowledge of all walks of social science to emancipate practitioners. A description of "scientific episodes or developments or processes," could, says Diesing, enable the readers "to see something of themselves there. Or, if not themselves, they may be able to recognize others" (p. 129). If this contribution succeeds in effecting "self-reflection," it could increase "awareness of the pitfalls and the nonrational influences on research" (p. 363) which could in turn lead to correction of weaknesses and construction on strengths (p. 128). In this, he is reinforcing the idea that self-reflection may lead to a better social science.

The book is structured in three parts. In Parts I and II, Diesing surveys a vast body of literature in social science as well as in philosophy/history/ sociology/politics of science to weed out the useful, workable, and realistic building blocks for the synthesis that comes in Part III. I suggest that readers commence with the last part as Diesing seems to forget his own finding: human cognition of complex structures, such as his, is limited. Reading the book out of the usual order, should make the too convoluted parts I and II less confusing and more palatable.

# II

It is not surprising to see that Diesing's starting point is positivism (logical empiricism). He echoes the long-existing concern that the normative prescriptions of positivism come from a point above science: the ideal of perfect knowledge. This is most untenable for it presumes the existence of neutral or detached scientists who look for and find observable data, equally neutral or detached from values, in order to test hypotheses that if verified/not falsified/ confirmed can be called *laws*. Progress in science is defined in terms of a linear movement towards the ideal, Truth with a capital T if you will. This flawed position holds that if ideal and practice are different, then practice should be blamed as deficient (p. 26).

In his arguments against positivism, Diesing is not alone. Positivism as we all know has had disastrous results for social science.

1.   The search for a healthy body of positive, value-free theory is not unlike that for the Holy Grail. In economics, we have witnessed the failure of welfare theorists to reach a positive set of theories. The theoretical apparatus that we have been left with is, as a result of this pursuit, full of *ad hoc* assumptions, devoid of policy relevance, but shot through and through with value judgments (Aslanbeigui, 1984). Kuhn, Lakatos, and other philosophers/historians of science have shown that the ideal of a perfectly positive science is a mere illusion. Values can creep in at many levels, for example, "theory produces the data that test it" and interpretations "always mediate between scientists and the world" (Diesing, 1991, p. 313).

2.   The positivists' exclusive emphasis on the observable and measurable has resulted in decades of "behaviorism in psychology and behavioralism in political science" (p. 311). Much similarly, one could exemplify the neoclassical theory of consumption. Empirical regularities that the positivists arrive at— Diesing is hesitant to call them laws because they impart permanence—are but one type of knowledge or truth in social science: external. Knowledge, structuralists have demonstrated, could also come in terms of "abstract structural dynamics that can be exemplified in empirical cases," for example, Keynesian economics. "Such structures, mathematical or nonmathematical, enable us to understand and predict the dynamics of some empirical system," or even propose policies, that is, a Keynesian policymaker can cure unemployment via fiscal policy (p. 306).

Hermeneutics, is a third type of knowledge (internal) in social science. It "deals with clarifying the meaning of a text, and by extension the meaning of any human action, product, or expression that can be treated as a text." *Texts* can include Supreme Court decisions, memoirs, interviews, books, dream reports, or "a small group session in an interaction process laboratory" (p. 105). The hermeneutic approach assumes that scientific neutrality is impossible;

scientists are active participants who try to understand and take part in life as it is lived, and who, again by extension, are enabled to understand their own lives better (p. 306).

Perhaps the reason why positivism excludes internal truth from the domain of "science" is its flawed belief that the contexts of discovery and justification are separate. Hermeneutics could, therefore, they may claim, belong to the former but not to the latter. Frame theory shows, argues Diesing, that a cognitive process—science is such a process—which involves search does not and cannot separate the two contexts. Justification occurs in a "larger context of discovery and takes its character from that context" (p. 308). This brings us to the next point, the role of testing in theoretical analysis.

3.   Social scientists do not use testing to falsify/disconfirm theories. In fact, positivism has a significant problem with the degree of confirmation. Goodman's Paradox has demonstrated that data do not only confirm the particular hypothesis at hand but an infinity of other hypotheses. "Consequently, the degree of confirmation for any one of this infinite set is zero" (p. 314).

Case studies from cognitive and experimental psychology prove to Diesing that in practice tests are mainly used for confirmation. Those who are not yet committed to their own theory will be persuaded by confirmatory data; "the theory is worth developing; it works." Those who are already committed to the theory use testing to persuade others who are not—it is a McClosky-type rhetorical device. Testing is further used to engage in Kuhnian puzzle solving: "work on details, find areas of weakness or vagueness, try a new area of application or new variant, suggest supplementary hypotheses, find a better definition of some concept such as *money*, and so on" (p. 311). Whatever its use, testing *is not* for falsification/disconfirmation.

4.   Truth does not come in the form of separate, confirmed laws as positivists argue but rather in such wholes as Kuhn's paradigms, Lakatos' research programs, and Stegmüller's structures. If the reader is unconvinced by these philosophers/ historians, Diesing brings to her evidence from psychology (frame theory) and artificial intelligence models which have demonstrated that "cognition and perception ... depend on the activation of complex multiply connected structures" (p. 307). Because human cognition of our complex society is limited and partial, we will never arrive at a unified theory of society especially if we take into account social, political and personal influences that affect scientists (see below).

Similar to such pragmatists as Dewey, Diesing holds that truth is not unchangeable or static; that there are no "permanent, unquestionable foundations." In other words, there is no Truth with a capital T or "progress toward any such timeless goal," as Popper has argued. Today's truth is built on past errors and "will in turn be reconstructed in the future" (pp. 307-308). Ours is an everchanging truth that is a "plurality of mutually incompatible theories and unrelated communities" (p. 358).

Social science produces a multiple, contradictory truth for our time—that is, a set of diversified perspectives and diagnoses of our changing, tangled, and contradictory society. These truths live in the practices and understandings of a research community, not in particular laws, and when that community peters out, its truth passes into history along with the society it tried to understand (p. 364).

## II.

The most fundamental failure of positivist methodology, finds Diesing, is that it comes from logic rather than from scientific practice. Science is a social activity, a manufactured product, and should therefore be studied as such.

A philosophical statement of how science should work and what its goal is should at least be compatible with an account of how it *does* work, since otherwise we cannot get from here to there (p. 303).

So, how *does* social science work? Diesing believes that Kuhn, Lakatos, Stegmüller, and Gadamer have all established that scientists operate within communities trying to work out "the implications of some founding theory, paradigm, metaphor, set of categories, or metaphysical idea" (p. 318). Thanks to the pioneering work of Kuhn, we know that developments in science— Diesing is reluctant to call them progress—are nonlinear. The origin of new paradigms need not, however, be the Kuhnian scientific revolutions. Particular models or hypotheses can set up long-term research programs (Lakatos). Traditions can ensue when an original model is applied to new cases, an imperfect fit leading to the development of a new variant (Stegmüller). Or, diversification will happen "by working out a plurality of interpretations of the original text and thereby enriching it" (hermeneutics) (pp. 318-320).

Scientific communities can appear and flourish because important changes in the real world "have awakened a strong social concern in an age cohort of social scientists, who have founded a research program." Or, because funding agencies (e.g., NSF, the Ford Foundation) support a specific research program, defining mainstream social science. Or, because certain social groups (e.g., government, the RAND Corporation) "use certain types of research and thus provide field experiments, practical tests of external validity. The result is an enriched, relevant theory, plus social encouragement to continue that line of research" (p. 361).

Because at any point in time, there is a multiplicity of research programs, individual scientists should use some criterion (criteria) to decide which one they want to join. Alas, there seems to be no common, or rational, criterion for the choice to abandon a degenerating research program or to join a progressive one. "Scientists do not join a research community to advance knowledge in general; they join either to advance their own careers or to advance some social or personal interest, or both" (p. 361). To be more specific, some scientists choose with respect to expected payoffs: "perceived opportunity to accumulate intellectual capital—get published, get discussed, get research grants" (p. 321), or get tenure. Others choose on the basis of "loyalty, identification with the mentor, rebellion, class identity, ethnic identity" (p. 322) or gender. Personality of the scientist should not be discounted either. Diesing himself presents as an example Max Weber's personality and its impact on his theory of the Protestant ethic. In economics, we can contrast very effectively Alfred Marshall, the cautious model-builder, with Keynes, the enthusiastic problem-solver.

## III.

There are two constant dangers that can lead to the degeneration of science, compromising scientific integrity. (1) If professionalization (formalization) dominates, then desires for egocentricism are unchecked. Individual scientists live "only for publications that show off the latest techniques and concepts." "Each new index or scale or concept rapidly becomes obsolete and forgotten because few others use it; they are busy developing their own" (p. 351). Diesing believes that psychologists and to a lesser extent economists have fallen into this trap. (2) If social scientists are heavily motivated by visions or social concerns, they can become dogmatic or use science for propaganda. Examples abound: Austrian economics, Marxist-Leninism, Monetarism, and so forth.

> A healthy science maintains some social interests and some connections to political actors, plus personal interests and a pure desire to know, but also maintains some political detachment and some connections with research groups having different but compatible interests. It also pays some minimum respect to the tenure-publication-convention rat race without becoming a complete society of Grant Swingers (p. 351).

The only way that we can keep science from degenerating into dogma, mindless formalization, or both, proposes Diesing, is by having a plurality of conflicting research programs, a position very similar to that of Feyerabend. "The continuous conflict prevents the researcher from simply accepting any received dogma, and forces conflicting viewpoints into his consciousness as well" (p. 321). Exposing weaknesses may not affect some who will choose to remain dogmatic but it may affect others who can generate creative solutions. Plurality can lead to cross fertilization among research programs, within or across disciplines, and therefore to progress.

In order to expose each other's weak points, however, Diesing holds that research programs need to understand each other, hence the need for hermeneutics, the medium through which people understand and communicate with one another. Despite his calls for the contrary, Diesing is pessimistic that social scientists are or will be communicative. Communication does exist within research programs that have a unifying social concern or among programs that have similar concerns (e.g., Marxists and left Keynesians). But when social concerns are very different, communication fails (e.g., pluralists and elitists) or becomes unproductively acrimonious.

## IV.

In the main, I agree with Diesing's analysis; how could one disagree with arguments that are ever so sensible?![2] I do, however, have some reservations about his conclusions.

1.    Although I find communication highly desirable, I do not find it either sufficient or necessary for cross fertilization. The Cambridge controversy shows that communication may not lead to cross fertilization. The neoclassical theory of capital did not become any richer after the debate was over (see Naples and Aslanbeigui, 1995). On the opposite side of the spectrum one can provide examples where communication has not existed but cross fertilization has occurred. New Classical and Keynesian economists may not communicate much but the rational expectations hypothesis has convinced some Keynesians that expectation formation is important. As a result, some Keynesian models assume such rationality at the individual level but go on to prove unemployment and policy effectiveness at the macro level. Another example would be economists' borrowing from physics without communicating with physicists or even understanding them (see Mirowski, 1989).

2.    Due to the transient nature of truth, we may not be able to define progress towards Truth. But we need not be so pessimistic as Diesing to say that progress over time cannot be defined at all. If it is possible to find progress in terms of techniques—Diesing himself says that we "are slowly learning to learn" (p. 363)—then we should be able to do the same for social science. After all, techniques also develop within the context of scientific communities.

I think Diesing's definition of truth allows for progress, that is, we can identify progress over time if we could understand, predict, and influence/manage our world better. The plurality of scientific programs in economics and social sciences today, compared to the time of Adam Smith, does create the *potential* of better understanding the world, although admittedly, there is more room for confusion as well. With respect to prediction, the jury may still be out. But I think, today, we are much more capable of influencing our world for the better. Have we not been able to control the depth of recessions or to avoid depressions since 1929?

Will Diesing's book induce social scientists to self-reflect or communicate better? It may, if they read the book, that is.[3] But even if they do not, we must behave *as if* they do; perseverance may also lead to progress! Diesing's book is a valuable contribution.

## ACKNOWLEDGMENTS

The author would like to thank Young Back Choi, Michele I. Naples, and Steven Pressman for their comments. The usual disclaimer applies.

## NOTES

1. Margaret Schabas (1992) has recently argued for the separation of history of economic thought from economics and for its inclusion into history of science. Economists of various persuasions have rejected the proposal (see, e.g., Caravale, 1992; Patinkin, 1992).

2. Given the detailed nature of the book, it is hard to agree with everything said in it. Hence, a few quibbles. First, Diesing's Keynes-in-a-nutshell on page 173 is not expressed accurately because it puts the emphasis on consumption rather than on investment. Second, I find it odd that Diesing should so fervently argue for interpretation of texts and historical studies without spending time on the associated problems, that is, canonization, rational versus historical reconstruction, and so forth (see Blaug, 1990; Brown, 1992). And last but not least, I find Diesing's assessment that "Pigou never understood Keynes" erroneous. Many Keynesians believe that Pigou's *Keynes's 'General Theory' A Retrospective View* (1950) was the epitome of his recantation. Although I do not believe that Pigou recanted, I do believe that he did come to a good understanding of Keynes' views.

3. I think Diesing shares the same problem with Feyerabend and hermeneutics: communication requires a certain will or motivation that may not exist in many social scientists.

## REFERENCES

Aslanbeigui, Nahid. 1984. *Modern Welfare Economics and Positive Science*. Ph.D. Dissertation, University of Michigan.

Blaug, Mark. 1990. "On the Historiography of Economics," *Journal of the History of Economic Thought*, 12(1): 27-37.

Brown, Vivienne. 1993. "Decanonizing Discourse: Textual Analysis and the History of Economic Thought." In *Economics, Language and Critical Theory*, edited by Willie Henderson, Tony Dudley-Evans, and Roger Backhouse. London: Routledge.

Caravale, Giovanni. 1992. "Comment on Schabas," *History of Political Economy*, 24(1).

Diesing, Paul. 1991. *How Does Social Science Work? Reflections on Practice*. Pittsburgh: The University of Pittsburgh Press.

De Vroey, Michel. 1980. "The Transition from Classical to Neoclassical Economics: A Scientific Revolution." Pp. 297-321 in *The Methodology of Economic Thought*, edited by Warren J. Samuels. New Brunswick, NJ: Transaction Books.

Hutchison, Terrence W. 1938. *The Significance and Basic Postulates of Economic Theory*. New York: Augustus M. Kelley.

Lavoie, Don, ed. 1990. *Economics and Hermeneutics*. London: Routledge.

McCloskey, Donald. 1986. *The Rhetoric of Economics*. Brighton, England: Harvester Wheatsheaf.

Naples, Michele I. and Aslanbeigui, Nahid. 1995. "What *Does* Determine the Profit Rate? The Neoclassical Answers Presented in Introductory Textbooks." *Cambridge Journal of Economics*.

*Mirowski, Philip. 1989. More Heat than Light*. New York: Cambridge University Press.

Patinkin, Don. 1992. "Comment on Schabas." Pp. 230-233 in *History of Political Economy*, 24(1).

Pheby, John. 1988. *Methodology and Economics: A Critical Introduction*. London: Macmillan.

Pigou, Arthur C. 1950. *Keynes's 'General Theory' A Retrospective View*. London: Macmillan.

Samuels, Warren J., ed. 1990. *Economics As Discourse: An Analysis of the Language of Economics*. Boston: Kluwer.

Schabas, Margaret. 1992. "Breaking Away: History of Economics as History of Science." *History of Political Economy*, 24(1): 187-203.

Weintraub, E. Roy. 1990. "Methodology Doesn't Matter, But the History of Thought Might."Pp. 263-279 in *The State of Macroeconomics*, edited by S. Honkapohja. Oxford: Basil Blackwell.

# Evaluating Diesing on Social Science

## How Does Social Science Work?

by Paul Diesing
(Pittsburgh: University of Pittsburgh, 1991; 114 pp.)

Review Essay by **Robert S. Goldfarb**

This is a quite remarkable book, both for the astonishing range of disciplines the author appears able to confront, and for the magnitude of the questions he undertakes to address. Not only did I benefit from reading the book, but I found myself constantly pleased to be doing so, despite the book's considerable length and ponderous subject matter, a combination with the potential for substantial drudgery.

At the very beginning Diesing indicates a set of large questions he intends to pursue:

> (1) What are the actual goals of the various current research methods? Call the goals 'truth' or 'knowledge'; then what characteristics does achieved truth have in the various methods? (2) What social, cognitive and personality processes occur or should occur during research, and how do they contribute to the outcome? (3) What persistent weaknesses and dangers appear in research, and what can we do about them?

He goes on to say that he is aiming at "raising consciousness about research." Moreover, "the reader who works through this material should develop a greater self-awareness, and also an understanding of alternative approaches to research. I am not arguing for one philosophy and one research method as the best way to truth; I leave that decision to the reader" (p. ix).

**Research in the History of Economic Thought and Methodology,**
Volume 13, pages 169-177.
Copyright © 1995 by JAI Press Inc.
All rights of reproduction in any form reserved.
ISBN: 1-55938-095-0

As the above excerpt suggests, the book can be read in two quite different ways. A first way is as a collection of essays about knowledge accumulation in a wide variety of fields, including philosophy of science (and social science), sociology of science, cognitive psychology, the Keynesian tradition in economics, the political science of science politics, and so forth. A second way is as a particular overview of how knowledge is accumulated in social science, an overview built around the three large questions in the quote above. Indeed, a major stylistic flaw of the book is that this second more general focus tends to get lost in the 300 pages lying between the 4-page introduction and chapter 11.

Each way of reading Diesing's book generates somewhat different broad reactions to it, and suggests somewhat different criteria for evaluating it.

## I.  REACTIONS BASED ON THE "COLLECTION OF ESSAYS" READING

Diesing provides a seemingly useful view of what has been going on in a remarkably wide range of disciplines. But is the seemingly useful view *actually* useful? An important critical criterion for a collection of "overview essays" would seem to be "does the author have the story right" or, perhaps more reasonably, "is his story a credible and/or usefully provocative rendition of what has gone on in each of the disciplines he describes"? How can a reader-critic with narrower disciplinary expertise judge if Diesing has reasonable stories about disciplines far removed from the critic's own areas of knowledge?

One possible strategy for evaluating the writer's views is to concentrate on those essays covering topics familiar to the reader-critic. Pursuing this strategy led me to focus on the relatively minimal coverage of economics, and the very sizable coverage of philosophy. The one substantial chunk of economics presents a hermeneutic interpretation of developments in Keynesian economics. As a micro-oriented economist, I found this interesting reading, but cannot evaluate it as a real student of macro might (I report below the reactions of several macro-economists to this section). There are other brief references to economics, most of which are "one-liners-in-passing;" the economist reader is likely to find them both a bit too glib and off the mark.[1] Given the much more sophisticated and extended treatments of other areas, it appears that Diesing has not devoted the same intense attention to trying to "get under the skin" of microeconomics that he seems to have devoted to philosophy of science and sociology of science. With the possible exception of the section giving a hermeneutic interpetation of Keynesian economics—and more about that below—economists should not look to this book for deep critical insights about economics.

The sections on philosophy are quite a different matter. I came to these sections with a reasonable amount of background knowledge, having spent a good deal of time reading and thinking about Kuhn and Lakatos, combined with background reading of philosophy of science texts, review articles, writers such as Laudan, Suppes, and Toulmin, extensive reading in the economic methodology literature, and so forth.

I found the sections on philosophy of science extremely interesting to read, and very beneficial. Discussions of familiar topics were illuminating, and discussions of unfamiliar ones at times quite intriguing. Therefore I would highly recommend these sections of the book to readers ranging from those with little familiarity with the area, all the way to those with considerable background. The essays about philosophy are in Part I of the book, entitled "Perspectives from the Philosophy of Science." It runs 143 pages, and includes 5 chapters: Logical Empiricism, 1922-1970; Popper and His Followers; Kuhn and Stegmuller; Pragmatism; and Hermeneutics: The Interpretation of Texts. A few of the many features that made these "essays" interesting and instructive were:

1. A nice discussion of the tortuous intellectual developments in logical empiricism from 1922 to 1970, culminating in the message that that literature has relatively little to tell social scientists about productive practice;

2. The capping of a measured description of Popper's work with a delightfully snippy discussion of Popper's attitude toward criticism of his own work. The discussion suggests that Popper does not display the intellectual attitude toward "close to home" criticism that his philosophy advocates;

3. A sympathetic presentation of the views of Feyerabend, who is often dismissed by writers on philosophy of science as a supporter of methodological anarchy.[2] This leads into a very interesting juxtaposition of the views of Kuhn and Feyerabend. Diesing indicates considerable similarities in their thought, but then points to some important differences that seem to have their source in very different ideas about the crucial bottlenecks impeding growth of knowledge.

4. Fruitful presentations of a number of writers with whom I was largely or completely unfamiliar, such as Churchman, Kaplan, and Stegmüller. The discussion of Churchman's Hegelian Inquirer seemed especially interesting.

5. Of the material that was completely new to me, the chapter on hermeneutics really stood out. My prior expectation was that this philosophical approach would be some combination of impenetrable, obscure, and fundamentally wrong-headed. Diesing presents a highly readable sympathetic rendition of this way of thinking, a discussion that

overturned my prior expectations. The very last section of the chapter explores the relation of hermeneutics to other philosophies of science, finding, for example, that "Popperian and Hermeneutic philosophies of science are compatible in various ways" (p. 143).

In short, when evaluating those topics with which I am relatively familiar, I came up with a very strongly positive verdict on the extensive material on philosophy of science, and a negative finding about the (very limited) nonKeynesian economics discussions.

But what about all the other areas covered by Diesing? A second strategy the reader/critic with limited expertise can use is to coerce qualified acquaintances to read and react to these other "essays." I succeeded in getting four knowledgeable and thoughtful people to read portions of the book that dealt with their areas of expertise. Two macroeconomists, each with considerable historical perspective, read the section giving a hermeneutic interpretation of Keynes. A sociologist read the sections on sociology of science and a political scientist read the section on science politics.

Despite their somewhat different orientations, both macroeconomists came up with similar verdicts about Diesing's hermeneutic analysis of Keynes's *General Theory* and the intellectual developments involving its interpretation. Both found flaws in some of Diesing's particular assertions about the Keynesian literature, but both had quite positive reactions to Diesing's general hermeneutic approach to the Keynesian tradition. One of the readers strongly approved of Diesing's general point that, when there are alternative ways of thinking about "the world," insightful translation of concepts and views between traditions is a very important activity. He thought that macroeconomics was a particularly appropriate area for applying this translation activity, because the theoretical constructs are not always logically "tight." The other reader thought that Diesing's tracing of the early history of interpretations of the *General Theory*, and his description of the working-out of what it all "really meant," was very well-done and basically correct. Thus, both readers basically liked what they read.

However, both readers had important objections to some of Diesing's particular interpretations. The reader who liked the early history thought that Diesing considerably overstated the span of time during which Keynes's emerging message remained mysterious. The other reader found a flaw in Diesing's underlying view that early critics of Keynes were confused, and that the "rightness" of Keynes became evident with the passage of time and the "clarification" of the message. This reader argues that the jury still is not in— those issues some of the early critics raised have in fact reemerged as of 1990 as possibly fundamental difficulties with Keynesian modes of analysis.[3]

Three additional brief comments are in order. First, the sociologist was very impressed by Diesing's discussion of Merton's work and his contributions to the sociology of science literature; this reader characterized the discussion as exhibiting a "deep understanding" of Merton's work. A second comment concerns my own reaction to this same sociology of science material. While I am not familiar with the underlying literature, I found Diesing's substantial discussion of that material very interesting, worthwhile, and provocative reading. Third, whereas the sociologist and the macroeconomists had positive overall reactions to what they read, the political scientist was unimpressed by the science politics chapter. Another critical reaction came from a reader with a strong background in philosophy. Whereas he agreed with my positive assessment of the sections on logical empiricism, Popper, and so forth, he thought there was too little emphasis on insights from the constructivist-rhetorical tradition in philosophy, focusing for example on discursive strategies and modes of argument.

So what is the implication of all this? Some of the essays are interesting and intriguing, and in my view make this book well worth reading, but there is the danger that other essays may be of considerably lower quality, and might even turn out to be wrong-headed.

## II. REACTIONS BASED ON THE "HOW KNOWLEDGE IS ACCUMULATED IN SOCIAL SCIENCE" INTERPRETATION

An alternative way of reading Diesing's book is as an attempt to address broad questions about knowledge accumulation in the social sciences. My reaction to this reading is that Diesing has not provided definitive answers to the three broad questions he poses in the quote at the beginning of this review (indeed, it would have been absurd to expect definitive answers). However, his views about processes of and problems with knowledge accumulation in the social sciences are certainly thought-provoking and deserve serious attention. Space constraints allow only a limited discussion of these views.

Diesing gives "one-line" summary answers to his three initial questions in the last two pages of the book. "As for question 1: Social science produces a multiple, contradictory truth for our time...diversified perspectives and diagnoses of our changing...contradictory society...[When] a research community.... peters out, its truth passes into history along with the society it tried to understand" (p. 364). The capsule answer to question 2 is that "(r)esearchers work within a research program or community or tradition to develop the potentialities of some 'new paradigm,' some creative and exemplary work that relates to their interests" (p. 363). Question 3 is addressed in terms of "two subquestions: (a) What maintains community and communication within and across programs? and (b) What sorts of degeneration occur in research programs?" (p. 363). The answer to (a) is not usefully quoted. The answer to (b) is in terms of two kinds of degeneration. First, an absence of "shared social concern" can lead to "the egocentric desire for recognition" going "unchecked" and "brand-name differentiation" running wild. Second, when the underlying intellectual "vision"and "the shared concern become urgent and political action becomes central, the theory and examples are used as propaganda to support and guide some political program. The theory becomes rigidified into dogma, as with orthodox Marxism-Leninism or free market individualism."[4]

Readers familiar with Kuhn and Lakatos will say that Diesing's answer to question 2 sounds like those writers. So, given this similarity, is there something new and useful (or at least provocative) in his description of what social scientists do, or in his elaboration of the nature of "social science truth"? There is, indeed. The following list is illustrative of the many thought-provoking elements in his discussion:

1.  Why, in opposition to the logical empiricists, "confirmed laws" are not the only kind of "truth" in social science. Diesing's list also includes "truth from the inside" and abstract structural dynamics of the kind captured in mathematical models. This list may not have it quite right, but the discussion is provocative.

2.  How data and "testing" contribute to searching for "truth" or to progress in a research program. Diesing says it is a mistake to view testing as separate from the process of finding hypotheses ("discovery"). "Testing occurs in a larger context of discovery and takes its character from that context. Thus, a separate 'logic' of testing is fundamentally misleading" (p. 308). This is summed up as "research is a process of search and discovery continuing over decades, and testing is a step in that process. Testing does not come after discovery as its culmination; it occurs within search" (p. 327). I think Diesing's contribution here is the rich array of social science examples that he uses to orchestrate a story that Kuhnians would (I think) not find surprising.

3.  What is a "test," anyway? Following the proposition flowing from Hanson and Kuhn that data are "theory-laden," so that "data are in part the product of theory," the notion of using data to test theory becomes much more problematical."What then does *test* mean? We are not testing a theory's correspondence to reality, but its ability to produce its own reflection in reality" (p. 314).

4.  Diesing approvingly cites Lakatos, Kuhn, Stegmüller and a hermeneutic interpretation as generally implying "that social science achieves knowledge through the development and diversification of traditions or research programs,"and that a number of traditions can "flourish simultaneously" (p. 320). He then points out that "this account leaves several gaps to be filled," concerning how such research traditions get started, and whether "there is a rational basis for choosing to join or abandon a research program" (p. 320).

This last issue is very Lakatosian, but Diesing produces an excellent thought-provoking discussion.

5. The Lakatosian rationality discussion leads Diesing to "another unsolved problem. If, according to Feyerabend, the conflicting traditions or communities need each others' criticisms to bring out their weak points, they must be able to communicate. What facilitates and maintains such communication?" This stress on the problem of translation between, and communication among, differing research approaches and traditions runs through many of the book's earlier chapters (including the Keynes discussion). It seems a major concern of Diesing's, and was for me one of the most valuable "consciousness-raisers" in the book.

6. The notion of "vision" (attributed to Schumpeter) is seen as providing a driving force for some research traditions. "A vision focuses the attention of a school of scientists on a set of phenomena and motivates them to study, search out, analyze. It sensitizes them to empirical traces of the vision, suggests interpretations of seemingly random events, and points to a deeper reality or structure beyond appearance" (p. 175). An example of an idealized vision in economics is "the perfect self-cleansing market devoid of all market failures" (p. 173). This "shared truth" or "shared concern maintains a community more effectively than either Mertonian norms or disciplinary socialization" (p. 348).

7. If visions can maintain research programs, the pull of social concerns on the one side and professionalism on the other can cause them to degenerate, and lose "scientific integrity" (p. 349). "Social science exists between two opposite kinds of degeneration, a value-free professionalism that lives only for publications that show off the latest techniques...and a deep social concern that uses science for propaganda" (p. 351). Diesing quotes from Klamer's 1984 conversations with economists to argue that Townsend represents excess professionalism, Friedman represents propaganda, and Tobin represents the hallowed middle ground: two of these attributions will offend many economists.

The above enumeration provides a partial list of topics Diesing discusses, and is meant to whet the reader's appetite. My bottom line is that, based on the second way of reading this book, the volume represents a thoughtful and valuable "consciousness-raising" treatment of important social science methodology questions. (This is not meant as an endorsement of each and every Diesing position. I disagree with a number of them.) The book should be of interest to those with considerable background in the methodology literature, but is also accessible to those with limited background, since it does a good job of laying out basic philosophy of science positions associated with Lakatos, Kuhn, logical empiricism, and so forth.

The one disputational discussion I would most like to have with Diesing would be to start with his aside that "A broader perception would enable a school to find weak points in its own treatment of a topic. It might also prevent the more dogmatic members of a school from pushing a good theory to an absurd extreme where it explains everything, as the rational choice people are now doing" (p. 356). I would read to him from Gary Becker some lines which suggest the view that one's *job* if one works within a paradigm (the economic approach, in this case) is to see how far one can get by pushing the central assumptions of the paradigm as far as they will go: "The combined assumptions of maximizing behavior, market equilibrium, and stable preferences, used relentlessly and unflinchingly, form the heart of the economic approach as I see it" (p. 110). Is it possible that "relentlessly and unflinchingly" trying to extend the application boundaries of a paradigm as far as they can go will result in knowledge growing faster than if we follow what seems to be Diesing's advice of not trying to push "a good theory to an absurd extreme where it explains everything"?

# ACKNOWLEDGMENTS

I would like to thank Michael D. Bradley, Marsha Goldfarb, Arjo Klamer, Ruth Wallace, Helmut Wendel and an anonymous political scientist for helpful comments.

# NOTES

1.   One of Diesing's asides about economics left me particularly puzzled about his acquaintance with some elementary facts about its textbook-level literature. He indicates that, in taking some courses in economics at the University of Chicago, "I never heard the name Keynes mentioned in any of my undergraduate and graduate courses...Our price theory text was Stigler, not Samuelson" (p. 348). Now Stigler wrote a classic undergraduate price theory text (*The Theory of Price*), but the famous Samuelson undergraduate text is not a price theory text at all, but a "principles of economics" text appropriate for the course *before* price theory. If Diesing is talking about this substitution in an undergraduate price theory course, he exhibits a real confusion about the nature of these texts. The statement also does not make sense if Diesing is instead talking about a graduate price theory course.

2.   Diesing argues that Feyerabend is *not* saying that "'Anything goes,' in the sense that people can use any method they please and get equally good results. This is a common misinterpretation of Feyerabend by people who take the 'Anything goes' out of context. Rather Feyerabend means that the method to be used should be appropriate to the research situation, including subject matter, theory, audience.... 'Anything goes' is not his rule at all; it is, he claims, the only rule a Popperian or Lakatosian historian can find that has no exceptions" (p. 52).

3.   A specific assertion of Diesing's—which struck me as quite bizarre when I first read it— drew the fire of both readers. In discussing Lucas's reaction to Keynes, Diesing says, "Obviously, Lucas has missed the point entirely" (p. 120). My immediate reaction was that Diesing is simply not knowledgeable enough about economics to provide a deep and sophisticated evaluation of Lucas's views. My two readers had much better ways of indicating what was wrong-headed about this Diesing statement. The reader who argued that Diesing considerably overstated the time period

during which Keynes' emerging message remained mysterious viewed this Lucas statement as symptomatic of Diesing's error. By the time Lucas was writing, the former "mysteries" were all widely understood, thanks to the existence of astrong explanatory literature, the very literature Diesing's account traces. This reader argued that a more plausible interpretation is that Lucas understands Keynes quite well: he just rejects the Keynesian message or mode of analysis as fundamentally wrong. That one could "rationally" and with full knowledge reject the Keynesian mode of analysis as incorrect does not seem to be a possibility that Diesing entertains, yet a large and talented pool of macroeconomists do exactly that. The other reader, who criticized Diesing's view that Keynes was right and the early critics confused, also saw the Lucas statement as symptomatic of this error. By ignoring the possibility that Keynes might in fact turn out to have been wrong, Diesing misses the possibility that Lucas understands Keynes perfectly well, but rejects Keynes' view of how the economy works. Incidentally, neither of my macroeconomist readers is a Lucas clone; one of them is much closer to being a Keynesian, while the other has an eclectic empirical orientation.

4. Economists of the neoclassical persuasion reading 3b will say, "that sure isn't relevant to economics," but Diesing disagrees. In addition to the above-quoted slap at "free-market individualism," there is the following statement. "We have been witnessing the degeneration of a good portion of economics into propaganda and even pseudo-science in recent years. The Austrian School...have provided some of the impetus in this direction" (p. 350).

# REFERENCE

Becker, Gary. 1986. "The Economic Approach to Human Behavior." Pp. 108-122 in *Rational Choice*, edited by John Elster. London: Basil Blackwell.

# Reflections on Practice:

## How Does Social Science Work?

by Paul Diesing
(Pittsburgh: University of Pittsburgh, 1991, 414 pp.)

Review Essay by **Andrea Salanti**

*How Does Social Science Work? Reflections on Practice* is a well documented, comprehensive and stimulating plea for a greater self-awareness among social scientists. However, despite its indisputable qualities, Paul Diesing does not seem to have completely succeeded in providing the reader with a coherent and convincing set of tools suited to the intended purpose. He surveys and comments upon an impressive amount of recent literature in all the different fields of social science (cf. the final bibliography, pp. 373-403), but on finishing the volume the undoubted impression of intellectual challenge stimulating further reflections is mixed with a feeling of residual confusion in need of further clarification.

At the outset of the introduction the author himself points out that his book

> [I]s intended for the practicing social scientist or social science student. It is concerned with actual research, and focuses on three main questions: (1) What are the actual goals of the various current research methods? Call the goals "truth" or "knowledge"; then what characteristics does achieved truth have in the various methods? (2) What social, cognitive, and personal processes occur or should occur during research, and how do they contribute to the outcome? (3) What persistent weaknesses and dangers appear in research, and what can we do about them (p. ix)?

**Research in the History of Economic Thought and Methodology,**
**Volume 13, pages 179-185.**
Copyright © 1995 by JAI Press Inc.
**All rights of reproduction in any form reserved.**
**ISBN: 1-55938-095-0**

Accordingly, the first part is devoted to the various perspectives from the philosophy of science that might be of some interest to the social scientist. In addition to three chapters where the main tenets of logical empiricism, Popper and Popperians (among whom some attention is paid to Agassi, Lakatos and Feyerabend), and Kuhn and Stegmüller are duly summarized, a fourth is devoted to pragmatism, while the fifth and longest (pp. 104-145) introduces us to the main concepts of hermeneutics. This part is meant to introduce the innocent reader to post-positivist debates in the philosophy of science and does so concisely and effectively.

Diesing's exposition stands out from other introductions of this kind especially addressed to economists (see, for instance, Blaug, 1980, Part I; Caldwell, 1982, Part I; Pheby, 1988; Redman, 1991; Stewart, 1979) because of the greater attention paid to pragmatism and hermeneutics, due to his conviction that "Pragmatism is ... the gate that can open up the study of hermeneutics for Americans, after positivism had walled it off as irrelevant to science" (pp. 143-144). I doubt, however, that his review of the various interpretations of Keynes (pp. 112-117) will really impress very much my economist friends. Their reaction to a five pages summary of well-known material that ends by concluding

> We see here a conflict between two opposed tendencies in a tradition. One tendency is to work out the implications of some central message in the original text: clarify it, correct errors of expression, expand it, enrich it, apply it to new cases and thereby bring it up to date as the legal scholars did with Roman law, and systematize it. The other tendency is to reject all these changes and return to the founder's original message. Both tendencies appear in psychoanalytic theory and recent Marxism (p. 117).

is very likely to be: "So what? We've known this all along, even if we didn't know anything about hermeneutics!"

This is not the only passage in the book which might bother practitioners of the "dismal science." At least the following deserves to be cited:

> [T]he vision of a free market has pushed aside the problem of externalities, has neglected or denied validity to the study of how tastes are formed and changed [...], has ignored advertising and addiction, has rejected the empirical study of investment and consumption decisions as irrelevant, has treated market power (except monopoly) as a temporary aberration of no theoretical significance. The concept *natural rate of unemployment* has brushed aside nonmonetary causes of unemployment as unchangeable and probably unknowable, and the other "natural" rates do the same thing (p. 177).

A defense of economics not being within the scope of a review article, I would limit myself here to asking why it is that some competent scholars in not-too-distant disciplines believe economists to be really so stupid. This because Diesing is not alone in his low esteem of economics (cf. for instance, Friedland

and Robertson, 1990). Unfortunately, no one today seems to be very concerned about this issue.

What instead is likely to appear to economists much less familiar, and therefore more interesting, is the second part of the book. Under the appealing title "Social Science Studies Itself" we find five dense chapters in which the author moves on to examine the sociological, cognitive and personal aspects of scientific activity.

Diesing starts (Chap. 6) by giving a sympathetic account of Merton's functionalist view of those values and norms that should enable scientific communities to solve their internal problems and possible conflicts between opposite rules, followed by a discussion of the social location of social scientists and the possible influence of their "vision" (in Schumpeter's sense). Such a discussion ends with the following recognition of Merton's views:

> [E]ffective empirical research requires some detachment from the visions and interests that drive one on, and even some skepticism [...] Too strong an attachment to one's class position turns one into a propagandist, unable to distinguish between vision/fantasy and deep reality, unable to concede the validity of other visions. Merton was right (p. 179).

In the same vein we find at the end of his survey of the microsociology of social science (Chap. 7) the conclusion that "Perhaps Merton was right. Perhaps humility is essential to science after all" (p. 206), and again (in Chap. 8, devoted to science politics) the following cautious judgment about political influences on social science

> The history of science policy in the United States, even a superficial history like this one, does not allow a simple generalization about the influence of the funding agencies on social science. And the more closely one looks at the lists of projects funded the more complex the picture gets. Nor have we touched on the topic of how governments use social research, which is even more complex (pp. 238-239).

Potentially more useful insights are gained in the following chapter, dealing with experimental psychology in the field of cognitive process and research on artificial intelligence. Both approaches are shown to converge on three main points: (1) reasoning is not (only) a process of formal logical deduction, but (also) an heuristic process of search and discovery; (2) formulation of hypotheses and interpretation of data rely greatly on background knowledge; and (3) practical rationality is quite different from rationality as maximizing choice over the set of all available alternatives.

The last chapter in the second part addresses the issue of personality influences in social science, but the author seems to be unwilling to emphasize their importance, with the result that some useful insights remain somewhat unexploited and, in a sense, hanging in the air.

As we have seen, in the first two parts of the book Diesing covers much heterogeneous material; the reader therefore expects a final overview. Indeed, the third and last part gets the promising title "Putting It All Together," but— as I have already pointed out from the very beginning—the author does not keep the promise in full. To be sure, putting together all these different matters would be a daunting task for anyone, and perhaps no one can presently claim to possess a fully satisfactory solution. Let it be said at once that Diesing's competence and scholarship are beyond question: the aim of the following critical remarks is simply that of promoting further reflections on such an important issue.

One of the reasons of my discontent is that Diesing leaves unanswered the question he himself encourages the reader to ask: how may it be possible to have good (that is, *progressive*) social science stemming from research that is performed by social scientists who are much more devoted to their self-interest than to the desirable values of scientific activity and usually follow patterns of reasoning that do not have the force of formal logic? Note that to put things that way implies two beliefs: first, that science is actually progressive,[1] and second, that there must be a sort of "invisible hand" at work in the competition between different groups of scientists (and therefore, because no invisible hand could ever function without visible institutions, a set of more or less enforced rules).

Admittedly, to put the question in these terms makes it exceedingly complex and the corresponding answer very difficult, and Diesing seems to be somewhat aware of the problem. Indeed, introducing chapter 7 he quotes from Ravetz (1971, p. 171) a question somewhat akin to the one I have just formulated, that is

> How does it happen "that out of a personal endeavour which is fallible, subjective, and strictly limited by its context, there emerges knowledge which is certain, objective, and universal" (p. 181)?

However, he does not (and in a sense does not even try to) provide us with his answer to such a question, probably because he does not believe that scientific knowledge is (or might ever be) "certain, objective, and universal." Of course I cannot but agree, but this is not a good reason for avoiding explicit discussion if (social) science, after all, is progressive or not.[2]

In his attempt to formulate seemingly simpler questions, Diesing tries to separate the two faces of the problem (cf. Chap. 11, "How Does Social Science Produce Knowledge?," and Chap. 12, "Problems and Dangers on the Road of Knowledge," respectively). He begins the conclusive part of the book observing that

> A philosophical statement of how science should work and what its goal is should at least be compatible with an account of how it *does* work, since otherwise we cannot get from

here to there. If cognitive psychology tells us that some recommended practice is impossible
or very unusual, we would do well to look for a different recommendation (p. 303).

On this basis he draws a number of negative conclusions nowadays
undisputable but mostly obvious (at least to all non-Popperians). Among these
I count, for instance, the statements that: (1) logical empiricists "made a
fundamental mistake when they sharply distinguished the contexts of discovery
and testing" (p. 308); (2) "the logical empiricist reduction of data to observables
has had disastrous effects on the social sciences for decades" (p. 311); (3) "the
early logical empiricist assumption that observable data are there ready to
collect ... has long since been discarded" (p. 313); (4) "evidence that 'confirms'
one hypothesis also 'confirms' an infinity of other hypotheses" (p. 314); (5) "the
rejection of any philosophy that separates testing and discovery applies to
Popper's philosophy as well" (p. 318); (6) "Popper's emphasis on falsification
as the only engine of scientific progress is totally wrong" (p. 318); (7) there
is "some difficulty with Lakatos's insistence that scientists working in a research
program are rational" (p. 319) and there is "no rational rule for choosing the
community that best advance science" (p. 325).[3]

What finally emerges is a picture of scientific activity based on Kuhn,
Feyerabend and hermeneutics[4] which, therefore, should not leave much space
for normative judgments. Nevertheless in the concluding chapter Diesing
ventures into a discussion of how social science ought to be done. Given such
premises, however, the results center on commonsensical but ineffective
recommendations against two opposite "dangers." We are told that

> Social science exists between two opposite kinds of degeneration, a value-free
> professionalism that lives only for publications that show off the latest techniques and
> concepts, and a deep social concern that uses science for propaganda. A healthy science
> maintains some social interest and some connections to political actors, plus personal
> interests and a pure desire to know, but also maintains some political detachment and some
> connections with research groups having different but compatible interests. It also pays
> some minimum respect to the tenure-publication-convention rat race without becoming
> a complete society of Grant Swingers (pp. 350-351).

but it remains far from clear who or what should prevent scientists from falling
into one of these two very temptations.

This shortcoming is the direct consequence of Diesing's contemptuous
rejection of epistemology, which deprives him of the tool needed to find a
convincing answer (it is of course impossible to obtain useful *normative* insights
from a purely descriptive assessment of what scientist actually do). In spite
of the hermeneutic enthusiasm now in fashion we should never forget that the
normative aspect of epistemology cannot be overlooked without paying some
cost. Though we may feel uneasy with Popperian prescriptions or Lakatosian
rationalizations, we cannot expect to venture into normative judgments armed
only with methodological anarchism and hermeneutics.

The above critical remarks notwithstanding, let me conclude by saying that this volume can be recommended to the intended readers (social scientists and social science students) for the impressive amount of literature surveyed by its author and for Diesing's thorough efforts at showing the many aspects of the question "How does social science work?" Despite these undisputable merits, however, the reader should supplement it with readings elsewhere, in order to obtain a more balanced view of what epistemology has to offer to social scientists.[5]

## NOTES

1.  With this I do not mean, however, that social sciences are *always* progressive in the short run: sometimes it may well happen that a theory or even a whole paradigm is superseded by one that is not better, or that conflicts and controversies between opposite approaches last for a long time. But I think, nevertheless, that there would be general agreement that our understanding of social phenomena has progressed if compared, for instance, with that of a hundred years ago.

2.  As on p. 325, where we read: "The truth that we produce is a temporary, changing truth for our time, not an absolute truth. These truths build on past knowledge and will in turn be discarded or forgotten or built on in the future. In retrospect, we can sometimes see signs of progress toward the present, or signs of cyclical change without progress; but the philosophers provide no guaranteed measure of progress or rules for how to advance science."

3.  Surprisingly enough, Merton survives better than Popper from this array of criticism. The problem with Mertonian (macro)sociology of science is the same as we have with Popperian methodology: it is both a descriptive account of shared values within the scientific profession, and a prescriptive set of norms suited to pursue the goal proper of scientific enterprise. Consequently, it is far from clear how we should judge different attitudes, opposite behavior, or contrasting external influences easily discernible in current scientific practice. Indeed, it would be quite easy to show that social (and "natural") scientists preach Mertonian values very often but practice them much less frequently (as economists do with Popperian falsificationism), concluding that more coherence would be warmly welcome. While Diesing (see also Chap. 2) openly recognizes this possible source of difficulty and ambiguity with respect to Popper (and logical empiricists, for that matter), he does not alert the reader from the beginning that the same kind of problem affects Merton's views. On the contrary, we find that

> The issue, however, is not whether scientists act according to Merton's norms; Merton himself asserted that they often do not, but pointed to expressions of disapproval as evidence that the norms were accepted and enforced as obligations. But they may have been ignoring one norm, and getting disapproval for it, in order to follow an opposite norm, as with Merton's original achievement-versus-humility pair. Thus the issue is what norms scientists do accept in practice, or believe they accept (p. 160).

It is ironic to see that Merton's sociology of science escapes Diesing's criticism simply because the assumed contemporary existence of both norms *and* counternorms makes it unfalsifiable.

4.  In Diesing's words: "[K]nowledge is produced by a community or tradition which develops the possibilities of some initial text, paradigm, method, or concepts. Communities diversify, form branches, combine or intermingle, and disappear. Community members develop their theory by

using it to produce data which then change the theory. They also develop theory by shifting to a new area requiring a different interpretation of the theory" (p. 325).

    5.   A good antidote on this matter might be, for instance, Rosenberg (1988).

## REFERENCES

Blaug, Mark. 1980. *The Methodology of Economics. Or How Economists Explain.* Cambridge: Cambridge University Press.

Caldwell, Bruce. 1982. *Beyond Positivism. Economic Methodology in the Twentieth Century*: London: Allen & Unwin.

Diesing, Paul. 1991. *How Does Social Science Work? Reflections on Practice.* Pittsburgh, PA: University of Pittsburgh Press.

Friedland, Roger and Robertson, A. S., eds. 1990. *Beyond the Market Place. Rethinking Economy and Society.* New York: Aldine de Gruyter.

Pheby, John. 1988. *Methodology and Economics. A Critical Introduction.* London: Macmillan.

Ravetz, Jerome. 1971. *Scientific Knowledge and Its Social Problems.* Oxford: Oxford University Press.

Redman, Deborah. 1991. *Economics and the Philosophy of Science.* New York: Oxford University Press.

Rosenberg, Alexander. 1988. *Philosophy of Social Science.* Oxford: Clarendon Press.

Stewart, Ian. 1979. *Reasoning and Method in Economics.* London: McGraw-Hill.

# The Great History Hold-Up

## The Origins of American Social Science

by Dorothy Ross
(New York, NY: Cambridge University Press, 1991; 308 pp.)

·Review Essay by **Robert A. Griffin**

American exceptionalism is the main concern of Dorothy Ross in her latest book, *The Origins of American Social Science.*

What is "American exceptionalism"? For those who need an introduction or a brief refresher course to the topic, Dorothy Ross offers the citation from E. R. A. Seligman, who as president of the American Economic Association in 1902, objected strongly to:

> the opinion either explicitly or implicitly shared by many of our thoughtful fellow citizens that this country has in some way a distinctive mission to perform, and that we are marked off from the rest of the world by certain inherent principles, relative, indeed, in the sense of being peculiar to America, but eternal and immutable in their relation to ourselves (p. 149).

From our earliest beginnings as a nation we have nurtured an ideological assumption, "an intellectual construct, the work of cultural and political elites," (Ross, p. 29) that American culture is somehow an exception to all previous developments in the history of Western civilization. In the case of political economy, this view has been explicitly stated from the time of Alexander Hamilton's "Report on Manufactures" through the writings of Amasa Walker and the Careys up to the work of Frank Knight and the Chicago School generally. Since Ross takes exception to the ideology of exceptionalism, she contrasts the prevailing view with those of dissenters in our history.

**Research in the History of Economic Thought and Methodology,**
Volume 13, pages 187-193.
Copyright © 1995 by JAI Press Inc.
All rights of reproduction in any form reserved.
ISBN: 1-55938-095-0

Dorothy Ross is the Arthur O. Lovejoy Professor of History at the Johns Hopkins University, and she clearly demonstrates the strength of her qualifications in the field of American intellectual history throughout this work. After describing the rise of our nationalist ideology of exceptionalism in the pre-Civil War period, the author focuses on three crises which have served to form the current models of American social science:

1. The crisis of American exceptionalism, 1865-1896
2. Social Upheaval and Progressive Social Science, 1896-1914
3. Political Crisis and American social science as the study of natural process, 1908-1929.[1]

In order to give an in-depth study of her theme, Ross has selected three social science disciplines for special treatment: political science, sociology and political economy. The author justifies her selection of subject-areas by arguing that other disciplines were closer to natural history in their origins and were but partially involved in all the discourse on American exceptionalism. Not everyone will agree with the selection of material, and her argument, to me at least, is unconvincing. Still, choices have to be made for any publication, and certainly scholars in the history of economic thought will appreciate the attention given to their field when so many authors have chosen easier, more popular paths to follow. Dorothy Ross is one of those rare minds who like to think ... otherwise.

"All countries," we are reminded in the epilogue, "nourish a nationalist sense of 'specialness' and as a historical fact, all countries are to some degree unique." Indeed, the Swiss feel deeply they are trading their democratic "Sonderfall" in history for a role in the new European Economic Community.[2] It is only in the nature of the case, therefore, that Ross argues American social science characteristically reflects the ideology of American exceptionalism, a *Weltanschauung* that our nation has a position exempt from historical change because of its republican government and extensive freedom of economic opportunity. As a result of our national self-conception, continues Ross, Americans believed they were destined for a heavenly millenium, free from the mass poverty and class struggles of Europe. In the pre-Civil War period, the ideology was promulgated to enlist "social scientists" into a national effort "to stay the hand of time."[3]

The crisis of the post-Civil War period, argues Ross, compelled Americans to confront the realities of industrialization and historical change. Our modern social science disciplines originated in that crisis and evolved as ways to avoid or pacify historical transformation while safeguarding exceptionalist ideals. Addressing herself to the respective disciplines of political science, sociology and political economy as they develop in each era together with their representative leaders, Professor Ross seeks to explain the various ways in which the disciplines retain their intellectual traditions while trying to cope with changes in historical consciousness, political needs, academic forms and newer conceptions of science. "Hoping first in the Gilded Age to sustain fixed laws of nature and history, social scientists in the Progressive Era linked American history to Western liberal history and its modernizing forces to capitalism, democracy, and science. But they hastened to subject that history to scientific control and tried to carve out a realm of nature that would perpetuate exceptionalist ideals. By the 1920s, driven to harder versions of technological control, the social sciences had transmuted the dismaying uncertainties of history into controllable natural process."[4]

To support her case as an advocate of "historicism" in opposition to the perpetuation of American exceptionalism, an essentially a-historical world-view, Dorothy Ross connects her facts from the history of American social thought to her own modified methodology derived from Max Weber. Here, as with Weber and the German neo-Kantian tradition, the main goal is "understanding," or *Verstehensphilosophie*. But, unlike Weber and the dominant voices of *Verstehensmetaphysik* at the universities of Heidelberg and Marburg in the early twentieth century, Ross wants a positive relationship with the Marxist radical science of history and argues that historical understanding implies our participation in social change. This is her "new interpretive tendency" of historicism.[5] Hoping to find a supporting framework for her case in her own version of neo-Kantianism[6] and an emphasis on critical understanding, Professor Ross is an avowed humanist with a humanist *Weltanschauung*. "A historical world is a humanly created one. It is composed of people, institutions, practices, and languages that are created by the circumstances of human experience and sustained by structures of power."[7]

Principally, however, Ross draws most of her methodological support from the work of Max Weber, whose "historical conception of sociology" she opposes to the "sociological naturalism" of Robert E. Park.[8] In the Weberian thought favored by Ross, the logic of natural science emphasizes the search for universals, while history and social inquiry depend on a logic of individuals. They are opposites in work and purpose; therefore, a natural science of society is logically possible, but pointless. So runs the argument. Scientifically, such argumentation was far behind the most advanced logic at the turn of the century, and today it would be quickly dissolved by computer analysis. I restate it chiefly to make its case clear and to recall that the author, with some modifications, relies heavily on it for organizing her account of historical events and personages.

For her narrative of events and personages in the area of political economy, Dorothy Ross draws heavily on the well established histories of Joseph Dorfman, and Gide and Rist. This wise choice allows her to breeze quickly and smoothly through the native traditions established by Alexander Hamilton. Curiously, Benjamin Franklin, who agreed with Hamilton on the desirability of immigration and industrialization but was more skeptical about our exception to social class history, does not even warrant a place of honorable mention in the book. Still, Ross has a basic empathy for the slaves, women and propertyless citizens who received no real benefits from the exceptionalist ideology. At the higher echelons of political economy, Jefferson and Madison were first exceptions to the exceptionalist philosophy and were but reluctantly persuaded that "America was, and in the foreseeable future would remain, different."[9]

In the description of political economy during the post-Civil War period as a "gentry science," there is an interesting, well-detailed biography of Francis A. Walker, his labor sympathies, and his unique criticism of the wages fund theory. Walker's argument that wages are tied to anticipated increases in production foreshadows the emphasis of Thorstein Veblen on the potential earnings of corporations as vital to any consideration of investment capital. The author, however, does not make this connection. She sees the greatest contribution of Walker as being "the first economist to work out distinctly the concept of perfect competition."[10]

Out of the rapid industrialization of America during the Gilded Age there arose the twin phenomena of large labor organizations and an ideology of socialist economics to which they were drawn. The new, radical theory of socialism, of course, emphasized historicist thinking and in the nature of the case posed a threat to American exceptionalism and its relationship to classical political economy. In this context, the marginalist economics of Fisher, Fetter and the more liberal Clark often were expressed as fear responses essential for the health and progress of a society where the educated could dominate and control the ignorant.[11] Alternatively, a sustained challenge to the dominance of marginalist theory was presented by the evolutionary economics of Thorstein Veblen. In opposition to the capitalist character of marginalism, Ross insists the political economy of Veblen is socialist. Her view in this matter is based on the early Veblen essay on "Some Neglected Points in the Theory of Socialism" in which Veblen analyses socialistic sentiments of the common people. Since Veblen was never an active political organizer in a socialist party, scholars have generally avoided labelling him "socialist," lending credence only to an old rumor of his students that Veblen always carried an IWW card on his vest pocket.

The study of the history and development of American social science ends with the belief that historicism has bequeathed to us an irreversible sense of the difference between the past and the future, and the need to act for the future without the assurance of the past. American exceptionalism for its part has adapted to the new historical awareness, modified its stance, and continued to wield the power to shape history to its purposes. Therefore, as the author sees it, rapid urbanization and conditions of anxiety and frustration born in and following the aftermath of World War I led social scientists to focus on various aspects of social change and control. In the case of political economy, the battle continued between institutionalism and the marginalist school, and in this narrative it ends with the demise of institutionalism after 1929 and the ascendancy of marginalism into the scientism of the Chicago School. Such, at least, is the perspective of the author. Historians of economic thought will easily recognize that quite a lot that has happened in more than half a century is simply left out or reduced to an occasional footnote.

While many books have been written on the individual histories of the different social sciences, the history of American social science by Dorothy Ross is important for being the first general study of the evolution of social science in America. It is also significant for the central importance it gives to the ideology of American exceptionalism.

At some point early in the perusal of the contents, it may occur to the reader to wonder whether we are dealing only with the reconstruction of the discourse within which social scientists have worked, that is, its special idiom or rhetoric, as the author says, or whether we are experiencing a demonology. Certain terms turn up regularly in a pejorative sense: for example, exceptionalism, positivism, aestheticism, scientism, professionalism, capitalism, technocratic, natural process, dissolving modernity, pluralist, elitism, and gentry. This list just as regularly has its elbow-pinching antonyms: working class, socialist critique, historicism and radical historicist analysis, Marxist theories, socialism, economic discontent, radical, social change, historical complex of social perspectives, dissenters, and, of course, figurative imagery of the masses of working classes, or demos, in opposition to the gentry. In the hierarchies of angels and devils, there are also subordinate devils such as liberal individualism and chauvinist ideas that call for exorcism by the critical historicist.

Certainly one could argue there are some "concrete realities" that seem to warrant the use of such labels; unfortunately, the author frequently lacks a cumulative account of the economic, material evidence to establish the causal linkages alleged. As a case in point, the transformation of American political economy and culture, which resulted from the organization of the railroads by means of management at a distance, is here reduced to a simple, modified expansion of industrial capitalism.

With her premature obituary of institutionalism, Ross is unable to take account of its resurgence as a topic of world interest. By handing victory laurels to marginalism, she has failed to note the Sraffa school has clearly demonstrated the fictional nature of the production function and the impossibility of deducing conclusions about the aggregate capital-to-labor ratio and the ratio of interest rates to wages.[12] Perhaps an expanded, revised edition of the book can remedy these defects.

Ernst Cassirer and Georg Lukács long ago showed the inherent irrationality and artificiality of the Rickert-Weber method of "understanding" history. Judgment is always an historical synthesis of universality and particularity.[13] By adhering too closely to Weberian methodology, Ross has weakened the causal emphasis she seeks to draw from the Marxian theory of history. Looking at the matter another way, the Faustian tradition of *Verstehens-metaphysik* in the book needs a stronger bond with the Mephisto-phelean tradition of Leibniz, Kant and Marx, and expressed so elegantly by Dr. Ernst Schroeder, German logician and friend of C. S. Peirce: "But if perhaps Lotze concludes his *Logic* with the wish that German philosophy should always rise to the test 'to *understand* the course of the world and not merely to calculate it', so it must be said: could we only *calculate* it in the first place! then we certainly would 'understand' it, also, as far as an understanding can be achieved on earth."[14]

# NOTES

1. Ross, Contents. My terms vary from those of the chapter titles to reflect the crisis theme more completely.
2. Ross 1991. *New York Times* (Aug. 11), p. 475.
3. Ross, Foreword abstract. My late friend, Rev. Raphael Hofman, characterized such efforts as attempts of intellectual hold-up men to hold up history.
4. Ross (1991, Foreword).
5. Ross (1991, pp. 4, 13).
6. Ross (1991, p. 9).
7. Ross (1991, Introduction, p. xiii).
8. Ross (1991, p. 27).
9. Ross (1991, p. 84).
10. Ross (1991, pp. 179-181).
11. Ross (1991, Introduction, p. xviii-xix).
12. See Sraffa (1973, p. 38); Hunt (1979, pp. 404-413); Pearce (1986, p. 343).
13. See Cassirer (1953, pp. 235-236, 247); Lukács (1953, pp. 474-489, esp. p. 483) where Lukács argues that Weber's purely constructed "ideal types" constitute the central task of his sociology. It follows that this analysis cannot result in an evolutionary line of reasoning, but only a succession of casuistically chosen and ordered ideal types.
14. Schroeder (1905).

# REFERENCES

Cassirer, Ernst. 1933. *An Essay on Man.* New York, NY: Doubleday.
Griffin, Robert. 1986. "Thorstein Veblen: The Theory of Evolutionary Economics as a Social Science." *Rivista Internazionale di Scienze Economiche e Commerciali,* XXXIII (12) Dic. 1986; "Antonio Labriola e Thorstein Veblen: l'economia del nuovo indirizzo evoluzionista"; *il Pensiero Economico Moderno,* Anno 7, N.4, Dic., 1987.
Hunt, E. H. 1979. *History of Economic Thought: A Critical Perspective.* Belmont, CA: Wadsworth.
Lukács, Georg. 1953. *Die Zerstörung der Vernunft.* Berlin, GDR: Aufbau-Verlag.
Pearce, David W. 1986. *The MIT Dictionary of Modern Economics,* 3rd ed. Cambridge, MA: The MIT Press.

Ross, Dorothy. 1991. *The Origins of American Social Science.* New York, NY: Cambridge University Press.

Sraffa, Piero. 1973. *Production of Commodities By Means of Commodities.* London, England: Cambridge University Press.

Weber, Max. 1953. *The Protestant Ethic and the Spirit of Capitalism.* New York, NY: Charles Scribner's Sons.

# Reflections on the Origins of American Social Science

## The Origins of American Social Science

by Dorothy Ross
(New York, NY: Cambridge University Press, 1991; 308 pp.)

Review Essay by **Humberto Barreto**

The historian of economic thought, because of the fact that the entire intellectual history of what today we call "economics" is grist for the mill, spends much time struggling with the basic "How did we get to where we are today?" question. In any discipline, if one school of thought or paradigm replaces another, it seems only natural to wonder about the reasons for the change. Did the old orthodoxy fail to explain newly observed phenomena or was the explanatory power of the challenger superior? Did new questions pop up or did the old ones get stale and/or frustrating? Did new rules for judging truth emerge? The list of follow-up questions grows quickly and in a variety of different areas—hence the morass that is methodology in economics today.

Although historians of economic thought think they have a panoramic view, the intellectual historian of social science has an even wider vista—changes in the social sciences as a whole are the material to be explained and discussed. The up side of having all of social science as your laboratory is that there is an incredible abundance of interesting observations; the down side is that complete answers to questions are impossible to find. If you think questions such as "Why was the classical school replaced by the neoclassicals?" or "Why did Monetarism rise and fall and rise again?" are tough, try your hand at "Why are the social sciences divided along their current lines?" or "Why did science and liberal individualism come to dominate American social science?"

**Research in the History of Economic Thought and Methodology,**
**Volume 13, pages 195-201.**
Copyright © 1995 by JAI Press Inc.
**All rights of reproduction in any form reserved.**
**ISBN: 1-55938-095-0**

This last question is the subject of *The Origins of American Social Science* by Dorothy Ross. Because of the sheer breadth and complexity of information that must be covered, attempts to wrestle with such a question may be informative and thought provoking, but are guaranteed to be difficult, frustrating, and never ending. The reader must be prepared to ponder interesting possibilities and partial explanations, while keeping supressed until the end a series of doubts and a strong desire for more detail. Likewise, the reviewer must accept, from the very beginning, that the nature of the question imposes severe constraints on the offered explanation.

With this caveat in mind, I propose to do the following: review Ross' explanation, analyze in more detail the application to economics, and, finally, offer my reactions and appraisal. Before beginning, however, a review of key words and phrases will make the ensuing presentation much clearer.

# I. A GLOSSARY OF TERMS

Taking center stage in Ross' explanation is *American exceptionalism:* "the idea that America occupies an exceptional place in history, based on her republican government and economic opportunity" (p. xiv). This isn't simple nationalism, says Ross, for it is embedded in the belief that America is unique and special. Furthermore, there are varying degrees of American exceptionalism. The strong form has religious overtones and was most prevalent in the Antebellum Period. It manifested itself in the belief that the United States was completely exempt from the conflict and strife that was ripping Europe apart:

> When national independence was won, fervent Protestants identified the American Republic with the advent of the millenial period that would usher in the final salvation of mankind and the end of history. American progress would be the unfolding of the millenial seed rather than a process of historical change (pp. 22-23, footnote omitted).

As Americans saw their own country suffering from the same ills as the rest of the world during the Civil War, the Gilded Age, and a series of political and economic crises, the strong form of American exceptionalism gave way to a less forceful, but still important feeling that America was somehow singular and destined for success:

> So long as the ideal of American perfection lived on, so long as the Americans continued to fear entrusting that ideal to history, the logic of American exceptionalism remained relevant .... Exceptionalism survived in the utopian ideal ambiguously both present and potential in American society. It survived in the willingness to place America at the forefront or the quintessential center of liberal change and to cast universal progress in specifically American shapes (p. 150).

By *historicism,* Ross means "the discovery that history [is] a realm of human construction, propelled ever forward in time by the cumulative effects of human action, and taking new qualitative forms" (p. 3, footnote omitted). The historicist sees the particular events unfolding in time as neither pre-ordained by God nor the product of some inevitable natural process (as in natural history). New events are simply caused by past events, yet they are qualitatively different from the past—implying an open ended future. Perhaps the most important effect of accepting this world view is that something else must be used to replace the old explanations of why things are the way they are and the old reasons for optimism. After all, how and why do actions today determine the future? And furthermore, if human actions today determine tomorrow's world, what assurance can there be that there will be improvement? The void caused by historicism and the clamor to fill it plays an important role in Ross' argument.

*Scientism* is its usual nebulous, never exactly defined self. It implies quantitative work (gathering numbers, use of statistics to make decisions, mathematical presentation) and requires allegiance to the scientific method (forming hypotheses, testing them with empirical evidence, and at least formally, replication), but it also brings a reliance on experts (because of the presumed objectivity of the scientific method) and specialized language. By proposing ever more accurate models and theories, science claims to provide ever better predictions (and, thus, control) and explanations of reality that are then used to fill the void left by historicism.

Finally, Ross notes that *liberalism* (or, more specifically, liberal individualism) is a term first used by European radicals in the early 1800s who wanted to replace governmental authority with individual power and freedom. For Ross, to be liberal implies confidence in the reason and initiative of the individual and a bias against government intervention and control. This is, of course, a position that economists are quite familiar with—that is, the belief that individuals know what is best for themselves and that they should have the liberty to choose and the responsibility that comes with choosing.

## II. THE ORIGINS OF AMERICAN SOCIAL SCIENCE

Having defined these key terms, the thesis can now be presented and understood clearly: Ross argues that American exceptionalism is the driving force that has determined the shape of modern American social science. More precisely, modern American social science is scientific, not historicist, and liberal, not Marxist, communitarian or anything else, because of American exceptionalism. The support for this position lies in a review of the history of American social science. By reconstructing the discourses of leading figures in the core disciplines of economics, political science and sociology, Ross hopes to show how American social science came to be what it is today.

Unlike their European counterparts, argues Ross, American social scientists remained essentially pre-historicist until the Civil War. The Industrial and French Revolutions caused enough upheaval in eighteenth century Europe that historicism destroyed the old world view and created a need for new answers to questions concerning change and progress. Montesquieu, Smith, Condorcet, and Herder responded to the challenge by creating explanations of reality based on natural law and history. American social scientists had it much easier during this time period since the strong version of American exceptionalism blocked the challenge of historicism. Faced with few social crises (no mass poverty or open class conflict) and supported by the cheery optimism of American exceptionalism, leading social scientists (including Francis Lieber, Francis Wayland, Amasa Walker, and Henry Carey) spent most of their time explaining why Europe was in trouble and relying on America's uniqueness to prevent the spread of contagion.

The period from 1865-1896 saw crucial changes in American social science because, says Ross, of a crisis in American exceptionalism. Although the change in intellectual authority from religion to science played a role, it was a series of easily observed and deeply felt shocks (especially the Civil War and the threat of socialism) that marked the rise of historicism and the end of pure American exceptionalism as a widely accepted explanation of American reality. Just as in Europe a century earlier, actual historical events forced a deeper awareness of historical change and, for the first time, created doubt that progress was guaranteed.

The challenge of historicism was met, during the formative decades of today's American social science (1870-1929), by scientism and liberalism. Faith in America's uniqueness was replaced by faith in science and the concept of natural processes. Since America's past was no longer seen as idiosyncratic and her future was uncertain, American social scientists replaced pure American exceptionalism with science and liberalism. The key, argues Ross, is that American exceptionalism limited the pool of available explanations—in particular, ruling out socialist and historicist interpretations of reality. Thus, American social science's reliance on science and a deeper, natural order was a product of American exceptionalism. In economics, political science and sociology, the same intellectual battle was played out: historicism's challenge and defeat of pure American exceptionalism was met by a combination of science and liberal individualism. The refusal to accept a purely historicist view and the requirement that the theoretical successor claim powers of prediction, explanation and control were all products of American exceptionalism. Thus, argues Ross, American exceptionalism was and remains the driving force behind today's social science.

## III.   APPLICATION OF THE THESIS TO ECONOMICS

In economics, the first part of the thesis, that is, strong American exceptionalism dominated an essentially pre-historicist antebellum American social science, is presented by a review of the works of Wayland, Walker and Carey. Authors of leading texts, they all claimed that the United States would be exempt from Malthusian or Ricardian problems and presented varying degrees of expansive optimism.

During the crisis of American exceptionalism (1870-1896), American economics rejected simple exceptionalism and began the search for an alternative answer:

> The recognition that America was changing in the Gilded Age was the central problem of all the gentry social scientists, and for the political economists, change meant that America could no longer opt out of the direction of history the classical economists had predicted (pp. 80-81).

As an example of the difference between the Antebellum and post-Civil War periods. Ross offers a comparison of Amasa Walker (1799-1875), the "pious father," and his son, Francis A. Walker (1840-1897). They disagreed on the existence of fundamental economic laws applicable to all societies (the son accepted, for example, the possibility of Malthusian and Ricardian outcomes in America), yet they concurred on the fact that America was best served by a decentralized, market, liberal, and republican system. For the father, the strong version of American exceptionalism was explicit in his explanation of reality; while, for the son, American exceptionalism was rejected as unscientific.

Since historicism forced economists to abandon explanations based on America's uniqueness, new explanations of economic reality were needed. After a long struggle, various forms of socialism and historical analyses were eventually rejected, says Ross, in favor of liberalism and marginalism because of American exceptionalism. The standard explanation is that marginalism was more "scientific"—that is, "more analytically general, logically stricter, and further removed from philosophical and political assumptions" (p. 176) and, thus, more attractive to the increasingly professionally and academically oriented economist.

Although the professional-scientific explanation of the rise of marginalism "carries some degree of truth," Ross argues that, "As Mark Blaug has pointed out, the social and political relevance of marginalism was its great attraction" (p. 178, footnote omitted). It was during the rise of marginalism (1890-1910) that American exceptionalism exerted its greatest force—the American economists had to come up with a scientific defense of modern capitalism, an explanation of the causes of the great changes taking place, and, most importantly, a theory that provided assurances of future stability and prosperity.

For Ross, marginalism defeated socialist and historicist explanations because the former provided the required rationalizations and optimism, while its competitors (Veblen, institutionalists, and Marxists) did not.

## IV.   APPRAISAL AND REACTION

The standard criticisms (e.g., problems concerning the case study method, differences in interpretation, or errors of omission) are not appropriate here—as stated above, a complete answer to the proposed question is plainly impossible. Thus, instead of the usual critique, I simply offer my reactions to the author's fundamental claim that American exceptionalism explains the modern day scientific and liberal foundations of American social science.

Unlike Ross, who sees American social science shaped by the particular American experience, I am struck by the commonalities between the intellectual histories of American and European social science. Although a close look certainly reveals differences, a more distant view shows a similar development: they both went through a pre-historicist period, followed by a period of crisis that destroyed their blind optimism, then responded to the challenge of historicism by erecting models of natural process and emphasizing science and liberalism. Instead of searching for a particularly American cause, such similarity suggests a common, root cause. To me, the core explanation of why social science is scientific and liberal can be found in the *Western need for order*. American social science became scientific, not because American exceptionalism forced an optimistic world view, but because Westerners believe that an orderly process underlies even the most turbulent surface. If you take away a pre-ordained, deterministic world view, you must replace it with a view that maintains a place for order and organization.

When applied to economics and the rise of marginalism, the magnetic force of the need for order is clear. American exceptionalism was not the key factor in causing turn-of-the-century American economists to embrace marginalism. I believe a much stronger effect was the belief that the equimarginal principle was at the core of all problems in economics. Imagine, a single idea to explain a wide variety of different phenomena! That revelation accounts for Philip Wicksteed's insistence that a single "law" (marginal productivity) could determine all factor rewards (*An Essay on the Co-ordination of the Laws of Distribution*) and a long list of social scientists (of every nationality) who have confessed their awe over the allure of marginalism.

I would also claim that this same attraction is at the heart of the current expansion of economics into the other social sciences. The idea that optimization and comparative statics, call it "the economic method," is a truly general tool that can be applied to any problem involving choice drives research in political science, organizational theory, law and economics, and even biology. What is the attraction? The claim that this economic method offers a single, fundamental explanation of all reality. This is not driven by American exceptionalism, but by our insistence that there is a pattern, however deep and complex, to our lives. Finally, I would also like to point out that this very same insistence on underlying order drives physicists as they search for their Holy Grail—the Grand Unification Theory.

## V.  CONCLUSION

I recommend *The Origins of American Social Science* because it broadens one's view of economics and all social science. Ross reminds us that Veblen, Knight, and others can be seen from non-economics perspectives and that the lines dividing the social science disciplines are not as sharp nor fixed as the layout of offices on the typical university campus would lead us to believe. The review of the reactions of economists, political scientists, and sociologists to socialism and other "radical" theories was informative and interesting. Finally, although Ross builds a convincing case for the importance of the awareness of historical change on social science and on the need to "historicize" American social science, I remain unconvinced as to the primary importance of American exceptionalism in explaining today's scientific and liberal American social science. But that is not a key failing in a book where the discussion itself is more important than any final answer. The fundamental question: "Why did science and liberal individualism come to dominate American social science?" remains interesting, thought provoking and—as it always will be—open.

The Life and Political Economy of Lauchlin Currie: New
Dealer, Presidential Adviser, and Development Economist

by Roger J. Sandilands
(Durham, NC: Duke University Press, 1990; 441 pp.)

Reviewed by **W. Paul Strassmann**

The catastrophic depression of the 1930s, extravagant wars afterwards, and
the unacceptable poverty of backward countries have provided the great
challenges for economics in the twentieth century. In taking on all three, no
economist has been more engaged than Lauchlin Currie. Born in a Nova
Scotian fishing village in 1902 and educated at St. Francis Xavier, the London
School of Economics and Harvard, he led in making the U.S. Federal Reserve
System a genuine central bank, in giving a rationale to compensatory fiscal
policy before Keynes, and in 1939 becoming the first economic advisor at the
White House, meeting with FDR twice a week. During World War II he also
directed Lend-Lease assistance to China and the Foreign Economic
Administration, activities that invited years of harrassment by right-wing
Senators and Congressmen and loss of U.S. citizenship in 1954. After leading
the first World Bank country mission in 1949 to Colombia and conducting
follow-up studies, Currie settled in that country, bought a dairy farm, and tried
to advise one Colombian president after another. Meanwhile, he forged his
macroeconomics reflections on the New Deal, and Colombian experience into
a unique concept of economic development. Austere in some ways, yet bold
in others, this theory, like those of von Thünen, Hotelling, Schumpeter, and
that of Currie's own mentor, Allyn A. Young, may have to ferment a while
before catching on.

Research in the History of Economic Thought and Methodology,
Volume 13, pages 203-209.
Copyright © 1995 by JAI Press Inc.
All rights of reproduction in any form reserved.
ISBN: 1-55938-095-0

## I. OVERVIEW OF THE BOOK AND THE MAN

Whatever suitability Currie's insights may have for speeding development, their acceptance has been fostered by Roger J. Sandilands' biography and survey, *The Life and Political Economy of Lauchlin Currie: New Dealer, Presidential Adviser, and Development Economist*. Sandilands, an economist at the University of Strathclyde, Scotland, first met Currie in 1967 at Simon Fraser University, British Columbia, where Sandilands was a graduate student. Since then the two have been associated in various projects, including the writing of this book during 1987-1990. Currie made available decades of memoranda, correspondence, and other documents; discussed related experiences in detail; and read a draft of the manuscript. According to Sandilands, Currie limited himself to correcting factual errors, mentioning gaps in coverage, and pointing out weaknesses in his own work.

Nevertheless, Sandilands' "overall impression is of a man forcefully driven since childhood not only to be right but to persuade others that he is right" (p. ix). In 1943 Keynes called him an old friend whom he knew well, "but there is no one more difficult to handle. He is extremely suspicious and jealous" (p.134). In Colombia, Douglas McCallum, among others, reported that Currie dominated meetings because "of his greater intellectual force, aggressiveness, and tenacity" (p. 266). The Colombians followed his advice only now and then but often enough to be the only major Latin American country to avoid the debt crisis and stagnation of the 1980s. The credit should be shared with other advisors, of course, and with dubious good luck, but Currie's contribution, direct and indirect via his students, was enough to earn him a series of homenajes (tributes and honorary dinners), including the country's highest decoration, the Cruz de Boyaca.

For an account of childhood and youth, Sandilands gives the reader 14 pages of Currie's own memoirs, written in 1952. Next come three chapters on 20 years at Harvard and in Washington, 1925-1945, followed by one on postwar America and the McCarthy period. Eight chapters cover four decades in Colombia, 1949-1989, roughly five years per chapter, adjusted to coincide with major projects and analytical priorities. An important contribution of the book is its thorough presentation of lengthy memoranda written for high officials, especially presidents, as well as reports and articles originally published in Spanish, polished by others since Currie's command of that language remained "relatively poor" (p. 330). A chronological bibliography lists 177 items, with a curious gap for 1955-1958, the dairy farming years. For three of those years, his Holstein herd won the prize for highest milk yields in Colombia.

Sandilands' expositions of Currie's economic theories are uniformly clear and judiciously appraised. Assessments of Currie's work by others in reviews and correspondence are presented at length but occcasionally with rather partisan, not altogether fair asides. Thus, Hirschman's "hiding hand" referred to a propensity for wishful thinking in the face of uncertainty, not a recommendation to "deliberately exaggerate the benefits and minimize the costs in order to persuade people to invest their money (not Hirschman's) in industry" (p. 215).

## II.  PRECONCEPTIONS

Currie's essential model and consequent policy recommendations cannot be understood without appreciating his underlying philosophy. He believed that "long sustained thinking in terms of symbols" about "hypothetical problems" led to irrelevant solutions for "people with emotions, beliefs, and vested interests" in a "continually emerging and fluid overall situation" (1964 report quoted on p. 216). "Material progress [had] to satisfy the deeper needs of man: man's craving for esteem and a sense of personal worth, his conformism, his emotional equipment inherited from a technically much more primitive time" (p. 330). This perspective led to an aversion to *ceteris paribus* assumptions and equilibrium models but did not make him insensitive to the requirements of sound finance.

## III.  CENTRAL BANKING AND THE NEW DEAL

In North and South America alike Currie insisted that central banks had to be concerned with the availability and growth of the money supply, avoiding both deflation and inflation via open market operations. Making profits, mobilizing saving, and promoting good quality loans was not their function. Currie was the first monetary theorist to hold the Federal Reserve responsible for precipitating the depression of the 1930s. He then provided the rationale for the New Dealers' deficit spending as "compensatory fiscal policy," and was considered their intellectual leader, the man who came "closer than any other American economist to anticipating Keynes" (p. 92, Mordecai Ezekiel quoted by Herbert Stein). Lacking were the simplifying assumptions about stable multipliers, wage rigidities, and so forth, that could lead to the IS-LM model that first made Keynesian theory dominant but then caused its decline as unrealistic.

In 1968 Currie's *The Supply and Control of Money in the United States* (1934, 1968) was reprinted with a foreword by Karl Brunner, who wrote that "Currie's explicit challenge to the ruling myth has been thoroughly vindicated in recent research bearing on monetary policy" (p.xxiv, quoted on p. 49 by Sandilands).

## IV.  DEVELOPMENT THEORY AND POLICY

Vindication of Currie's development theory may take longer although it changed little while the fashions for other theories rose and fell. He never favored import-protected industrialization and state-operation of sectors at "the commanding heights." Hence he opposed (unsuccessfully) the steel plant erected at Paz del Rio. Structuralism and dependency theory were not for him. Nor did he participate in the shift to agriculture first, the informal sector, small-is-beautiful, decentralization, and basic needs. All this he deplored as "pseudo-economics and sentimentality" (p. 189). "What is sound is generally unpopular; what is popular is generally unsound" (a 1989 paper, quoted on p. 374).

But unlike the "Chicago boys" who tried to bring the non-interventionist gold standard back to the "Southern Cone" nations, Currie did not believe that free markets alone would sufficiently accelerate growth. It was regrettable that Latins wanted to over-control and to regulate all sectors, wages, and prices. But at strategic points intervention could indeed be helpful: selective action guided by respect for underlying economic forces, raising productivity by promoting a shift to demand-elastic sectors beyond the current trend of markets. Through such expenditure-switching, reminiscent of Harry G. Johnson's views, growth could be accelerated without inflationary finance.

Currie's concept of underlying forces went back to Jean Baptiste Say's law, as reinterpreted and extended by his Harvard professor, Allyn A. Young. The right kind of supply and demand stimulation in leading sectors could create demand throughout the economy, and vice versa, in a chain reaction involving latent technological advances, external economies of scale, capital formation, and improved deployment of labor. Thus all these input improvements were endogenous changes that did not have to come first. Whatever growth rate an economy had, whether stagnation, a Hindu 4 percent, or a Little Tiger 10 percent, that rate was likely to become built in, generating the inputs and technology to keep an economy going at just that rate. The trick of strategic intervention was to jolt an economy out of a low growth rate into a higher rate.

Currie was thus sympathetic to concepts of take-offs, critical minimum efforts, and Big Pushes. He differed from the proponents of these notions, however, in his choice of leading sectors, not infrastructure nor high-tech manufacturing, but exports and housing. He selected these sectors, not because of comparative advantage or other supply characteristics, but because of the ease of promoting an initial discontinuity in demand with general financial policies. Thus, suitable foreign exchange and trade policies could allow a country to tap vast foreign markets, as the Far Eastern "Tigers" have now demonstrated, but that was not at all obvious in the 1960s when the Tigers were seen as authoritarian sweatshops with a dubious future.

## V.   HOUSING AS A LEADING SECTOR

Less accepted so far has been Currie's other leading sector, housing for the middle classes. He was not part of the worldwide lobby of "housers," devotees of the sector because of the physical characteristics of its production and consumption. Some of those devotees saw housing as an outlet for surplus-labor and spending in trade-deficit countries because its construction can be labor-intensive, small-scale, low-tech, and using local materials. Others have seen shelter as producing health, productivity, self-reliance, and community spirit. Insofar as these views led to low-density, low-cost, subsidized housing for the poor, Currie was opposed. They attacked symptoms as mindlessly as Harpo Marx followed each pretty woman passing by, now in this direction, now in that. The policies were unaffordable give-aways that inhibited growth, made for poor urban design, and ignored the most important source of housing—reassigning the existing stock of dwellings.

Curry favored middle class housing because of its abstract economic characteristics: expensive, durable, but subject to elastic demand if finance were available. Indeed, high housing costs made finance necessary and durability made it possible by providing collateral. The needed policy intervention to get construction and turnover of the old stock going was the establishment of viable financial intermediaries with mortgage instruments suitable for both depositors and borrowers. In the inflationary Latin American setting, such instruments needed indexation, liquidity, and long maturities. With such a system new savings could be generated, underused factors could be mobilized for construction, residential mobility would rise, and vacated housing could be transferred to the poor, while productive activity would be galvanized indirectly throughout an economy, moving it to a higher Say-Young growth path. Workers would migrate from unproductive small farms and towns to modern industries and services in the largest cities.

For these ideas, as set forth in *Accelerating Development: The Necessity and the Means* (Currie, 1966), Currie won a competition sponsored by McGraw-Hill and the Society for International Development. In 1972 a system of private Savings and Housing Corporations was actually set up in Colombia along lines recommended by Currie and with himself as President Misael Pastrana's representative on the supervisory board. Within two years the system had 125,000 depositors and launched such a volume of construction that it could not simply be canceled by more lukewarm later national administrations. Nevertheless, against Currie's opposition, the extent of indexing was progressively moderated and housing subsidies for the rich and poor were reintroduced in a way that probably retarded both building and economic growth.

## VI.   URBAN DESIGN

Promotion of exports and housing finance led to rapid urbanization and the need for a third type of intervention: urban land use. Like others before him,

Currie saw that urbanization provided unearned betterment values for some, which should be taxed, and negative externalities for others through sprawl and congestion, which should be prevented through zoning and appropriate infrastructure. According to Currie, employment should be decentralized to major clusters within an urban area, and half of housing should be four and five story walk-ups and half high-rise condominia, as in Singapore. These views were spelled out in "cities-within-cities" policy recommendations that the Colombians never fully adopted though Currie "battle[d] relentlessly" against "economic illiteracy" (pp.265, 279). The plan indeed had flaws as well as major insights, and in any case was better than actual urban trends.

## VII.  GENERAL REFLECTIONS

Thus outside of his prize-winning dairy farm and iris gardens, Currie's policy recommendations were rarely given a full trial; and his theories have no assured recognition among economists. Milton Friedman and Anna Schwartz could write *A Monetary History of the United States* (1963) without mentioning his name; and Nicholas Stern (1989) could write an 88-page survey of the development literature without once referring to Currie. Although the list of economists who have met and corresponded with him is close to a Who's Who of the field, his work has not become part of the curriculum studied and cited by all.

If anything, Currie's effect on academia has been less than that on policy, a common fate of pioneers. Problems like depressions, wars, and urban dislocation arise and require informed action before academically respectable formulations can evolve. Eventually the most cosmetic slow distillations of recipes concocted rapidly in the heat of crisis will have greater longevity. But who is to say who made the greater contribution, the pioneer or the craftsman? Academics will naturally praise whatever is most academic, but problem-solvers—when they have time to reflect at all—are likely to choose the man who first pointed clearly in the right direction. What that direction may be is often not clear until the effective and the misleading have proven themselves as such, perhaps after years have passed.

Currie's once maverick theory of a soundly financed but rapidly expanding housing sector as crucial for stable development has now found an echo in research at the World Bank by Robert Buckley, Stephen Mayo, Bertrand Renaud, and others in a way that seems destined for application. Forty years earlier when Currie led the World Bank mission to Colombia, housing was not accepted at all as a legitimate concern for the Bank. Housing conditions were hopeless and irrelevant for the time being. Now the view is spreading that neither labor markets nor the financial system can function well without a healthy and dynamic housing sector.

No one can foresee how much luster the name of Lauchlin Currie will retain in coming decades. The inertia of events and human learning is often disappointing, but the very appearance of a biography like Sandilands' shows that lags are not insurmountable.

# REFERENCES

Currie, Lauchlin. 1968. [1934]. *The Supply and Control of Money in the United States.* Cambridge, MA: Harvard University Press. Russell and Russell.

―――――. 1966. *Accelerating Economic Development: The Necessity and the Means.* New York: McGraw-Hill.

Friedman, Milton, and Schwartz, Anna. 1963. *A Monetary History of the United States.* Princeton: Princeton University Press.

Stern, Nicholas. 1989. "The Economics of Development." *Economic Journal,* (September): 597-685.

# The Rhetoric of Reaction

## by Albert O. Hirschman

## Reviewed by **Torbjörn Tännsjö**

# I. INTRODUCTION

Albert O. Hirschman's new book, *The Rhetoric of Reaction* is extremely well written with both wit and irony but, as I will try to show, a complete failure, even on its own terms.

Hirschman sets out to examine three successive waves of "reactionary" opposition to the "progressive" ideas of the French Revolution and its Declaration of the Rights of Man, to the drive towards universal suffrage in the nineteenth century, and to the welfare state in our own century. He observes three modes of argument invariably used: (1) the perversity thesis, whereby any action to improve some feature of the political, social, or economic order is supposed to result in the exact opposite of what was intended, (2) the futility thesis, predicting that attempts at social transformation will produce no effects whatever: and (3) the jeopardy thesis, according to which the cost of a proposed reform is unacceptable because it will put into jeopardy previous hard-won accomplishments. The author illustrates these propositions by citing writers across the centuries such as de Maistre, Burke, Alexis de Tocqueville, Herbert Spencer, George Stigler, Jay Forrester, Charles Murray, and Gordon Tullock.

The book can be read either as a contribution to the history of ideas or to political philosophy proper. Both readings, however, are problematic.

As a contribution to the history of ideas it strikes the reader as unreliable. The reader fears that the examples picked by the author may not be *representative*. The author does not even attempt to show that they are, and he does not search systematically for recalcitrant, disconfirming evidence for his hypotheses.

Research in the History of Economic Thought and Methodology,
Volume 13, pages 211-221.
Copyright © 1995 by JAI Press Inc.
All rights of reproduction in any form reserved.
ISBN: 1-55938-095-0

As a contribution to political philosophy the book is wanting for the simple reason that the author does not even *attempt* to give charitable interpretations of the arguments he identifies. Moreover, he makes no serious attempt to assess the soundness of the arguments. Yet, for all that, he leaves the reader with the impression that the arguments are hopelessly flawed.

The main thrust of Hirschman's book is the claim that the patterns of reactionary argumentation he identifies are stereotypes and that, as such, they are *dangerous*. For those who aspire to the genuine dialogue that characterizes a truly democratic society, these stereotypes, just like similar stereotypes of the extreme left, function *rhetorically*, as contraptions making debate impossible. By exposing them, Hirschman wants to pave the way for a better intellectual climate. According to Hirschman (1991) modern democracies are characterized by a "...systematic lack of communication between groups of citizens, such as liberals and conservatives, progressives and reactionaries" (pp. ix-x). He goes on to claim that the "...resulting separateness of these large groups from one another seems more worrisome...than the isolation of anomic individuals in 'mass society' of which sociologists have made so much (p. x). "However, even if his diagnosis is correct, it seems to me that Hirschman does not help us to overcome this separateness. My main point in this notice is not only that he fails to do so, but that he fails *completely*. Not only is his attempt in vain, what he produces is the very *opposite* of what he sets out to do. What he accomplishes, when his book is read and admired, is the perverse effect that a critical discussion between reactionaries and progressives becomes *more* difficult.

## II.   A TERMINOLOGICAL OBJECTION

A common feature of the three patterns of argument examined by Hirschman is that the authors do not attack the underlying *rationale* of the progressive ideas against which they are directed. They do not care to attack their adversaries "head-on," they do not question that it *would* be a good thing to achieve what the progressives propose but, rather, they question whether this *can* be achieved. They accuse the radical either of being insincere or of being naive; the radical *knows*, or *should* know better. What he attempts will fail and what he will accomplish is either the opposite of his express goal (perversity), nothing at all (futility), or, only too little at much too high a price (jeopardy). This means the the word "reactionary" is not well placed as a name of these patterns of argument. Moreover, because of its negative emotive meaning, "reactionary" is a bad word to use for Hirschman for strictly methodological reasons. I suggest that, instead he should have used the word "conservative." These patterns of argument are typical of conservative thinkers such as Burke and de Maistre, but not of, say, a truly "reactionary" thinker such as Plato. de Maistre made the same point when he remarked that, "Nous ne voulons pas la contre-révolution mais le contraire de la révolution." Anthony Quinton (1978) more recently, has put it like this:

> A conservative proper is not a reactionary. His belief in continuity with the past is not a belief that some ideal state of affairs in the remote past ought to be reinstated by a radical change now, a negative revolution" (p. 19).

If it is kept in mind that what the conservatives want is to hold on to the continuity with the past, the patterns of arguments identified by Hirschman look less like stereotypes. How else *could* these authors argue when they want to oppose attempts at radical change of society, one might ask. *Must* they not argue in conformance with *some* of Hirschman's patterns. This need not mean that their arguments are stereotypes. In particular, if put into *context*, it seems very likely that they turn out to be both varied and respectable. At least sometimes, they are, but, because of his rigid classification, Hirschman is not capable of noticing when this is the case. He disposes of the "reactionaries" in a truly rhetorical manner. I think he should instead have gone more into detail with some of them. He should have tried to make charitable interpretations of their statements, taking into account the context where they were put forward, and he would have found, I conjecture, much of interest.

## III.   DIFFERENT LINES OF INTERPRETATION

The three patterns of argumentation identified by Hirschman allow themselves to be interpreted in three very different directions. They have something in common, viz., that they question a proposed change or reform, without questioning the *aim* of it. However, it is not clear what *kind* of arguments they prepare the ground for. Is the conservative point only that *this* measure will fail, since, when trying to bring *it* about, we will obtain the opposite of what we set out to accomplish (perversity), or, we will not achieve anything at all (futility), or, we will achieve something, but at too high a cost (jeopardy)? Or, is it that this measure will fail, since *any* attempt to bring about a change or a reform must fail in either of the described ways? Or, can we find an interpretation somewhere in between these two extremes? Could we find some conditional principles to the effect that, attempted reforms of a certain *kind* tend to fail?

Hirschman (1991) himself seems not to have recognized these fairly obvious differences. In his own statement of the three patterns of "reactionary" rhetoric he oscillates between them. When he states the perversity thesis, his stress on "any" indicates that he states it in its generalized version:

According to the *perversity* thesis, any purposive action to improve some feature of the political, social, or economic order only serves to exacerbate the condition one wishes to remedy (p. 7).

When he states the futility thesis, it is not clear in what version he intends it:

The futility thesis holds that attempts at social transformation will be unavailing, that they will simply fail to "make a dent" (p. 7).

And when he states the jeopardy thesis his stress on "the proposed change or reform" indicates that he intends it in a not generalized version:

Finally, the *jeopardy* thesis argues that the cost of the proposed change or reform is too high as it endangers some previous, precious accomplishment (p. 7).

Obviously, it is of the utmost importance along which line we interpret the "reactionary" critics of human rights, democracy, and the welfare state. Do they argue that the proposed changes must fail because *all* attempted changes for the better fail? But this is absurd! Or, do they argue that the proposed changes fail, for specific reasons, relating to each of them in a particular situation? But this seems trivial. How else *could* these critics, who are not prepared to question the *goal* of the proposed reforms, argue? Or, do they base their repudiation of the attempted reforms on some less radical, but yet principled stance against radical change *under certain conditions*? My conjecture is that they sometimes do, and, when they do, their arguments are of much interest. To this I will return.

## IV.  THE PERVERSITY THESIS

In his statement of the perversity thesis Hirschman tends towards the generalized version. We saw this in the quotation above, and he repeats it, for example, in the following way:

Attempts to reach for liberty will make society sink into slavery, the quest for democracy will produce oligarchy and tyranny, and social welfare programs will create more, rather than less, poverty. *Everything backfires* (p. 12).

Consequently Hirschman ascribes this generalized version of the perversity thesis to the "reactionaries" to which he turns for textual evidence. However, upon examination it turns out that only *one* of the quotations he makes from various different "reactionaries" is even compatible with such an interpretation. This is the following bold statement by de Maistre, in his *Considération sur la France*:

If one wants to know the probable result of the French Revolution, one only needs to examine the points on which all factions were in agreement: all wanted the…destruction of universal Christianity and of the Monarchy; *from which it follows* that the final result of their efforts will be none other than the exaltation of Christianity and Monarchy.

All those who have written or meditated about history have admired this secret force which mocks human intentions (p. 18).

*All* the other quotations are at variance with Hirschman's claim that the authors adhere to the perversity thesis in its a generalized version. Hirschman simply misrepresents these authors, obviously without noticing himself the difference between the generalized and more restricted versions of the thesis. This is perhaps most obvious when he makes the following quotation from Jay W. Forrester—I quote now from Hirschman:

At times programs cause exactly the reverse of desired results! For example, most urban policies, from job creation to low-cost housing, range from ineffective to harmful judged either by their effect on the economic health of the city or by their long-range effect on the low income population (p. 32).

And then goes on to say:

In other words, Joseph de Maistre's vengeful Divine Providence has returned to the stage in the guise of Forrester's 'feedback-loop dynamics,' and the result is identical: any human attempt to improve society only makes matters worse (p. 32).

Obviously, this is not a fair statement of Forrester's point. One must wonder how on earth Hirschman can have failed to notice the difference between the view actually put forward by Forrester, concerning *most urban policies*, and nothing else, and the (generalized) view Hirschman ascribes to him, which concerns *any* human attempt to improve society. It is difficult not to suspect that he misrepresents Forrester and other "reactionaries" because, if he did not, they would not at all turn out to be the kind of "stereotypes" he accuses them of being. However, this kind of misrepresentation of the views of an adversary cannot really render easier communication; quite to the contrary, it probably blocks a rational exchange of views.

A problem with Hirschman is that he does not take seriously the arguments he identifies. He is only too quick to classify them in accordance with his rhetoric patterns. Instead he should have examined them closer, and put them into context. He would then have found, not only some interesting arguments, built on particular traits of the proposed reforms and of the situations where they were put forward, but also some interesting ideas of a more general kind.

Hirschman does notice that a source of the perversity thesis may be the observation made during the Scottish Enlightenment of unintended effects of human action. But he does not observe a much more interesting source of the thesis. I think of a more general conservative critique of our ability to improve human conditions through conscious political action. This kind of critique appears in most conservative writings, for example in Burke, but it is perhaps put forward with most force by Michael Oakshott, in particular in his book *Rationalism in Politics and other Essays*. Oakshott does not say that *no* improvement of human affairs is possible through conscious political action, but he questions too much optimism about what he calls "rationalism" in politics, a stance which can be contrasted with "traditionalism." Let me elaborate on this point a little bit, since it constitutes one good example of what Hirschman would have been forced to discuss, had he taken his "reactionary" critics seriously.

According to rationalism,[1] when making political decisions, we ought (1) to investigate which are the alternatives facing us; we ought (2) to investigate which are the possible outcomes of these alternatives; we ought (3) to be explicit about our values and assess the value of these possible outcomes; we ought (4) to assess how probable these outcomes are, and, having done so; we ought (5) to apply the principle of maximization of expected utility, in order to reach a decision.

In contrast, the traditional way of taking political decisions is to be faithful to an existing and well established practical knowledge of how to conduct a certain activity.

Why should we adhere to rationalism in politics? I suppose that the standard answer to this question is that, if we do, and do it consistently, then, probably, in the long run, we realize our goals more fully than if, consistently, we adhere to some other method of reaching political decisions. I have discussed this view in Chapter 2 of my *Conservatism for Our Time*. My thesis there, which I will not belabor in the present context, is that, even if the rationalist stance may often seem rational to adopt, to adopt it may not be so rational in some situations. I think in particular of situations where our probability estimates are of very poor quality, or of situations where, depending on how we act, there may not be any "long run" where our goals can be realized. In the circumstances, a belief in the superiority of the rationalistic model seems to reflect nothing but blind faith. Of course, a less instrumentalistic argument could be given in defense of the model. To stick to it is, in a particular sense, to attempt to achieve *consistency* between beliefs, values, and actions. Consistency may be a good thing to achieve for its own sake. However, a very similar kind of rationale exists for the traditionalist model. After all, what the traditionalist is after is a kind of faithfulness to, or consistency with, an existing and well established practical knowledge of how to conduct a certain activity. This too may be of value in itself.

If this is correct, there may be more to Oakshott's criticism of rationalism than at first meets the eye. And I suppose that much of the conservative opposition to various proposals for social change, such as the proposals explicitly discussed by Hirschman, could very well be understood in the light of this kind of pessimism concerning rationalism in politics. Perhaps some of these suggested changes have been based on very poor estimates of the probability of the outcomes of them. Perhaps the traditional scepticism concerning at least some of these proposed changes, at least at some times, has been well placed.

This must not be taken to mean, of course, that, had these radical proposals been implemented, they would necessarily have resulted in exactly the opposite of what the reformers set out to accomplish. However, at least in some circumstances, it is not at all implausible that they would have. What we confront here is a line of conservative argument completely neglected by Hirschman but which deserves to be taken seriously.

## V. THE FUTILITY THESIS

Above I have given one quotation from Hirschman where he states the futility thesis in a less than general version. However, he also sometimes states it as a quite general thesis. The following is an example of this:

> The argument to be explored now says...that the attempt at change is abortive, that in one way or another any alleged change is, was, or will be largely surface, facade, cosmetic, hence illusory, as the "deep" structures of society remain wholly untouched. I shall call it the futility thesis (p. 43).

In his discussion of various critiques of human rights, democracy, and the welfare state, Hirschman does *not* ascribe any generalized version of the argument to the critics, however. It is also quite obvious that these critics do not adhere to it in its most generalized version. In the chapter about the futility thesis we get a traditional overview of fairly well-known arguments to the effect that the French Revolution did not achieve anything of substance (de Tocqueville), to the effect that the broadening of the franchise will not change the fact that, in each society, some rule others (Mosca, Pareto, and Michels), and to the effect that, no matter how well-intentioned the attempts may be to improve the social situation of the poor, such attempts will fail (George Stigler, Gordon Tullock, Milton Friedman, and others). This means, of course, that, from the point of view of Hirschman's main thesis, this chapter is a failure. He does not really succeed in showing that the authors he discusses have much in common. This fact goes unnoticed by the author, however.

Hirschman notes in his chapter about the futility thesis that, in their scepticism about democracy and the welfare state, "reactionaries" put forward arguments that have also been used by people on the extreme left. It is surprising, however, that Hirschman does not seem to notice that the theme he is here touching on is the main focus of Popper's *The Open Society*. At least according to Popper there are adherents of the futility thesis in its most generalized version, "historicists," who *are* really prepared to give arguments for the generalized thesis that *any* alleged change "is, was, or will be largely surface, facade, cosmetic, hence illusory." According to them, the only way people can consciously interfere with history is in the manner of lessening its "birth-pangs." Strangely enough, not one single reference is made to Popper in Hirschman's book.

## VI.  THE JEOPARDY THESIS

As we saw above, Hirschman's canonical statement of the jeopardy thesis is a non-generalized version. According to this thesis, "...the cost of the proposed change or reform is too high as it endangers some previous, precious accomplishment" (p. 7). No attempt is made by Hirschman in his chapter about this thesis to attribute it to any "reactionary" writer in a generalized version. This means that, according to Hirschman, the authors discussed in this chapter are more "commonsensical" and "moderate" than are the authors that have been reviewed in the chapters about the perversity and the futility theses. But then one must wonder what point there is in just *identifying* and *classifying* these arguments. For this means that there is no "shame" in being classified as an adherent of the jeopardy thesis. This is not really to believe in any suspect "thesis" at all. It consists mainly in having held that some attempt sometimes to introduce human rights, democracy, or a welfare state, may have been premature. Again it goes unnoticed by the author that he has failed to identify any stereotyped argument at all.

In this chapter he *does* touch upon *one* more general line of thought which may be an intellectual source of some arguments to the effect that a proposed reform may put into jeopardy earlier hard-won accomplishments. I think of the "slippery slope" or "the thin edge of the wedge" kind of argument. However, he only mentions it, he does not discuss it. He notes that this argument is widely used and misused (p. 83), but he does not try to find out what distinguishes a proper from an improper use of it. There exists a good deal of literature about this,[2] and it is a pity, again, that Hirschman does not take seriously the kind of argument he has identified.

Another possible intellectual source of the jeopardy thesis is the kind of defence of status quo that is put forward by David Hume in his defence of the right to property, cast in more modern terms by Thomas Schelling in his seminal book, *The Strategy of Conflict*. Hirschman does not notice this possibility of giving substance to the "reactionary" critique he is so eager to expose. I have discussed this strand of quite respectable conservatism elsewhere and will not repeat my argument in the present context.[3]

## VII.  CONSERVATIVE VALUES

From Hirschman's exposition, based on solid historical hindsight, the reader gets the impression that definitely most of the "reactionary" criticism was misplaced. The reforms, when eventually implemented, did not cause the disasters predicted by the critics. This, however, reflects in my opinion a much too simplistic view of the evidence, taken by the author. First of all, even if the consequences of the reforms did not turn out to be devastating, when eventually they were implemented, this does not mean that it *would* not have meant disaster, had they been put into practice, when *at first* they were brought upon the political agenda. Some people are criticizing Gorbachev today, because he put into office people who were later to make an attempted coup d'état, directed at him and his perstroika policy. However, it *might* very well be the case that, had he not put them into office, the coup would have come earlier, and, if it had come earlier, it might have succeeded. In a similar vein, it is possible that much of the criticism of radical proposals of reform in the past was much better placed than we are today capable of recognizing. Moreover, and this is perhaps even more important, when Hirschman seems to take for granted that many of the radical reforms in the past did no harm, this conclusion is based on certain (individualistic) *values*, never explicitly mentioned by him. This means that he does not take seriously a certain strand of conservative thought built upon the (collectivist) idea that well-established institutions ought to be retained, either because their continued existence is of value in itself, or because, unless we retain them, people who sustain them will lose their sense of identity. Even if, after the old institutions are gone, there is no one there to complain about what happened, since the people living in the societies where these institutions existed, are not really there any more—they too have changed—the change may have meant a definite loss! Again we have come across a line of conservative thought which deserves to be taken seriously but which Hirschman does not even consider.[4]

## VIII.  CONCLUSION

The express intention with Hirschman's book is to cast doubt upon the "reactionary" critique of human rights, democracy, and the welfare state. By demonstrating that the same stereotypes recur over and over again Hirschman wants to suggest that the reasoning is frequently faulty. A "... general suspicion of overuse of the arguments is aroused by the demonstration that they are invoked time and again almost routinely to cover a wide variety of real situations" (p. 166). He flatters himself with the belief that, upon his inspection, these arguments put forward by some "deep thinkers" who had invariably presented their ideas as original and brilliant insights, "... are made to look rather less impressive, and sometimes even comical" (p. 164).

A first quick reading of his book made me concur in this assessment. However, upon closer examination, I have found appearances to be deceptive. In the first place, Hirschman does not really succeed in showing that the authors he discusses exhibit any stereotyped arguments at all. In order to convince the reader that they do he often has to misrepresent their views. He has to represent them as adherents of the absurd view that the particular proposed reforms they oppose *must* fail because *all* kinds of conscious reform is doomed to failure. Few if any of the "reactionaries" adhere to such a generalized version of the perversity, or futility, or jeopardy "thesis." Not being prepared to attack the radical proposals "head-on," they argue in the only manner open to them, that the reforms will fail, either because they will produce unwelcome side-effects, or make no "dent" at all. Secondly, what contributes to the comical appearance of the scepticism of the "reactionaries" is that, with the help of a historical hindsight, Hirschman gives the impression that, obviously, they were very often simply *wrong*. However, this assessment is founded on a much too simplistic view of the evidence. It does not take seriously the possibility that, had some of the reforms come *earlier*, the result may well have been devastating. Moreover, it is a matter open to dispute whether some of the reforms really were such a success. This depends on value assumptions never discussed by Hirschman. Third, and perhaps most important, what contributes to the impression that the basic arguments of the "reactionaries" are such stereotypes, is the fact that Hirschman never cares to give *charitable* interpretations of them. He oscillates between an interpretation of their views that makes them absurd (the generalized version) and an interpretation that makes them trivial. However, there exist interesting conservative ideas *between* these extremes. I think here of such ideas as Oakshott's criticism of rationalism in politics, and Hume's and Thomas Schelling's defense of the status quo.

The final judgment of the book must be that, for all its wit and good humor, it is an intellectual failure.

## NOTES

1. I draw here on what I write in Chapter 2 of my *Conservatism for Our Time* where I make a "rational reconstruction" of Oakshott's characterization. This means that it is cast in a terminology known from modern decision-theory, which allows me also to improve on his *argument*. I hope that Oakshott would have approved of my way of handling his argument, but this I know nothing about, of course.

2. In particular, it has been discussed in the context of medical ethics. See for example, and for further references, David Lamb's *Down the Slippery Slope*.

3. In my *Conservatism for Our Time*, Chapter 2.

4. In Chapter 3 of my *Conservatism for Our Time* I pursue this line of thought more thoroughly.

# REFERENCES

Hirschman, A.O. 1991. *The Rhetoric of Reaction, Perversity, Futility, Jeopardy*. Cambridge, MA: The Belknap Press of Harvard University Press.

Lamb, D. 1988. *Down the Slippery Slope*. London: Croom Helm.

Oakshott, M. 1962. *Rationalism in Politics and other Essays*. London: Methuen.

Popper, K.R. 1945. *The Open Society and its Enemies*. London: Routledge & Kegan Paul.

Quinton, A. 1978. *The Politics of Imperfection*. London: Faber & Faber.

Schelling, T. 1960. *The Strategy of Conflict*. Cambridge, MA: Harvard University Press.

Tännsjö, T. 1990. *Conservatism for Our Time*. London: Routledge.

The Reach and Grasp of Policy Analysis:
Comparative Views of the Craft

by Richard I. Hofferbert
(Tuscaloosa, AL: The Institute for Social Science Research,
The University of Alabama Press, 1990; 1995; 192 pp.)

Reviewed by **James Duncan Shaffer**

This is an interesting book for practitioners and teachers of the craft of policy analysis. It makes observations about the craft which are useful in thinking about the roles of policy analysis and policy analysts and different approaches to policy analysis. The book is not comprehensive nor focused on a theme. It does not promote a particular approach to policy analysis, unless being pragmatic is considered an approach. It does not provide a systematic evaluation of success and failures of policy analysis. It is a set of eight thoughtful papers, each of which was originally written for a conference or journal.

Part 1 is three essays discussing lessons from the U.S. experience in the exercise of the policy analysis craft.

The emphasis is on policy evaluation which is defined as "... the effort to employ social scientific research tools to measure to what extent, under what conditions and at what costs public programs attain their objectives" (p. 4). Hofferbert argues that the policy evaluation industry flourished between 1960 and the late 1970s and has since been in erratic decline. The industry, to a large extent supported by government but undertaken by organizations separated from government, grew on the basis of optimistic views of the capacity of government to design programs to directly improve the lives of the disadvantaged, at least in part by changing behavior and a belief that social science had the tools to help design effective programs. The decline in the industry is related to three things: a disillusionment with analysis because it failed to help design programs which delivered desired outcomes, a migration of the evaluation activity from outside of government to the inside, and a shift in political power and ideology in government.

Research in the History of Economic Thought and Methodology,
Volume 13, pages 223-228.
Copyright © 1995 by JAI Press Inc.
All rights of reproduction in any form reserved.
ISBN: 1-55938-095-0

Hofferbert makes a distinction between what he calls product and process research. Product research delivers an evaluation of a program. Or it may be designed to test a theory. It was done mostly by research groups outside of the agencies responsible for implementing the program. It was generally aimed at the policy makers and academics not the administrators responsible for making the programs work. Much of the product research delivered bad news. Proof that the programs evaluated were delivering on their promises was scarce. "Rather than serving as an aid to management, the cumulative lesson of policy evaluation, at least as translated through the media and the receiving instruments of policy makers, was not so much to suggest means for improving program management as to challenge the theoretical foundations of the programs. Even the conventual statistical tools of social science, such as tests of statistical significance, loaded the evidence against demonstration of positive results of policies and in favor of falsifying the hopes of policy makers" (p. 14). It turned out that the effective demand (i.e funds) for this type of analysis was scarce as well.

Process research is more oriented to the problems of how to make programs work. It is concerned with the process of implementation. It is much more client friendly. Thus there is more demand for this type of analysis among those who have responsibility for making the programs work. It is also more compatible with the on going functions of an agency and more attractive as an in-house activity. Hofferbert argues that process research is more likely to be useful than product research.

Interesting to me was the association of process research with the tradition of the land grant universities emphasizing the concept of service, providing practical information to organizations and people in a position to use it. Its hallmark is identifying practical problems and working with people to solve them.

I agree that policy analysis has neglected the problems of implementation. Many program failures or poor performance have been due to failures in implementation. And policy analysis did not contribute to the design of programs taking into consideration the difficult problems of implementation. I also agree that implementation research can be much more effective if analysts develop effective relationships with the policy makers and administrators. And I agree very much with his pragmatic emphasis. It is what he doesn't say or deal with that bothers me.

Hofferbert directs his attention to program analysis rather than to the broad spectrum of policy analysis. Policy is concerned first of all with the rules of the political economic game. Here understanding how the system works and the effects of specific rules and expected effects of changes in rules is critical. Such research is not necessarily best targeted to the interests of particular policy makers or administrators. One problem with the idea of process research is that it may play down the role of the analyst as social critic. One of the difficult selling jobs for the social disciplines is funding of independent analysis critical of government policy and programs. In a democratic society decisions on policy and programs are influenced by many groups and individuals—not policy makers in the narrow sense.

It may be that the decline in demand for policy analysis is due to the poor quality of the product. Theory and methods are not up to the tasks of evaluation and design of policies and programs in modern complex political economies. The social disciplines are especially handicapped by the use of counterfactual assumptions in order to simplify complex analysis, then drawing conclusions which necessarily are misleading when applied to the real world of policy. Long run demand for and usefulness of policy analysis would be enhanced by honesty in labeling the products and delivering on more modest promises. Policy analysis may be able to make significant contributions to policy debate without the pretense of a comprehensive policy evaluation and prescription.

The second and largest part of the book is called "Policy Analysis for Export to the Developing World." The author's summary of the three papers of this part includes the following:

"Chapter 4 ...examines specifically the relative fit to a Third World context of the simple systems model generally adopted by political scientists studying policy in the West. By and large, a positive report is delivered on the utility of the approach, so long as certain key cautions are observed.

Chapter 5 argues that the mix of analytical tools used by policy analysts must be adapted to the actual priorities pursued in the countries studied. Particularly, I suggest that our research tactics to date have been ill-fitted to the major thrust of development policy toward basic needs of the poor in the poorest countries.

Chapter 6 proposes an additional view or stance for enhancing the utility of policy research in some of the most poor parts of the world. Based on observations made in Nepal, particularly with respect to the development of domestic water systems, the argument in Chapter 6 is for adding a 'bottom-up' approach to the strategies of development research that are commonly pursued" (pp. 57-58).

Hofferbert's discussion raises a classic problem for policy analysts. He argues that policy analysis must be adapted to the actual priorities pursued in the countries studied. He also argues the "Policy analysis, at its most useful, at its most inter-subjective, and at its most objective, reveals normative preferences and then arrays evidence to support hypotheses about the maximization of these preferences" (p. 58). Later in the book he says, "I expose myself as an unabashed, old-fashioned liberal, who takes a pretty unequivocal stand for the advancement (and even the export) of systems of popular control, call them "democracies," "polyorchis," "representative systems," or whatever. Prescribing for that advancement, on the basis of our very best, most rigorous modes of inquiry, is a moral objective I hold to be worthy of the efforts of my discipline" (p. 136). He also makes a very good point that there are two very different traditional views of the role of government which he refers to as the idea that the role of government is to serve the people, contrasting to the idea that the role of government is to control the people. What then is the role of the policy analyst in a country where the goals of the government are to control and manipulate their citizens in the interests of the ruling elite?

Allow me a few observations on policy analysis in the less developed countries based upon more than 25 years of frustrating experience.

First, I believe that one of the most important questions for the social disciplines is to provide an explanation of the very great differences in levels of productivity and levels of living among countries, regions and classes of people. What is it that leaves the greater part of the world's people destitute given the technological capacity to greatly increase their productivity and well being? I believe that the answer lies in the political economic institutions. The rules of the game, the standard operating procedures of firms, and the way people relate to each other contain perverse incentives and barriers to increased productivity and equity. We need better paradigms for understanding these relationships. But the transition to more productive systems will come from a combination of grubby work in policy analysis and heroic efforts of those influencing rule making.

Policies obstructing productivity and equity may be due to lack of knowledge about the consequences of existing and alternative policies and the power of interest groups, including members of the government. Frequently it is both. Understanding the objectives and power of the participants in the policy process is important in producing useful analysis. Take exchange rate policy as an example. There are some important questions of fact about the consequences of specific policy. However, the existing policy cannot be understood without recognizing that exchange rate control requires the allocation of foreign exchange and that this creates opportunities to give valuable favors, easily converted to political and economic benefits for the administrators and their bosses. The head of state may or may not know how the policy is used for personal benefits. Tactics become an important factor in doing useful analysis.

Legitimizing policy analysis and the idea that the policies and actions of the Government can make a significant difference is a first step in instituting useful analysis. If government leaders believe the state of their country simply reflects God's will or that government is helpless to really solve the basic problems or that policy analysis has nothing to offer them there will be little demand for policy analysis. Since it is frequently the case that a number of policies and programs with highly desirable stated objectives exist, but are obviously failing to deliver on the objectives because of problems in implementation, process research addressing these problems may be an effective point of entry without challenging powerful interest groups.

For the long run it is important to promote the establishment of organizations to do policy analysis. To create such organizations local analysts are needed who have both some competence and the belief that policy analysis can be useful. My experience suggests that formal training is important but seldom sufficient. Most effective is a collaborative project. Learning by doing. It is often the case that providing simple objective information relevant to a particular policy of interest to policymakers will contribute to both legitimization and training. For example, a price support for beans was undertaken in Rwanda. Beans are by far the most important staple crop and are grown by most farmers. The assumption was that by increasing the price of beans poor farmers would be made better off. Data from farm surveys was collected and presented which showed that most farmers were net buyers of beans, almost all of the poorest farmers were net buyers, and that Rwanda was a net buyer of beans from neighboring countries. In a seminar with selected policy makers it was not necessary to emphasize the importance of these data, they were quick to see it themselves. It created a demand for more information and a new belief by young analysts that they could make a difference. Several of my colleagues have written an article discussing procedures for undertaking useful policy analysis in less developed countries. I list it as a reference.

On a different level books integrating accumulated knowledge about the relationships of institutions and political economic performance might make a great contribution in the developing world in the next decade. The demand for new political economic systems and ideas for instituting them must be at an all time high. What do we have to offer?

This brings me to the third part of the book entitled "The Disciplinary Mix." Here the point is made that policy analysis is a shining example of an interdisciplinary endeavor but that interdisciplinary cooperation is seldom evident in practice. More importantly, in my opinion, is the atomization of policy research: "... It is not only across disciplines that mutual awareness of policy analytic tactics is lacking but within the work of leading political scientists themselves" (p. 135). Important points are made about tactics for policy analysis and the different roles for the disciplinary social scientist.

My own view is that interdisciplinary research is difficult. Specialists talk past each other and the transaction costs of coordinating activities often comes at a high cost. I believe this is due in part to the inconsistent paradigms held in the heads of the specialists. Perhaps an effort to reunite the social disciplines would help? Can the specialists in the study of economic thought help?

Of particular importance is the fragmentary nature of the policy studies. There is very little cumulative record. There is no generally accepted framework on which to hang the findings and give them meaning. There is no coordinating mechanism for assimilation and integration beyond highly specialized areas.

I found Hofferbert's essays provocative. I am glad I took the time to read them.

# REFERENCE

Weber, Michael T., Staatz, John M., Holtzman, John S., Crawford, Eric W. and Bernsten, Richard H. 1988. "Informing Food Security Decisions in Africa: Empirical Analysis and Policy Dialogue." *American Journal of Agricultural Economics* 70(5): 1044-1052.

# The Production of Commodities:
# an Introduction to Sraffa

by John E. Woods
(Atlantic Highlands, NJ: Humanities Press International)

Reviewed by **David Andrews**

## I. INTRODUCTION

Piero Sraffa's *Production of Commodities by Means of Commodities: Prelude to a Critique of Economic Theory* is:

> ...an extraordinary little book, whose title [is] almost as baffling as its content...The book contain[s] no introduction or conclusion, no discussion of assumptions, no justification for its analysis...What it seem[s] to be about [is] Ricardo's old problem of finding an invariable standard with which to measure prices, such that they will not depend on the level of wages and profits...But what the book is really about has been the subject of a heated debate (Blaug, 1985, p. 237).

On one hand, Pierangelo Garegnani, John Eatwell, and Allesandro Roncaglia, among others, have written of the "Sraffa Revolution" and the "Revival of Classical Political Economy." According to this interpretation, the work of Sraffa provides a decisive critique of "neoclassical" or "marginalist" economic theory as well as the foundation of a positive theory and thereby paves the way for a paradigm shift, from the neoclassical theory to a Sraffa inspired alternative.

On the other hand, Paul Samuelson, Mark Blaug, Frank Hahn, and Edwin Burmeister, to name a few, representing the orthodox neoclassical theory, have argued that there is nothing in Sraffa's analysis that should be viewed as threatening to standard theory. On this interpretation it is accepted that Sraffa's reswitching example demonstrates restrictions on the applicability of aggregate production functions, but the consequences of this are considered to be relatively minor. Sraffa's analysis is simply another special case of the neoclassical orthodoxy.

**Research in the History of Economic Thought and Methodology,**
**Volume 13, pages 229-248.**
Copyright © 1995 by JAI Press Inc.
All rights of reproduction in any form reserved.
ISBN: 1-55938-095-0

In addition to the "heated debate" over the meaning and implications of his work, Sraffa the man presents a fascinating picture. He was a personal and intellectual intimate of some of the most brilliant and influential thinkers of the twentieth century, for example, Antonio Gramsci, John Maynard Keynes, and Ludwig Wittgenstein; although he was apparently a committed Marxist, some of the most important figures of orthodox economics have been among his admirers, for example, Schumpeter and Samuelson. All this despite the fact that he was apparently very quiet and published very little.

Despite the prominence of the participants in the debate over the significance of Sraffa's work, the gravity and scope of the issues involved, the degree of disagreement which remains, and the abundant evidence of his extraordinary intellect, John E. Woods would seem to be correct in his assertion that "the general level of awareness of Sraffa's work among economists [is] lamentable," and in his perception that there is "a clear need for a book which explained in the simplest terms possible the line of argument in Sraffa's *Production of Commodities by Means of Commodities*, chapter by chapter, even section be section."

In his book, *The Production of Commodities: An Introduction to Sraffa*, Woods sets out to satisfy this need, and for this reason the appearance of the book must be applauded. The stated goals of the book are modest in scope. Woods emphasizes that his primary purpose is not to provide a full scale interpretation of the significance of Sraffa's work, but rather only a simplified statement of the substance of Sraffa's book. The main purpose of the book, according to Woods, is "to provide an account of what Sraffa actually said."

There is one obvious nuance to Woods' treatment of Sraffa about which Woods is quite explicit:

> There is one respect in which my analysis differs noticeably from that in PCMC. Sraffa considers general multisector models with $n$ industries and $n$ commodities. In this book, I deal with only two-sector models (p. 3).

This simplification involves several judgments which go beyond "what Sraffa actually said" and Woods offers several justifications for this self-imposed restriction. "While the restriction precludes the derivation of some results, the loss is of second order importance: the essential theory can be presented in terms of two-sector models." It is difficult to dispute that much of the text of PCMC would become irrelevant with only one sector. "Why not more than two?" Because "mathematical considerations dictate that there should be at most two" (Woods, p. 4). This is consistent with Sraffa's intent as expressed in the preface to *PCMC* as his concern for the non-mathematical reader, but it goes beyond anything Sraffa said about what constitutes the "essential theory." One of the most peculiar aspects of Sraffa's book is that he gave no indication of his conception of what is most essential. Hence Woods' two sector restriction exceeds "what Sraffa actually said."

## II. EXISTENCE

The material in the first three substantial chapters, on "A Subsistence Economy," "Production with a Surplus: Subsistence Wage," Production with a Surplus: Wage above Subsistence," "follows PCMC quite closely." Woods focuses on simple models of the type with which Sraffa begins:

$$280 \text{ qr. wheat} + 12 \text{ t. iron} - 400 \text{ qr. wheat}$$
$$120 \text{ qr. wheat} + 8 \text{ t. iron} - 20 \text{ t. iron}$$

The sharp difference which appears in these chapters between the approaches of Sraffa and Woods is the latter's concern with questions of existence. "Result 1" of Woods' book, for example, is that "there is a positive solution to [the quantity equations] which is unique up to scalar multiplication, if and only if [certain restrictions on the technical coefficients obtain]" (p. 15). Such "Results" appear throughout the book.[1] Such results are generally absent from *PCMC*.

"Existence" here is used in a somewhat peculiar sense, that is, that in which it might be said that the existence of general equilibrium has been proved. "Existence" has another sense, that is, that in which the existence of the Loch Ness monster might be debated. The former sense, as Don McCloskey has observed, has been appropriated by economists from mathematicians. The latter sense, surprisingly, has not been important in many economic analyses.

Sraffa was evidently not very concerned with questions of existence in either sense. His method in *PCMC* is to assume existence in the mathematical sense, "Let us consider an extremely simple society which produces just enough to maintain itself" (Sraffa, 1960, p. 3). That is to say, he restricts his analysis by assumption to cases in which mathematical existence is not an issue.

Presumably, Sraffa is simply not interested in economic systems which do not exist in the mathematical sense. This is not surprising in that existence results have been a primary concern of neoclassical economists, and Sraffa intends to provide the basis for a critique of neoclassical economics. Unless one projects upon him the interests and concerns of the tradition he takes as the object of his critique, it is very difficult to see why he should be interested. "An extremely simple society which produces just enough to maintain itself" is quite easy to conceive; the additional insight gained by noting the more or less trivial conditions this places on the technical coefficients is negligible.

Sraffa is also not interested in existence in the sense relevant to the Loch Ness monster. There is "no reference to market prices" (p. 9) and Sraffa states quite clearly that he is concerned only with a logical construct: "...we are all the time concerned merely with the implications of the assumption of a uniform price for all units of a commodity and a uniform rate of profits on all the means of production" (p. 91).

Rather than being concerned with existence in either sense, Sraffa takes existence as given and investigates the implications thereof. To assume that "existence results" are important in "An Introduction to Sraffa," or to suggest that the absence of such results in Sraffa's work represents a "lacuna" requires a tacit assumption that Sraffa shares or ought to share an important element of the orthodox methodological approach, an assumption for which there is no basis in any of Sraffa's work.

## III.  THE STANDARD COMMODITY

After presenting the simplest single product industries version of the model with a surplus, Woods moves on, as does Sraffa, to consider the effects of changes in the distribution of income between wages and profits on the prices of individual commodities with the methods of production unchanged. This issue arises from the analysis of Ricardo who argued that an increase in wages, ceteris paribus, would have the effect of altering the system of relative prices such that some prices would rise and other prices would fall.

This leads to a problem: as Sraffa says,

> The necessity of having to express the price of one commodity in terms of another which is arbitrarily chosen as standard complicates the study of the price-movements which accompany a change in distribution. It is impossible to tell of any particular price-fluctuation whether it arises from the peculiarities of the commodity which is being measured or from those of the measuring standard (Woods, 1990, p. 58; Sraffa, 1960, p. 18).

Ricardo's solution to the problem was to consider a hypothetical "invariable standard of value" which would be free of any such "peculiarities."

These "peculiarities" arise due to the inequality of the proportions in which labor and capital are employed in the various industries. It is not simply the case that a wage increase will lead to an increase in the price of the product of an industry with a relatively high ratio of labor to means of production and a fall in the price of a product of an industry with a relatively low ratio of labor to means of production. The relative price movements might be precisely the reverse.

> The reason for this seeming contradiction is that the means of production of an industry are themselves the product of one or more industries which may in their turn employ a still lower proportion of labour to means of production (and the same may be the case with these latter means of production) (Sraffa, 1960, p. 14).

Sraffa's solution to the problem is his Standard commodity. This is a composite commodity

which consists of the same commodities (combined in the same proportions) as does the
aggregate of its own means of production—in other words, such that both product and
means of production are quantities of the self-same composite commodity.

The question is, can such a commodity be constructed (Sraffa, 1960, p. 19)?
Sraffa maintains that such a commodity can be constructed and that it is free
of the troublesome "peculiarities."

Although Woods appears to understand the purpose of having an "invariable
measure of value" in the sense described by Ricardo and Sraffa, he obscures
the project when he states of the Standard commodity: "Trivially, if chosen
as numeraire, it would be invariable—an observation that applies to any
numeraire" (Woods, 1990, p. 65). Apparently he means that if the absolute
value of one commodity is fixed arbitrarily as a standard in which the relative
values of other commodities can be measured, then the absolute value of the
commodity is fixed. This, however, is different from the problem at issue as
it has been traditionally discussed, that is, the problem of finding a commodity
the relative value of which is invariant with respect to changes in the distribution
of income. This is not a property of any numeraire.

Sraffa begins with a system that produces iron, coal, and wheat in the
following manner:

90 t. iron + 120 t. coal + 60 qr. wheat + 3/16 labor —> 180 t. iron
50 t. iron + 125 t. coal + 150 qr. wheat + 5/16 labor —> 450 t. coal
40 t. iron + 40 t. coal + 200 qr. wheat + 8/16 labor —> 480 t. wheat

Giving in total 180 t. iron, 285, t. coal, 410 qr. wheat, and 1 unit of labor.
The Standard system derived from this system is

90 t. iron + 120 t. coal + 60 qr. wheat + 3/16 labor —> 180 t. iron
30 t. iron + 75 t. coal + 90 qr. wheat + 3/16 labor —> 270 t. coal
30 t. iron + 30 t. coal + 150 qr. wheat + 6/16 labor —> 3600 t. wheat

The proportions in which the three commodities are produced in the new
system (180:270:360) are equal to those in which they enter its aggregate means
of production (150:225:300). The composite commodity sought for is
accordingly made up in the proportions

1 t. iron:1 1/2 t. coal: 2 qr. wheat.

The Standard commodity, therefore, consists of iron, coal and wheat in these
proportions.

The logic behind choosing such a commodity to solve the problem of price
fluctuations consequent upon a change in the distribution of income can be

illustrated with Sraffa's notion of surplus and deficit industries. Suppose that prices remained constant in the face of a decrease in wages and, correspondingly, an increase in the rate of profits.

> Since in any one industry what was saved by the wage-reduction would depend on the number of men employed, while what was needed for paying profits at a uniform rate would depend on the aggregate value of the means of production used, industries with a sufficiently low proportion of labour to means of production would have a deficit, while industries with a sufficiently high proportion would have a surplus, on their payments for wages and profits (Sraffa, 1960, p. 13).

The Standard commodity simulates the product of a hypothetical industry that has a proportion of labor to means of production which is a "medium" between the surplus and deficit industries. Following a wage reduction, such an industry "would show an even balance—the proceeds of the wage-reduction would provide exactly what was required for the payment of profits at the general rate."

Woods claims to have found a counter-example in which the Standard commodity does not "show an even balance" but is instead a "surplus" industry. He begins with the system:

$$1 \text{ t. iron} + 1/2 \text{ labor} \longrightarrow 1 \text{ qr. wheat}$$
$$1/4 \text{ qr. wheat} + 1/2 \text{ labor} \longrightarrow 1 \text{ t. iron}$$

and derives the Standard system

$$2/3 \text{ t. iron} + 1/3 \text{ labor} \longrightarrow 2/3 \text{ qr. wheat}$$
$$1/3 \text{ qr. wheat} + 2/3 \text{ labor} \longrightarrow 4/3 \text{ t. iron}$$

These Standard quantity equations give price equations

$$((2/3)p_2)(1 + r) + 1/3w = 2/3p_w$$
$$((1/3)p_1)(1 + r) + 2/3w = 4/3p_i$$

Woods assumes that the initial distribution of income has the rate of profit $r^1 = 0$ and wage $w^1 = 1$; therefore the price of wheat is equal to $4/3$ and the price of iron is $5/6$.

Next assume, following Woods, that the rate of profits rises to $r^2 = 1/10$. What is the appropriate corresponding wage to use? Woods acknowledges that the validity of his counter-example hinges on the choice of the wage. Woods chooses to use $279/315$ as the new wage.[2] He derives that as follows: from the original system he gets price equations

$$(1+r)p_2 + w_y/2 = p_1 \qquad\qquad (5.32a)$$
$$(1+r)p_1/4 + w_y/2 = p_2 \qquad\qquad (5.32b)$$

Using the net output of the original system as numeraire implies

$$3p_1/4 = 1 \qquad\qquad (5.31)$$

Where $p_1$ is the price of wheat, $p_2$ is the price of iron, and $w_y$ is the real wage. From (5.31) and (5.32) he obtains an equation representing the wage profit-tradeoff

$$w_y = (1-(1+r)^2/4)/(3(r+2)/8) \qquad\qquad (5.33a)$$

which, with $r^2 = 1/10$, gives $w_y = 279/315$. With this result, the revenues of the Standard system are greater than its costs, implying that rather than having an "even balance" following the wage reduction, the Standard system is a "surplus industry."

Woods notes "one caveat", viz., that it is possible to find a wage rate that would generate Sraffa's desired result, that the Standard system break even with the new distribution of income and the original prices, in this case 9/10; but Woods claims that with respect to "[w]hich wage rate should be chosen...Sraffa throws no light on the question" (Woods, 1990, p. 70).

This calls for two comments. First, the choice of 279/315 for the new wage is mistaken: It is obtained with equation (5.33a), which is derived from equations (5.32). These latter equations, however, are mutually inconsistent in the case under consideration, that is, with the original prices and with the new rate of profit $r^2 = 1/10$: at these values equation (5.32a) gives $w_y = 5/6$ and equation (5.32b) gives $w_y = 14/15$.

Second, although Sraffa does not address the issue explicitly, he does "throw light on the question." Throughout the book Sraffa assumes that the whole of the surplus is distributed between wages and profits. In the case of Woods' example, in the Standard system at the original prices, with the rate of profit $r_2 = 1/10$, total profits are

$$(2p_2/3 + p_1/3)(1/10) = 1/10$$

The value of the net output is equal to one by the definition of the numeraire (5.31). Hence, after total profits are deducted, there remains 9/10 of net output to be distributed to one unit of labor, necessitating a wage rate of 9/10. This is precisely the wage rate which, according to Woods, sustains Sraffa's result. Thus, Woods' claim to "have raised doubts about Sraffa's method of constructing the Standard Commodity" must be rejected.

# IV.   RESWITCHING OF TECHNIQUES

Considering the tremendous volume of literature to which Sraffa's discussion of "Switch in the Methods of Production" has given rise, it is remarkable that Sraffa himself devotes only six and one-half pages to his chapter with that title. Woods' chapter on "Choice of Technique" runs about 50 pages; there he describes the nature of the problem of different methods of production; analyzes the problem in a very simple case; generalizes the simple case; and explores the implications of the analytical results.

Reswitching of techniques occurs when it is most profitable to choose one technique at two distinct levels of the rate of profits when there is a different technique which is most profitable at intermediate rates of profits.

The implication to which Woods justly devotes the most attention concerns the relationship between the quantity of a commodity used as an input into production and its price. According to standard neoclassical theory, the relationship should be inverse, that is, as the quantity used of a factor increases, the amount that a firm or an industry is willing to pay should be decreasing. This relationship is expressed in the downward sloping firm or industry demand curve for a factor.

Reswitching implies that the price of a particular produced input (or even a non-produced input) need not exhibit an inverse or monotonic relationship between its price and the quantity employed in production. Woods also shows that although reswitching is a sufficient condition for the absence of an inverse monotonic relationship between the quantity of a commodity employed in production and its price, it is not a necessary condition.

As Woods notes, the failure of the claim that the quantity of an input employed and its price have an inverse monotonic relationship has considerable import for conventional microeconomics: "In particular, the notion of substitution—which seems to rely on the changes in input quantities being in the opposite direction to the respective price changes—is called into question" (Woods, 1990, p. 117).

That the demand curve for a factor should slope downward and therefore that the relationship between the quantity of an input employed and its price should be inverse, is also a central aspect of the theory of derived demand. According to this theory, which was an essential aspect by which the early marginalist writers distinguished their theory from that of Ricardo and his followers, the value of "factors" of production derive their value from that of "final" products. Wieser writes:

> The classical political economy really examines only the value of...produced consumption goods. So far as factors of production are concerned, it looks upon them, on the one side, as sources of income...: on the other side as the elements which go to form the *costs of production, and are considered to decide, principally, the value of the products.*

> But when one compares with this the endeavors which, explicitly or implicitly, guide the new writers on the theory of value, we find... the relations between the values of utilities and the value of production goods is turned just the other way about—the former being considered as determining, the latter as determined... the proposition which may serve as a starting-point for the whole theory... [is] that *production goods receive their value from the value of products which they serve to create.* Gossen, Jevons, Menger, and Walras are all agreed on this point (Wieser, 1956, p. 71, n. 1.).

Thus, reswitching of techniques points to a fundamental critique of the conventional theory of value, for without the demand for factors analysis, the supply and demand explanation for the determination of relative prices is left with a gaping hole.

The analysis of reswitching of techniques also has implications for macroeconomic theory, insofar as the aggregate demand curve for labor is thought to play some role in determining the level of employment: "I have shown... that the aggregate demand curve is not downward sloping in the presence of reswitching: indeed... it is not even monotonic. Reswitching is sufficient, not necessary, for the aggregate demand curve for labour not to be downward-sloping" (Woods, 1990, p. 117).[3]

Sections 7.4 to 7.6 of Woods book provide a very useful extension of the analysis of choice of technique. Here the notion of capital reversal is introduced, which involves a shift to a technique of production with a larger capital to output ratio following an increase in the rate of profit. Standard neoclassical microeconomics suggests, on the contrary, that an increase in the rate of profit should lead to a shift toward a less "capital intensive" technique. Woods demonstrates that reswitching is a necessary but not sufficient condition for capital reversal. Moreover, both reswitching and capital reversal generate non-concavities in aggregate production functions. Woods concludes that much of traditional macroeconomics and growth theory are called into question.

# V. MULTIPLE PRODUCT INDUSTRIES

In Chapters 8 to 11 Woods follows Sraffa in the extension of the original single product industries to a multi-product industries system. Sraffa treats fixed capital, following Torrens and Ricardo, as a joint product. That is, the product of labor and an n year old piece of capital is considered to be output plus an n+1 year old piece of capital.

Woods's chapter on Fixed Capital begins with an examination of a method of treating fixed capital which is an alternative to that proposed by Sraffa, viz., the method of a priori specified mortality coefficients. The point of doing this is to demonstrate its inadequacy, "To impose a priori specified mortality coefficients as part of a general treatment of fixed capital cannot be justified on theoretical grounds because the profitability of a machine, and hence its economic lifetime, depend on prices; the imposition of mortality coefficients means that the lifetime of each sector has been specified at the outset without regard to essential economic considerations" (Woods, 1990, p. 173). This point is important but not necessarily obvious to a reader of Sraffa's *Production of Commodities*.

The method of considering fixed capital as a joint product, as Woods demonstrates, following Sraffa, provides an "acceptable" and "proper" treatment. As opposed to the mortality coefficients approach, the fixed capital approach does take the essentially economic aspects of the problem into account. Woods begins with the solution of an extremely simple model of fixed capital as a joint product; then he deals with the problem of negative old machine prices and choice of technique, and finally discusses various generalizations of the model.

Woods undertakes a similarly detailed analysis in his chapter on land. Following Sraffa, he examines extensive rent and intensive rent, including the question of choice of technique. Woods substantiates Ricardo's claim that 'Corn is not high because a rent is paid, but a rent is paid because corn is high'; but he refutes Ricardo's claim that lands of different quality can be ranked according to a technically given order of fertility and that this order will correspond to an ordering according to the level of rents paid for use of the various lands. On the contrary, it turns out that, in general, the order of fertility depends on prices and the distribution of income. This is a very interesting and significant result that has not received much attention in the literature.

In contrast with Sraffa, Woods discusses the general case of joint production after he discusses the special cases of land and fixed capital. This appears to be the result of a difference in emphasis: whereas Sraffa writes that "the interest of Joint Products does not lie so much in the familiar examples of wool and mutton, or wheat and straw, as its being the genus of which Fixed Capital is the leading species" (Sraffa, 1960, p. 63), Woods seems to attach considerable importance to "intrinsic joint production" of the wool and mutton variety.

The major interest of Woods' Chapter 12, in which intrinsic joint production is discussed, is Woods' claim to have found errors in Sraffa's analysis. First, Woods claims that "[i]n section 96 of PCMC, Sraffa argued that the cost minimizing technique could be identified as that supporting the highest real wage. The numerical example, (11.43), demonstrates Sraffa's arguments to be false in the joint production case" (p. 280). The method is again one of providing counter-examples: "...if negative results are to be derived, the provision of appropriate numerical examples suffices" (p. 278). While this method is legitimate, the example upon which Woods rests his claim, (11.43), does not "suffice."

Woods' example (11.43) is as follows. Consider the technology:[4]

    (I) 3 t. iron + 4 cwt. coal + 1 labor —> 6 t. iron + 5 cwt. coal
    (IIg) 2 t. iron + 3 cwt. coal + 1 labor —> 3 t. iron + 8 cwt. coal
    (IId) 3 t. iron + 2 cwt. coal + 1 labor —> 5 t. iron + 6 cwt. coal

Letting iron be the numeraire he derives the price of coal $p$ and the wage $w$ for each of the two techniques $g$ and $d$ made up of process (I) and (IIg) and process (I) and (IId) respectively:

$$p^g = (2\text{-}r)/(4 + r)$$
$$w^g = (14\text{-}18r + r^2)/(4 + r) \text{ and} \qquad\qquad (11.44)$$
$$p^d = 1/(3 + 2r)$$
$$w^d = (10\text{-}7r\text{-}6r^2)/(3 + 2r). \qquad\qquad (11.45)$$

In order to determine which technique is more profitable, Woods compares the surplus or loss relative to normal profits of method d at the prices of system g and of method g at the prices of system d. This criterion seems to give the same answers as Sraffa's method in the examples cited, but is difficult to understand why anyone would care about the profits of a technique under a price system with which it is inconsistent. It is apparently intended to simulate the choice a firm would make based on the irrational assumption that the introduction of a new technique would not lead to changes in the system of relative prices.

Switch-points occur when it is equally profitable to produce with more than one technique at a given rate of profits. "[S]uch points necessarily have also the same commodity-wage and the same system of relative prices"(Sraffa, 1960, p. 82). From the price equations it can be seen that in this example there are no switch-points.

Equating (11.44) and (11.45) Woods finds that the wage-profit curves intersect at $r = 1/4$, which, given that there are no switch points, is certainly not a switch-point. For $r < 1/4$, technique g supports the higher real wage, and for $r > 1/4$, technique d supports the higher real wage. For $r < 1/4$, then, g is not the cost minimizing technique, but it does support the higher real wage. Thus, Woods concludes, Sraffa's argument "that the cost-minimising technique could be identified as that supporting the highest real wage," is contradicted.

Yet to draw this conclusion is to misunderstand Sraffa's statement in section 96. In that section he is dealing with the problem of determining which process of production will be superseded when a switch in methods of production does occur. In the single product industry case, alternative techniques produce the same product. Therefore, the technique which produces more profitably and at a lower cost can be identified immediately as the one which generates the lowest price for that product.

In the multiple-product industries case the situation is more complex, because there may be several processes which produce the same commodities in different proportions. Thus, it may not be obvious when a new lower cost process becomes available, which process is to be superseded.

Sraffa's argument runs as follows (p. 86): Begin by considering "that rate of profits at which *each* of the...commodities is produced, whether by the new method or by the old ones, at the same price," that is, a switch-point. At this point, the wage and the rate of profits, as well as the system of relative prices, will be the same for all of the different techniques.

"Suppose now that the rate of profits is raised by a very small fraction above that point. For all the...systems the resulting wage will be lower than before: but it will be different for each of the systems." The method to be superseded is the one excluded from the system with the highest wage, because that system is the most profitable. "If we regard the wage, instead of the rate of profits, as being given, we shall find that this system will...be the most profitable one since, given *any* of those wages, it will allow the payment of a higher rate of profits than does any other system."

In general Sraffa argues that comparisons of profitability are impossible across different relative price systems. At switch-points meaningful comparisons can be made, and also at points very close to switch-points. This is because within a very small neighborhood of a switch-point the differences between the relative price systems can be made arbitrarily small. It is therefore essential for Sraffa's claim that the rate of profits be in the neighborhood, a "very small fraction" above a switch-point.

In Woods' alleged counter-example there is no switch-point, hence there is no neighborhood around a switch-point, above or below. The context with which Woods concerns himself, and in which he claims to have found an error in Sraffa's analysis, is different in essential aspects from the context with which Sraffa is concerned. The alleged counter-example turns out not to be a counter-example at all, and does not serve to show that Sraffa's analysis is mistaken.

Interestingly, Woods misattributes to Sraffa precisely the false assumption that would make his own counter-example valid. Woods claims that Sraffa "identifies intersections between w-r curves as switch-points between techniques" (Woods, 1990, p. 289). If such an identification could be made, then Woods' "counter-example," which includes an intersection between w-r curves but no switch-point, would be justified. Yet Sraffa does not make this identification and Woods provides no textual reference for his assertion. Sraffa implies that w-r curve intersections occur at switch-points, but he does not suggest that switch-points necessarily occur at w-r curve intersections.

Woods also takes issue with Sraffa's exclusion of production processes which generate negative prices. After noting the possibility of negative prices Sraffa says:

> This conclusion is not in itself very startling. All that it implies is that, although in actual fact all prices were positive, a change in the wage might create a situation the logic of which

required some of the prices to turn negative; and this being unacceptable, those among the methods of production that give rise to such a result would be discarded to make room for others which in the new situation were consistent with positive prices (Woods, 1990, p. 287; Sraffa, 1960, p. 59).

Woods claims that "[t]he only reason for a change in the process of production is that capitalists have a cheaper alternative." Hence he interprets Sraffa's statement to mean that "... a positive price system comes about ... through cost minimisation." Woods produces an example in which negative prices are cost minimizing, and therefore claims that Sraffa is mistaken.

But Sraffa never makes the argument which is attributed to him; he merely says that negative prices are "unacceptable." Previously Sraffa said that "only those methods of production are *practicable* which ... do not involve other than positive prices" (Sraffa, 1960, p. 44, emphasis added). It would seem quite reasonable to base this claim on experience: no cost minimization argument is required.

Apparently Woods, as opposed to Sraffa, believes that negative prices are acceptable and practicable; but he provides no explanation for this curious view. Given the absence of negative prices in the world of experience, it would seem that Woods has proved either that his claim that changes in the process of production only occur for cost minimization reasons is wrong, or that his example is irrelevant.

Thus, while there may be problems with Sraffa's analysis of choice of technique for joint production, Woods has failed to find any. His claim that Sraffa's theory presented in section 96 is "erroneous" must be rejected.

## VI. RETURNS TO SCALE

The "never ending debate" (Levine, 1990, p. 161) over the role of the assumption of constant returns in *PCMC* is now almost 30 years old.[5] In accordance with the recommendation of Keynes, Sraffa included an "emphatic warning" in the preface that the assumption is not implicit in his analysis, "no such assumption is made" (Sraffa, 1960, p. v). Woods makes the assumption nevertheless, appealing to the authority of Pasinetti and Garegnani, but offering no explanation for its inclusion in his "Introduction to Sraffa."[6]

Sraffa states that if the assumption of constant returns "... is found helpful there is no harm in the reader's adopting it as a temporary working hypothesis" (Sraffa, 1960, p. v, emphasis added). The word "temporary" implies that it must eventually be jettisoned, that is, that there is harm if it is maintained more than temporarily. Hence despite its explicit intent to the contrary, Woods' analysis seems to ignore "what Sraffa actually said."

Keynes' suggestion apparently followed from his acceptance of Marshall's interpretation of Ricardo.[7] Jevons had claimed that Ricardo, "... shunted the car of Economic science on to a wrong line..." (Jevons, 1965, p. li)," due to the determining role of costs of production in Ricardo's theory of value. Marshall argued, in opposition to Jevons, that Ricardo's theory of value was essentially no different from his own (Marshall, 1961, Appendix I).[8]

In Marshall's marginal utility theory of value, the role of demand in price determination is closely bound up with questions of returns to scale: long run price depends on unit costs; unit costs depend on scale; scale depends on demand and utility. In the framework of this theory this chain can be broken and demand can be ignored in the determination of value if constant returns is assumed. Thus, in order to argue that Ricardo's theory was simply a special case of his own, Marshall attributed to Ricardo a tacit assumption of constant returns to scale (Marshall, 1961, p. 814). Keynes seems to have foreseen that Sraffa's apparent neglect of demand would be viewed as "neo-Ricardian" by "neo-Marshallians," who would be inclined to see the same tacit assumption.

Sraffa therefore implicitly takes issue with Marshall's interpretation of Ricardo, other aspects of which he disputes in his Introduction to Ricardo's *Principles*. Sraffa's insistent warning implies that the failure of demand to play an important role in *PCMC* is not because it represents a special case of marginal utility theory, but rather because it represents something fundamentally distinct.

The effects of changes in scale are avoided because the analysis in *PCMC* abstracts from changes in demand: the composition of output is taken as given and fixed. Sraffa gives us no reason to think that it is not determined by demand; nor does he argue that demands never change in the world of experience or that variable returns to scale would have no effect on prices if the composition of demand were to change. He simply does not address the issue in his book.

Sraffa examines the effect of changes in demand on prices in his 1926 article. There he points out that due to the interconnectedness of production, if one does not assume constant returns, then in general there are no simple statements which can be made about relative price movements consequent upon a change in the composition of demand. This excludes statements characteristic of Marshallian partial equilibrium analysis, for example, an increase in the demand for good X ceteris paribus, leads to an increase in the price of good X.

In general, due to the interconnectedness of production, any influence that returns to scale are likely to have on the costs of one commodity is likely to be just as great on other commodities:

> [The Marshallian] point of view assumes that the conditions of production and the demand for a commodity can be considered, in respect to small variations, as being practically independent, both in regard to each other and in relation to the supply and demand for all other commodities... But..the assumption becomes illegitimate, when a variation in the

quantity produced by the industry under consideration sets up a force which acts directly, not merely on its own costs, but also upon the costs of other industries (Sraffa, 1926, pp. 538-539).

Hence if a change in demand occurs such that variable returns to scale are significant, then the prices of several commodities are likely to be affected. If the prices of several commodities are affected, and in varying degrees, then statements about relative price changes, for example, an increase in the price of good X, become problematic. An increase in demand for good X need not lead to an increase in its price relative to all other goods. It might lead to an increase in price relative to some commodities and a fall relative to others.

The one case in which this will not happen is the case in which the relevant economies or diseconomies of scale "are external from the point of view of the individual firm, but internal as regards the industry in the aggregate" (Sraffa, 1926, p. 540). That is, as the scale of output increases, the kinds of economies which are permissible from the Marshallian partial equilibrium point of view are only those which are peculiar to an industry. If they are not "external from the point of view of the individual firm," then they will not affect all producers of a commodity, and therefore will have no general effect on price; if they are not "internal as regards the industry in the aggregate," then they are not conclusively determinative of the relative price of a particular commodity. According to Sraffa, such economies "constitute precisely the class which is most seldom to be met with."

Sraffa concludes from the fact that in the presence of variable returns there are no simple statements to be made regarding the effects of changes in demand on the system of relative prices, that "as a simple way of approaching the problem of competitive value, the old and now obsolete theory which makes it dependent on the cost of production alone appears to hold its ground as the best available" (Sraffa, 1926, p 541). The argument is not that constant returns characterize the world of experience, only that variable returns are not adequate for the purposes of Marshallian analysis.

## VII. REDUCTION TO DATED LABOR AND COMMODITY RESIDUE

It is somewhat surprising that a book devoted to "what Sraffa actually said" fails to include any discussion of the "Reduction to dated quantities of labor."

Sraffa relates his discussion of "Reduction" to a criticism made by Marx throughout *Capital and Theories of Surplus-Value*, of the treatment of reproduction in the analysis of classical political economy after Adam Smith. Although the influence of Quesnay can be found in the work of Smith and Ricardo, Marx considered Smith and Ricardo to have taken a step backwards in their understanding of reproduction.

Marx writes of "...an incredible blunder in analysis, which pervades all political economy since Adam Smith" (Marx, 1967, Vol. III, p. 815), as he refers to "...the fundamentally erroneous dogma to the effect that the value of commodities in the last analysis may be resolved into wages + profit + rent" (p. 821) without any 'commodity residue.' Smith claims that

> In every society the price of every commodity finally resolves itself into some one or other, or all those three parts [viz. wages, profits, rent]...A fourth part it may be thought, is necessary for replacing the stock of the farmer or for compensating the wear and tear of his labouring cattle, and other instruments of husbandry. But it must be considered that the price of any instrument of husbandry, such as a labouring horse, is itself made up of the same three parts: the rent of the land upon which he is reared, the labour of tending and rearing him, and the profits of the farmer, who advances both the rent of his land and the wages of his labour. Though the price of corn, therefore, may pay the price as well as the maintenance of the horse, the whole price still resolves itself either immediately or ultimately into the same three parts of rent, labour and profit (Marx, 1967, Vol. II, p. 373, Vol. III, p. 821; Marx, 1968, Vol. I, p. 98; Sraffa, 1960, p. 94).

Marx comments on this passage as follows:

> This is verbatim all that Adam Smith has to say in support of his astonishing doctrine. His proof consists simply in the repetition of the same assertion...The contention that the entire price of commodities resolves itself "immediately or ultimately" into v + s would not be a hollow subterfuge only if he were able to demonstrate that the commodities whose price resolves itself immediately into c (price of consumed means of production) + v +s, are ultimately compensated by commodities which replace those "consumed means of production," and which are themselves produced by the mere outlay of variable capital, i.e., by a mere investment of capital in labour power. The price of these last commodities would then be v + s. Consequently the price of the former, c + v + s...would also be ultimately resolvable into v + s (Marx, 1967, Vol. II, pp. 373-374).

The price equation for commodity A to be associated with Smith's analysis is

$$(A_a p_a + B_a p_a + \ldots + K_a p_k)(r) + L_a w = A p_a$$

rather than the equation

$$(A_a p_a + B_a p_a + \ldots + K_a p_k)(1 + r) + L_a w = A p_a.$$

The difference between these two equations is the term

$$(A_a p_a + B_a p_a + \ldots + K_a p_k)$$

which is analogous to what Marx calls 'constant capital'. Constant capital is characteristic of an economy that reproduces itself, and constitutes the quantitative link between the condition of reproduction and the value of commodities. It enters into the value of commodities representing the value of commodities used up in the production process and which therefore must be reproduced. It is not relevant if and only if reproduction is inessential.

Sraffa's 'Reduction' proceeds as follows: "Take the equation which represents the production of commodity 'a'...:[9]

$$(A_a p_a + B_a p_a + \ldots + K_a p_k)(1+r) + L_a w = A p_a.$$

> We begin by replacing the commodities forming the means of production of A with *their own* means of production and quantities of labour; that is to say, we replace them with the commodities and labour which, as appears from their own respective equations, must be employed to produce those means of production; and they, having been expended a year earlier, will be multiplied by a profit factor at a compound rate for the appropriate period, namely the means of production by $(1+r)^2$ and the labour by $(1+r)$. (Sraffa, 1960, p. 34).

This process is then repeated by replacing these latter means of production with their own means of production and labor, multiplying by the appropriate 'profit factor' for one more year, $(1 + r)^3$ for the means of production and $(1 + r)^2$ for the labor. This process can be repeated indefinitely such that a 'reduction equation' for product 'a' can be written as an infinite series

$$L_a w + L_{a1} w (1 + r) + \ldots + L_{a1} w (1 + r)^n + \ldots = A p_a^{10}$$

> How far the reduction need be pushed in order to obtain a given degree of approximation depends on the level of the rate of profits...Beside the labor terms there will always be a 'commodity residue' consisting of minute fractions of every basic product; but it is always possible...to render the residue so small as to have...a negligible effect on price (Sraffa, 1960, p. 35).

This represents a formal statement of the process that Smith suggested in the passage cited above. The produced means of production are 'reduced' to the value of their means of production and labor.

> Samuelson takes this to mean that Marx's criticism of Smith is mistaken:...Marx's erroneous belief that Adam Smith cheated in claiming to break down a good's price and a society's national income into the eclectic triad of wage component, land-rent component and interest component. Marx suspected that a fourth component of used-up capital goods somehow escaped inclusion... (Samuelson, 1990, p. 266).

But, this analysis only applies in the case of single product industries. With joint production, and especially with fixed capital, which is treated as a species of joint production,[11] the situation is different. "The equations for fixed capital make it easy to see how an attempt to effect the 'reduction' of a durable instrument to a series of dated labour quantities will in general fail."[12]

Sraffa's analysis thus shows that Marx's criticism of Smith and Ricardo is correct and that Samuelson's criticism of Marx is incorrect; not that Ricardo is necessarily guilty of excluding fixed capital, only that in a system which reproduces itself one component of the value of each commodity is 'constant capital', that element over and above factor costs which accounts for the replacement of the means of production consumed in the production process. Moreover, that element does not "resolve itself" into factor income as Adam Smith believed. This is absolutely clear in the case with fixed capital, which is certainly the case that Marx had in mind, but even in the case without fixed capital, Sraffa shows that "there will always be a 'commodity residue'..." Hence in the value of total output and in the value of individual commodities there must be included an element of 'constant capital'.

## VIII.  CONCLUSION

John E. Woods' *Production of Commodities: An Introduction to Sraffa* is a useful and simple account of some of the technical issues involved in Sraffa's analysis. It contains numerous examples and exercises which are very useful for getting a firm grasp on the mathematical subtleties. It is quite rigorous and considers its material in considerable detail. The book also contains a relatively simple and straightforward discussion of the implications of reswitching and capital reversal for conventional micro- and macroeconomics. And it achieves all this without making any great mathematical demands on the reader and without assuming any familiarity with Sraffa's work.

In accordance with its goal, it focuses more on "what Sraffa actually said" than Pasinetti's *Lectures on the Theory of Production* or Mainwaring's *Value and Distribution in Capitalist Economies: An Introduction to Sraffian Economics* and it contains less explicit interpretation than Roncaglia's *Sraffa and the Theory of Prices*.

Nevertheless, the book has important limitations. As described above, there are several places in which the mathematical treatment is less than completely satisfactory. The book does contain an implicit assumption that orthodox methodological concerns, in particular, existence results, are of great significance for Sraffa's analysis. It also presents some ideas not found in Sraffa, for example, that the analysis of $PCMC$ should be viewed as a positive theory rather than as simply providing the basis for a critique and an analysis of the implications of a growing labor force. The book also fails to discuss several key issues that are included in $PCMC$, for example, the significance of the absence of the assumption of constant returns to scale and Reduction to dated quantities of labor.

# NOTES

1.   Results 2, 4, 6, 8, 11, 15, 16, 17, 18, 19, 20, and 21 are all existence results.

2.   The number that appears in the book is 275/315, but this appears to be a typographical error, as it is inconsistent both with the equation from which Woods claims to have derived it, and with the results he derives from it.

3   Cf. John Weeks, 1989, pp. 157-161.

4   What is given differs slightly from the example actually given by Woods—the term "4 cwt. coal" in the input to process I is "6 cwt. coal" in the text—but this is apparently an error, as the rest of the analysis follows only if the correct number is 4.

5.   Alternatively, it might be said that the debate dates from Sraffa's discussion with Keynes in 1928, or as will be discussed below, from Marshall's discussion of Ricardo in the famous Appendix I of his *Principles of Economics*.

6.   Garegnani and Pasinetti do not accept that the assumption of constant returns to scale is required for PCMC. While perhaps they adopt it in various other contexts, both accept Sraffa's claim.

7.   In 1924 Keynes had been certain that Marshall was correct on this point (Keynes, 1951, p. 182); but by 1936 he entertained doubts (Keynes, 1951, pp. 290-291).

8.   Cf. J.A. Schumpeter, 1954, pp. 920-921.

9.   The wage and prices are expressed in terms of Sraffa's 'Standard commodity'.

10.   Where the $L_{ai}$'s are the successive aggregate quantities of labor collected at each step.

11.   Following Torrens, see Sraffa, 1960, pp. 94-95.

12.   "To take the simplest case, suppose that a machine has a life of two years and its efficiency is constant. The equations would be

$$(M_0 p_{m0} + A_g p_a + B_g p_a + \ldots + K_g p_k)(1 + r) + L_g w = G_{(g)} p_g + M_1 p_{m1}$$
$$(M_1 p_{m1} + A_g p_a + B_g p_a + \ldots + K_g p_k)(1 + r) + L_g w = G_{(g)} p_g$$

"Now the first step toward the 'reduction' of the one-year-old machines $M_1$ to a series of labor terms is to subtract the second equation from the first so as to isolate $M_1$, leaving it as the sole product on the right-hand side. As a result of this there appears a similar quantity $M_1$ among the means of production; it has, however, a negative sign and its price is multiplied by $(1 + r)$.

This is by itself sufficient to show that we are engaged in a blind alley: for when we come to the 'reduction' of the negative term containing $M_1$, there will appear among its residual means of production a positive $M_1$; and so, with successive steps, $M_1$ will constantly reappear, alternately positive and negative, and in each case multiplied by a higher power of $(1 + r)$. This will make it impossible on the one hand for the residual aggregate of commodities to tend to vanishing-point and on the other for the sum of labour terms to tend to a limit" (Sraffa, 1960, pp. 67-68).

# REFERENCES

Bharadwaj, Krishna and Schefold, Bertram. 1990. *Essays on Piero Sraffa: Critical Perspectives on the Revival of Classical Theory*. London: Unwin Hyman.

Blaug, Mark. 1985. *Economic Theory in Retrospect*. Cambridge: Cambridge University Press.

Jevons, William Stanley. 1957. *Theory of Political Economy*. New York: Sentry Press.

Keynes, John Maynard. 1951. *Essays in Biography*. New York: Norton.

Levine, A.L. 1990. "The Sraffa Model, Constant Returns to Scale and Empirical Implications." In *Essays on Piero Sraffa*, edited by B. Schefold and K. Bharadwaj.

Mainwaring, Lynn. 1984. *Value and Distribution in Capitalist Economies: An Introduction to Sraffian Economics*. Cambridge: Cambridge University Press.

Marshall, Alfred. 1961. *Principles of Economics*. London: Macmillan.

Marx, Karl. 1967. *Capital*. New York: International Publishers.

———. 1968. *Theories of Surplus-Value*. Moscow: Progress.

McCloskey, Donald. 1985. *The Rhetoric of Economics*. Madison: University of Wisconsin Press.

Pasinetti, Luigi. 1977. *Lectures in the Theory of Production*. New York: Columbia University Press.

Roncaglia, Alessandro. 1978. *Sraffa and the Theory of Prices*. New York: Wiley.

Samuelson, Paul. 1987. "Sraffian Economics." In *The New Palgrave Dictionary of Economics*, edited by J. Eatwell, M. Milgate, P. Newman.

———. 1990. "Revisionist Findings on Sraffa."

Schumpeter, J.A. 1954. *The History of Economic Analysis*. New York: Oxford University Press.

Sraffa, Piero. 1926. "Laws of Returns under Competitive Conditions," 1926: December. *Economic Journal*. 36: 535-550.

———. 1960. *Production of Commodities by Means of Commodities: Prelude to a Critique of Economic Theory*. New York: Cambridge University Press.

Weeks, John. 1989. *A Critique of Neoclassical Macroeconomics*. New York: St. Martin's Press.

Woods, John E. 1990. *The Production of Commodities: An Introduction to Sraffa*. Atlantic Highlands, NJ: Humanities Press International.

# The History of the International Association of Agricultural Economists.
# Towards Rural Welfare Worldwide

by J.A. Raeburn and J.O. Jones
(Brookfield, MA: Dartmouth Publishing Company; 1990, 187 pp.)

Review by **A.W. Coats**

Generally speaking many, if not most, professional economists have tended to regard their agricultural counterparts as a separate, if not alien and inferior breed; and it is certainly true that as a segment within the larger disciplinary community agricultural economics has had a quite distinctive organizational, sociological and intellectual development. Although there were, as always, antecedents, agricultural economics emerged as the most clearly identifiable and organizationally distinct subdiscipline of economics immediately after World War I and soon acquired a unique role as a species of expertise within national governments in the United States and the United Kingdom (although there were doubtless well-established precedents in continental European countries). As a field it has always been heavily applied problem-and policy-oriented, hence its inferior status among mainstream economists who generally regard high theory as the Ark of the Intellectual Covenant; and to the best of my knowledge of continuing international organizational history that is presented in the volume under review.

Institutional histories do not often make exciting reading, and that generalization is not disconfirmed by Raeburn and Jones's volume. However, their approach is by no means uncritical and the book is full of invaluable information about the strains and stresses as well as the achievements in the 60 year record of conferences and publications. This small (especially in the print) book is full of useful factual information about personalities, papers delivered, topics discussed, problems of finance and government discrimination against unwelcome foreign scholars, and so forth. The organization's records

**Research in the History of Economic Thought and Methodology,**
**Volume 13, pages 249-250.**
Copyright © 1995 by JAI Press Inc.
All rights of reproduction in any form reserved.
ISBN: 1-55938-095-0

have obviously been faithfully preserved, for there are numerous tables and graphs of membership and conference attendees; and, in one Chapter, to illustrate the intellectual activities involved, there is a careful and revealing effort to produce systematic content analysis of a series of conferences on two particular topics: "deep poverty in rural areas of the tropics and subtropics" (p. 63ff), and "human birth and death rates" (p. 71ff). The second of these demonstrates a point frequently made in the text, namely that agricultural economics is a multidisciplinary field involving "holistic thinking" (pp. 63, 82, 164); and one is reminded of the high praise bestowed on the field by Wassily Leontief in his provocative Presidential Address to the American Economic Association.[1]

As might be expected, given the opening remarks of this review, there is little evidence of close relations between the International Association of Agricultural Economists and other economists' organizations, whether at the national or international level. However, the roster of speakers listed includes a significant number of very distinguished economists, several of them Nobel prizewinners whose major works fall squarely within the AEE's subject area.

There are, of course, colorful characters and charming anecdotes. But it is more important to stress the solid contribution to disciplinary and professional history this volume contains. It is to be hoped that other subdisciplines in economics will soon produce their own historians.

## NOTE

1.   An exceptional example of a healthy balance between theoretical and empirical analysis and of the readiness of professional economists to cooperate with experts in the neighboring disciplines is offered by Agricultural Economics as it developed in this country over the last fifty years. While centering their interest on only part of the economic system, agricultural economists demonstrated the effectiveness of a systematic combination of theoretical approach with detailed factual analysis (Leontief, 1971, p. 5).

## REFERENCE

Wassily, Leontief. 1971. "Theoretical Assumptions and Nonobserved Facts." *American Economic Review* 61: 1-7.

# The Political Economy of Soviet Socialism: The Formative Years, 1918-1928

by Peter J. Boettke

(Boston: Kluwer Academic Publishers, 1990, $49.95,)

Reviewed by **Howard J. Sherman**

This book is a right-wing ideological diatribe, pretending to be an academic treatise. In the first place, Boettke attacks and discards all of the usual sources on the Soviet Union in this period, including E. H. Carr, Stephen Cohen, Maurice Dobb, Alec Nove, Isaac Deutscher, Alexander Gerschenkron, and many others. It is always possible to attack the main authorities and be correct, but one must supply an extensive proof. In his case, however, the nature of his "proof" is quite unusual. He specifically states that he is not concerned with refuting anyone's statistics, so there are very few statistics offered in the book. He is concerned with (1) "economic theory" (by which he means exclusively the Austrian version of neoclassical theory) and (2) what the actors in history had to say about what they were doing.

With respect to economic theory as applied to socialism, he naturally attacks Oscar Lange. His chief authorities with many, many references throughout the book are: Ludwig von Mises (12 of whose works are cited), Frederick Hayek (ten of whose works are cited), James Buchanan (seven of whose works are cited), and Paul Craig Roberts (three of whose works are cited). Unfortunately, none of these people have ever written in any detail on the specifics of the Soviet Union. Thus, at the very least it would seem that the book says nothing new about its presumed subject, the USSR in 1918 to 1928. Rather, the objective is to "apply economic theory" to the Soviet experience in order to draw anti-socialist conclusions, discussed below.

With respect to what the actors had to say, two examples may suffice. In the first place, he cites Mikhail Gorbachev saying that his reform program

**Research in the History of Economic Thought and Methodology,**
**Volume 13, pages 251-257.**
Copyright © 1995 by JAI Press Inc.
**All rights of reproduction in any form reserved.**
**ISBN: 1-55938-095-0**

(perestroika) is really a return to Leninism (Boettke, p. 13). One would think it apparent that Gorbachev needed to say that at a certain time to calm his enemies, whether or not it was true. Therefore, to use this self-serving statement as evidence that perestroika is not new, but is mainly a return to Leninism, is rather unpersuasive. Another example is the use of Bukharin to say that War Communism was a true model of communism. Of course, Bukharin and all the other Bolshevik leaders had to claim that this was so to support their current operations during War Communism. Once again, such self-serving statements do not constitute persuasive proof.

The main substantive argument of the book is as follows: contrary to the weight of authority of all the writers who knew the Soviet Union in great detail, the period of War Communism was not merely a forced reaction to extreme circumstances, but was the ideal system toward which this faction of Russian socialists had striven. This follows from the thesis that Marxian socialism means central planning, which is its main goal. Most socialists have always thought that the abolition of exploitation and establishment of a non-exploiting, free and democratic society was the goal of socialism. Boettke, however, knows socialist goals better than socialists. He follows to some extent the convoluted argument of Paul Craig Roberts (who is frequently cited) that Marx was more concerned with alienation than exploitation, so Marx's main solution was central planning, which abolished the anarchy and alienation of the market.

After proving to his satisfaction that the Bolsheviks saw War Communism as the perfect form of socialism, he next proves that War Communism was a failure by 1921. Since everyone agrees that the Soviet economy was a mess by 1921, it is amusing that this is the only place where he cites considerable data. The Communist Party itself reached the conclusion that the system was a failure and Lenin proposed the New Economic Policy as "one step backward and two steps forward." Boettke, on the contrary, sees the NEP as the admission that socialism had failed and would always fail. His argument is a simple syllogism: War Communism is the ideal of Marxian socialism; War Communism failed; therefore, all of Marxian socialism is a failure. He writes: "The Soviet experience with communism from 1918 to 1921 bears directly on the calculation argument advanced by Mises. The Marxian project of economic rationalization proved unrealizable in practice" (Boettke, 1990, p. 91). To claim that this hastily improvised system, bearing little relation to the pre-revolutionary program of the Bolshevik party, was the intended goal of Marx and Marxian socialists is quite surprising. To claim that 3-4 years under extreme war time conditions is a reasonable test of any economic system is quite amazing.

As is well known, Mises argued his own syllogism: that socialism means no markets, that no markets mean no rational prices, that no rational prices mean no rational planning. Boettke ignores all of the long debate that has refuted this syllogism.

Furthermore, Boettke gives the argument made famous by Hayek, that central planning—or any large amount of government intervention—must inevitably lead to dictatorship. He states that: "The existence of a liberal political order and central planning are incompatible" (Boettke, 1990, p. 37). But he provides no empirical proof of this key statement. Instead, he merely gives us a lengthy quotation from Hayek, who naturally agrees with him.

In summary, rather than describe and explain the empirical facts about the Soviet Union, Boettke uses his particular authorities to prove that socialism equals planning equals dictatorship. His emphasis on thought as opposed to institutional structure, class relations, or actual economic operation and performance, comes from a deep methodological belief. On page 1 of the book, he quotes Mises: "There is for history nothing beyond people's ideas and the ends they were aiming at motivated by these ideas." This is the methodological stance sometimes called psychological reductionism or mentalism or idealism. It is highly controversial and certainly not proven to be correct because it is stated by Mises.

Scholars interested in the Soviet Union will find little of interest in this book, despite its name. Scholars interested in the curious far-right ideology of the United States, circa 1990, will find it a fascinating example.

## I. ALTERNATIVE THEORIES ON THESE ISSUES

Boettke does raise some important questions. These questions may be restated as follows: (1) Does dictatorship automatically tend to be created by socialism—or by capitalism? (2) Does inefficiency tend to be created by socialism—or by capitalism? These two questions—and much of the vast literature on them—have been discussed in detail in my book (Sherman, 1987, Chapters 10-16); so only the highlights are briefly considered here in the context of Boettke's book (and the reader may consult my book for all references).

Before we can answer these questions, one must define "socialism" and ask whether the Soviet Union (pre Gorbachev) was socialist? Socialism is commonly defined as "public ownership." But "public" implies a democratic political system; the government of the Soviet Union was ruled by a small clique, which in turn owned and ran the economy. Socialism, to Marx and to most socialists, means economic democracy, the extension of democratic rule from the political sphere to the economic sphere. Under the normal definitions of democracy and of socialism, the Soviet Union was neither democratic nor socialist (though it claimed to be both), and Western critics never took the claim of democracy seriously. Therefore, why did they assume that the claim of socialism was true?.

The questions must first be answered in theory for a perfect model of democratic socialism and a perfect model of democratic capitalism; then they may answered for actually existing systems and countries, including the Soviet Union. A democratic socialist country would tend to be far more democratic than a democratic capitalist country because capitalism means enormous concentration of wealth. Concentrated wealth means concentrated political power (see Sherman, 1987, Chapter 8), which means that Congress, the President, and the courts usually follow the interests of the capitalist class (though other classes certainly have influence in varying degrees). The media under capitalism are privately owned and therefore biased in favor of the interests of the capitalist class that owns them. Under socialism, one alternative is public ownership of the media with strict fairness rules, as is done by the Public Broadcasting System in the United States or BBC in England. Another alternative is cooperative, non-profit ownership, such as the Pacifica broadcasting radio stations in the United States.

In a socialist economy, all public employees can be covered by civil service protection, so as to prevent political pressure. Under pure capitalism, however, all jobs are controlled by the capitalists, so there is dictatorship within enterprises and subversive views may be punished by termination. Thus, if two countries start off with identical democratic institutions, but one is pure socialist and one is pure capitalist, it is likely that, all other things being equal, the socialist country will have a higher degree of democracy than the capitalist country. (Of course, as shown below, all other things were not equal between the United States and the Soviet Union in 1917.)

A pure socialist country should be equally efficient with a pure capitalist country in a narrow definition of efficiency—and far superior in a broader definition of efficiency. A socialist economy must, by definition, be non-privately owned (except for small business, according to most socialists), but it may make use of a market or of central planning. Assume first that it is centrally planned. In the narrow definition of efficiency of Pareto optimality, it has been proven that optimal efficiency is possible either by a pure and perfect market economy or by a pure and perfect centrally planned economy (that is, where there is complete information and perfect calculation, see Sherman, 1987, Chapter 14, for details of the argument). In a broader sense of economic efficiency, meaning how well the economy performs for human needs, pure capitalism will pollute and destroy the environment (since that is external to the profit and loss calculation) and it will be subject to cyclical depressions, with mass unemployment and declines in output (see Sherman, 1991, for theoretical and factual argument on this point). Thus, democratic socialism with pure and perfect central planning could better meet human needs because it would have full employment and could incorporate environmental protection in the objective function of central planning.

Of course, Hayek argued that a centrally planned socialist economy can never be perfectly planned because of the lack of information and lack of computing ability. It is certainly true that microeconomic planning of every nut and bolt in a modern economy would probably be totally inefficient for these reasons. But three points must be stressed. First, capitalist competition is also always going to be far from pure and perfect because capitalist competition always produces vast monopoly power, which means that the economy is far from optimal efficiency. Second, socialism can be accomplished partly or wholly in the form of market socialism. Under market socialism, enterprises may be run by worker-appointed or by state-appointed managers, whose goal is to maximize profits for the worker-owners or for the state. There is no reason to believe that market socialism should be any less efficient than market capitalism. Third, it must also be stressed that we have no evidence as to the efficiency of a centrally planned democratic socialism because none has ever existed—the Soviet Union was centrally planned, but surely not democratic socialism.

## II.  LESSONS OF SOVIET HISTORY

Within this theoretical framework, Soviet history can be examined for its lessons on democracy, socialism, and planning. First, why did the Soviet Union end up with a one-party dictatorship? On the eve of the 1917 revolution, conditions were not favorable to democracy: (a) the persistence of feudal power by some landlords over their former serfs, (b) illiteracy, (c) poverty, (d) lack of democratic traditions, and (e) a tradition of underground politics by the Bolsheviks. Then dictatorship was established as the result of (a) the devastation of World War, (b) the ruin of a Russian civil war, and (c) foreign intervention. In war periods, countries generally trample on democratic rights; remember the anti-civil liberties actions of the United States during the world wars and the Civil War. The main reason for the continuance of the dictatorship was the attempt to force a super-rapid growth by the unpopular means of squeezing the peasantry, who constituted over 80 percent of the population, but the peasanty could only be squeezed through an undemocratic, repressive dictatorship. The existence of dictatorship with extreme central planning meant a class structure in which the ruling class had every motivation to preserve the dictatorship. Witness its bitter resistance to the reforms, even in the 1990s, both through everyday politics and bureaucracy and through a coup attempt.

Capitalism, on the other hand, is no guarantee of democracy on the basis of actual historical experience. If Africa, Asia, and Latin America are included, then most capitalist countries in the last century have been dictatorships. South Africa is an industrialized capitalist country, but it is also a repressive dictatorship. In capitalist countries like the United States, there is a considerable degree of democracy, which is important to its people (and has resulted from many protest movements, each removing some barrier). Yet, in the United States and similar countries the economic wealth of the capitalist class, as well as the structure of capitalism, affect politics in such a way that most political decisions have been made in their interest.

Extreme central planning was not a part of pre-revolutionary socialist ideology, which rather focused on the slogan of the free development of all people. Central planning in its extreme form was instituted mainly as a tool with which to conduct the industrialization drive; after initial industrialization, the tendency was toward decentralization, beginning with Khrushchev in 1957. So central planning was not a cause of the initial dictatorship, but an effect of its early decisions—though central planning then also became a convenient tool for extending the power of the dictatorship and its ruling class.

Is central planning efficient? The question cannot be answered in the abstract because all other things are not equal. What is known from Soviet experience is the performance of central planning under a one-party anti-democratic socialist, dictatorship. It appears that central planning and dictatorship can lead to rapid industrialization of an underdeveloped country; that is shown by the Soviet performance in the 1930s (no matter whose data are believed). It was the extreme contrast of successful Soviet planning versus the Great Depression of the capitalist countries that gave the Soviet Union considerable popularity (enhanced by its successful defense against the Fascists in the war).

For initial industrialization, central planning with dictatorship has advantages because it can collect all of the resources and put them all to work. It may not be efficient in the Pareto optimal sense, but it can get the job done (at great cost). When the economy is industrialized and must move into the modern era, however, extreme centralization and dictatorship proves to be a disaster. It puts more and more resources into growth, but less and less comes out. The increasing complexity of the Soviet economy—and an increasing need for technological innovation—guaranteed a lower and lower rate of growth for the Soviet economy. This economic crisis eventually led to the revolutionary situation that ended the Soviet Union. Because the ruling class could no longer rule and the working class would no longer accept their rule.

With the end of Communism and dictatorship, the way is cleared for democratic socialism. The Soviet Union may not go to democratic socialism because of the awful stink of the word "socialism" resulting from the Communist experience. For the rest of the world, however, the greatest obstacle to the advance of democratic socialism has been removed. Now that the Communist Soviet Union has disappeared, the Boettkes of the world will find it much more difficult to attack democratic socialism.

# REFERENCES

Boettke, Peter J. 1990. *The Political Economy of Soviet Socialism: The Formative Years, 1918-1928*. Boston: Kluwer Academic Publishers.

Sherman, Howard J. 1987. *Foundations of Radical Political Economy.* Armonk, NY: M.E. Sharpe.
Sherman, Howard J. 1991. *The Business Cycle: Growth and Crisis Under Capitalism.* Princeton, NJ: Princeton University Press.

# Alfred Marshall in Retrospect

edited by Rita McWilliams Tullberg
(Hants, England: Edward Elgar Publishing Ltd., 1990; 228 pp.)

Reviewed by **James F. Becker**

In America after the Civil War, the widening and deepening of industrial accumulation was accompanied by a rapid spread of incorporation—a growth in number and scale of administative superstructures reflecting ongoing technical changes in industry, finance, marketing and administration. The proliferation of "bureaus and offices" (Sir W. Petty) stimulated demands for specialized varieties of social labor, industrial and pecuniary alike (Veblen, 1919, pp. 279-323), and greatly encouraged a growth in size and number of colleges and universities, their transformation from church colleges to corporate universities, and the creation of whole new faculties in both the social and natural sciences capable of supplying the personnel in demand. The university was becoming "the central powerhouse" reshaping American industrial society.[1]

In England, a not dissimilar process had earlier overtaken organizational structures and, need one add, a pre-existing and pervasive order of class alignments reflecting a feudal past. From a base of consolidations effected during the Napoleonic wars, the expansion involved the schools in accommodating the flow of personnel into a format of traditional relations. Here, too, the corporate suction caught up small business and other sections of "the middle classes," bringing new schools and recruits into an educational "powerhouse" long since attuned to social discrimination, spewing them out in graded wavelets of function and status.

The middle classes most directly involved in these social reassignments had assumed distinctive characteristics in a centuries old welter of mercantile and productive activities comprising what Veblen (1931, p. 233) termed "the educative action of the economic life of the community." Decisive for the

**Research in the History of Economic Thought and Methodology,**
**Volume 13, pages 259-269.**
Copyright © 1995 by JAI Press Inc.
All rights of reproduction in any form reserved.
ISBN: 1-55938-095-0

development of economic thought, this action had put into ever sharper opposition the interests and viewpoints peculiar to each. The classes had split openly during the seventeenth century wars, and in the eighteenth aroused Smith's alarm for a mercantile "spirit of monopoly" at odds with a productive "natural" system of liberty. They came into the nineteenth century riven with such profound differences that Marx could weave the divisions between them into a general theory of capitalist development (Dobb, 1963, Ch. 4).

The Victorian accumulation widened the social breach. On the one hand, the bureaucratic blow-up was serving as a system of indoor relief for the middle classes, and as such was viewed appreciatively by growing numbers of administrative acolytes.[2] For its beneficiaries the movement portended an improved status and well-being than had been provided by that older mode of administration once referred to derogatorily by Jeremy Bentham as the "establishment." On the other hand, the industrial intelligentsia, represented by men like Augustus de Morgan (of symbolic logic) and John Cairnes (of the theory of non-competing groups), were impelled to rise up in support of the heightening needs of productive labor. Within this coterie William Morris was a leader in rallying workers to cope with the threat to art and science posed by the degradation of labor. Contemplating fundamental labor values, he came quickly to the crux of the issue. He wrote "...these (modern) civilized States are composed of three classes—a class which does not even pretend to work, a class which pretends to work but produces nothing, and a class which works, but is compelled by the other two classes to do work which is often unproductive" (Morris, Vol 1966, p. 23, 100). Like Richard Wagner, Morris felt the pathos of the legendary struggle between the Völsungs and the tribes of lesser endowment but higher privilege (Morris, Vol 1966, p. 283ff).[3]

It was from a markedly accommodationist standpoint that Marshall's sensibility responded to circumstances. No Völsung he in his reaction to the flux of social relations. Unhappily, in the Tullberg collection's approach to the subject, the failure to proceed from the relational point of departure is serious. As in other collections of the genre, the failure seems to rest upon a fixed principle of neoclassical historiography: one is not to be shown how the microcosm of economic thought reflects the larger tensions, and how its contributors so often came to be ruled by them. No doubt a pure science should be free from mundane influence, but the emancipation of the scientist cannot be realized if the determinants of his interests he cannot identify.

Not that the essayists ignore altogether the social aspect, but the larger scene comes forth only suggestively, typically indirectly, and all too timorously. R. H. Coase reveals for us, hardly inadvertently, how circumstances of the British accumulation bore down upon upon Marshall's family forebearers, a background he skillfully details following imaginative and industrious research (Tullberg, pp. 9-27). The familial carnage that he uncovers calls to his mind, as it might to ours, Keynes' biographical glossing over of this aspect of his teacher's background. As aspirants to a higher service whose requisites they similarly conceived, was there between these pioneers a conspiratorial element within a network of larger loyalties? Was, and is, the professional bond a tolerably amusing ploy, as the old boy chain is so widely regarded? Or is discrimination in "scientific" taste and style a weapon of ambush in some carefully unidentified social contest? With how much fervor, and by what means, must scholars oppose establishmentarian "combinations" in restraint of the scientific trade?

Contemplating the derogatory evidence surfacing in this volume, one must conclude that much was amiss, if not remiss, with the subject himself. It may occur to the reader, as it perhaps did to some essayists, that in the contests of Marshall's time, even as in our own, the competitor is wise to conceal, even from ones self, all treacherous deficiencies in argument. In a fine unravelling of Marshall's theory of competitive price, revealing starkly its contradictions, John K. Whitaker is struck by "puzzling passage(s)" in Marshall's presentations of a theory "baffling and fraught with apparent inconsistencies..." (Tullberg, pp. 29-48). Remarkably, in this day of ubiquitous maskings of partisan tripe, Whitaker does not mistake obscurantism for scholarship. But why, one wonders, does he rest content, leaving it to the reader to ponder the meaning of the artifacts turned up; why, having shown the sea into which the argument sinks, does he persist in hoping that subsequent investigators should be able to make it walk on water?

Were Marshall's inconsistencies by-products of strenuous effort to secure and hold position and place? For the middle-class entrepreneur of his time, British and American alike, retreat from the fray was cut off by a social crisis featuring dwindling opportunities within old lines of small business and among the non-competing groups of the classical professionals, while to the fore lay a tantalizing vista of economic and social opportunities accessible through the higher learning—a prospect the more tantalizing should physical handicap limit one's maneuverings. Caught in the breach between the industrial and "commercial" proletarians below, and above, the old upper class of aristocratic and classical professionals in law, medicine, and the academy at large, how desperate it all must have been.[4] The restructuring of political economy, concealing its political bent in a cloak of illogic, was born of this desperation.

The unwonted residuals of an induced hypertension to which contrivance comes as relief and competitive theory as sublimation of the unbearable, show up again in an excellent essay by Philip Mirowski: "Smooth operator: how Marshall's demand and supply curves made neoclassicism safe for public consumption but unfit for science" (Tullberg, pp. 61-90). Mirowski points to the "drive to formalization" of supply and demand theory, so much a feature of that century, and is amazed at the persistence and force of scholarly energy expended in this promotion. In explanation of Marshall's participation in the action he alludes to his conversion to "the energetics revolution," to the influence upon his thinking of Herbert Spencer and Benjamin Kidd, to a certain fascination with the conservation of energy, and to sundry "ties to evolution and biological metaphor so prominent in Marshall's thought." Like Whitaker in insisting upon the essential futility of Marshall's theoretical contrivings, he enlarges our appreciation of *ad hoc* improvisations in support of an ill-defined "dynamic" ideal. On the other hand, the ideal itself along with its social significance remain undefined, for Mirowski as for other of our essayists. We return shortly to this problem.

While Mirowski documents admirably Marshall's lack of originality, lack of consistency in argument, jerry-building tendencies in theoretical construction, and so on, he does not relate these failures to the social origins of bias and scientific incontinence. His commentary upon institutional eccentricities of the emerging "science" is provocative, but the distressing "hundred years in a rut" (Culbertson, 1986) of modern economics is only to a limited degree comprehensible from within the restrictive confines of a science taken to be properly endogenous. However, Mirowski's final comment on the god-head is worth repeating, though one would hope not to discourage the reader from examining the details of his case: "It was this persona of the dour schoolmaster, pruning-shears in one hand and scissors in the other, which brought about the textbook reconciliation of the classical trope of supply and demand with the neoclassical image of free-floating energy in commodity space."

In A. W. Coats' essay, "Marshall and ethics" (Tullberg, pp. 153-177), we perceive the steadfastness of the Second Wrangler in coping with "certain practical issues" (as Marshall put it) of political economy. Marshall's clever exploitation of classicism, abetted by his talent for elusive abstraction, were distinctive features of man and work, yet his attempt to reconcile polarities, historical, theoretical and political, is seen as a dextrous expression of talents rather than an exercise in deconstruction. From a biographical standpoint, such attenuation of impulse might well lead one to the social origins of moral provocation rather than to an ingenuity in disjointed ethics. From this angle the historian's premises are as much at issue as those of his subject: one perceives in both parties an adherance to normative standards that frustrates a larger inquiry into behavioral determinants. The constriction is effected, defense of the normative buttressed, by avoiding analysis of why it exists in the first place. The avoidance itself lends an aura of rationality to argument since, as everyone knows, the hopelessness of debate on norms is long since proved: on the unassailable the unexaminable is preserved.

As Marshall's career suggests, conservatism in economics is closely bound up with a ritual observance of style and manners. In its more neurotic manifestations such observance is often protected by make-shift adaptations in "scientific" semantics, such as his own "biological" metaphor with its semiotic props, or the more recent "instrumentalism" of the static theoretician, devices calculated to protect and defend the metaphysical. Even in journalism, one encounters no holds barred in interchange. In economics a reverential dedication to proprieties envelopes the sacred in vibrations of taboo, therewith sparing the knowledge or acknowledge of common prejudice. This rite of passage renders acceptable the vestal's "scientific" offerings, however corrupt the corpus of offerings. When the incense is potent, decades may pass before the truth emerges. As Kenneth Arrow notes, there is a vulgar odor in Marshall's attribution of Ricardo's fondness for abstraction to his "Semitic" heritage.[5] As an economist outside the historian's province, Arrow may be forgiven his desecration of the idol—provided he lays the topic henceforward to rest. Such are the usual gentlemen's agreements.

In the soft sciences, the tradition of manners is an intergenerational complex of proprieties concealing what must be hidden if the reputation of doctrinaires is to be preserved. Historically, the clusters of iconographic signs pressed into introvert signalling have shifted from parietal geometrics of the paeleolithic to linguistic circumlocutions of the Victorian indirection to the non-operational mathematics of the contemporary hustings. In the so-called "economic analysis," the net effect of these bolsterings of the rites of provincial domain is that, miraculously, the looming spirit of the revered departed, speaking through the voice of his medium, may modestly decline its own exorcism. Ecclesiastical forbearers are in these slick waxes preserved, if, hopefully, not forever.

There are the usual genuflectories in this volume. Coates attributes an influence of Marshall's theorizing upon the development of economics: "...absorbed so effectively into twentieth century mainstream economics that it takes a conscious effort of historical reconstruction to identify it." Yet it is less the influence of theoretical insight than of the old inter-generational signalling that prompts the reproductive conception. Marshall was indeed "the very model of a model," as the libretto put it, and, as with other popular models in the standard line, one readily perceives an indefatigible if, as it turns out, socially defective instinct of workmanship, cloaked in the preferred motley of social contaminations. The complex strikes the rock of native preconceptions from which comes the stream of standard response: neo-Austrian, neo-liberal, neo-conservative "methodological individualisms," intellectually rugged, of course. The combination of cant with Crusoe is marvelously applicable to the desired narrowing of discourse, wonderfully suited to subliminal reception of ideological cues for spontaneous rebroadcast. And so, as the neoclassical historian surveys the transmission of signs from past to present, it appears incontrovertible that later practice is influenced by precedent rather than by social programming.[6]

The reality is that the ephemera of current practice have virtually nothing to do with authenticated sources, just as Marx and Christ have nothing to do with Communism and the Inquisition respectively. Today's "imbecile institutions" are not the contributions of distant worthies, but only the cumulative flotsam of generations caught up in similar circumstances. They are grown out of demands for an effective daily practice over a century and more of pressurings under the weight of the higher imperatives. So flattened is the latest generation that, even when practices are normalized, enforced by paternalistic if commonly ignorant administrations flouting the usual club insignia, the grotesqueries of command decision fail to offend. They fail because they conform to sensibilities long dulled by exactions of tribute to overbearers as well as forebearers, themselves sanctified because roasted to a turn on the very same racks. The historian's attributions of influence thus smack of necromancy and bootlicking. The imputation of influence forestalls reflection on how and why the scientific insensibility has come to be what it is.

For those whose youthful aspirations run willy nilly to the contrary, it is always in the end a question of what will wash in too small a basin. The maverick is overwhelmed with discriminate behests either engraved or about to be engraved in faculty handbooks, departmental conventions and sundry testaments to true value, so that sooner or later the free-form is eliminated by conformists to that "educative action" to which, as in Marshall's case, the mercantile recruits all too hastily succumb. All the long-gone casualties should of course be resurrected, albeit not so reverently. Only by scientific study of mutations induced by prolonged exposure can we hope to understand, and so learn to cope with, the gradual removal of economics from the realm of social science. Or can the phenomena of levitation and abdication themselves be denied?

In the usual reconstruction only the doilies appear on the Victorian chairs as upholsterers hasten with laces to cover degenerate features. This saves embarrassment in polite company (Let us hear no more of Marshall's anti-semitism!) Thus, the present volume passes by Marshall's abiding but utterly confused animosity to the rising "materialism" of his day: he is attracted to Adolph rather than Richard Wagner, and to wallpaper rather than to work-a-day predicaments of social labor. We are not told whether his aversion was to material self-indulgence or to scientific materialism or to both. The aversion to the scientific, of course, shows up in his methodology as well as in disdain for the social views of William Morris, poorly masked by uncomprehending approval of Morris' commercial design. His shallow misinterpretation of Marx fits well with his Christian socialism and the sentimental humanism of the Oxford movement, while his admiration for the strategic conceptions of Captain Mahan sinks him in the rank pool of missionary ideology.[8] Nevertheless, given the long term rate of deviation of economics from the public service, it is not surprising that Marshall's own perception of the social location of the economist should have been in closer and even franker contact with actuality than would appear from *Alfred Marshall in Retrospect*. To explain, we turn briefly to those exogenous determinants that Marshall was so careful not to emphasize unduly.

It may be going too far to see him as a utilitarian, or at any rate a consistent one, yet his theory of the surplus, to which we find but two casual references (Tullberg: Mirowski, p. 62; Gallegati, pp. 142-143), falls back upon the hedonic calculus. As everyone knows, he sees both the "producer" and the "consumer" receiving a net of satisfaction above the price of their respective services. He combines this algebra with his own methodological individualism in summing it up: "The intimate connection between both of them...is shown by the fact that, in estimating the weal and woe in the life of Robinson Crusoe, it would be simplest to reckon his producer's surpluses on such a plan as to include the whole of his consumer's surplus." (Marshall, pp. 831) If this is what Marx called a "Robinsonade," its social bearing is not immediately evident; the metaphor only gives the clue that something is up.

He concludes that the various nets may be algebraically aggregated, presumeably on the basis of definitions of producers and consumers whose social spirits first materialize in his discussion of "Agents of Production" (Marshall, 1938, pp. 138-143). Following the lead of his definition of the principal social agent as the "worker," we find in Appendix K that the "worker" is also the capitalist whose entrepreneurial contributions to production, together with his contributions of "saver's surplus," put him, too, into the "worker" or "producer" category. The significance of his aggregation "plan" begins to become apparent.

This aggregation of surpluses across social classes is obviously directed immediately to undercutting the implication of exploitation belonging to quite a different surplus value theory: he declares our capitalist world to be one of mutual sharing of psychic surpluses, immaterial perhaps, but surpluses nonetheless. With this blow he deep-sixes those embarrassingly material and wholly political classical distinctions between productive and unproductive labor, productive and unproductive consumption, producers and consumers, and so on. In their stead he develops a harmony thesis worthy of the reactionary classicism, the apologetics that he throughout fails to distinguish from the old Liberal radicalism arising out of the humanistic aspirations of the more enlightened strain. With the aid of this historical error, if that is what it is, he defines classicism in terms of its peripheral, low profile qualities. This strengthens his plea for a weak-kneed and illiberal "classicism." So we come to the point of it all.

His political economy emerges when we combine the foregoing with his theory of "sensibility," that economically and administratively invaluable characteristic of the "natural" leader on whom he expatiates (Marshall, 1938, Ch. VI). Here is the real substance of his "organismic" thesis. In passages easily mistaken for mere "philosophical" digression, he analyzes the labor-capital division of labor with its problems of education and training. We are told that one of these two "agents of production" is more frequently "naturally" equipped—it was certainly more strategically placed—to render those sensitive judgments so vital to economic efficiency. While both types of "workers" contain within themselves some measure of sensibility, or can be brought to this rare point by formal education, only one of them contains the overwhelming relative mass of the required talent: "The laws which govern the birth of genius are inscrutable. It is probable that the percentage of children of the working classes who are endowed with natural abilities of the highest order is not so great as that of the children of people who have attained or inherited a higher position in society" (Marshall, 1938 p. 212). Is this Edmund Burke? Or the liberalism of Adam Smith? What impoverished classicism have we here!

For Marshall it is the producer-capitalist who embodies the natural dominion of "art" over "technics," the two fundamental talents ranging from a to b within a private hierarchy of values. Here is the Robinson whose artistic sensibilities a properly economical administration demands, the artist who, should he not be such naturally, may be made into such, albeit only in a certain relative frequency, by an appropriate "education in art." Marshall's psychology is evidently not so much an individual as it is a social psychology. It is a drab, supplicant psychology of imputed class characteristics. There is something ominous as well as aquiescent in his invitation to the principle of social discrimination: "...(while) differences between individuals might be neglected...it might be necessary to consider whether there were some special reasons for believing, say, that those who laid most store by tea were a specially sensitive class of people... *then a separate allowance for this would have to be made before applying the results of economical analysis to practical problems of ethics or politics"* (Marshall, 1938, Ch. VI, p. 130. Underlining mine).

Marshall's devotion to devising special allowances for the "new class" was a direct outgrowth of personal aspirations. The emergence of an administrative hierarchy within which the old was becoming a new managerial petty bourgeoisie he promoted with a tedious skein of argument woven by day into his theory and unravelled by night in his political practice. Within his Platonic conception of the ideal, as his modelling reveals, the economist enters as aide-de-camp to the natural decision makers. This class hierarchy was still largely inchoate in America at the century's end, but the direction of movement was enouraged by accumulation throughout the Anglo-American world, a shared motion accounting for the popularity of an "economics" recounted in a common language. The *Principles* recommends to the economist the same social function and status as were then, and remain still, the objective of Social Darwinians and sundry small class entrepreneurs. The "artists" over the technicians was to Marshall the quite visible and desireable object of a "biological" movement. This explains why his organismic metaphor has never been theoretically realized, by him or by anyone else.[9] It has long since been a cover-up for an established feature of capitalist development.

Marshall's political economy, with its natural decision makers and their educating and rationalizing auxiliaries, is essentially that of today's economists—and for essentially the same material reasons in support of the unconscious as were his in the first place. By the same token, it remains an ideal that its supporters prefer to conceal; after all, the myth of the "independent" scientist is at stake here. The mainstream compound with its scientific pretensions and political conservatism is nowadays well constructed to implement these ignoble ideals, while the neoclassical history of thought shrouds the whole in mythology.

The essays of this collection thus fall within that mythopoeic misconception of a social and scientific economics emerging inexorably from a self-contained, endogenous process. Paradoxically, this very matrix, narrowed with the aid of the historian, threatens now to expel from its monopolized precincts as an unessential discipline the history of economic thought itself. One by one the introvert dynamic has cast off the fragile ties of economics to social serviceability, leaving a servile discipline whose shrunken interests coincide with those of the managerial bourgeoisie. With the abandonment of the social interest, minimally compensated by private gain, the practitioners move on an Hegelian circuit ranging from ideological palaver to irresponsible silence, and return. While the contraction means the finish of economics as a social science, the neutering and dismissal of the real history of thought puts the seventh seal on the tomb.

The collection contains, among others, essays by John Maloney on "Marshall and business," offering insight into further connections within that relationship. Phyllis Dean's "Marshall on free trade," examines yet another realm of the subject's theoretical equivocation, enveloped, as usual, in his obsequious modesty.

## ACKNOWLEDGMENT

Research for this review enjoyed the support of the C. V. Starr Center for Applied Economics, New York University. I thank Robert Griffin for helpful critical comment.

## NOTES

1. See H. Perkin, "The recruitment of elites in British society since 1800," *Journal of Social History*, 12, 1979, 229, cited by Roy Lowe, "English elite education in the late nineteenth and early twentieth centuries" (Conze and Kocka, pp. 147-162).

2. The domestic system is incremental to the British rule in India described by James Mill as "a system of outdoor relief for the upper classes."

3. For him the Völsungs were symbolized by such as Watt Tyler and John Ball, spiritual heirs of the legendary Siegfried. Like Wagner,he fought the mercantile corruption in poem, music and deed, promoting the cause of the tribe of art and craft in this phase of its development. Morris'

comment on his development as a socialist is interesting: "I put some conscience into trying to learn the economical side of socialism, and even tackled Marx, though I must confess that, whereas I thoroughly enjoyed the historical part of "Capital," I suffered agonies of confusion of the brain over reading the pure economics of that great work. Anyway, I read what I could..." (Morris, 1938, p. 278). While the details of Wagner's relations to socialism are to some extent still wanting, I believe, the influence of Ludwig Feuerbach upon both him and Marx was significant. There was for Wagner the unforgettable experience of the Dresden barricades and for both of them the travail of exile. Marx's early theory of alienation, including the role of the division of labor within it, may have affected Wagner's thinking. Marxian interpretations of Der Ring des Niebelungen are not all that wide of the mark.

4. The intensity of social competitions is well described by an American member of the new leadership. Henry Adams' assessment of what he termed the "Darwinian" challenge well expresses the academic spirit of the age: "For the young men whose lives were cast in the generation between 1867 and 1900, Law should be Evolution from lower to higher, aggregation of the atom in the mass, concentration of multiplicity in unity, compulsion of anarchy in order; and he would force himself to follow wherever it led, though he should sacrifice five thousand millions more in money, and a million more lives" (Adams, 1918, p. 232). With economic necessity to the rear, and to the fore the material and social prospects of the higher learning, the cowboys surged into the open spaces of the academic frontier.

5. In Marshall's presumed fondness for Ricardo, Arrow observes, there is "...more than a touch of condescension. Ricardo is given to an excessive love of abstraction, no doubt, says Marshall, the result of Ricardo's "Semitic" heritage." He further notes, "The great biological developments of the nineteenth century had their dark side in the use of science to justify racism, and this example is far from the only one in Marshall" (Arrow, p. 71). I thank Bruno Stein for drawing this to my attention.

6. The seminality imputed to leading figures may even be strengthened by discrete admission that the current forms of reproduction may take an unfortunate turn. In the way we live now, it is seen to be faintly regrettable that a quasi-pleasurable addiction to "workaholism" should have come upon us like censeorial smokes, sanctifying the current taste for unrelenting deductive rigor and hard-nosed quantification. The agnostic, of course, might entertain the thought that the saints and their overworked virtues can hardly be responsible for the catastrophe.

7. In the context, be it noted, of an imperialistic scholarship of his own design (Marshall, 1938, p. 776).

8. "The promise of Marshall's organismic-biological approach has yet to be realized" (Coats, p. 170). An interesting consideration of the analogy is Neil B. Niman's "Biological Analogies in Marshall's Work" (Niman, 1991) which, however, fails to perceive the ideal to which Marshall points so obliquely.

# REFERENCES

Adams, Henry. 1918. [1961] *The Education of Henry Adams*. Boston: Houghton Mifflin.

Arrow, Kenneth J. 1991. "Ricardo's Work as Viewed by Later Economists." *Journal of the History of Economic Thought*, 13:70-77.

Conce, Werner, and Kocka, Jurgen, (hrsg). 1985. *Bildungsburgertum im 19 Jahrhundert*, Stuttgart.

Culbertson, John M. 1986. "American Economics: 100 Years in a Rut." *The New York Times* (January 12).

Dobb, Maurice. 1963. *Studies in the Development of Capitalism*. London: Routledge and Kegan Paul.

Marshall, Alfred. 1938. *Principles of Economics*, eighth ed. London: Macmillan and Co.

Morris, William. 1966. *The Collected Works of William Morris*. New York: Russell and Russell.

Niman, Neil B. 1991. "Biological Analogies in Marshall's Work." *Journal of the History of Economic Thought*, 13(10): 19-36.

Smith, Adam. 1937. *An Inquiry into the Nature and Causes of the Wealth of Nations*. New York: The Modern Library.

Veblen, Thorstein. 1931. *Theory of the Leisure Class*. New York: The Modern Library.

―――――. 1919. "Industrial and Pecuniary Employments." *The Place of Science in Modern Civilization*. New York: Modern Library.

# Thomas Tooke: Pioneer of Monetary Theory

by Arie Armon
(Ann Arbor, MI: The University of Michigan Press, 200 pp.)

Reviewed by **Samuel Hollander**

This book incorporates the substance of several of Arie Arnon's published articles (1984, 1987, 1989). Part I sets the theoretical and factual stage, relying heavily on Feavearyear (1963) for the latter, and includes a chapter on Ricardian monetary thought; Part II on Tooke the Follower—of mainstream monetary theory, largely Ricardo (excluding the posthumous paper *Plan of a National Bank*)—takes the preparatory material further by outlining Tooke's pre-Banking School views in what is called the 'stable conceptual framework' of his first published work, *Thoughts and Details on the High and Low Prices of the Last Thirty Years* (1823) through the first two volumes of *A History of Prices and of the State of the Circulation...* (1838). But the core of the book is to be found in Parts III and IV. Part III (Tooke, the Innovator) contains three chapters—one on Tookean Banking School principles as they appear in *An Inquiry into the Currency Principle* (1844), a second on the Transition to those principles which Arnon dates largely from 1838 (though in Part II reference is made to some early dissensions from Ricardian orthodoxy even in the 1820s), and a third on the post-1844 years. Part IV (An Attempt at Perspective) comprises two chapters, one on Tooke's knowledge of price trends considering his neglect or ignorance of index numbers; and the second, which contains the substance of the *O.E.P.* paper, on the applicability of the competitive solution to money and credit.

It is a central theme of the book, reflected in the choice of title, that Tooke was a major contributor to monetary theory, a view contrasting with that of

**Research in the History of Economic Thought and Methodology,**
Volume 13, pages 271-276.
Copyright © 1995 by JAI Press Inc.
All rights of reproduction in any form reserved.
ISBN: 1-55938-095-0

Schumpeter but in line with that of T.E. Gregory (and of course J.S. Mill). The early Tooke defended convertibility on the 'Bullionist' lines characteristic of the Currency School that prices are determined by the quantity of the medium in circulation (coins plus banknotes), which quantity should behave as would a pure gold circulation. This position is abandoned in the 1844 *Inquiry* which (a) rejects the distinction between notes and other means of payment; (b) denies the quantity theory, reversing the causal relation between quantity of means of payment and prices—the 'money supply' becoming an *endogenous* variable—with prices themselves determined by consumer income (pp. 3, 97). The primary question exercising Arnon is *when* and *how* this Transformation occurred. Gregory, the target throughout, had maintained in his 1928 Introduction to the *History of Prices* that the break was *sudden*, occurring in 1840 immediately after publication of the third volume, and reflected an altered perception of the role of deposits, more specifically the abandonment of the view that deposits are 'unemployed and inert' money distinct from the note issue (p. 3). For Arnon, the transformation was *gradual*, and reflected in its fundamentals the more basic issue of the applicability of free trade to banking, Tooke abandoning his original opposition to free trade in note issue in favour of competition. The chapter devoted to The Transition Period elaborates the thesis that the key years are those following the 1838 volumes and preceding the 1844 pamphlet, during which period 'Tooke was gradually rejecting certain of his earlier premises but had not yet consolidated a complete alternative theory' (p. 120).

Gregory's position that it was only *after* Volume III of *A History of Prices* but *before* the evidence given to the Committee on Banks of Issue later in 1840 that the transition occurred (Gregory, 1928, p. 71, cited Arnon, p. 120) is said to be misleading, Tooke having already *rejected* the strong distinction between deposits and banknotes in favor of a more balanced position. When this particular change occurred is an open question; it might, one supposes, have been at any time between 1838 and 1840, even in 1840 itself. Potentially significant is the further thesis that the Transformation was a gradual one lasting until 1844, turning on various additional reasons for the altered position apparently neglected by Gregory. But Arnon somewhat undermines this potentiality by insisting also that these reasons are already to be found *in Volume III itself*—(a) the argument that banks cannot increase the amount of notes in circulation, the basis for 'the famous law of reflux'; (b) the denial that excess issue of bank notes is responsible for speculation; and (c) an income theory of prices in place of the quantity theory—in which case his difference with Gregory regarding timing may reduce to a few months in 1840. As for the abandonment of the sharp contrast between notes and deposits that 'did not change after Volume III' and reappears as such in 1844 (p. 122). And though Tooke 'still appears indecisive' about the above-mentioned novelties, one can already distinguish the emergence of those new principles which were to make him an opponent of the Currency School' (p. 124). In fact, we are told, the testimony given later in 1840 to the Bank Issue Committee 'add[ed] almost nothing new to Tooke's arguments in Volume III of *A History of Prices*'.

The 'indecision' just alluded to is said to have dissipated by the 1844 *Inquiry* (p. 129), the process of clarification reflecting the resolution of a tension between Tooke's 'meta-theory' relating to Free Trade and his specifically banking principles (p. 126f). Although his new monetary theory minimizing the Bank's influence on prices should have suggested to him an extension of free trade to banking, Tooke did not take this line immediately and continued to maintain the original exclusion in 1840—*'free-trade in banking is synonymous with free trade in swindling'*; *'the issue of paper substitutes for coin is no branch of productive industry. It is a matter of regulation by the state...'* (cited Arnon, p. 129). In 1844 this tension is resolved when Tooke accepted 'that free trade in banking is not dangerous to the production of wealth, its influence on prices is negligible, and so there is no reason not to leave this business outside the "province of police" ...'. Arnon has some interesting observations here and elsewhere in the book on technical or analytical innovation relative to alterations in broader ideological perspective (e.g., pp. 126, 130, 166, 180).

Here we might profitably consider a broad question raised by this study— the quality of Tooke's theorizing. The innovations alluded to thus far in the context of application of free trade to banking as a reflection of the new monetary theory relates to *note issue*. Arnon allows that his admiration for Tooke as theorist does not extend to the status of free trade with regard to *credit*. That is referred to as 'a critical lacuna,' 'a strange omission,' and 'the weakest point in his analysis' (pp. 115, 131, 173). The mature theory 'seems to avoid and bypass ...the status of free trade with regard to credit,' Tooke failing to build a 'complete system' and engaging rather 'in attempts to discredit his rivals' arguments,' so that despite his recognition that (unlike notes) credit does not adjust automatically to the needs of the economy through the law of reflux, he failed to draw the formal conclusion that free-trade principles are *inappropriate* in the case of credit (p. 131).

This 'failure to develop a theory of how credit should be controlled, leaving it totally to the Bank Director's discretion', is one exception to the representation of Tooke as a major theorist: 'If Tooke deserves criticism for being atheoretical, it is in this context' (p. 4, cf. p. 175). And though there was some progress after 1844, even in the last volumes of *A History of Prices* (1857) there remains 'a gap between Tooke's theories of money and credit and his proposed banking regimes' (p. 142). But what is one to make of the relation between meta-theory and analytical innovation considering so great an exception as the control of credit? And surely Arnon exaggerates when he insists against Gregory on 'a complete reversal in Tooke's attitude to free trade in banking' (p. 132).

The foregoing is by no means the only major reservation allowed by Arnon. There is also the fact that Tooke's original theory of interest (recognizing only a transitory impact of monetary phenomena on the interest rate and emphasizing an effect of the level of the interest rate on the level of prices) remains unchanged despite all the subsequent major revisions: 'In view of the radical changes in his other positions this is somewhat odd' (pp. 86, 116). And there is the puzzling question how Tooke managed to arrive at his accurate conclusion regarding price trends despite the absence of formal indexation, 'even when these [data] were not compatible with his general [theoretical] position on the determinants of prices' (p. 160). Considering Arnon's high opinion of Tooke as theorist, these anomalies require further attention.

The significance of Tooke's theoretical contribution emerges also in the context of filiation of ideas. Tooke's notion that banks cannot increase the amount of their notes in circulation is said to reflect partial acceptance of 'Gurney's argument that any additional supply of notes by the Bank would find its way back to the Bank, which "would lock them up in their tills"' (p. 123). This idea, it is pointed out, was later developed into the 'famous law of reflux' (Arnon, pp. 99, 179, contrasts Tooke's restriction of the doctrine to *notes* only with Adam Smith's version). But that law was *not* due to Tooke, but to Fullarton (p. 135), despite which fact it is Tooke who is represented as 'the innovator of the Banking School' (p. 179).

Much more then should have been said of the relation between Fullarton and Tooke. Only brief mention is made of another major Banking School exponent, James Wilson. Above all, I miss any concerted effort to elaborate on the relationship both from a theoretical and policy perspective between Tooke and J.S. Mill. Mill does not even appear in a brief paragraph in the Introduction on influence or in an Epilogue touching on influence (pp. 4, 184).

A word is in order on the representation of the great classics, especially Smith and Ricardo. As for Smith, I am not sure of the edition of the *Wealth of Nations* Arnon has used, since his discussion of Smith's case for free trade in banking opens with the assertion that "Adam Smith discussed money before discussing the division of labour in the fourth chapter of Book I entitled 'The Origins and Use of Money'" (p. 21). More seriously, the exposition of Smith is too neat and tidy. Arnon asserts that 'Smith's theory assumes that a mixed convertible circulation, one based on commodity money, needs no regulation or control. The quantity of the circulating commodity—money—will always be the right one' (p. 24). But the truth is far more complex, since Smith actually maintained that banks *do not necessarily understand their own interest*, and might therefore be responsible for an excessive money supply over an extended period by way of an on-going process of inappropriate discounting, illustrating the case of a circulation 'overstocked with paper money' by Bank of England notes, issued in 'too great a quantity' and this 'for many years together' (1937,

p. 286). Here is a nice instance of a potential clash between technical monetary theory and the free trade 'meta-theory.'

Arnon has much of interest to say on Ricardo's posthumous paper *A Plan for a National Bank* (1824), particularly its distinction between paper issue as substitute for gold, a function to be carried on by a Commission; and the business of loans which was to be left to competition. This rejection of free trade in note issue, Arnon maintains, has generally been understood as involving *passivity* of the issue authority which was to *respond* to gold movements (pp. 31, 38, 98-9, 177). Readers of this pamphlet, including both the main Currency School authorities and Tooke, failed to recognize that it actually constituted a major break with Ricardo's earlier thinking, one which reflected 'growing mistrust in ..."natural" forces', leading Ricardo to recommend discretionary open-market operations by the Bank to alter the note supply (pp. 99, 177, based on Ricardo, 1951, IV, pp. 296-297). Arnon insists then on differentiating the Currency School from the late Ricardo, considering the latter's rejection of the meta-theory of free trade in the monetary sphere and 'adoption of a basically central banking theory.'

All this is very difficult and doubtless the last word has not been said on the interpretation of Ricardo's banking principles. Years ago I myself wrote that Ricardo in 1824 'allowed some discretion to the authority by way of the issue of notes against government securities in the event of an improvement of the exchanges and a fall in the market price of gold and the sale of government securities under the opposite conditions' (1979, pp. 492-493). It was not clear to me then, and it is not clear now, precisely what to make of this allowance, but I have the impression that Arnon makes too much of it since the 'discretion' in question is in fact to be strictly a *passive reaction* to movements in the bullion price and exchange rate. It is a major theme of this book that insofar as the mature Tooke (by 1857 at least) and Ricardo (1824) were both pointing towards active Central Bank interventionism—Ricardo for notes and Tooke for credit (p. 180)—there is more in common between them than anyone, Tooke himself and his contemporaries as well as later and modern commentators, ever realized. Because of the various reservations noted above regarding both Ricardo and Tooke, I would say that this position should be viewed as a hypothesis still requiring confirmation.

The reader is not helped by an inadequate index—for example, there is no listing for Gregory, though so much of Arnon's case is directed against him, or for many other characters mentioned in the text including Gurney (we are never told which Gurney), Grenfell, King and Wheatley, and the entry under *Plan for the Establishment of a National Bank* omits the main page references. Throughout one encounters a veritable menagerie of strange creatures such as Lord Grenfeld, Pascue Grenfel, Weatly, Honer, Malet, Sir George Schuckbury Evelyn. The Bibliography extends far beyond works actually cited, which practice breaks a useful convention. And some attention might profitably have been paid to Pivetti's contribution on Tooke for the New Palgrave (1987) which also represents Vol. III of the *History* as a new stage in Tooke's thought.

# REFERENCES

Arnon, A. 1984. "The Transformation in Thomas Tooke's Monetary Theory Reconsidered." *History of Political Economy* 16, 311-326.

_____ . 1987. "Banking Between the Invisible and Visible Hands: A Reinterpretation of Ricardo's Place Within the Classical School." *Oxford Economic Papers* 39: 268-281.

_____ . 1989. "The Early Tooke and Ricardo: A Political Alliance and First Signs of Theoretical Disagreement." *History of Political Economy* 21: 1-14.

Feavearyear, A. 1963. *The Pound Sterling: A History of English Money*, 2nd ed. Oxford: Clarendon Press.

Gregory, T.E. 1928. "Introduction to Tooke and Newmarch." *A History of Prices... From 1792 to 1856*. London: King & Son.

Hollander, S. 1979. *The Economics of David Ricardo*. Toronto: University of Toronto Press.

Ricardo, D. 1951. *Works and Correspondence of David Ricardo*, ed. P. Sraffa. Cambridge: Cambridge University Press.

Pivetti, M. 1987. "Tooke, Thomas" Pp. 657-659 in *The New Palgrave: A Dictionary of Economics*. London: Macmillan.

# Theorists of Economic Growth from David Hume to the Present: With a Perspective on the Next Century

by Walt Whitman Rostow
(New York: Oxford University Press, 1991; 712, pp.)

## Reviewed by **Mark Perlman**

Let me start with my paramount conclusion. This is an important book by one of our profession's most versatile and profound current scholars. Reading it, if an awesome experience, is also something of an exhausting pleasure. Yet, what makes the reading of this study so essential for those seeking an exhibition of how someone can put the parts together to form a whole are (1) the range of Rostow's historical and philosophical knowledge, (2) his capacity for evaluating and employing the generalizations developed by others, (3) his capacity for identifying and refining his own intuitions, and (4) his command of language. For those not averse to working with tag-end threads in the filiation of ideas, the book has all the qualities of a rich golden tapestry.

As Professor Rostow's career is no longer universally known, I start by noting some of its historical sequence. His university training was principally at Yale and at Oxford (where he was a Rhodes Scholar during the 1930s, particularly during the years of the Baldwin-Chamberlain appeasement). His academic career includes service at MIT (1951 to 1961), and at the University of Texas (since 1969), and shorter professorial stints at Oxford (The Harmsworth Chair, 1946-1947) and Cambridge (The Pitt Chair, 1949-1950). He has seen much governmental service, including military and State Department during World War II, and he served as a (and later *the*) principal administrative national security counselor to Presidents Kennedy and Johnson during their administrations (1961-1968).[1]

His previous bibliography is monumental, including such standard works as *The Growth and Fluctuations of the British Economy, 1790-1850*, with

**Research in the History of Economic Thought and Methodology,**
**Volume 13, pages 277-283.**
Copyright © 1995 by JAI Press Inc.
**All rights of reproduction in any form reserved.**
**ISBN: 1-55938-095-0**

A. D. Gayer and Anna Schwartz (which had been written before World War II but was not published until 1953), his 1953 *The Process of Economic Growth*, and the 1960 *The Stages of Economic Growth; A Non-Communist Manifesto*.

*     *     *     *     *     *

As for this book—it has four major parts, not including an intriguing Introduction and a lengthy Appendix. The book is in the Marshallian *Principles* tradition, because in addition to a seemingly crystal-clear prose text, it contains a mathematical appendix. Also like Marshall's, Rostow's book attempts to combine many views in order to offer wisdom rather than learning.

The first Part deals with six classical period economists: Hume and Smith; Malthus and Ricardo; John Stuart Mill and Marx. Part II surveys the rise of the Marshallian neo-Classical tradition and the switch from economic growth at Center Stage, to its place "at the [disciplinary] periphery, 1870-1939." Part III, dealing with economic growth analysis after World War II, covers (1) some of the usual master figures (i.e., Harrod-Domar, Kaldor, Joan Robinson, Solow, and some efforts at collateral development (including Hicks, Hansen, Duesenberry, Matthews, and Burns and Mitchell); (2) the overwhelming statistical influences, principally introduced by Kuznets and extended by Denison, are combined with discussions of the significant but "lesser" (in the sense that stars do come in magnitudes) works of Bauer, Colin Clark, Hirschman, Lewis, Myrdal, Prebisch, Rosenstein-Rodan, Singer, and Tinbergen. In the end there is a general lengthy statement of his own synthesis, somewhat (but only slightly) revised from his earlier works. The fourth Part deals with the future—"What Don't We Know About Economic Growth?" and "Where Are We? An Agenda in Mid-Passage."

In several critical senses Rostow goes well beyond his own earlier works on the theory of economic growth. For one thing, this book offers an interpretation or a commentary on the vast historic literature on the subject of growth. His earlier work focused not on the literature, but on the specific roles of pecuniary saving and investment and the "momentum" that they could generate. For another, he assesses quite critically (but always along the line of his economic institutionalism) his earlier reasoning and his resulting conclusions. By turning to a review of the literature we can see how he has broadened extensively his analytical framework, and how he has replaced what had been "a theory" of economic growth with a rich matrix into which he fits data to give a "causes-of-growth profile."

Of the *Introduction* I report only selectively because my space is limited. But, it deals with Rostow's analytic method; in particular, with the question of whether life's experiences really do or do not shape individual theorists' ideas; and whether ideas are shaped in the tradition of Aristotle (where empiric input matters) or in the tradition of Plato (where only the essence or kernel of truth, alone, matters). Rostow's argues his

> conviction that an economic truth useful for either historical or contemporary analysis ... must embrace endogenously the demographic transition, treat science and invention as investment sub-sectors and the capacity to innovate as a creative task distinguishable from profit maximization with fixed or incrementally changing production functions, account for the tendency of major innovations to cluster ..., demonstrate the intimate linkage between growth and cyclical fluctuations of differing periodicity *with major innovations and the generation of the inputs of food and raw materials accounted as endogenous to the system* (p. 7, emphasis added).

Rostow is an institutionalist in the Aristotelian tradition, and his analytic method involves initial observation and cognitive comparison and then formal generalization.

When it come to his approach to the literature on economic growth, he examines what each writer has employed, often but not always explicitly, as his:

- theory of population
- assessment of the determinants of investment
- views regarding the impact of new technology
- concern with the vagaries and effects of business cycles
- attitudes towards the relative roles of the cultivation of raw materials and manufactures
- criteria, if any, relating to comparative regional or national development, from the standpoint of per capita national income
- concern with the limits of growth, if any
  blinterest and ways of handling non-economic variables

In *Part I*, Rostow chooses to use the pairing of contemporaries in his study of the period from about 1750 until 1870. Hume is contrasted to his advantage with Smith—they were close friends (each asked the other to be his literary executor) and were in most things in general agreement (Hume explicitly disagreed only with Smith's treatment of rent); but Hume, in Rostow's assessment, comes out the better because he was both the more analytical as an economist, and he managed always to fit his superb analysis more successfully into a comprehensive framework about the way (what was for both of them in the future) industrial civilization was going to work. In an aside Rostow urges the reader to let Friedman and Bauer (probably mistakenly) venerate Smith's ideology, but his final lines in the chapter are:

> In terms of development theory of the 1950s and 1960s Hume and Smith might not fully qualify as "structuralists"; but it is clear that they did not believe competitive market

economics would, without government intervention, maximize the wealth of nations, and
they would have understood with sympathy Paul Rosenstein-Rodan's case for a Big Push
to expand infrastructure in an underdeveloped economy... (p. 50).

The pairing of Malthus with Ricardo differs from the previous comparison
mostly in the sense that the two close friends disagreed about a great many
things. Part of that disagreement, no doubt, was that Ricardo held onto
Malthus's earlier concern about the speedy application of the laws of
diminishing returns long after Malthus had backed away from that view. But
a larger cause was Malthus's explicit criticism that "scientific writers on political
economy" try too precipitously "to simplify and generalize" (p. 53). Rostow's
assessment of Ricardo's growth economics is that it does not reveal any of
the kindly compassion or quest for tolerance which in other ways truly
characterized the man.

It is with the pairing of J.S. Mill and Marx that Rostow has the most to
report. While both men were great economists, neither saw his economic
analysis as much more than an important intermediate product on the way
to a much more important interpretation of the social process and the
formulation of social history. Again, lacking space, I cannot go into the reasons
why Rostow finds Mill, the founder of modern economic environmentalism,
so wise and prescient, but his is a judgment well worth study. Rostow analyzes
Marx, not from the usual standpoint of his general theory of history, but based
on his formal economics analytical system (a choice he credits to Joan
Robinson with having persuasively made earlier), and this choice makes the
object of his assessment seem intellectually impoverished, ideologically driven,
and empirically careless.

While there are a many great names and proper nouns cited as theorists
in *Part II*, including Marshall (and his younger colleagues and successors), the
Austrian School, Irving Fisher, the National Bureau of Economic Research,
Schumpeter, John H. Williams, both the "younger" and the "older" Simon
Kuznets, and Harrod, the thrust of these chapters is based not so much on
original theoretical constructs as it is on efforts to quantify observations and
analyze the numbers. There is a shift from the study of already industrialized
to industrializing economies—thus, it is typical that a chapter starting with
the subtitle, "The Great Enterprise of Simon Kuznets," quickly moves to a
discussion of the works of Hollis Chenery and others.

In general, it is fair to say that Rostow admires the work of John Stuart Mill
and Alfred Marshall above all others. Marshall's study of economic development
was intensive, but time-, place-, and culture-defined. Nonetheless, the breadth
and depth of Marshall's intended "reach" (doubtless exceeding his "grasp") served
to create the bases for the modern discipline of economic development. What
Kuznets did was to extend that by "a collective reach" to cover not only
industrialized societies (influenced as they were by late nineteenth-until mid-

twentieth developments), but through his Social Science Research Council large grant for studies of industrializing societies, to something approximating the present "collective grasp," including developing economies.

Of *Part III* (Growth Analysis Post-1945: A Three Ring Circus), I chose to focus on Chapter 17. "[Modern] Development Economics" organizes the current discipline's development into six "phases," of which the *first* was tied in with developments during World War II, the *second* with movement from concern only with the post-war reindustrialization of the industrialized nations to third-world economies, and the *third* which involved the pressures introduced by the facts of the Korean Civil War. Rostow's *fourth* phase included the halcyon period of the Alliance for Progress and the efforts of the OECD to do for Asia what was being tried for Latin America and the disillusionment with the lack of results which became all too apparent, even before the decade of the 1960s. The *fifth* phase was the period of transfer of leadership from national or regional (AID or OECD-type) programs, to truly internationalized programs such as those sponsored by the World Bank and other development banks; this phase lasted until the era of the Second Oil Shock which served to all but crush the development schemes.[2] There then follows a sequential analysis of contemporary growth theorists: Bauer, Colin Clark, Hirschman, Lewis, Myrdal, Prebisch, Singer, and Tinbergen.[3] Of these Rostow gives major recognition to Lewis whom he puts in the class of John Stuart Mill and Marshall.

Chapter 18 is a new statement of Rostow's own theory of economic growth, or to use his explanatory phrase, "[it] is an exercise in summation, not intellectual biography" (p. 428). Even so, it does contain powerful autobiographical bits, and, incidentally, offers a persuasive (to me) claim that his view of the decline of the Soviet behemoth was seen by him as a growth economics problem rather than the question of any leadership's loss of confidence in its capacity to govern politically or economically. Some, particularly those who have long opposed Rostow's views because of his Viet-Nam stance, might find this assertion self-serving. That may be so, but that does not make it less correct.

While *Part IV* has three chapers, it is on the penultimate Chapter (20), again couched in terms of the available literature, which focuses on Rostow's essential *deus ex machina*, the dual nature and complexity of technological change that I chose to comment. His partial rejection of the reasoning in his earlier complex view that the world had progressed beyond trying to cope with Kondratieff long cycles is well argued. He now advances new and better arguments. The text concludes with a statement of the current agenda (Chapter 21). Rostow being Rostow, he sets out to do more than merely state its elements; he suggests that the danger of an inappropriate resolution will bring on a modern French-type revolution, but phrased in terms of the Armageddon of civilization.

The book concludes with an Appendix, written in cooperation with Michael Kennedy (RAND Corporation) presenting formally (mathematically), but nonetheless containing considerable explanatory prose, the various models of economic growth discussed earlier.

*   *   *   *   *   *

While I have made it abundantly clear that I am much impressed with Rostow's conceptual apparatus and the way he has employed it, it is nonetheless desirable to note some reservations, which others might find likely, about this work.

First and foremost is the question of what really constitutes an economic theory? While there have been many who claim that theory must offer a quantitative test, both retrospective and prospective, such in my judgement is far too a specialized view of the nature of theories; certainly one which Marshall would have thought far too narrow. The lessons of Machlup's decades-long debate with Lester are still far from clear, but what does emerge is that theory may explain only one kind of "rational" action (what may vary is the kind of rationality, not merely any purported single universal test of imminent criticism), and that if "theory is only what theory can do," the game is not to expect it to do everything. In other words, the validity of a theory may depend upon what rules of rationality one chooses to employ—Newtonian mechanics, probabilities, simple explanatory assistance, and so on. And although theory can be made to explain everything in a game with fully specified assumptions, in the game of normal living (to use a Marshallian word of art) a theory is only as good as it can be used practically.

Second, Simon Kuznets, upon whose empirical and conceptual work Rostow clearly draws heavily, thought that any stages theory, as such, had to admit of explicit definition of each stage and overwhelming evidence that the stage sequence could be quantitatively defined and was in and of itself necessary and invariable unidirectional. Kuznets's earlier (1960) criticism of Rostow's stages theories is well-known and requires no repetition here. It was forcefully put, and doubtless served to persuade a generation of economists that Rostow's claim was premature. But, Rostow has gone beyond what he previously asserted ("the take-off had necessary requisite and invariable consequences"), and he now offers us a richer and broader view.

But, there is another side to the Kuznets coin. While Kuznets averred in his 1954 American Economic Association presidential address that he retained a faith in the eventual identification of a theory explaining economic growth, neither then nor later did he ever produce a theory which satisfied his expectations. My question then becomes, "Does Rostow come as close to a theory as we have, and, if so, should his formulation be so considered until something better comes along?"

I am not averse to drawing a comparison with Pareto's "Law [of Income Distribution]" and Rostow's "Theory." The beauty of Pareto's discussion of his "Law," is that he clearly prescribed it as a generalization, one true only until something more refined came along, as indeed Robert Gibnat's did. Neither Pareto nor Rostow deserve to be evaluated in terms of an insincere "politesse"; but if mere man is in the clear granting to Pareto points for the time and place value of his Law, I see no reason for mere man to hesitate to grant to Rostow points for the time and place value of his theory. He offers a matrix broad enough to encompass Colin Clark, Gunnar Myrdal, and the older and younger Kuznets. That he identifies John Stuart Mill and Marshall as his preferred theorists merely explains what I have tried to say; neither of them thought that economic theory was the appropriate goal. Theory was learning; understanding was knowledge. Their appropriate goal was an understanding of the complexities of economic life, that is of the possession of knowledge. In the end, I think that what Kuznets couldn't find but still hoped existed, doesn't exist. There is no theory of economic growth; what there is is a bundle of varieties of knowledge. Pope chose his words carefully when he wrote that "a little *learning* is a dangerous thing." What Kuznets probably came to realize and Rostow now offers, is that the answer is not a theoretical model, it is an understanding of how human society approaches economic growth.

I think that this book contains a fine, and even rare, statement of current knowledge.

## NOTES

1.  His hardline Viet-Nam position has served to give many purportedly self-conscious *scientific* academicians an essentially negative but irrelevant view toward all of his scholarly achievements. This last point is important, because while there may or may not be reason to admire his foreign policy assumptions and views (and having studied them in some detail, I tend to admire them), there is no clear reason to me to explain how one cannot but admire and envy the range of scholarship—particularly as revealed in the book at hand.

2.  Obviously the book, published in 1990 and therefore written earlier, could not take into account the rash of events in Central and Eastern Europe in 1990 and 1991.

3.  Lest anyone think that Adelman, Myint, Nurkse, Rosenstein-Rodan, Streeten, and Viner are carelessly omitted, be reassured. They get much of their due; Rostow's explains his choices.

# Carl Menger and His Legacy in Economics

edited by Bruce Caldwell
(Durham, NC: Duke University Press, 1990, 407 pp.)

Reviewed by **Peter Boettke**

In April 1989 a conference was held at Duke University to commemorate the acquisition of Carl Menger's papers by Duke. In fact, over the past several years Duke has worked to acquire the papers of several outstanding figures in the history of economics, a strategy which solidifies that institution's position as perhaps the leading center for research in the history of economic thought. The volume that emerged from the Duke conference represents the third volume of collected papers devoted to a critical assessment of Menger's work available to English language readers that has appeared in the last 20 years. John Hicks and Wilhelm Weber edited a volume, *Carl Menger and the Austrian School of Economics* (1973), which developed out of a 1971 conference to celebrate the 100th anniversary of the publication of Menger's *Grundsatze*. Richard Wagner also collected a series of assessments of Menger in a special issue of the *Atlantic Economic Journal* (September 1978).

Menger scholarship has definitely been on the increase. The social science index, for example, shows that in the period between 1966 and 1970 Menger received only 14 cites, whereas during that same period William Stanley Jevons received 45, Leon Walras 62 and Alfred Marshall 316. However, while Menger does not overcome his marginal revolutionary contemporaries in the post-1970 era, attention to his work steadily rises. In the period between 1971-1975 Menger received 59 cites, 38 between 1976-1980, 70 between 1981-1985, and 122 between 1986-1990. Between January and August 1991, the *Social Science Citation Index* recorded 60 cites (no doubt in large part because of the Caldwell edited volume), whereas Marshall recorded 83, Jevons 20 and Walras 19.

Research in the History of Economic Thought and Methodology,
Volume 13, pages 285-293.
Copyright © 1995 by JAI Press Inc.
All rights of reproduction in any form reserved.
ISBN: 1-55938-095-0

An assessment of Menger could take one of at least four tracks. It could proceed in the first instance as an examination of the ideas that influenced Menger and his intellectual development as well as his own contributions to economic science and social science methodology. Second, it could proceed as an examination of the development of Austrian economics in the first two decades of this century and its subsequent spread to the English speaking world in the interwar period. A third method of assessment could be a critical appraisal and reconstruction of Menger's methodological writings in light of modern developments in the philosophy of science. And, finally, a critical appraisal and reconstruction of Menger's economics in light of modern developments in economics and the Austrian tradition could prove very fruitful. *Carl Menger and His Legacy in Economics* does touch all four topics, and offers the reader a wealth of information on Menger.

Unfortunately, I did not come away convinced of the merit of several of the articles. History of thought, for history of thought's sake is interesting, but it does not get us very far toward understanding the meaning of an author. The more interesting questions, at least for me, are those which attempt to appraise and reconstruct an earlier author—to ask what the author's message *means* to us today. The majority of the articles collected in this book simply do not address that question. They, on the contrary, contain much information, some bold conjectures, and generally some rather odd interpretations of Menger. The one point sorely missing from the volume is a really thorough treatment of the meaning of subjectivism that permeates Menger's work, and what that entails for our construction of modern economics along Mengerian lines.

The chapter by Jeremy Shearmur does address the question of subjectivism, but mainly from the point of view of pointing out the inherent weaknesses of *radical subjectivism*. Shearmur argues that radical subjectivism implies an economic nihilism toward welfare propositions that he perceives as undesirable. Shearmur believes that a return to Menger's concern with human nature, grounded in biological notions and a willingness to make "common sense" interpersonal utility comparisons would provide a better foundation for modern Austrian economics than the radical subjectivism of Ludwig Mises, F. A. Hayek, Ludwig Lachmann, and G. L. S. Shackle.

But, Shearmur's concerns arise from a failure to recognize the limits of economics. Economics per se may be best understood as dealing with what men think and believe, and not the objective properties of things. If that limits the confidence with which economists can say something about the equilibrium properties or welfare consequences of policies, then so what? Shackle's argument in *Epistemics and Economics* that economics is fundamentally about thoughts, and that "as far as men are concerned, being consists of continual and endless fresh knowing" about sums up the subjectivist perspective even if it implies certain indeterminacies in our thought (1972, p. 156). Lachmann argued in his last book, *The Market as an Economic Process*, following Shackle that the market is best understood as the "meaningful utterances of the human mind" (1986, p. 165). The implication of these statements by Shackle and Lachmann are wide ranging—influencing not only the questions economists should ask, but also defining how we should attempt to find appropriate answers. What economists give up in terms of their ability to make statements about "best" or "better" social arrangements, they may gain in terms of a richer understanding of the phenomena they are studying—like market exchange or interest. It is a trade-off that economic science should be willing to make.

This does not mean that economists have nothing to say about alternative social arrangements. As an economist, I cannot tell you which property rights system is "right" or "wrong," but I can say something about the effect different property rights arrangements can have on the pattern of economic activity. Property rights create expectations, and expectations guide actions.

Subjectivist economics provides the analyst with general insights concerning the effects which alternative institutional environments can have on human behavior. While these insights do not provide the information necessary for designing mechanisms of social control, they do provide information that the analyst can employ in discussing social arrangements that cultivate economic progress.

The goal of the subjectivist economist is, first and foremost, to understand human action in terms of the purposes and plans of individuals, and, secondly, trace out the unintended consequences of those actions. Recognizing the problem of economic calculation, for example, emerged out of a subjectivist understanding of the exchange ratios that are formed on the market.[1] By translating the subjective trade-offs of some into effective knowledge for others, the price system provides a social means for separating out from the numerous array of technologically feasible projects those which were economically feasible. The individual trading activity of economic actors produces a relative price structure, which, while not of anyone's intention, was the composite result of their actions, and serves as a social backdrop upon which economic decisions are based.

Interference or abolition of this social system of learning, a learning process which Mises argued was anchored deep in the human mind, would distort or destroy the signals which guide human actions in allocating scarce resources.[2] This is not to argue that the process of economic calculation in a private property order is a perfect mechanism for allocating scarce resources, but rather, as Mises argued, that it provide all that practical life demands.[3] Despite its imperfections, the relative price structure existing in the market gets the job done through a process of error detection and entrepreneurial discovery.

Don Lavoie's contribution to the volume addresses this issue of interpretation of market signals and how economic actors come to understand one another and the market signals that guide them to act in concert with one another. Lavoie, drawing from developments in philosophical hermeneutics, rejects the "copy" theory of communication which perceives human communication as analogous to fax transmissions or machine communication between computers. Instead, Lavoie argues, all human communication requires interpretation and mediation. If, as Hayek has argued, the main function of the market is one of communicating information to economic actors, then Lavoie's suggestive essay points us in a direction of research that is invaluable in gaining a better understanding of the communicative properties of the price system.

Karen Vaughn's essay, which I think is the most interesting in the collection, also highlights the importance of the communicative properties of the market system, and specifically, the importance that the issue of economic calculation has had for steering the direction of modern subjectivist economics. Vaughn's essay is a contribution to contemporary intellectual history as she details the resurgence of the Austrian school in the 1970s. But, in her historical account she also examines some of the nagging questions that the modern Austrian school is still grappling with concerning the nature of market processes, the meaning of equilibrium, and the central concern among Austrians in explicating how the competitive market process communicates dispersed knowledge.

The point here, contra Shearmur, is that *only* by pursuing a radical subjectivist research agenda can the economist arrive at a proper understanding of the dynamic, non-equilibrium nature of the competitive market economy, and, as such, highlight the problems that intervention in this process will confront. If that does not yield the determinate conclusions that, say, Walrasian economics does, then so much the better because the goal is conceptual understanding of the economy and economic institutions and not determinate solutions.[4] In addition, the subjectivist project is somewhat less ambitious than what Shearmur expects of economics. Economics per se cannot make statements about everything—there is an intellectual division of labor.

The subjectivist economist need not be a moral or cultural relativist once the bounds of economics are crossed. In fact, Shearmur's conclusion seems to suggest that only an interdisciplinary approach to welfare economics can solve the problems he raised. In this, I think he is right. But, then why all the fuss about subjectivist economics? The contribution of economics to the issue lies precisely in the realm of providing a subjectivist understanding of economic activity, and nothing more. Ethics, history, psychology, and so forth, alongside economics, all have their role to play in formulating a social theory. And, in the end, it is a comprehensive social theory that will change the world in the direction that Shearmur desires, not economics per se.

Roger Garrison's chapter on the development of Austrian capital theory demonstrates the point that by pursuing the radical subjectivist agenda, errors in economic reasoning are eliminated. Bohm-Bawerk's greatest error was precisely that he did not safeguard the subjectivist domain from the unwarranted intrusion of objectivistic concepts. As a result, Bohm-Bawerk was vulnerable to the criticisms of J. B. Clark and later Frank Knight, and provided the foundation for Knut Wicksell's reformulation of Austrian capital theory along formalistic lines. Garrison, who is not only a very clear expositor of the history of capital theory, but also a significant figure in the reconstruction of modern Austrian capital theory, argues that Menger's reservations about Bohm-Bawerk's capital theory were warranted and that by pursuing the radical subjectivist, non-formalistic mode of analysis Menger suggested, economics will develop a better understanding of the capital using economy.

Many essays in this volume attempt to address Menger's philosophical system. One of Eric Streissler's papers, for example, addresses Menger's belief system in terms of public policy—as does the paper by Israel Kirzner. Streissler derives his interpretation of Menger's policy position from Menger's lectures to the Crown Prince Rudolf. As an undergraduate, I had heard about the Rudolf lectures from Hans Sennholz—he placed great weight on these lectures and the Crown Prince's suicide as evidence of Menger's classical liberal perspective and his prescience with regard to the decline of liberalism in Europe. Menger's pessimism about the plight of liberalism was invoked by Sennholz to explain Menger's inactivity in the late stage of his career. Streissler's paper seems to corroborate Sennholz's tale. Kirzner's paper, on the other hand, deals more directly with the substantive content of Menger's work and its implication for public policy. Kirzner argues that Menger's approach, when consistently pursued, generates a policy position which may be much more radical in its adherence to laissez-faire than even Menger was aware.

The other paper by Streissler analyzes the state of German economic thinking prior to Menger. It is a very informative essay, demonstrating that German economics had already developed along lines that anticipated Menger's innovations. Paul Silverman's paper pursues a similar theme. He argues that the usual interpretation of Menger as an Aristotelan, associated with the work of Emil Kauder, does not possess the evidence usually assumed. Menger was indeed a Aristotelan, but not directly. Rather, Silverman argues that Menger inherited his Aristotelan framework indirectly through the Cameralist writers. Silverman's thesis is interesting, but it unfortunately diverts our attention from Menger's philosophical connection to continental philosophers.

Austrian economics is best understood as the peculiar by-product of classical economics (perhaps in the form of the older German historical school) combined with the continental philosophies of interpretation and understanding. Max Alter's paper, for example, does have the strength of placing Menger firmly within the *verstehende* tradition, but his fundamental misunderstanding of that philosophical tradition and Menger's system of thought render his provocative chapter highly suspect—as Lawrence White's rebuttal demonstrates. Only the chapter by Barry Smith actually seems to capture Menger's spirit, even if Smith fails to do justice to Mises's philosophical project and its direct connection to the philosophical project that influenced Menger via Franz Brentano, i.e., phenomenology.

The radical subjectivist position follows from a concern with gleaning meaning. The essentialism of Menger, the a priorism of Mises, and so forth, have the same goal—to obtain a fundamental understanding of the meaning of social phenomenon.[5] The teleological perspective that is adopted follows from the fact that it is only at the level of the individual that we can attribute meaning to actions. The Austrian perspective *never* denied collective entities; rather, the whole point was to try to understand the being and becoming of such entities.[6]

The Mengerian system of thought can be divided into methodological propositions and modes of analysis. The methodological propositions amount to: methodological individualism, methodological subjectivism, and concern with processes as opposed to end states. In terms of the mode of analysis we can talk of: exact theory, which has the goal of generating universal laws; applied theory, in which the universal laws are still in operation but yield different results depending on the alternative institutional arrangements assumed; and economic history and public policy, where interpretations are detail specific and unique.

The Mengerian criticism of historicism amounted to an argument that all facts were theory laden. Historical interpretation is based on a theoretical framework, made up of components from the realms of exact and applied theory. It is through this framework that historical facts are distilled. History simply cannot be done without the aid of theory. The question is not theory or no theory, but rather, articulated theory subject to peer criticism or non-stated theory. Those who try to reason without theory simply tend to reason with implicit and perhaps bad theory. Menger was trying to justify theoretical investigation in an intellectual culture of German-language economics that tended to denigrate theory. *Causal* explanations that sought to get at the essence of social phenomenon, however, required a well-articulated theoretical edifice to aid the researcher.

Exact theory, for example, is confined to examining *reflectively* the basic principles that guide human behavior. The fact that individuals have goals and strive to obtain these goals possesses implications. Logical principles such as diminishing marginal utility, the notion of opportunity cost, and economizing behavior all follow from examining the logic of action. These interpretive principles do not need to be tested. Rather, the very limited set of principles that constitute the realm of exact theory are derived from our *intersubjective* experience of being human.

We have access to information as social scientists because we are what we study. Because we dwell within the world we are hoping to understand, we are actually in a better position with regard to the status of our knowledge than the natural sciences.[7] Whereas the natural science begin with an arbitrary starting point, the social sciences begin with knowledge of the shared human experience. This is not private introspection, but the intersubjective experience of the life-world that phenomenologists like Edmund Husserl have discussed at length. Mises, for example, was influenced by Husserl both directly and indirectly through Alfred Schutz. In fact, Schutz's *Phenomenology of the Social World* (1932) provides a key that unlocks many of the philosophical and language mysteries of the Austrian project that have produced many misinterpretations throughout the years, and, unfortunately, in the volume presently under discussion. There is not a single reference to Schutz in the entire volume, yet many of the authors offer interpretations of the development of Menger's philosophy by the subsequent generation of Austrian thinkers.

Schutz attempts in *The Phenomenology* to resolve some of the remaining issues from the methodenstreit for social theory by way of reconstructing Max Weber's interpretive sociology with the aid of the philosophical writings of Husserl and Henri Bergson.[8] Schutz was influenced in this direction by Mises. It is important to remember that Mises considered his development of praxeology as the further development of Weber's project. Much of the peculiar language of the Austrians and the direction of research they pursued disappear if these philosophical roots are understood. For example, in Machlup's paper on verification in economics, contrary to usual interpretations, he is actually worlds apart from Milton Friedman's "as ifism." By invoking the criterion of "understandability" to judge basic propositions, Machlup alludes to his phenomenological roots, and adopts a philosophical perspective which is alien to the Friedmanite position, yet this is bypassed by most readers (1955, p. 17).

In terms of understanding the thrust of Menger's philosophical message, his general connection to the concerns of the *verstehende* tradition, and specifically, his direct connection to the emergence of phenomenological psychology with Brentano, are essential, as Barry Smith has argued in several papers in recent years.[9] The implications of this general philosophical approach to studying the social world are vast, and probably received their fullest statement by Hayek in *The Counter-Revolution* (1952).

In Philip Mirowski's book, *More Heat than Light* he puts forth the idea that the rejection by the economics profession of Hayek in the late 1940s and early 1950s, after a decade of being one of the dominant figures in the profession, had as much to do with his alien philosophical approach as it did with his anti-socialist, anti-Keynesian policy conclusions (1989, 412, fn. 1). I tend to think Mirowski is right. Unless the philosophical tradition is understood, the project that emerged from Menger's writings and continues to be developed will not be appreciated. Unfortunately, it is precisely this philosophical spirit which the authors of a majority of the papers in this volume do not understand.

*Carl Menger and His Legacy in Economics* contains much useful information, and may get individuals thinking about the foundational issues that are of concern to Austrian economists, but it does not get us much closer to an understanding of the meaning of Menger today for the reconstruction of economic methodology and economic reasoning. Caldwell did an outstanding job of organizing the conference and editing this volume which contains so many diverse readings of Menger, but it remains unclear to this reviewer how much most of these papers add to Menger scholarship. If, however, this volume leads scholars to examine these issues in more depth, then perhaps the result will confirm one of Menger's most important insights— that many socially beneficial institutions (such as the growth of scientific knowledge) are the result of human action, but not of human design.

## ACKNOWLEDGMENT

I would like to thank Gilberto Salgado, Warren Samuels, and Charles Steele for comments on an earlier draft. Remaining errors are exclusively my own.

## NOTES

1. Ludwig von Mises argued that "To understand the problem of economic calculation it was necessary to recognize the true character of the exchange relations expressed in the prices of the market. The existence of this important problem could be revealed only by the methods of the modern subjective theory of value" See Mises (1922, p. 186).

2. As Mises wrote, "The process by which supply and demand are accommodated to each other until a position of equilibrium is established and both are brought into quantitative and qualitative coincidence, is the higgling of the market. But supply and demand are only the links in a chain of phenomena, one end of which has this visible manifestation in the market, while the other is anchored deep in the human mind" See Mises (1912, p. 153).

3. See Mises (1922, pp. 100-101).

4. For a general discussion of the price economics as a science pays for the overriding emphasis on producing determinate solutions see Samuels. (1989).

5. Because positivist and Popperian notions of science preclude in principle discussions of "meaning," the papers by Karl Milford and Jack Biner, while providing interesting reading, simply miss the boat with regard to understanding Menger's methodological system. Uskali Maki's attempt to reconstruct Menger along the lines of scientific realism is provocative, but fails in the final analysis to do justice to Menger's continental roots and the project of economic understanding that follows.

6. See Mises (1949, p. 42), where he states that "Methodological individualism, far from contesting the significance of such collective wholes, considers it as one of its main tasks to describe and to analyze their becoming and their disappearing, their changing structures, and their operation. And it chooses the only method fitted to solve this problem satisfactorily."

7. This argument has been made forcefully by Michael Polanyi (1958).

8. For a general discussion of this project see Predergast (1986).

9. See Smith (1986, 1990).

# REFERENCES

Hayek, F. [1952], 1979. *The Counter-Revolution of Science*. Indianapolis: Liberty Classics.

Lachmann, L. 1986. *The Market as an Economic Process*. New York: Basil Blackwell.

Machlup, F. 1955. "The Problem of Verification in Economics." *Southern Economic Journal*, 22(1): 1-21.

Mirowski, P. 1989. *More Heat Than Light*. New York: Cambridge University Press.

Mises, L. [1912], 1980. *The Theory of Money and Credit*. Indianapolis: Liberty Classics.

Mises, L. [1922], 1981. *Socialism: An Economic and Sociological Analysis*. Indianapolis: Liberty Classics.

Mises, L. [1949], 1966. *Human Action: A Treatise on Economics*. Chicago: Henry Regnery.

Polanyi, M. 1958. *The Study of Man*. Chicago: University of Chicago Press.

Prendergast, C. 1986. "Alfred Schutz and the Austrian School of Economics." *American Journal of Sociology*, 92(1): 1-26.

Samuels, W. 1989. "Determinate Solutions and Valuation Processes: Overcoming the Foreclosure of Process. *Journal of Post Keynesian Economics* 11(4): 531-546.

Schutz, A. 1932. *The Phenomenology of the Social World*. Evanston: Northwestern University Press.

Shackle, G. 1972. *Epistemics and Economics*. New Brunswick, NJ: Transaction Publishers.

Smith, B. 1986. "Austrian Economics and Austrian Philosophy. Pp. 1-36. In *Austrian Economics: Historical and Philosophical Background*, edited by W. Grassl and B. Smith. New York: New York University Press.

Smith, B. 1990. "On the Austrianness of Austrian Economics. *Critical Review* 4(1-2): 212-238.

# Discursive Acts

by R.S. Perinbanayagam
(Hawthorne, New York: Aldine De Gruyter, 1991; 211 pp.
$43.95 cloth; $23.95 paper)

Reviewed by **Robert E. Babe**

It is highly significant that the publisher of R.S. Perinbanayagam's *Discursive Acts* requested a review in this annual. It is equally remarkable that the editor undertook to provide it.

For Perinbanayagam's book, which analyses the dynamics of human conversations from the perspectives of rhetoric, semiology, psycholinguistics and hermeneutics, does not address directly what many would consider to be "economic" phenomena at all. Economists, after all, are inclined to limit their professional attention to those human interactions or exchanges mediated by money, barter being a notable but minor exception. *Discursive Acts,* in contrast, focuses on non-monetarized, verbal, symbolic interactions, thereby calling attention to a bifurcation of the field of human interaction—into the realms of the "economic" and the "non-economic" (or what I will term here the "purely communicatory").

This bifurcation may make sense or at least be harmless if, as Gary Becker contends, all human relationships *are* essentially commodity relationships (Becker), or alternatively if the two systems or modes of interaction are essentially independent of one another. On the other hand, if economic relations tend to overwhelm and transform otherwise non-commoditized or purely communicatory interactions (what some critics refer to derisively as "labor commoditization," or "information commoditization," for example), or if the non-commoditized sector affects in complex ways the economic, then interrelations between economic and communicatory processes need to be explored more fully than has been the case hitherto (Babe, 1996). Preliminary to such exploration, however, is a reappraisal of the economists' conception of information.

Research in the History of Economic Thought and Methodology,
Volume 13, pages 295-301.
Copyright © 1995 by JAI Press Inc.
All rights of reproduction in any form reserved.
ISBN: 1-55938-095-0

Certainly over the 32 years since George Stigler lamented information's occupancy of "a slum dwelling in the town of economics" (Stigler, 1960/1968), information has moved up-scale, so to speak. Today, a still-burgeoning "Information Economics" literature is in place, which focuses primarily on theoretical implications for economic behavior of "imperfect information" in capital, labor or product markets (Stiglitz; Lamberton, 1984, 1990; Spence; Jonscher). Moreover, information's new-found prosperity is underscored by pointing to a less voluminous but nonetheless highly influential "Information Economy" literature, proposing the predominance for the macro-economy of information production, processing, storage and distribution (Machlup; Porat; Hepworth; Serafini and Andrieu).

But, to extend Stigler's metaphor a bit, this heightened attention afforded information (of a certain type) distracts attention from the discrimination now being practiced in the town of economics. For "Information Economists" recognize and honor but one type of information. In the words of Kenneth Arrow, a seminal figure in the field: "The meaning of information is precisely a reduction in uncertainty" (Arrow, 1979 p. 306).

Such an impoverished conceptualization of what information is results in, at best, a superficial and inadequate comprehension of communication as well. To mainstream (neoclassical) economists, human relations are monetarized exchange relations wherein sellers dispose of items or of labor power in order to attain products or labor services that they value more highly. In this paradigm, human interaction is means to an end, namely the disposal and acquisition of products or services to attain higher satisfaction. "Information," (i.e., reduction in uncertainty) facilitates such exchanges by helping buyers and sellers locate one another, and also by making them more aware of the properties or qualities of the commodities bought and sold. It is a major virtue of R.S. Perinbanayagam's book that it implicitly challenges economists to explore more deeply than hitherto the complexities and profundities of information and communication, and to reconsider the adequacy of current treatments.

Before enlarging on the challenges posed to mainstream economics by fuller understanding of information/communication, I attempt first to synthesize the theoretical first half of Perinbanayagam's book, and also to summarize briefly the book's second half which illustrates preceding theories through analyses of recorded conversations.

It is Perinbanayagam's contention that "conversations lead to the emergence of selves, and selves in turn create conversations" (p. xi). Likewise, communication both produces and is a product of human relationships. For adequate understanding, then, symbolic exchanges need to be studied in the context of on-going and developing relationships.

Perinbanayagam declares that "meaningful interactions are not just an [sic] exchange of meaning with the help of symbols.... [but] should rather be viewed as selves participating in encounters" (p. 7). In discourse, the initiator, upon articulation, surrenders control of the meaning of the message to the respondent whose job becomes one of "working upon" the message, reconstructing it, interpreting it—prior to framing a response. Such reconstructions and interpretations, however, Perinbanayagam writes, can be as much "full of a self as the articulations of the initiator" (p. 66), making the interpretive chain "replete with uncertainty" (p. 68). By engaging in communication, therefore, "a person enters a life with others, opening himself or herself up to responsive acts" (p. 114).

Following semiologist C.S. Peirce, Perinbanayagam contends, "in acts of discourse the initiator and the respondent practice mutual semiosis", semiosis being defined as "an action or influence which is, or involves, a co-operation of *three* subjects, such as a sign, its object, and its interpretant, this tri-relative influence not being resolvable into action between two pairs" (p. 31). Tri-relative influence implies that initiator and respondent may have quite different interpretations ("interpretants") for a given message or "sign," if and when their experiences of the external world ("object") differ. In summary, discursive acts "elicit active and responsive interpretations that *to some extent* are dependent on the original acts and their constituent features" (p. 86, emphasis added).

The last half of Perinbanayagam's book applies these observations and theories of human interaction to recorded conversations of various categories: first, to different *forms* of discourse (such as requests, instructions, compliments, insults, retorts, commands, jokes, scoldings, rebuttals, etc.); next, to different *emotions* in discourse (anger, frustration, catharsis, love, jealousy, joy, shame, malice); and finally following Kenneth Burke, to *drama* in discourse (act, scene, agent, agency, purpose, attitude, mimesis, play and display of self).

Perinbanayagam, it may be concluded, paints a much different picture of information and of human communication than do "Information Economists." This is because Perinbanayagam views people as "selves" experientially constituted through discursive interaction and engaged in on-going discursive acts. For the author, freedom characterizes conversation due to ambiguities and uncertainties in interpretations and responses, calling for creativity and adaptive strategies. How different is this view of human interaction from that of economists who insist that people are behavioral units, mechanically maximizing utility (subject to income constraint) by buying and selling in depersonalized markets (Scitovsky). Whereas economists define information precisely as a "reduction in uncertainty," Perinbanayagam insists that symbolic exchange *creates* uncertainty, launching dialogic partners onto paths that take unforeseeable twists and turns. Far from viewing personal interaction as taking place solely between autonomous others intent on satisfying pre-existing wants through commodity transfer, Perinbanayagam insists that we all live in and hence share a semiological field ("a signifying culture") wherein symbolic interactions create self-identities as well as "interpersonal presence and interactional resonance and engagement" (p. 4). Communication, that is symbolic interaction, affects others, and all are affected.

Furthermore, as Perinbanayagam notes, the "tri-level" nature of communication means not only that the "interpretant" of a sign can vary in accordance with one's experience with the sign's "object," but conversely that signs (or texts, or discourses) can in turn modify experiences with "objects". An example provided in the book concerns food:

> One feels hunger and eats not just food "but various natural substances that have been turned into hamburger or steak, pasta or pudding. In semiotic terms, a sign selected for an object is replaced by another one before it is presented for the elicitation of an interpretant.... In this method of transformation, human experiences are perceived, defined, and represented in such a way that their significance is essentially altered. These experiences are typically carried in linguistic forms (p. 56).

Or, to coin another example, economic theory (a "sign" or text), does not merely stand for or describe an external reality (its "object," namely economic processes), but also transforms perceptions of, or experiences with this "object." Recognition of this "active" role of economic theory and analysis has spawned an emerging literature on "Economics as Discourse" (Samuels; Klamer et al.), from which it is but a small next step to view mainstream economics as ideology, as persuasion, as means of control, leading to a political economy approach to economic "knowledge." (Adams and Brock).

Moreover, Perinbanayagam's analysis invites us to explore the implications for economic theory of comprehending artifacts or commodities as "signs" or as texts to be "read" or interpreted, rather than merely as "objects." Thorstein Veblen well understood that commodities are simultaneously "objects" and "signs" (Veblen), but his insights have been largely ignored by the modern theorists. If, however, commodities are not demanded solely for their utilitarian properties but also (often more so), for the messages they impart to buyer and to others, then "users" of such commodities are not merely those who own or display them but also those who "read" them as messages. Our on-going conversations then are not merely verbal (the focus of Perinbanayagam's book), but also artifactual. If selves exist and develop, as Perinbanayagam contends, in symbolic interactions, then commodities owned, used and displayed contribute to such existence and development. Moreover, if symbolic interaction is to be studied in the context of on-going and developing relationships, as Perinbanayagam insists, then so too should the signifying properties of commodities. Commodities, the theories of discourse imply, are symbols or signs in flux. The meanings that people ascribe to artifacts, of course, derive in part from how these artifacts are circulated and used, and upon the meanings ("interpretants") that vendors (advertisers) attempt to attach to them, as well as personal histories with things (Miller; Csikszentimihalyi and Rochberg-Halton; Appadurai; McCracken).

The implications for the economic theory of consumer behavior of viewing commodities as signs, then, may be quite revolutionary. If each commodity is a sign in a semiological system that a "self" uses to "compose" statements concerning self-identity and relations with others, then *all* goods become "complementary goods," modifying one another syntagmatically. Indeed, Perinbayanagam views the self as a "maxisign," that is a "system of symbols and meanings" (p. 10). People can think only with signs, the author contends, and every conception people have, including that of self, is "cognizable," that is "signable" (p. 9). Among the universe of signs used to constitute a particular self, are commodities. Quoting G.H. Meade, Perinbayanagam notes: "The self as an object ... is dependent upon the presence of other objects with which the individual can identify himself" (p. 13). As the self changes through continued discourses, so too will the meanings of the commodities selected, and also the selection of commodities.

A further implication of treating objects as signs, potentially devastating for neoclassical theory, is that all economic transactions become replete with "externalities": all live in communicating, signifying systems in which objects are means of communication. No person is an island in his/her use of goods.

Commodities-as-signs challenges also the efficacy of static economic analysis. For in conversation, participants enter into relationship with unforeseen eventualities, and commodities as signs means that commodities participate in these uncertain and evolving relationships. As Perinbanayagam expresses it (p. 4), "Like Shahrazade's stories, all discourses are embedded in other discourses, which are embedded in other discourses, through which we make ourselves and our worlds." Commodities-as-signs, or as discourse, implies that the foregoing statement can be applied to economic goods as well.

Perinbanayagam's analysis of dialogic interaction, for this reviewer/economist, certainly crowds out the more specialized and reductionist conception of human symbolic interaction countenanced by neoclassical theory and by "Information Economists". Far from economics being "the imperial science" (Stigler, 1988, pp. 191-205), the mainstream discipline should be seen as giving inadequate rendering to even commoditized human interactions.

In my view, R.S. Perinbanayagam's informative and lucid book, *Discursive Acts,* is but one of many possible entry points whereby a fuller and deeper comprehension of information/communication can burst neoclassicism apart at the seams. A fuller rendering of symbolic interaction challenges neoclassical "truths" of: methodological individualism, static analysis, equilibrium, harmony, optimality, efficiency, and exchange.

Of course, neoclassicists will continue to attempt to bar the door, maintaining that "the meaning of information is precisely a reduction in uncertainty." But their insistence in this regard has more to do with the political economy of discourse than with the search for truth. As Perinbanayagam remarks:

Theories should not be treated as commodities demanding fetishistic loyalties or as religions but as incomplete programs forever demanding critique and development (p. xii).

## REFERENCES

Adams, Walter and James Brock. "Economic Theory: Rhetoric, Reality, Rationalization." In *Information and Communication in Economics,* edited by Robert E. Babe. Boston: Kluwer Academic Publishers.

Appadurai, Arjun. 1986. *The Social Life of Things: Commodities in Cultural Perspective.* Cambridge, MA: Cambridge University Press.

Arrow, Kenneth. 1979. The Economics of Information. Pp. 306-317 in *The Computer-age. A Twenty-Year View,* edited by Michael Dertouzos and Joel Moses. Cambridge, MA: MIT Press.

Babe, Robert E. 1992. "Communication: Blindspot of Western Economics." In *Illuminating the Blindspots,* edited by M. Pendakur, J. Wasko and V. Mosco. Norwood, NJ: Ablex Publishing Corporation.

Becker, Gary. 1976. *The Economic Approach to Human Behavior.* Chicago: University of Chicago Press.

Csikszertmihalyi, Mihaly and Eugene Rochberg-Halton. 1981. *The Meaning of Things: Domestic Symbols and the Self.* Cambridge, MA: Cambridge University Press.

Hepworth, Mark. 1990. *Geography of the Information Economy.* New York: Guilford Press.

Jonscher, Charles. 1982. "Notes on Communication and Economic Theory." Pp. 60-69 in *Communication and Economic Development,* edited by D.M. Lamberton and M. Jussawalla. Elmsford, New York: Pergamon Press.

Klamer, Arjo, Donald, McCloskey, and Robert Solow, eds. 1988. *The Consequences of Economic Rhetoric.* Cambridge, MA: Cambridge University Press.

Lamberton, Donald M. 1984. "The Economics of Information and Organization." *Annual Review of Information Science and Technology.* 19: 3-30.

Lamberton, Donald M. 1990. "Information economics: 'Threatened wreckage' or new paradigm?" CIRCIT Working Paper 1990/1991. Melbourne: Centre for International Research on Communication and Information Technologies.

Machlup, Fritz. 1961. *The Production and Distribution of Knowledge in the United States.* Princeton, NJ: Princeton University Press.

McCracken, Grant. 1988. *Culture and Consumption: New Approaches to the Symbolic Character of Consumer Goods and Activities.* Bloomington/Indianapolis: Indiana University Press.

Miller, Daniel. 1987. *Material Culture and Mass Consumption.* Cambridge, MA: Basil Blackwell.

Porat, Marc. 1977. "The Information Economy: Definition and Measurement." Special publication 77-12(1). Washington, D.C.: Office of Telecommunication, U.S. Department of Commerce.

Samuels, Warren J. 1990. *Economics as Discourse: An Analysis of the Language of Economists.* Boston: Kluwer Academic Publishers.

Scitovsky, Tibor. 1976. *The Joyless Economy.* New York: Oxford University Press.

Serafini, Shirely, and Michel Andrieu. 1981. *The Information Revolution and Its Implications for Canada.* Ottawa: Minister of Supply and Services.

Spence, Michael. 1974. "An Economist's View of Information." Pp. 57-78 in *Annual Review of Information Science and Technology, Vol. 9,* edited by C. Caudra, A. Luke and L. Harris. Washington: American Association for Information Science.

Stigler, George. 1960. "The Economics of Information." Pp. 171-190 in *The Organization of Industry,* edited by George Stigler. Homewood, IL: Richard D. Irwin.

Stigler, George. 1988. *Memoirs of an Unregulated Economist.* New York: Basic Books.

Stiglitz, Joseph E. 1985. "Information and Economic Analysis: A Perspective." *The Economic Journal,* 95:21-41.

Veblen, Thorstein [1899] 1953. *The Theory of the Leisure Class.* New York: New American Library.

Selected Papers from the History of
Economics Society Conference 1989
Volume V:    Themes in Pre-Classical, Classical and
Marxian Economics
Volume VI:    Themes in Keynesian Criticism and
Supplementary Modern Topics

edited by William J. Barber

Reviewed by **John B. Davis**

The sixteenth annual History of Economics Society meetings at the University
of Richmond in June 1989 were the occasion for presentation of more than
120 papers by scholars from 21 countries. Of the 43 sessions involved, nearly
half were devoted to Keynesian and methodological issues, with about the same
number of sessions on each subject. Also notable were two sessions on the
two-hundredth anniversary of the French Revolution and two sessions on the
nature of the economics profession. Other sessions included discussions of the
world of Adam Smith, John Commons, Knut Wicksell, Frank Knight, W.H.
Hutt, and such topics as "Visions of the Fate of Capitalism," "Free Trade
Doctrines Reconsidered," and "Topics in Italian Economics."
    It fell to William J. Barber who had organized the conference to select the
papers to be collected in these two *Perspectives* volumes. His selection of 20
papers largely put aside the specifically methodological papers to produce five
thematic sections: in Vol. V, *ASPECTS OF PRE-CLASSICAL ECONOM-
ICS, VARIATIONS ON CLASSICAL THEMES, ASPECTS OF CLASSI-
CAL CONTROVERSIES OVER MONEY AND BANKING,* and *TOPICS*

Research in the History of Economic Thought and Methodology,
Volume 13, pages 303-310.
Copyright © 1995 by JAI Press Inc.
All rights of reproduction in any form reserved.
ISBN: 1-55938-095-0

IN THE ECONOMICS OF MARXISM; in Vol. VI, *INTERPRETATIONS OF KEYNES' POLITICAL AND EARLY ECONOMIC WRITING, THE RECEPTION OF KEYNES'* THE ECONOMIC CONSEQUENCES OF THE PEACE, *CRITIQUES OF THE KEYNESIAN PERSPECTIVE,* and *SUPPLEMENTARY TOPICS.* Across these sections, three general orientations can be distinguished. First, there are papers which might be termed excavational studies, that is, papers that are principally meant to uncover aspects of past thinking that are largely unknown to or unappreciated by contemporary scholars. Second, there are papers which seek to improve our understanding of contemporary traditions in economic thinking by reviewing past debates and controversies. Third, there are papers that attempt to explain how economic ideas get established, both in the sense of explaining their reception and uptake, and in the sense of explaining how that reception and uptake reflects the historical context of those ideas.

Not all of the papers collected here fit neatly into this division, but a case can be made for saying that most do more than not. It would thus be interesting to consider whether these different orientations are complementary, or whether they reflect conflicting conceptions of the tasks appropriate to the history of economic thought. Perhaps more importantly, it would be interesting to consider whether the methods each of these orientations adopt are complementary or conflicting. Orientation I's method is largely directed toward the exegesis of primary sources of a single author or tradition with some reference to the historical context. Orientation II's method takes modern authors and debates as a point of reference for a parallel (though not identical) elaboration of past authors and debates. Orientation III's method examines discursive contexts contemporary and subsequent to past works as the most important means to their explanation. How do these methods stand in relation to one another? Before attempting an answer to this question, a brief survey and classification of the papers of these two *Perspectives* volumes according to orientation is in order.

a.  Excavational work employing the method of exegesis is represented by the papers of Baeck, Lapidus, Murphy, Kennessey, O'Donnell, Dimand, and Yeager. Louis Baeck's "The economic thought of classical Islam" unveils a large body of Islamic economic thinking driven by the moral injunctions of the Koran and the commercial imperatives of Mediterranean trade. The paper makes available generally unavailable sources, and structures the literature according to a view of its progressive unfolding. Andre Lapidus' "Information and risk in the medieval doctrine of usury during the thirteenth century" seeks to sort out contradictions in the medieval doctrine of usury, not by finding a modern understanding of negotiation, information, property, and risk in the doctrine, but by using these notions in a form specific to the thirteenth century to assist in the explanation of the doctrine. The paper builds on the particular market experience of the time to demonstrate the rationales for the Church's evolving views. Antonin E. Murphy's "John Law: aspects of his monetary and debt management policies" provides an account of the development of Law's pre-French Revolution thinking in a way to emphasize that this thinking linked the financial system and the real economy. His paper rehabilitates Law's arguments, despite their association with eighteenth-century speculative disasters. Zoltan Kenessey' "Why *Das Kapital* remained unfinished" presents the results of much archival work to suggest that Marx found explanation of the business cycle more difficult than he had originally imagined. This paper makes a judgment on Marx's more familiar works from the vantage point of the under-exploited archives. R.M. O'Donnell's "Keynes' Political Philosophy" gives a broad survey of many of Keynes' less often cited writings to distinguish Keynes' views on this score from his better known ones in economics. The paper seeks to add a further dimension to philosophical thinking about Keynes. Robert W. Dimand's "'A prodigy of constructive work': J.M. Keynes on *Indian Currency and Finance*" offers a full account of this rarely discussed work of Keynes' in the conviction that it represented a first careful consideration of certain international finance issues on Keynes' part. His paper places the early Keynes in the Classical tradition of Ricardo, Mill, and Marshall. Finally, Leland Yeager's "Hutt and Keynes" re-acquaints us with the work of the recently deceased W.H. Hutt, a longtime critic of Keynesian thinking. The paper surveys Hutt's different writings, and contrasts Hutt's explanation of unemployment with Keynes'.

b.  Studies meant to illuminate current debates by reference to past thinking are represented by papers written by Lowry, Dimand and Dimand, Humphrey, Dostaler, Brems, and Sandelin. S. Todd Lowry's "Understanding ethical individualism and the administrative tradition in pre-eighteenth-century political economy" adds to the modern concept of individual economic rationality an emphasis upon administrative efficiency that dates back to Plato. His argument is meant to extend the contemporary view of individual decision-making by demonstrating its relationship to a developed literature in the administrative tradition. Mary Ann and Robert W. Dimand's "Moral sentiments and the marketplace: the consistency of *The Theory of Moral Sentiments* and *The Wealth of Nations*" examines this classic issue from the contemporary perspective of general equilibrium theory. Offering a new view of the relationship between these two works, this paper has as much to say about general equilibrium theory from Smith's perspective as about Smith's two famous works. Thomas M. Humphrey's "Kaldor versus Friedman in historical perspective" demonstrates that the debate between these two modern figures has extensive antecedents in the bullionist controversy and the currency school-banking school debate. Humphrey uses these earlier disputes to give a fuller characterization of the terms of the Kaldor-Friedman debate. Gilles Dostaler's "The debate between Hayek and Keynes" traces the exchanges between these two figures and their followers in the 1930s. Dostaler sees the same issues afoot today, and seeks to better illuminate them by showing how Hayek and Keynes each responded to each other's argument. Hans Brems' "The Austrian time-interest equilibrium" extends Bohm-Bawerk's model of circulating capital to a fixed capital framework to determine the more general adequacy of the model's predictions. His conclusion that a lower interest rate does not necessarily entail a lengthening of the period of production is meant to enlighten modern Austrian capital theorists about the more general nature of the period of production approach. Finally, Bo Sandelin's "Wicksell's Wicksell effect, the price Wicksell effect, and the real Wicksell effect" re-consider recent judgments of Wicksell's views that arose in the Cambridge controversey on capital. The paper shows that real Wicksell effects, as defined in that modern controversy, had a place in Wicksell's own analysis, and thereby suggests that Wicksell has more to offer on the topic of capital to contemporary theorists.

c.  Papers written to explain how economic ideas get established and how their reception influences their understanding are contributed by Vint, Alborn, Lonnroth, Hemery, Blitch, da Empoli, and Clark. John Vint's "The 'rigid' wages fund doctrine: McCulloch, Mill and the 'monster' of money" systematically applies the Lakatosian methodological framework to explain the rise and fall of the Classical wages fund doctrine. His strategy is to use this example as a case study in the Lakotosian analysis of defense and abandonment of theory. Timothy L. Alborn in his "Commercial therapeutics and the banking profession in early Victorian England" likens developments in nineteenth-century thinking about banking to contemporaneous developments in the medical profession in Britain. He argues that views of therapy and well-being were common to the two, and that developments in the two were mutually influencing. Johan Lonnroth in "The defeat of Marxism as economics: the Swedish example" charts the reception of Marx and Engel's ideas in Sweden through the commentaries and interpretations of early Swedish economists. He emphasizes the adequacies and inadequacies of these readings to show how Marx and Engels came to be understood in Sweden in contrast to their reception elsewhere. John Hemery in "Something and nothing: the impact of J.M. Keynes' *The*

*Economic Consequences of the Peace* in Britain," Charles P. Blitch in
"American responses to Keynes' *The Economic Consequences of the
Peace*," and Domenico da Empoli in "The impact of Keynes' *The
Economic Consequences of the Peace* in Italy, 1919-1921" all take the
occasion of the seventieth anniversary of Keynes' influential book to
examine the progress of its notoriety in their respective national contexts.
Their three papers show there to have been very different views of the
book in each country according to the arrays of political interests
operative in each at the time. Finally, Charles M. A. Clark in his
"Naturalism in economic theory: the use of 'state of nature' explanations
in the history of economic thought" traces a specific metaphysical vision
at work in the development of economic thinking to demonstrate how
economists thinking about social behavior has relied on natural law
presuppositions. His paper explains the perceived coherence and logic
of economic thinking in terms of its grounding in philosophy.

Some of the authors here might well contest their being ascribed only one
or even the particular orientation by which I have classified their papers.
Nonetheless, the broad classification into three orientations seems to
adequately describe most of the contributions to these two volumes of
*Perspectives*, so that the issue remains, how do these orientations and their
methods compare? Guidance on the matter is offered in Barber's own
subsequent Presidential Address to the History of Economics Society (1990),
"Does Scholarship in the History of Economics Have a Useful Future?" Here,
taking as its immediate stimulus the recent opening up of the Eastern bloc and
the likely transmission of Western economic thinking to the countries
abandoning planned economies, but also drawing on his own considerable
scholarship on American political economic experience (1975, 1981, 1985, 1987,
1988, 1989), Barber advances elements of a theory of the international transfer
of economic ideas that makes the general question of the reception and uptake
of economic ideas a central concern.

Chief among the concepts advanced in the Presidential Address is that of
selective filtration. Looking across three historical episodes in the development
of American economic thinking, Barber takes care to describe how ideas
imported from other countries, principally Britain and Germany, were
transformed in their significance and application by American economists
intent upon adapting those ideas to American needs. In the early nineteenth
century, for example,

what came through was not a carbon copy of the originals. Selective filtration was applied.
Most of the American interpreters systematically purged crucial points in the European
classical perspective. Banished was the pessimism of early nineteenth-century classicism
about the dismal prospects associated with the approach of the stationary state. This

outcome seemed inapplicable in the American setting where there was no threat of land
scarcity and the Malthusian population devil was nowhere to be seen. Similarly, overtones
of class conflict were painted out of the picture. This was a European conception which
seemed not to belong in free-soil America (1990, p. 113).

Economic ideas, then, take on their meaning for different audiences according
to the systems of interpretation those audiences inevitably apply to them.
Purists may assert that the study of this process of selective filtration is of
secondary importance in the history of economic thought, and that a Ricardo
or Marx transported and transformed is no longer the true Ricardo of the
*Principles* or Marx of *Capital*. Yet the implication of Barber's analysis is that
this traditional methodological approach is essentially misconceived. Though
the episodes of American interpretation and appropriation he cites are
remarkable for the very considerable transformation of imported ideas,
nonetheless, in principle the same process of interpretation and appropriation
should also be thought present in any and every episode of the interpretation
of economic ideas. The international transfer of ideas, just because it involves
different national contexts, magnifies the exigencies of local interpretation. The
so-called purist, however, also brings his or her own requirements of
interpretation to the texts that he or she studies, and thus the model of selective
filtration Barber offers must ultimately be a very general one. This seems to
be the message of his Presidential Address, and indeed it is a theme that recurs
throughout his scholarly discussions of American political economy.

Orientation III, accordingly, with its focus on ideas' reception and uptake
has pride of place in the two *Perspectives* volumes considered here. This is
perhaps best reflected in the inclusion of the entire session on the reception
surrounding Keynes' *The Economic Consequences of the Peace*. Reading
through these papers in succession is sufficient to disabuse any historian of
economic thought of the presence of a single, definitive message in Keynes'
influential work. But it would be hasty to conclude from this that orientations
I and II represent misguided methodologies in the history of economic thought,
or that these methododologies in some sense conflict with orientation III. In
the optimistic words of his Presidential Address on the future importance of
the history of economics, Barber urged historians of thought to remember that
they are "more likely to think in terms of choices between competing models
and to ponder the conditions under which specific choices are made at
particular moments in time" (1990, p. 111) than traditional theorists who are
generally less methodologically aware of the complexities of reception and
uptake. Orientation II, which seeks to illuminate the choices contemporary
theorists make in light of the similar but different choices made by past
theorists, thus takes just this comparative context and occasion of theory choice
as its implicit backdrop. Relatedly, orientation I, with its excavational
perspective, though certainly susceptible to the bias of the purist, is also

reasonably employed when pursued with sensitivity to controversies in current interpretation.

Nonetheless, it is the emphasis on the reception and uptake of economic ideas which seems central to the principle of selection adopted in these two *Perspectives* volumes. This is particularly interesting in light of the attention economic methodologists have recently devoted to questions surrounding the interpretation and reading of texts (see Samuels, 1990). Barber's own particular emphasis on the reception and uptake of economic ideas, it is fair to say, supports this recent focus by making the historical and social context of a text's reading an important part of its interpretation as a text. Thus, while recent attention to economics as discourse has been chiefly concerned with the linguistic dimensions of text interpretation, that is, considerations largely internal to texts themselves, Barber's interest in the historical spread of ideas rather draws upon the developing social contexts in which economic discourse is embedded. These two approaches—the internalist economics as discourse and the externalist spread of ideas—can be regarded as complementary, though there certainly have been conflicts between some proponents of the two viewpoints over the relative merits of their respective contributions (McCloskey, 1983; Caldwell and Coats, 1984; McCloskey, 1984).

This, however, is not the occasion for a discussion of such issues. Rather, it suffices to note here that in as much as Barber's selection of papers for the two *Perspectives* volumes representing the 1989 History of Economics Society meetings itself reflects well-considered methodological convictions, it seems naturally to follow that historians of economic thought ought themselves be more sensitive to the methodological principles operative in their scholarship. This would almost certainly enhance the quality of their work. Yet it might also, in line with Barber's hopes, add to the credibility of the history of economics in the eyes of the more conventional members of the economics profession. And, a more historically and methodologically aware economics profession that might well emerge from this appreciation can hardly be doubted desirable.

# REFERENCES

Barber, William J. 1975. "The Kennedy Years: Purposeful Pedagogy." In *Exhortation and Controls: The Search for a Wage-Price Policy, 1945-1971*, edited by Craufurd D. Goodwin. Washington, DC: Brookings Institute.

Barber, William J. 1981. "The United States: 'Economists in a Pluralistic Polity'." In *Economists in Government: An International Comparative Study*, edited by A. W. Coats. Durham, NC: Duke.

Barber, William J. 1985. *From New Era to New Deal: Herbert Hoover, the Economists, and American Economic Policy, 1921-1933*. New York: Cambridge University Press.

Barber, William J. 1987. "The Career of Alvin H. Hansen, in the 1920s and 1930s: A Study of Intellectual Transformation." *History of Political Economy* 19:191-205.

Barber, William J., ed. 1988. *Breaking the Academic Mould: Economists and American Higher Learning in the Nineteenth Century*. Middletown, CT: Wesleyan.

Barber, William J. 1989. "The Spread of Economic Ideas between Academia and Government: A Two-way Street." In *The Spread of Economic Ideas*, edited by David Colander and A. W. Coats. Cambridge, MA: Cambridge University Press.

Barber, William J. 1990. "Does Scholarship in the History of Economics Have a Useful Future?" *Journal of the History of Economic Thought* 12:110-123.

Barber, William J., ed. 1991. *Perspectives on the History of Economic Thought*, Vols. 5 and 6. Aldershot: Elgar.

Caldwell, Bruce and A. W. Coats. 1984. "The Rhetoric of Economists: A Comment on McCloskey" *Journal of Economic Literature* 22: 575-578.

McCloskey, Donald. 1983. "The Rhetoric of Economists." *Journal of Economic Literature* 21:481-517.

McCloskey, Donald. 1984. "Reply to Caldwell and Coats." *Journal of Economic Literature* 22:579-580.

Samuels, Warren J., ed. 1990. *Economics as Discourse: An Analysis of the Language of Economists*. Dordrecht: Kluwer.

# Marx's Critical/Dialectical Procedure:

by H. T. Wilson
(New York: Routledge, 1991; 248 pp.)

## Reviewed by David F. Ruccio

"Is there any part of Marxism that has received more abuse than the dialectical method?" Thus begins a recent article on the role of abstraction in Marxian dialectics (Ollman, 1990). It is against the background of this question that H. T. Wilson's interpretation of Marx's "critical/dialectical procedure" must also be assessed. My own view is that, unfortunately, Wilson's attempt to render the critical potential of Marxian dialectics finally serves to mute—and thus "abuse"—that critical potential.

The sense of "lost opportunity" stems from the fact that, as Wilson himself clearly recognizes, slavish adherence to positivist calls for a "unity of method" has all but ruled out serious attention to—let alone the further elaboration of—alternative analytical approaches, dialectics included. For Wilson, Karl Popper is the main adversary (although Friedrich Hayek and, especially, Peter Wiles receive their share of criticism). Today, of course, a sustained criticism of dialectics or of any distinct Marxian method emerges from the work of the so-called analytical Marxists (especially John Roemer and Jon Elster) who argue that there is a single, "modern" method in economics and the other social sciences—one based on methodological individualism, the "tools" of neoclassical economics, and so on—and that Marxists have no claim to a distinct approach to epistemology or explanation.

So a contemporary treatment of Marx's "critical/dialectical procedure"—one that is concerned with formulating and perhaps extending the more disruptive or destabilizing implications of that procedure—would surely be welcome. As Don Lavoie (1989) has recognized, Marx's "dialectical approach" emphasizes the "radical significance of time" and other features that are

Research in the History of Economic Thought and Methodology,
Volume 13, pages 311-317.
ISBN: 1-55938-095-0

disruptive of the prevailing modernist approach to economic and social theory; therefore, it points in the direction of what Lavoie considers to be the "new view of science" associated with chaos theory. Wilson, however, only succeeds in containing or domesticating the radical implications of dialectics by harnessing Marx's critique of political economy to a combination of liberal criticisms of positivism, Aristotelian categories of explanation, and a rendering of critical theory that is closer to the Frankfurt School (Theodor Adorno, Max Horkheimer, Herbert Marcuse, and company) than to Marxism.

Both the critical potential of Marx's procedure and Wilson's ultimate "abuse" of that potential can be glimpsed early on in the book. Wilson begins by noting that Marx's "intellectual practice" entailed a rejection of "identity and certainty as possible and desirable goals of inquiry" (p. xiii). Thus, Marx is credited with developing a "full blown counter approach to knowledge and knowing" (p. xiii). But even before leaving the Preface, he seeks to tame the more unsettling implications of Marx's "counter approach" by formulating the following "proof" of Marx's procedure: a "full, rather than truncated, intellectual procedure" shows us that reality is, in fact, "active and dynamic rather than passive and static" (p. xvi). So, finally, there is some form of certainty concerning—a "true" conception of—social reality!

The tension that marks the Preface is characteristic of Wilson's treatment of "materialist dialectics" throughout the entire book. In the first part (roughly the first four chapters), Wilson focuses on Marx's epistemological critique of the classical political economists. This is where he develops his understanding of Marxian "dialectics." In the second part (Chaps. 5 through 7) he focuses on Marx's alternative "materialist" analysis of social reality based on the labor theory of value. In both cases, the tension surrounding the (more or less) critical potential of Marx's critique of political economy is evidenced.

1.   In the first part, Wilson appears to glimpse, and often succeeds in formulating, some of the more "unsettling" implications of Marxian epistemology. In fact, he explains his preference for the term "procedure" over "method" based on what he considers to be "Marx's own resistance to the idea of method as 'one best way', an idea central to the traditional theory which he found so problematic in political economy and other disciplines" (p. 24). Thus, Marx's approach is best understood as an "anti-method" (and, elsewhere, as a "counter method") in which there are no guarantees, no "promised results"; instead, whatever methods are used have to be "adapted to problems or invented anew" (p. 31). Coupled with the previous comments concerning Marx's rejection of "identity and certainty," Wilson's interpretation comes very close to what another tradition in Marxian thought—stemming from the work of Louis Althusser—has termed Marx's "epistemological break." According to Althusser and others whose work has been influenced by him (Etienne Balibar, Stephen Resnick and Richard Wolff, and an ever-growing circle of

"overdeterminist" Marxists), a Marxian theory of knowledge rejects any and all "foundational" truth claims, whether of a singular logic or the facts of "experience." All truth claims (those of Marxism included) are considered to be "internal," and therefore relative, to the discourse or theory within which they are formulated. In addition, each theory (including its truth claims) is conceived to be a complex product of the social environment—languages, politics, patterns of property ownership, forms of class exploitation, and so on—within which the process of theorizing takes place. A Marxian dialectical conception of knowledge therefore represents a break from—and poses an alternative to—all theories of knowledge in which there is a claim of "identity and certainty," a relationship of adequacy between knowledge and its object "out there."

Wilson contrasts this dialectical conception of the process of theorizing with the positivists' "preoccupation with the possibility of identity and certainty, coupled with the frustration at their impossibility" (p. 36). Wilson's various assaults on positivism throughout the book will probably ring "true" for many practitioners of alternative approaches to economics today—from Marxists and radical political economists to institutionalists, post-Keynesians, and Austrians, especially the growing body of economists who are interested in the languages and "rhetorics" of economic discourses. Wilson constantly chides positivist economists and other social scientists for their "will to power"—their presumption that the world is both "knowable and controllable" (p. 36). And, in a restatement of views put forward in an earlier work (Wilson, 1977), he charges positivists with holding and promoting a set of views through which "the present system is sustained and extended" (p. 36).

Ultimately, however, Wilson truncates the more destabilizing implications of the Marxian view that the world is "differently knowable" according to different discourses—and therefore that there is no "neutral" or final arbiter of different truth claims—by grounding the "unknowability" of reality in the properties of reality itself. This is a move reminiscent of a long line of Frankfurt School "critical theorists" and of contemporary "realists" (for example, Roy Bhaskar, Derek Sayer, Andrew Collier, and others) who share Marxists' antipathy to positivism but who recoil at the more "relativist" implications of a dialectical epistemology. For them, positivists are "wrong," not because they attempt to provide a "true" representation of reality—and therefore accept a "mirror of nature" epistemology—but because they refuse to get beyond the "mere appearances" of things, to their natures and essences. Therefore, the positivists (and others like them) fall short of providing an "accurate" representation.

According to Wilson, the reality that exists "out there" is a seamless, contradictory web of nature, society, and "man." Positivists make the "mistake" of splintering the "true" interdependence of facts and of considering them in an "atomistic" and piecemeal fashion (hence their complicity with the piecemeal social engineering that keeps the current "system" in place). This exclusive attention to surface phenomena, rather than the proper use of "abstraction" and "concretion" to get "behind" and "below" those phenomena, was the mistake of the classical political economists—and it is one that continues to haunt contemporary (positivist) economists.

Wilson uses the following passage from Marx's introduction to the *Grundrisse* to illustrate his approach:

> if I were to begin with the population, this would be a chaotic conception [*Vorstellung*] of the whole, and I would then, by means of further determination, move analytically towards even more simple concepts [*Begriff*]...until I had arrived at the simplest determinations.[1]

One interpretation of this passage is that the move from "the whole" to "simplest determinations" varies according to the theoretical framework in which the move is made. Different thinkers would arrive at different "simplest determinations" and then proceed to concretize their conception of the whole in different ways. Or, as Marx continued, "from there the journey would have to be retraced until I had finally arrived at the population again, but this time not as a chaotic conception of the whole, but as a rich totality of many determinations and relations." Different thinkers—Smith, Ricardo, Marx, Samuelson, and so on—would finish their theoretical journey with different conceptions of "the whole." According to Wilson, however, there are not different sets of "simplest determinations" from which different "wholes" may be concretized but, rather, a single correct procedure—in his view, Marx's— and the "mistaken" approach of the political economists whose "subsequent act of recapitulation which (re)aggregates... *fundamentally violates reality* (p. 130, emphasis in original).

Wilson's interpretation can only be sustained on the basis of a "foundationalist" view of the process of theorizing according to which theories are more or less adequate to their extra-theoretical object. And this is exactly what he presumes when he states that reality "*is* contradictory" (p. 139, emphasis in original) or that "the dialectic must be understood as a feature of *Society* and historical development, and not just the pattern taken by human *thought* (p. 189, emphasis in original). There are not, for Wilson, different "concrete" conceptions of reality—with their different concepts and conceptual strategies, different social conditions and effects. Instead, there is a single standard—"Society"—according to which different theories can be declared valid or not.

Wilson is therefore left to resolve the apparent difference between this "absolutist" epistemology with his initial claim, later restated, that there is always a "non-identity of reality and knowledge" (p. 139). The answer he supplies does not, as it turns out, come from Marx but, rather, from Aristotle's "incontrovertible claim regarding the non-contradictory nature of truth" (p. 139). Wilson's "resolution" of the problem thus rests on the presumed lack of correspondence between the contradictory nature of reality, as it exists "out there," and the non-contradictory "foundations" of thought. He therefore succeeds in containing the more nihilistic implications of Marx's epistemological break by reaching back 2,000 years to find the "knowledge" of our "lack of certainty"!

2. If Wilson's interpretation of Marx's dialectical epistemology succeeds in blunting its critical potential, his rendering of the "materialist" elements of Marx's critique of political economy has similar effects. According to Wilson, Marx was obliged to "develop an alternate conceptual and theoretical structure, and with it an alternate approach to inquiry" (p. 145) once he realized the shortcomings of existing political economy. A key feature of this "alternate approach" is, of course, the labor theory of value.

In treating the status of Marx's value theory, Wilson makes a distinction between what he calls the "analytic" beginning and the "real" beginning. The first half of the book focuses on the "analytic" beginning, in Marx's critique of the epistemological "errors" of the classical political economists; the second half is concerned with the "real" beginnings. In fact, Wilson is somewhat apologetic for holding his discussion of "what grounds" Marxian theory until the later chapters. But this is exactly where still more "problematic" features of Wilson's interpretation can be found. And, again, it is his being wedded to an approach that borrows from Aristotle and the Frankfurt School, rather than the more "overdeterminist" approach pioneered by Althusser and others, that undermines the critical potential of his interpretation of Marx's procedure.

To his credit, Wilson is quite straightforward in his theoretical allegiances. On the first page of Chapter 5, he declares Marx's theory of value to be "objective in the sense that labor *really* is the essence of human collective life and the historical reality of humanity as a species-being" (p. 93, emphasis in original). Having already "solved" the epistemological problem of the adequacy (if non-identity) of thought to reality in the first part, he can now declare Marxism to "capture" the "real" nature of human beings and society in thought. This "anthropology" of human beings is, in turn, justified by recourse to an Aristotelian conception of "essentialism" (pp. 93-95). Together, the notions of laboring human beings and essential causes serve, not to separate Marxism from political economy and modern-day economics, as Wilson presumably would wish, but to close that gap.

The effect of Wilson's formulation of the "ontological underpinnings" of Marxian value theory is to reproduce—rather than to criticize and thus undermine—the "humanism" of classical political economy and contemporary (neoclassical and Keynesian) economics. In both cases, the economy is conceived to be a closed, homogeneous space that corresponds to *homo oeconomicus*, whether the laboring "man" of the classicals, the rational agent of the neoclassicals, or the "mass psychology" of the Keynesians. The only theoretical space that Wilson leaves open for Marx is to show that "labour really was the source of all value, that both workers and capitalists could, would, or already had come to know this from experience, and that political economy had (apparently) insulated itself against this realization by the development of its so-called method" (p. 153).

The idea that what Marx's critique of political economy accomplished was a radical questioning of an "economy" that corresponded to human nature—that he "decentered" the classical conception of the economy from production and a presumed set of human needs and "opened" the economy to the noneconomic aspects of society such as politics and culture—is therefore displaced by Wilson's interpretation. What has disappeared, too, is what Resnick and Wolff have argued is Marx's discursive "focus" on classes and class struggle—and hence the concrete conditions under which class exploitation takes place within a capitalist social formation. Instead, Wilson's approach makes classes the alienated form of labor associated with the commodity form; class exploitation is therefore considered to be an effect of the opposition between use-value and exchange-value. What this means is that class exploitation would, on Wilson's account, cease to exist with the "overcoming" of the domination of exchange-value over use-value, with the reassertion of the "real value of labour and its products" (p. 160).

According to Wilson, what Marx's "critical/dialectical procedure" reduces to is the "discovery" that there was, at some point in the past, an organic relation among nature, society, and "man" which was mediated by labor; that capitalism has "distorted" this relationship, at once reflected in and extended by the opposition between use-value and exchange-value; and that a "correct" perception of this relationship will lead to the end of "alienation" and the "coming to be of human being, the realization of its true nature or essence" (p. 159). What this "end of history" also means is that social contradictions would cease to exist. Thus, the correspondence between thought and reality that is denied in a capitalist society would also be restored: "labour would be social, while at the same time it would be *known* to be social" (p. 161, emphasis in original).

It is this "end of alienation" thesis that represents the final step in Wilson's "abuse" of the critical potential of Marx's dialectical procedure. In it, Wilson betrays his nostalgia for the "certainty" that he otherwise denies to contemporary positivists. And, as he is reunited with Popper—if only in a "next" world of "unalienated" human existence—he has effectively blunted the potential critical contributions of dialectics to contemporary economics.

# NOTE

1.  Marx (1973, p. 100); Wilson focuses on this passage at the beginning of Chapter 3.

# REFERENCES

Lavoie, D. 1989. "Economic Chaos or Spontaneous Order? Implications for Political Economy of the New View of Science." *Cato Journal* 8: 613-635.

Marx, K. 1973. *Grundrisse*. Translated by M. Nicolaus. New York: Vintage Books.

Ollman, B. 1990. "Putting Dialectics to Work: The Process of Abstraction in Marx's Method." *Rethinking Marxism* 3: 26-74.

Wilson, H. T. 1977. *The American Ideology*. Boston: Routledge & Kegan Paul.

# Economics and the Philosophy of Science

by Deborah A. Redman
(New York: Oxford University Press, 1991; 252 pp.)

Reviewed by **A.W. Coats**

Deborah Redman's book is certainly timely. According to her calculations (pp. 91, 97), more than fifty books on economic methodology have appeared since 1970, and heaven knows how many scholarly articles. And the flood is still rising, but to what end?—in either of the two obvious sense of that work.

Already the compiler of a comprehensive *Economic Methodology: A Bibliography with Reference to Works in the Philosophy of Science (1860-1988)*, published in 1989, Redman hardly needs to argue to case for "a concise, neutral, accurate introduction to the vast philosophy of science literature so that economists and other social scientists can become well informed with the least possible expenditure of time and energy" (p. 5). Whether optimum efficiency in these matters can be achieved by studying her book is a moot point, to be considered later. What is undeniable, however, is that hardly any practicing professional economist, and very few specialist economic methodologists, will be familiar with the entire range of works she cites so lavishly. Here, as in all scholarly fields, some reliance on authority is unavoidable.

Aiming to combine honesty with accuracy while "lending support" to her own interpretation, it would be surprising if Redman satisfied every reader, especially given the controversial status of many of the views she presents. Yet no other book I know of so successfully conveys the content and flavor of the rich and varied topics she surveys. On the whole summary predominates over commentary and interpretation, and "neutrality," one of her desiderata, is adequately maintained except in the final chapter, where she displays less restraint in examining the development of economics as a profession.

**Research in the History of Economic Thought and Methodology,**
**Volume 13, pages 319-321.**
Copyright © 1995 by JAI Press Inc.
**All rights of reproduction in any form reserved.**
**ISBN: 1-55938-095-0**

Part I: "Philosophy of Science: Rationality, Growth, Ignorance, Objectivity, Criticism" proceeds through brief accounts of "Problems", and "The Decline of logical Positivism" to a survey of "Sociological Explanations in Science" (featuring the work of Michael Polanyi, the unduly neglected Ludwig Fleck, and the inevitable but overexposed Thomas Kuhn). There follows an examination of "The Popperian School" (covering the master himself, his unruly pupils Imre Lakatos and Paul Feyerabend, together with the most recent contributor, William Bartley); a discussion of "Whiter the History of Science?" (focusing on Stephen Toulmin and Norwood Russell Hanson); and a brief statement of Conclusions.

Part II contains chapters on "Philosophy's Influence on Economics: Early Exchanges" (mainly J. N. Keynes, T. W. Hutchison and F. Machlup); "Sir Karl Popper's Philosophy of the Social Sciences: A Disjointed Whole"; and "Lakatos and Kuhn: Science as Consensus." There are also brief appendices on "the Is-Ought Problem" and a somewhat idiosyncratic list of books by economists "whose first work or works deal with methodological and/or philosophical topics." This is followed by a massive 49 page bibliography, which is daunting enough to scare off anyone who aspires to master the literature.

Needless to say, Redman cannot cover everything. She may be too modest in confessing that she has introduced the reader to only "a small portion" of the important relevant literature. But while she claims to have represented as many methodological positions as possible, "including both mainstream and nontraditional" (p. vii), she is eventually obliged to list some of the relevant philosophies of science that have been excluded from her account (p. 180). Moreover, with respect to the economic literature, she does much less than justice to the recent institutionalist writings and to Austrian economics and other species of subjectivism. Constructivism does not appear in the index, and the recent, perhaps transitory, vogue for rhetoric is relegated to a single substantial footnote. Most significant among the omissions, however, is the growing recognition that economic methodologists are nowadays trying much harder to study and understand what economists actually do, rather than more conventional and remote philosophical notions of "science" as applied to economics. This is indeed a most welcome, albeit long overdue trend.

Unfortunately, despite her laudable initial objectives, Redman's book contains far too many typos, proof reading errors, confusing quotations and references, and factual and historical inaccuracies. And while I have considerable sympathy for her perception of the economics profession (pp. 152-167); see also pp. 167-172, on the "Communis Opinio Doctorum", it hardly qualifies as "neutral." Far too many of the matters discussed so summarily here—such as the discipline's power structure, pressures of conformity, and "the stifling of competition among theories and schools of thought" (p. 167) are based on opinion rather than reliable evidence; and when evidence is available, there is usually ample room for sharply differing interpretations. The sociology of economics is an essential part of every economist's education. But as a field of research it is still in its early stages, and has limited value in the absence of careful comparisons between economics and other disciplines. Above all, it needs to be carefully distinguished from that amorphous and sprawling species of semi-popular commentary on "the state of economics," usually a prime occasion for breast-beating and other lamentations.

Redman's book is a useful introduction to its field. It could, however, so obviously have been much more.

# Theory of Property

by Stephen R. Munzer
(New York: Cambridge Unversity Press, 1990; $59.95 491 pp.)

Reviewed by **Randall Bartlett**

One of the central defining characteristics of any society is its system of property, that is, its socially defined and defended rights, privileges and obligations regarding things. At base that system is more concerned with relations between persons than between persons and things. While property as an institution is always important intellectual concern with the character of property has ebbed and flowed. Property was a central concern of classical economics with its emphasis on the functional distribution of income and the labor theory of value. With the rise of neoclassical economics the social character of property slipped into the background of mainstream economic inquiry but remained important to institution-alists, legal scholars and others. While economics textbooks fell into the trap of defining market transactions as simply a trading of goods, the Uniform Commercial Code continued rightly to define the sale of goods as "the *transfer of legal title* for a price."

The last twenty-five years have seen a resurgence of broad-based, explicit consideration of property rights. Mainstream economics' new field of law and economics is concerned with the efficiency of rules of law, including property rights. Demsetz (1967) argued that property rights come into existence for, and are to be understood as a means of, internalizing externalities. Coase (1960) argued that what often appears to be a failure of markets is in fact a failure fully to define and vest property rights. Property can be seen as an element in promoting efficiency.

Research in the History of Economic Thought and Methodology,
Volume 13, pages 323-328.
Copyright © 1995 by JAI Press Inc.
All rights of reproduction in any form reserved.
ISBN: 1-55938-095-0

The 1970s also saw a resurgence of moral philosophers' interest in property as a factor in defining social justice. Rawls (1971) derived his maximin principle as a universal standard for a just distribution of income and wealth. Nozick (1974) responded with a theory of justice in distribution based on the fairness of the process of creating distributions of property rather than the pattern of the outcome.

In the same period, institutionalists, who never really abandoned a concern with property as a fundamental social institution, tried to keep the rekindled discussion honest. Samuels (1971) emphasized the endogenous nature of property rights. They are created by social processes which in turn do not stand apart from all of the other elements of social life. Property in any society reflects the evolutionary interactions of its entire fabric. Meanwhile Marxists continued to view property as the defining characteristic of classes and as such central the understanding of the unfolding dialectic.

Property has clearly again been in the spotlight on many an analytic stage. Stephen Munzer has attended all of the performances and is well qualified to act as critic. Not content simply to review, he seeks also to author the definitive final act in his ambitious new book, *A Theory of Property*. On one level the book is a useful and accessible survey of thinking about property. He reviews all the major trends, both "classical" and modern and identifies many of the flaws and inconsistencies within and between traditions in that broad based survey. That alone would have been a valuable contribution, but he is ambitious enough to attempt a resolution of the conflicts and a synthesis of the ideas into a comprehensive, "pluralist" normative theory of property.

The book opens with a useful taxonomy of rights. Part I borrows heavily from Hohfeld (1919) refining the concept of property, distinguishing for example "claim rights," "privileges," "powers" and "immunities." What we conceive of as property is not simply an item in one's possession but a complex bundle of various forms of "claims," "immunities," and so on. He could, then, have gone on in strictly positive form, exploring rules of law and fitting them into these categories, but he chose a different route. He wants to develop standards to judge the superiority of different rules of property. Not content to explain what property is, he wants to be able to tell us what it ought to be. Munzer, of course, is not the first to ask that question and so, as a foundation for his answer, he takes us through the issues and answers offered by others.

In Part II he surveys work done on the justifiability of initial acquisition via "incorporation" and "projection." He then explores what rights people have in themselves and their bodies and what role those rights play in promoting desirable social and personal ends, such as the relationship between property and moral character.

Part III is the most ambitious for it is his survey and synthesis of normative standards for judging property rules. Judgments about property have most often been based upon one of three principles. Some argue that good rules are those which promote "efficiency and maximum utility." Others hold that the correct standard for judging property arrangements is "justice and equality," while still others have argued for arrangements reflecting "labor and desert". He reviews these theories, points out their strengths and weaknesses, and exposes their contradictions. He then tries to overlap and combine these principles into a "pluralist" theory of property that draws from the strengths of each and while overcoming the flaws and inconsistencies.

There are two conceivable target audiences for such a discussion, "academics" who are curious observers of social processes defining property, and "lawgivers" who are the actual participants in those processes. By the time Part III is underway it is clear that Munzer wishes to be able to offer guidance to the latter group. He does not just wish to converse with the academics. He wants to direct the lawgivers. To do so successfully he will have to (a) give real operational content to each of the principles and, (b) unambiguously overcome the conflicts between them.

## I.  CONTENT ISSUES IN THE PLURALIST THEORY

Content—Utility and Efficiency: Because he is so thorough in relating the problems within each principle he has difficulty overcoming them. For example, Munzer recognizes that 19th century utilitarianism has fallen into disregard, at least among economists, because of the failure to find any "objective" standard for interpersonal utility comparisons. He notes the problem and tries to step around it, but in a manner not wholly satisfactory. He argues that while we cannot feel others' pain we can be sure they feel it. We can all predict that bending someone's harm violently behind her back will cause that person pain (p. 199). Though true, identifying others' pain isn't the problem. The obstacle to operation is that I have no way of knowing whether her sore arm hurts worse than his toothache. If you both report pain I will accept your self-evaluation, but neither I, nor she nor he has any way of measuring whose pain is worse.

Economists tried to overcome this with the Hicks-Kaldor compensation principle and Munzer notes this possible "solution." However, it has been set aside by economists as technically flawed, practically inapplicable, and not really morally justifiable. Munzer knows of these difficulties. He notes them, but then goes on to use the principles as if the difficulties had been overcome rather than simply presented. After his discussion of the inoperability of utilitarianism he still proposes that

> The combined principle maintains that property rights should be allocated so as (1) to maximize utility regarding the use, possession, transfer and so on of things and (2) to maximize efficiency regarding the use, possession, transfer and so on of things (p. 202).

The combined principle is no more operational than its constituent parts. Indeed it may be less operational for he even abandons the self-definition of welfare and preferences which is the foundation of utilitarianism in most forms (p. 219). We need not even take preferences as we find them. "We" might be able to make people better off by providing them with superior preferences and then satisfying those! If preferences are endogenous and can be influenced, then there is not even a fixed standard for measuring a single individual's welfare, let alone for making interpersonal utility comparisons. Lawgivers may find that it is not really clear what the combined principle means.

Content—Justice and Equality: Munzer's pluralist theory also absorbs a justice principle, taking equality of holdings as the standard, accepting unequal property holdings only "if (1) everyone has a minimum amount of property and, (2) the inequalities do not undermine a fully human life in society" (p. 227).

Again, obvious operational difficulties abound. What is the necessary "minimum" and what is a "fully human life in society?" He knows that question needs an answer. He provides one.

> The answer, insofar as it relates to property, is: a life freed from the conditions that undermine the ability to live with self-respect and healthy self-esteem in society (p. 247).

But then what defines "healthy self-esteem?" Something more fundamental than self-perception. As with preferences, there seems to be some objective standard by which we can judge someone's healthy self-esteem independent of their own self evaluation. For example, he addresses the possibility that someone in a lower caste could subjectively believe himself to be of equal worth with those in a higher caste, but merely called in this life to a different plane. For Munzer that person is not experiencing "fully human life" because people can be "mistaken about their levels of self-respect and self-esteem" (p. 250). If false consciousness is a possibility, how can "lawgivers" have faith in their own, or judge the falseness of others?

Content—Labor and Desert: Munzer's pluralist theory also incorporates arguments justifying property because of labor and effort put forth. For Locke that was a central theme. It is implicit in Marx's labor theory of value. Munzer, however, finds that in its classical form the principle is based upon unrealistic assumptions. In Chapter 10 he provides modifications and qualifications to make the principle applicable by "lawgivers." He is unable to provide a short and simple statement of the qualified principle comparable to those proposed for the first two principles. Instead there is an extensive list of qualifications, but even with detailed discussion they remain unusably vague. For example, number 3 on the list states that "Existing property rights can be diminished if post-acquisition changes in situation have the result that acquisition would traverse some moral restriction" (p. 284). Some more content may be necessary to make that fully operational.

## Conflict and Resolution

Conflict Among Principles: To be operational Munzer's pluralist theory of property must provide specific and detailed guidance. He has developed it out of three broad principles which are combined in a pluralist whole. If we overlook the remaining content ambiguity, is the theory ready for the "lawgiver"? Not yet, for as he readily notes, "these may not be the only principles that makes up a satisfactory moral, political, and legal theory of property [though] they are by far the most important" (p. 292). The pluralist theory is not wholly complete but to move on he assumes it complete enough. More important, within it situations might arise when the three included principles come into conflict.

In most cases a resolution will be possible, he asserts, though the details remain quite vague. "Such resolution involves defensibly adjusting the scope of one or more principles, creating an exception to one or more principles, devising a priority rule to resolve the conflict or revising the background normative, psychological, and socioeconomic account of property" (p. 302). What makes an adjustment defensible or what grounds are to be used establish exceptions, etc. are not spelled out. Still, at this stage Munzer believes that conflicts between principles can be resolved within the mind of a "lawgiver."

Conflict Among Principals: That vision of the "conflict" issue is revealing. He sees the interesting problem to be a conflict between abstract principles, not a conflict between interested parties (p. 312). There is fundamental flaw in that vision. Munzer does not see legal rules as endogenous, as part of a evolutionary institutional whole. His audience of "lawgivers," judges, legislatures and lawyers, seem able to pick what ever property rules they choose, with no constraints other than timeless moral principles. Even though players in the game may have "false preferences" or may be deceived about their levels of "self-esteem" those who make the law are not socially selected or affected. They have true consciousness and pure hearts and so stand above society. They can be counted upon to act in pursuit of objective "social good."

To explore the salient issues in conflict resolution in Chapter 11, Munzer begins with a hypothetical example. "...imagine that a legislature has asked a social planner to formulate an income policy based on the three principles" p. 292. Conflict comes after this stage when the social planner is attempting to "solve" the technical problem using the pluralist standard. It is an interesting abstraction but it is wholly divorced from what legislatures do or how income policies are established. Property is not an exogenous technical problem solved by philosopher kings. It is an endogenous social one solved by contentious political processes. One might as easily imagine a flock of migratory elephants flying across the Atlantic. It provides an interesting mental picture but it ignores the nature of the beast.

Munzer clearly wishes his theory to be a useful guide to both "academics" interested in debate and "lawgivers" interested in setting real world property rules. It is an interesting book, but it fits better the first audience than the second. As a survey of thought about property Munzer's book is quite valuable. As a realistic guide to defining optimal rules it is too vague to be operational. As a vision of how property fits into a real world social context, it is hopelessly naive.

# REFERENCES

Coase, Ronald. 1960. "The Problem of Social Cost." *Journal of Law and Economics* 3: 1-44.
Demsetz, Harold. 1967. "Toward a Theory of Property Rights." *American Economic Review* 50: 347-373.
Hohfeld, W. N. 1974. *Fundamental Legal Conceptions.* New Haven, CT: Yale University Press.
Nozick, Robert. 1974. *Anarchy, State and Utopia.* New York: Basic Books.
Rawls, John. 1971. *A Theory of Justice.* Cambridge, MA: Harvard University Press.
Samuels, Warren. 1971. "Interrelations between Legal and Economic Processes." *Journal of Law and Economics* 5: 435-450.

# Economic Theories, True or False

## by Mark Blaug
### (Aldershot and Brookfield: Edward Elgar, 1990; $59.95; 250 pp.)

## Reviewed by **Terry Peach**

Mark Blaug needs no introduction. In this, the latest volume of his collected writings, he presents ten essays, all reprinted from various sources. Although only five essays are focused directly on methodological issues, with the other half grouped under the heading "History of Economic Thought," a general concern with theory-appraisal surfaces throughout the book. While I have some reservations, mostly concerning Professor Blaug's methodological position, the essays demonstrate his enviable talent for raising fundamental questions in a bold and stimulating fashion.

The first two essays concentrate, respectively, on the internal coherence and the predictive record of Marxian economic theory. Relying heavily on the Sraffa-inspired critique of Marx's transformation of values into prices of production, Blaug concludes in the first essay (1980) that the Marxian system "is logically inconsistent" (p. 33), which is itself rather at odds with an earlier claim, made in the introduction to the collection, that "there are no serious logical inconsistencies in the Marxian system" (p. 7).[1] If the former view is correct, then, according to Blaug, "there is no point in appraising Marxian economics in the light of its prediction" (p. 33), since "a logically inconsistent theory is compatible with any and all events" (p. 17). Yet in the second essay (1980) the exercise is undertaken just the same, with particular attention given to the falling rate of profit argument and the associated breakdown-of-capitalism thesis. The essay concludes, stentoriously:

**Research in the History of Economic Thought and Methodology,**
**Volume 13, pages 329-335.**
Copyright © 1995 by JAI Press Inc.
**All rights of reproduction in any form reserved.**
**ISBN: 1-55938-095-0**

> Perhaps there are still some among you who think that economic theories can be decisively refuted by the historical record and that there is no need for Popperian rules that positively forbid arbitrary revisions of a theory to accommodate growing anomalies and repeated refutations. If so, study the history of Marxism and consider the error of your ways (p. 51).

Radical economics, although "undoubtedly" inspired by Marxism (p. 59), fares better in the third essay ("A methodological appraisal of radical economics," 1983) than its 'parent' doctrine did in the previous essays. Some of the work done by radical economists "commits itself to definite empirical implications" and is "content to rest its case against orthodox economics on the strength of the supporting evidence" (p. 80). Moreover, unlike "orthodox economics," which "does sometimes have all the appearance of a subject in which issues of no great consequence are carefully examined while those of momentous consequence are consigned to the outer darkness" (p. 81), the 'radicals' do at least raise fundamental questions, such as that concerning the relationship between economic and political freedom. In spite of these virtues, however, Professor Blaug ends his critical survey "as I began-an unconverted neoclassical economist" (p. 81).

In the fourth essay, "Second thoughts on the Keynesian revolution" (listed as 1990, but published in the Summer 1991 edition of *History of Political Economy*), Blaug defends his thesis that Keynesian economics succeeded because of its prediction of "novel facts": it constituted a (theoretically) "progressive" scientific research programme in the sense of Imre Lakatos. The fifth essay, "John Hicks and the methodology of economics" (1988), contains a scathing assessment of Hicks' contribution (or, rather, lack of it) to economic methodology. Hicks' writings are said to "suffer from a continuous unwillingness to face up to the question of how it is that we ever discover whether a piece of positive economics is true or false" (p. 111). Professor Blaug concludes, "It is impossible to extract any coherent methodology of economics from the writings of Hicks" (p. 116).

With "The economics of Johann von Thunen" (1985), the sixth essay in the collection, Professor Blaug is found in a more antiquarian mood. The essay follows the pattern of a chapter in his *Economic Theory in Retrospect*, with a biographical sketch and a reader's guide to the first and second volumes of Thunen's *The Isolated State*. In the introduction to the essay Blaug recalls Alfred Marshall's wish that "someone would care for von Thunen" and, despite some general criticism of Thunen's *magnum opus* ("a formless monster," p. 122), and more specific criticism of Thunen's treatment of distribution, the caring role has clearly been adopted with some enthusiasm. However, something less than clear—at least to me—is how Thunen's work illustrates the point that "in a subject like economics, highly abstract theories are nevertheless occasionally capable of throwing surprising light on the real world" (p. 10). For example, do we really need Thunen's "highly abstract theory" to illuminate the point that "forestry is carried on near the market because, compared with grain ... [it] requires high transport costs relative to its value" (p. 133)?

The seventh essay, "Classical economics" (1987), is a reprint of Blaug's magisterial contribution to *The New Palgrave. A Dictionary of Economics* (London, Macmillan, 1987). Blaug takes issue with both the Sraffa-based "surplus interpretation" of classical economics, according to which the so-called "core" of classical doctrine is equivalent to the theoretical approach adopted in Part I of Sraffa's *Production of Commodities by Means of Commodities* (Cambridge, C.U.P., 1960), and Samuel Hollander's "neoclassical" interpretation (or translation) of Ricardo. Although I am in substantial agreement with Blaug, there are a number of points on which we must part company. Concerning Ricardo I disagree with Professor Blaug's claim that the invariable standard adopted by Ricardo in the third edition of his *Principles* represented a "*weighted* average of the entire spectrum of capital-labour ratios" (p. 148, my emphasis); I am more inclined than Blaug to accept a loose (non-Sraffian) "surplus" interpretation of Ricardo's theory; I take the view, contrary to Blaug's, that Marshallian demand and supply analysis is, *in principle*, entirely foreign to Ricardo's approach; and I disagree with Blaug's suggestion that Ricardo took an optimistic view of Britain's growth potential "*only* if the Corn Laws were repealed" (p. 155, my emphasis).[2] Also, it is a pity that exaggeration should spoil what is, in other respects, an admirable critique of Samuel Hollander's misinterpretation of Ricardo. Thus, Hollander does *not* claim that Ricardo "never entertained the corn model even implicity, never assumed that corn alone enters the wage basket ... [and] never assumed that real wages remain constant" (p. 150) (which does not mean that Hollander supports either Sraffa's version of the corn model interpretation, or the traditional, subsistence-wage interpretation).

The eighth essay, "Marginal cost pricing: no empty box" (1985), traces the "tortured history" of the debate surrounding the marginal cost pricing doctrine: a doctrine endorsed by Blaug as "a method, not a dogma ... [I]t is a systematic check-list of what to look for in pricing a public service" (p. 183). Then, in the ninth essay (1989), Blaug offers a review and assessment of Nicholas Kaldor's work on growth. Kaldor is praised for a "willingness to rework his pet theories when they are upset by the discovery of some hitherto unsuspected fact" (p. 186), and for attempting to explain 'facts' in "a genuine, causal sense" (p. 194), even though these 'facts' turn out to be fictions. But the overall verdict is negative: "judged by academic, rather than political, standards, his ideas must be judged as having failed to take off" (p. 206).

The final essay, "Economics through the looking glass" (1988), is likely to be the most controversial in the collection. The gist of Blaug's argument is that the three Sraffian editors of Macmillan's *The New Palgrave*, John Eatwell (since ennobled for his services to the British Labor Party), Murray Milgate and Peter Newman succeeded in pulling off a gigantic confidence trick. Through their manipulation of editorial levers it is alleged that the trio vigorously promoted their favored, minority brand of Sraffian economics, together with its associated historiography, while endearing themselves to mainstream economists (or rather, those more gullible than Professor Blaug) through the inclusion of mathematically sophisticated entries of "mind-boggling obscurity" (p. 213). While allowing that "there is much gold amidst the dross" (p. 214)—entries of which Professor Blaug approves—the alleged bias in the choice of entries, together with "the omission of entries for many important topics ... and many recognized branches of economics-the economics of education ... comparative economic systems, cultural economics, and the history of economic thought" (pp. 214-215), led Blaug to conclude that the *Palgrave* "gives a hopelessly distorted picture of where economics is now" (p. 224). He adds, ruefully:

> when one considers that a dictionary of this kind only appears every 20-30 years and stands as a testimony to an entire generation of professional economists, one can only tear one's hair out at the magnitude of the opportunity that has been missed (p. 235).

Blaug's is certainly a provocative thesis, and one not arrived at painlessly (he testifies to having spent five weeks reading the *Palgrave* from cover to cover, without food or sleep, p. 214). From my own browsing acquaintance with the four volumes—at no cost in terms of food or sleep, I must confess—and a more searching reading of entries related specifically to my interests (history of economic thought generally and Ricardo-related topics particularly), I have little doubt that the editors did "ringfence" topics of importance to "Sraffians." To take a singular instance: why include only one, very lengthy piece on Ricardo, by a confirmed "Sraffian" (G. de Vivo), at a time when Ricardo-scholarship is riven by disputes over the legitimacy of Sraffa's interpretation? The answer, I fear, does little credit to Lord Eatwell and his fellow editors.

On various other matters I find Professor Blaug's argument rather less convincing. First, as to the "hopelessly distorted picture" of *mainstream* economics, he perhaps confuses (much of) economics as it is with economics as he would like it to be. Thus, he accepts that "a revelling in [mathematical] technique for technique's sake, is certainly a feature of much modern economics" (p. 213). But when he adds that "an encyclopedia of economics would hardly seem an appropriate place to advertise it" (p. 213), he merely discloses his antipathy to highly mathematical economics (especially of the general equilibrium variety). Needless to say, the representation of a subject one disapproves of is not the same as a misrepresentation of that subject.

I also find unconvincing Professor Blaug's strictures on Sraffa's economics. Granted, Sraffa's work does appear to be over-represented in the *Palgrave* in proportion to its representation in the global academic community,[3] but that is no excuse for distorting its purpose, and then criticising it for failing to achieve objectives which were never set. When Professor Blaug describes "Sraffian economics" as "totally moribund," and when he writes, "surely, it is time to ask whether it is perhaps something about the very nature of Sraffa's approach that has so far made it totally irrelevant to practical issues" (pp. 225-226), he apparently misses the point that "Sraffa's approach" was *purely* theoretical: *all* that Sraffa claimed for his work (in *Production of Commodities*) was that it should form the basis for a logical critique of "mainstream" (or "marginalist') economics. In this connection it is perhaps noteworthy that Professor Blaug should shrug off Sraffa's critique of 'mainstream' economics on empirical grounds (p. 224), while praising, fulsomely, the Sraffa-inspired, logical critique of Marxian economics.[4]

I turn, finally, to a brief consideration of the dominant theme in the collection, namely that theories are to be judged, above all else, in terms of their (comparative) predictive records.

On the face of it Professor Blaug's position is unequivocal. Assuming that a theory has passed the necessary test of logical consistency (pp. 7, 17), empirical evidence is "the final arbiter of [its] truth (p. 3)."[5] When one probes deeper, however, a less well-defined picture seems to emerge.

First, with regard to the criterion of logical consistency it is perhaps surprising to be told that theories "that are eminently relevant to practical questions are rarely rigorous analytically" (p. 226), because this might suggest that logical consistency is something that can be compromised (though not, it seems, in the case of Marxian economics). An unsympathetic reader might, indeed, impose just such an interpretation on Professor Blaug's "empirical" defense of (one version of) neoclassical theory, since it is precisely the internal incoherence of that theory, involving a notion of aggregate "capital" and its relationship to the interest rate, which the "Sraffians" have exposed.

Secondly, on the "litmus paper test" of prediction, Professor Blaug allows that it also matters whether or not assumptions are "realistic" (p. 3); and, furthermore, he regards it as desirable that theories should aim to discover "the causal forces at work in the economic system" (p. 3, cf. pp. 108, 194). In other words the predictive accuracy of a theory, by itself, is *not* all that counts; as Professor Blaug concedes to Bruce Caldwell, economic theories "are not simply instruments for making accurate predictions about economic events but genuine attempts ... to depict things as they actually are" (p. 3). Unfortunately, the independent (i.e., non-predictive) criteria for judging a 'good' theory *qua* depiction of things "as they actually are," never receive adequate clarification.

Thirdly, although certain of Professor Blaug's remarks may lead one to think otherwise, he is not, in fact, condemning all non-empirical work in economics. Even "Sraffian" economics, devoid as it is of empirical content, is described as an "advance in economic theory" which has cast "new light on the ideas of the past" (p. 163). Moreover, it is significant that Professor Blaug should single out the "relationship between economic and political freedom" as a long-overdue subject of debate "between Marxist and mainstream economists" (p. 32), since it might be expected that such a debate could not be conducted solely (if at all?) in terms of falsifiable, empirical propositions. The message is that economists are not necessarily to be rebuked for engaging in 'non-empirical' activities, although the criteria for evaluating such activities are never fully spelt out.

Professor Blaug's position is, then, rather more flexible than some of his more uncompromising statements may suggest. But this flexibility is not without cost, at least with regard to "the crucial question of whether we are ever permitted to place any bars on the proliferation of possible economic theories" (p. 108). If an economic theory need not necessarily be rigorous, if it can represent an 'advance' without having *any* empirical content, if non-empirical work can address itself to worthwhile questions, and if "the empirical track record" is not, in any case, sufficient for the identification of "good" applied theory, then the criteria for answering Professor Blaug's "crucial question" must remain even more elusive than he himself allows.[6]

In conclusion, this is a stimulating, not to say provocative, collection of papers which I can recommend enthusiastically. To be sure, one may not always agree with Professor Blaug, but it would be dull person who found his work uninteresting.

## ACKNOWLEDGMENTS

I should like to thank Alistair Edwards (Department of Government, University of Manchester) and Ian Steedman (Department of Economics, University of Manchester) for their helpful advice and comments on a previous version of this review article. I must also thank Mark Blaug for his good natured remarks on the earlier draft. The usual disclaimer applies.

## NOTES

1.   Professor Blaug does qualify the latter statement when he adds, "or at any rate none that cannot be repaired by post-Marxian refinements" (p. 7). However, it is unclear how these "post-Marxian refinements," which involve the abandonment of either the "labour theory of profits," or the "labour theory of prices" (p. 25), or both, can truly be said to *repair* the Marxian system. Indeed, Professor Blaug appears sceptical on precisely this point (p. 28).

2.   I substantiate these claims in my *Interpreting Ricardo* (Cambridge, C.U.P., 1993).

3.   However, Professor Blaug's implied suggestion (p. 210), that Manchester University's economics department is a strong refuge for "Sraffians," does not conform to my own perception. On the same theme of mistaken identity, neither can I recognize the description of Ian Steedman

as a "Sraffian *Marxist*" (pp. 27, 30), still less as an unqualified "Marxist," even of the "better" variety (p. 34, n. 2).

4. Thus: "we can witness the enormous liberating value of Sraffa's *Production of Commodities by Means of Commodities*" in helping to "open the eyes of those who want to employ Marxian tools to the analysis of these laws [of motion of present-day capitalism]... [I]t took Sraffa's highly abstract model to convince some Marxists that they had been pursing the will-o'-the wisp for over a century" (p. 28, "A methodological appraisal of Marxiian economics I"): cf. the reference to "Ian Steedman's brilliant book. *Marx After Sraffa* ... [which] employs Sraffa's apparatus to argue that the labor theory of value in Marx is not only redundant but actually unworkable as soon as joint products and choice of technique are admitted into the analysis" (p. 222, "Economics through the looking glass").

5. Cf. "In the final analysis, nothing matters but the empirical track record" (p. 60), and "the predictive record of a theory ... is the ultimate acid test of correct understanding" (p. 63). By "truth" and "correct understanding," Professor Blaug should not be understood as implying *apodictic* truth for, according to his methodological position, *provisional* truth is the best that can be achieved. As Blaug himself states, "although a confirming instance does not prove truth, a disconfirming instance proves falsity" (p. 3). In this regard, it is unfortunate that "truth," without any qualification, is occasionally represented as an achievable objective (cf. statements on p. 111).

6. He does concede that the appraisal of theories "is more like an 'art' than a 'science'" (p. 3).

# Reaching for Heaven on Earth:
## The Theological Meaning of Economics

by R. H. Nelson
(Savage, MO: Rowman & Littlefield, 1991)

Reviewed by **John P. Tiemstra**

Nelson begins with the proposition that for most modern people economics has become theology. He claims that people invest their material standard of living and the economic arrangements of their lives with such importance that they believe that all human problems could be solved and we could achieve heaven on earth if only we could increase incomes to a high enough level. Because economics has this ultimate significance, all disagreements over economic structures and policies are religious in nature, and can only be resolved by secession. That is, all people should be allowed to live in states where the economic structures and policies conform to their own economic (read religious) beliefs.

The evidence that Nelson offers for the notion that economics has become the source of ultimate meaning is rather thin. The most persuasive are the quotations he reproduces (pp. 2 and 224) from John Maynard Keynes' famous essay, "Economic Possibilities for Our Grandchildren" (1933). If one takes that essay at face value, it would seem that Keynes believed that the problem of scarcity would one day be solved, and many other social problems with it. However, there is so little evidence of this point of view in the rest of Keynes' writings that it is difficult to know how to take that essay. Other quotations used to prove this point come from unnamed social and natural scientists and popular sources such as *Time* magazine (pp. 4-5). Most of them seem to be casual social ethics done by people who are not social ethicists, and somewhat overstated. That may explain the passage from Keynes, too.

Research in the History of Economic Thought and Methodology,
Volume 13, pages 337-343.
ISBN: 1-55938-095-0

Nelson also produces a wealth of quotations from economists and intellectual historians comparing economics to religion (e.g., Galbraith on p. 203, McCloskey on p. 284). However, these quotations also do not help his case. These critics of conventional economics are using religion as a metaphor to highlight many of the unscientific things that go on in the name of economic science. They certainly do not mean to say that they or anyone else take economics to be the meaning of life.

The reason Nelson has such trouble proving his point is that it is incorrect. Only the most rigorous materialist would believe the things that Nelson claims to be the common faith of our age, and most economists are not rigorous materialists. It is one thing to say that economics is important—it is quite another thing to say that it has ultimate importance. It is one thing to say that religious ethics has consequences for economic behavior—it is another thing to say that economic theory is the same thing as religious ethics. It is one thing to say that theology has economic implications—it is another thing to say that economics is theology. This confusion lies at the foundation of the entire book.

Keynes aside, I don't think many economists believe that standards of living will ever be high enough to effectively eliminate human conflict. To start with, there are many non-economic sources of human conflict. Furthermore, because satiety causes a lot of technical problems in doing economic theory, and hence brings its relevance into question, most economists have taken some trouble to convince themselves that satiety is not possible. There is a great deal of evidence that human happiness depends more on relative position in the income hierarchy than on absolute standard of living. (Easterlin, 1973; Scitovsky, 1976; Hirsch, 1978). Throughout history societies have reached and surpassed levels of income that once would have been inconceivable without the slightest hesitation. As we pass the sixty-second anniversary of that Keynes essay, we have to wonder if we are indeed approaching satiety and the redemption Nelson says comes with it. Looking around at the members of my generation, young enough to be Keynes' grandchildren, I do not see any diminution of material desire. Rich beyond our grandparents' wildest dreams, we seem to be no closer to earthly or heavenly bliss. Even as we continue to pursue wealth, we know full well it does not hold the answer to the meaning of life.

Though Nelson does not acknowledge it, there is a long-standing disagreement within the economics profession about whether economic growth is even a good thing. While many economists still operate on the assumption that growth is good, and a few even defend that position vigorously (e.g., Simon, 1981), there are a number of economists who have elaborated the disadvantages that come with economic growth, and who have questioned whether economic growth without end is even sustainable (e.g., Mishan, 1967; Daly, 1977).

So Nelson's case that economics is religion fails. Of course, that is not to say that there is no religious dimension to economic life. There is a very large literature addressing the question of the implications of Christian theology for economic theory and economic life. (Two reviews of this literature are Gay, 1991 and Tiemstra, 1993.) Some of it is addressed to the question of the desirability of economic growth, and both sides of the debate are represented. (Against growth see Daly and Cobb, 1989, chap. 3; Hoksbergen, 1983; Goudzwaard, 1979; Hay 1989, chap. 8; Sider 1990, chap. 2. For growth see Beisner, 1990.) But the point is that these Christian thinkers start out with answers to the fundamental questions about the meaning and purpose of life, the causes of human suffering and conflict, and the ultimate salvation of the human race and the restoration of creation. With those answers in hand, they proceed to discuss the role that economics plays in human life. Nelson has run across some of these titles—he lists a few of them on page 336, in the endnotes to the preface. But there is no evidence that he has read any of this material, since he does not discuss it substantively. Instead he strikes out in his own direction, arguing that economics provides the answers to the questions of meaning, of sin and alienation, and of salvation. Since he has the sequence backwards, his efforts fail to convince.

In his finale, Nelson uses his understanding of economics as theology to justify his vision for a new world order. He sees a world of rather small, Balkan-style nation states linked by international institutions in the style of the NATO or GATT. Each nation would manage its own internal economic affairs, and there would be free international trade and free immigration and emigration. Security would be managed by international institutions, which would ban all nuclear weapons. These international institutions would also handle any voluntary international income transfer programs. Global environmental matters would be handled by negotiations over rights to environmental amenities, in the spirit of current "debt-for-nature" swaps.

Nelson is not the first observer to describe a new world order combining small nation-states with large-scale international institutions (Lawday, 1991). Usually such an arrangement is justified on the ground that matters of culture, education, language, and religion are the most sensitive issues, and hence are best determined within relatively small, culturally homogeneous regions, thus minimizing conflicts. On the other hand, economic policies are better determined on a continent-wide scale, since larger markets are more dynamic and efficient, and since larger economic units are likely to capture economies of scale and internalize most externalities.

But Nelson believes that people are relatively indifferent to culture, language, ethnicity, and (real) religion, and extremely sensitive to matters of economics. Since economic institutions and policies are matters of religion, the only way to avoid religious conflict is to make sure that each and every person on earth can live under an economic regime that is consistent with that person's beliefs. This requires the large number of small states, each with a great deal of policy autonomy in economic matters. It also requires the free movement of people, so that everybody can leave their ethnic and cultural heritage behind to live in a state that conforms to their economic preferences. (More numerous and smaller states help to minimize this movement.) Since security is a matter of relative indifference, compromises can be reached at an international level. Other forms of international relationships would have to meet the test of the market, which allows the maximum amount of choice for individual persons and states.

The problems with this view are many. It may be the case that the American Civil War was at bottom a fight over economic institutions, though many would argue that slavery was more a moral issue than an economic one. But most civil wars are over ethnicity, language, and religion, not economics. Witness the current events in the former Soviet Union, the former Yugoslavia, and now the former Czechoslovakia. The people there agree on the direction of economic reform. What has led to the breakup of those states is culture, not economics.

The economic matters that will have to be handled at the international level in Nelson's new world order are many. There will be a market in environmental amenities. Who will determine the initial distribution of property rights? How will contracts be enforced? How will third-party issues be handled? Each nation-state will be allowed to determine its own international trading policy. How will international trade agreements be negotiated and enforced? How will international payments be cleared, and balance of payments problems handled? I have no doubt that there is a solution for each of these problems. The trouble from Nelson's point of view is that each of these solutions requires the participating state to give away some autonomy and compromise an economic (read religious) issue. If states refuse to compromise, these international public goods will remain inefficiently allocated. That may not bother Nelson, since he's something of an Austrian and a libertarian. But to many others, the ecological survival of planet Earth is more important than a commitment to certain economic policy positions.

The largest part of this book is devoted to a history of economic thought that takes us from Plato and Aristotle down through Charles Schultze and Donald McCloskey. Nelson's grand scheme classifies each of these thinkers into one of two categories: "Roman" and "Protestant." The key to this classification is the role of rationality in human existence and the possibilities of finding rational solutions to human problems. Romans believe "that there exist rationally grounded laws of nature and that mankind is both ethically bound and has strong practical reasons to behave in accordance with these laws" (p. 28). Romans are optimistic about solving problems and enjoy the good life. Protestants believe that "alienated from their true reason and from their true nature, men have fallen into a trap in which, like a man drowning in quicksand, they have nothing to grasp and must simply hope for divine or other outside mercy" (p. 51). Protestants are pessimistic and ascetic. A whole cluster of characteristic positions is developed for each category, but the role of rationality is the dividing line.

As the reader can imagine, this attempt to force all of Western thought into only two pigeonholes runs into problems. Any thinker of any subtlety or complexity holds these ideas of rationality and alienation in tension. Both ideas represent something true about the human condition. Since we are in the context of the Christian West here, and theologians figure importantly on both sides of Nelson's divide, it is also fair to point out that rationality and alienation are ideas held in tension in all authentic Christianity, whether Protestant or Catholic. To make the scheme work, Nelson has to flatten out the views of his subjects, making them a good deal less interesting than they really are. It also allows the author to be somewhat arbitrary in classifying certain thinkers whose characteristic opinions land them on both sides of the great divide, depending on the issue.

As a result we have some real classification oddities. James Buchanan ends up as a Protestant, sharing that category with Kenneth Boulding, Donald McCloskey, and Karl Marx. On the other side, Milton Friedman is a Roman, sharing that distinction with Charles Schultze, John Kenneth Galbraith, and John Maynard Keynes. Now I know that there are differences between Friedman and Buchanan, but if I were putting all of western thought into just two categories, I would make sure that those two were on the same side!

A deeper problem is Nelson's identification of the United States of America as the archetypical Roman society. By that he means to say that we are congenitally optimistic, pragmatic in approaching our problems, and worldly in our lifestyle. That is no doubt accurate. But how did a predominantly, almost aggressively Protestant country become Roman? Nelson understands that this is a problem, but he doesn't really resolve it. He cites the American Catholic theologian John Courtney Murray on the affinity between American constitutionalism and Catholic natural law theology (pp. 171-176). But Murray was trying to figure out how Catholics could become Americans, not how Americans became Catholics. In my view, this historical difficulty points up the problem with the whole scheme. Since there are only two baskets and one rather simple divider, not only thinkers but sometimes whole countries end up almost arbitrarily classified in a philosophical or theological category where historically they don't belong. The other leading case of this problem is the Puritan John Locke, who ends up on the Roman side of Nelson's ledger (pp. 90-95).

Another great oversimplification is Nelson's attribution to Protestants of the view that "the poor receive the fate they deserve; charity undermines the will to improve" (p. 54). It is certainly true that a great many present-day American Protestant people believe that. But it is a view that has nothing to do with authentic Christianity in any form, and certainly was not held by many of the great thinkers that Nelson calls Protestants. Nelson in particular attributes this position to John Calvin (pp. 78-79). This is not correct. Calvin believed that it is the duty of Christians to help the poor, and that government should take the lead in doing so. Nelson goes wrong because apparently all he knows about Calvin he got from Weber and Tawney, not by going to modern Calvin scholarship, let alone to the primary sources. (The modern scholarship begins with Graham, 1971.) I believe it is also unfair to attribute this view of the poor to Augustine, Luther, Marx, and probably most of the other Protestants on Nelson's list. Indeed, one of the remarkable areas of agreement in the present-day literature on Christianity and economics is that authentic Christianity demands concern and care for the poor. It is remarkable because these authors come from all kinds of theological backgrounds and from all points of the political compass. Of course, they would disagree about what should be done and who should do it. But none would subscribe to Nelson's "Protestant" view of poverty. Where did this view come from? I suspect it is a product of secularized, rationalized, Enlightenment-style thinking rather than any branch of Christianity. It reaches full development in the work of Herbert Spencer, but contra Nelson, Spencer was a disciple of Smith and Darwin, not John Calvin (pp. 143-150). While Protestant Christianity shares some of the blame for introducing individualism into Western thought, there is no way it can be honestly used to defend neglecting the poor.

The source of some of these problems with accuracy may be Nelson's tendency to rely very heavily on secondary sources. One of the very annoying things about reading this book is the frequency with which Nelson tries to prove his point by quoting a secondary source that he will not name in the text, but only in the endnotes. If he is trying to appeal to authority, he should name the authority in the text. If he is merely cribbing somebody else's notes, he should go back and do his own research.

The strategy of dividing all of Western thought into two categories might be understandable if it had some payoff for the larger argument of the work. In this case, it doesn't. To make the case for his new world order Nelson only needs to show that economics is theology and that there is more than one economic "church." He does not need to show that economic "religion" is in any way connected to Christian theology, as he seems to be trying to do when he traces the Roman tradition from Aristotle through Aquinas and down to Charles Schultze, or the Protestant tradition from Plato through Augustine and Luther and down to Mancur Olson. To call for a "right of free secession," Nelson only needs to show that economists disagree. One would think that to be pretty easy. There is no need to insist that there are exactly two positions on every issue. In short, the author is much too ambitious in this work, trying to do much more than he has to do to draw his conclusions, and trying to go much further than his scholarship allows.

Nelson has not convinced me that economics is religion. Neither has he convinced me that any authentically Christian theological tradition has had much influence on the mainstream economic thought of our day. A former colleague of mine once put out a book under the title *Life is Religion*, but after reading Nelson I would put it the other way around. Life is not religion, and economics is not religion. Religion is life. Religion can be economics. Truly religious people are the ones who allow their convictions about life's deepest questions to determine the way they think and the way they live. That is the kind of life that is truly worth living. It is sad to see intelligent people, economists or anyone else, let the ordinary business of life determine the way they answer the great religious questions.

# REFERENCES

Beisner, E. Calvin. 1990. *Prospects for Growth.* Westchester, IL: Crossway.

Daly, Herman E. 1977. *Steady-state Economics.* San Francisco: Freeman.

Daly, Herman E., and John B. Cobb, Jr. 1989. *For the Common Good.* Boston: Beacon.

Easterlin, Richard A. 1973. "Does Money Buy Happiness?" *The Public Interest* 30: 3-10.

Gay Craig M. 1991. *With Liberty and Justice for Whom? The Recent Evangelical Debate Over Capitalism.* Grand Rapids: Eerdmans.

Goudzwaard, Bob. 1979. *Capitalism and Progress.* Grand Rapids: Eerdmans.

Graham, W. Fred. 1971. *The Constructive Revolutionary: John Calvin and His Socio-economic Impact.* Atlanta: John Knox Press.

Hay, Donald. 1989. *Economics Today.* Grand Rapids: Eerdmans.

Hirsch, Fred. 1978. *Social Limits to Growth.* Cambridge, MA: Harvard University Press.

Hoksbergen, Roland. 1982. "The Morality of Economic Growth." *Reformed Journal* 32: 10-12.

Keynes, John Maynard. 1933. "Economic Possibilities for Our Grandchildren," from *Essays in Persuasion.* London: Macmillan.

Lawday, David. 1991. "My Country Right...or What?" *The Atlantic* 268:22-26.

Mishan, Ezra. 1967. *The Costs of Economic Growth.* London: Staples Press.

Nelson, Robert H. 1991. *Reaching for Heaven on Earth: The Theological Meaning of Economics.* Savage, MD: Rowan and Littlefield.

Scitovsky, Tibor. 1976. *The Joyless Economy.* New York: Oxford University Press.

Sider, Ronald. 1990. *Rich Christians in an Age of Hunger,* 3rd edition. Dallas: Word.

Simon, Julian L. 1981. *The Ultimate Resource.* Princeton: Princeton University Press.

Tiemstra, John P. 1992. "Christianity and Economics: A Review of the Recent Literature." *Christian Scholars' Review* 22.

# Economics, Philosophy and Physics

by Ching-Yao Hsieh and Meng-Hua Ye
(Armonk, New York: M.E. Sharpe, 1991; 170 pages).

Reviewed by **Richard B. Norgaard**

Professors Hsieh and Ye of George Washington University seek to portray for students of economics the relationships between theoretical developments in physics, philosophical debates in general, and the development of economic theory. The objective is certainly noteworthy given the interesting developments in both physics and philosophy during the twentieth century and the increased willingness of economists to re-examine the influence of Newton's mechanics on the development of economic thought.

Hsieh and Ye argue from the beginning how the philosophy of any period reflects the science of the period. They furthermore argue that since physics is the preeminent science, philosophy mirrors physics. The authors' unquestioning acceptance of this widely-held, but now widely challenged from within philosophy, view sets the tone of the book. Physics is central and preeminent to philosophy, indeed, philosophy is metaphysics. Philosophical thought independent of or in competition with physics is peripheral and wanting by definition. The authors, in short, mirror and perpetuate physics envy in economics in an age when philosophy itself has abandoned metaphysics.

The authors' 20-page plus introduction prior to Chapter 1 provides a glimpse of Aristotelian philosophy and economics, an overview of the philosophy and economics of St. Thomas Aquinas, and then moves rapidly on to the accomplishments of Newton and his impact on philosophy and economics. Philosophers with romantic notions, even Kant, for he questioned the limits of science, are portrayed as pessimists. While the potential effects on economics of twentieth century physics is ventured, the last philosopher

Research in the History of Economic Thought and Methodology,
Volume 13, pages 345-348.
ISBN: 1-55938-095-0

mentioned is Hegel. The authors effectively render philosophical developments during the last two centuries, the period during which economics itself takes significant form, as irrelevant. Clearly we are heading into a very spotty, selective portrayal of history.

Chapter 1 shows the parallels between Newton's mechanics and neoclassical economics. Several pages are devoted to how Newton influenced Locke and thereby modern political theory as well as on how Locke tried to formulate a quantity theory of money. From here, however, the authors jump to the mathematics of modern day textbooks with only minimal and occasional passing reference to the economists at the end of the nineteenth century who adapted, some say stole, Newton's equations for economics. The historical context and reasoning of those who made economics like mechanics are ignored while the modern day likeness is portrayed as somehow making economics right.

Chapter 2 presents a scattered, negative portrayal of romantic protests against the Newtonian world view. This chapter mixes a poor portrayal of evolutionary theory, some interesting commentary on Comte's and Marx's humanism, with miscellaneous comments on the German historical school. The tone and depth of the text is conveyed in the following passage:

> Unfortunately, in 1826 John Stuart Mill, the perfect specimen of the enlightenment, experienced a mental crisis: he began to explore the writings of such English romanticists as Thomas Carlyle ...

Chapter 3 summarizes the challenge to economics presented by the second law of thermodynamics. The authors draw on the work of Nicholas Georgescu-Roegen, ignoring the prior century of challenges of energeticists documented by Juan Martinez-Alier (1988). Georgescu-Roegen argued that economic activity increases entropy, an argument the authors do not dispute. Unfortunately, however, Hsieh and Ye are unable to put Georegecu-Roegen's argument in the context of the earth as an open system receiving energy from the sun for another 3.5 billion years. Indeed, the authors mistakenly argue that Darwin's theory of evolution and evolutionary process in general confirm progress and thereby defy the second law (p. 57). The second law has challenged the Western idea of progress and biological evolution for nearly a century (documented in Norgaard, 1988). Hsieh and Ye, however, like Georgescu-Roegen himself, prefer to philosophize independently of others. This chapter includes interesting commentary on Herman Daly and other "anti-growth" theorists, portraying them as remnants of romanticism past. Having muddled the latter half of nineteenth century physics and its relation to economics, the authors argue that new developments in physics promise to resolve the tensions between mechanics and thermodynamics and, of course, propel economics beyond its current controversies with respect to long-run resource scarcity as well.

Chapters 4, 5, and 6 present interesting summaries of twentieth century developments in physics. The authors provide scant evidence, however, that twentieth century physics has had any influence on economics. Einstein's theory of relativity supposedly has affected economics because:

> Although Popper has not completely conquered the philosophy of science, he is certainly a force to be reckoned with in the area of economic methodology. Since Einstein's philosophy of science is closer to that of Popper, we therefore suggest that Einstein has had an indirect effect on economic methodology (p. 82).

The authors suggest Kenneth Boulding's reference in his AEA presidential address to the Heisenberg principle, wherein he used it as an analogy, and his comment that economists are busily creating the world they study are adequate to document the influence of quantum mechanics on economics (p. 103). Fortunately, there is some evidence that chaos theory has influenced economics, and so Chapter Seven is a little more convincing, though the investigation of chaos theory is not particularly centered in physics.

In Chapter 8, the last, Hsieh and Ye ponder the future of economics in light of twentieth century physics. This chapter is somewhat redeemed by its emphasis on the methodological pluralism of physics at the end of the twenty century. And yet it is difficult to find any coherence in their ramblings about current issues in economic theory and their methodological parallels in philosophy and physics. We are provided miscellaneous reflections on Popper, strange comments on current dilemmas in mathematical economics, interesting comments on the institutionalists and their faults, and a few more words on anti-growth theorists. Charles Peirce is referred to several times as Pierce and as the founder of hermeneutics but the influence of pragmatism, interpretation, and language on the abandonment of metaphysics and the key actors are not mentioned (Rorty, 1982). The authors see the possibility that their sociologist colleague at George Washington University, Amitai Etzioni, might provide constructive avenues for institutional economists in his push for a socioeconomics. But the style is weakly inferential to the end, with Hsieh and Ye even trying to portray the rise of socioeconomics as consistent with physics:

> Although the new socioeconomists have not mentioned the revolution in physics, yet their basic tenet that economics and other social sciences are interrelated is compatible with the perception of the new physics that the universe is a network of relations. Hence we suggest that this new perception of reality could be the scientific foundation of the new discipline.

The highly scattered, weakly inferential style, and, for me, the misportrayals of biology and evolutionary theories, mean the authors have not become authorities I can trust. The authors at least refer to recent descriptions of developments in physics; their understanding of philosophy seems to come through their reading of physicists' reflections. The portrayal of the development of economics and its methodological problems also leaves me unimpressed. Frankly, I have had some difficulty interpreting what drove the authors to write the book. The text is not sufficiently structured to serve in the classroom, it never pursues any argument sufficiently in its wanderings to make a scholarly contribution, and it certainly does not rally old ideals with new ideas to stir a potential revolution in thought. Physics envy seems to be the driving force; it has certainly driven the profession in the past, and perhaps it is simply a deficiency on my part which prevents me from being tantalized by physics. So much more could be said about physics, philosophy, and economics so much more coherently. As truly scholarly efforts with quite a different slant, the books of Philip Mirowski (1988, 1989) provide far deeper insights into the relationships of physics and economics with exceptional documentation.

# REFERENCES

Martinez-Alier, Juan with Klaus Schlüpmann. 1987. *Ecological Economics: Energy, Environment, and Society*. Oxford: Basil Blackwell.

Mirowski, Philip. 1988. *Against Mechanism*. Totawa, NJ: Rowman and Littlefield.

Mirowski, Philip. 1989. *More Heat than Light: Economics as Social Physics: Physics as Nature's Economics*. Cambridge: Cambridge University Press.

Norgaard, Richard B. 1986. "Thermodynamic and Economic Concepts as Related to Resource-Use Policies: Synthesis." *Land Economics* 62:325-328.

Rorty, Richard. 1982. "Pragmatism and Philosophy." *Consequences of Pragmatism*. Minneapolis: University of Minnesota Press.

# Adam Smith's Legacy:
## His Place in the Development of Modern Economics

edited by Michael Fry
(New York: Routledge, 1992; 203 pp.)

Reviewed by **Spencer J. Pack**

Adam Smith's legacy for the twentieth century is complex and multilayered.

First, in a broadly "political" vein, the twentieth century can be viewed as the rise and fall of the Soviet Union. From this perspective, Smith can be seen as a great spokesperson for "capitalism" and against "communism." Smith's vision of how a "commercial society" ought to work is second to none; he provides powerful political and ideological weapons against communism and its chief supporter, Karl Marx. This "political" or "ideological" legacy of Smith is perhaps facilitated if one ignores or downplays the critical elements in Smith's thought, and Smith's own severe reservations concerning the moral desirability of the "capitalist system" (Pack, 1991).

Second, in a more "sociological" vein, the twentieth century can be viewed as noteworthy for the general rise of professionalism, the emergence of specific professional academic disciplines, and particularly, the emergence of the unique academic discipline of "economics," the queen of the social sciences (see, e.g., Proctor, Whitley, Burkhardt, and Canterbery). Academic disciplines function partly by solving analytical problems in a prescribed manner using standardized techniques. Among other things, the standardization of economists' intellectual skills, language and paradigm may be viewed to act as a prophylactic device, protecting the phalanx of priestly professional economists from intruding criticisms by secular outsiders. From this perspective, the wonderful systematic nature of Smith's work in the *Wealth of Nations* allows him to be cited as

Research in the History of Economic Thought and Methodology,
Volume 13, pages 349-357.
Copyright © 1995 by JAI Press Inc.
All rights of reproduction in any form reserved.
ISBN: 1-55938-095-0

the very first economist, and the founder of the academic discipline, helping to bestow legitimacy upon the economic professsion. This "professional" or "sociological" use of Smith is perhaps facilitated if one ignores or downplays Smith as a moral philosopher, the author of *The Theory of Moral Sentiments*, and the teacher of natural theology, ethics, natural jurisprudence, and rhetoric and belles lettres; instead, this particular legacy of Smith focuses concentration on Smith as the creator of economics.

Third, economics as a "science" in the twentieth century can be largely characterized as witnessing the development of econometrics, mathematical economics, elegant extensions of marginal neoclassical price theory, and Keynesian economics. Here, the "scientific" legacy of Smith to twentieth century "mainstream" economics is more problematic: Smith thought little of political arithmetic; in spite of his admiration of Newton (and Quesnay) and his apparent mathematical abilities, Smith did not try to develop mathematical "models"; Smith considered neither short-run business cycles nor conditions of underemployment "equilibrium"; and Smith's price theory was quite different from neoclassical price theory. It is largely (although not entirely) this problematic third "scientific" aspect of Smith's legacy which provides a great deal of tension in the book edited by Fry, *Adam Smith's Legacy: His Place in the Development of Modern Economics*. Some of this tension is creative.

A conference was held in Edinburgh in July 1990 to mark the bicentenary of Smith's death. Ten Nobel laureates apparently responded to the request to "look again at *The Wealth of Nations* from today's perspective"; or to discuss "modern applications of Smith's analysis" or to comment on the "condition of modern economics" (pp. xii-xiv). I will briefly comment on each of their resulting papers in roughly the reverse order they appear in the book (Klein and Schultz will be considered out of this sequence). Since the ticket to admission into the body of this book was possessing a Nobel laureate in "Economic Science," I conclude with a brief comment on the utility of this relatively new yet august club.

Lawrence Klein in "Smith's Use of Data" studies Smith's use of wheat prices in Chapter XI "Of the rent of the land" at the end of Book I. Klein is concerned with how Smith handled or interpreted the data, and with whether Smith could have been expected to see a "business cycle." Klein finds Smith's analysis of the data to be mainly descriptive. Among other things, Klein himself does a periodogram analysis of the wheat prices from 1594-1764. Klein also studied correlations between Smith's wheat price data and various series gathered by J.H. Wilson on physical production to see if there was any relationship between the two cyclical series. Klein concludes that there was indeed quite little evidence that Smith should have been able to observe business cycles in his lifetime. Yet, there is an important question which is not addressed: would Smith himself have had so much faith in the accuracy of the data to handle these manipulations?

Jan Tinbergen in "Economics: Recent Performance and Future Trends" evaluates the development of economic science; locates it in the universe of all sciences; samples recent results of economic thinking; and, speculates about where the science ought to go. Among other things, Tinbergen instructs that the birth of econometrics "meant the transformation of economics into a mature science" and that "econometrics introduced the standard scientific process into economics" (p. 152). Tinbergen patiently explains how "a hypothesis is formulated and tested by requiring sufficient similarity between observations and the theory. If the similarity is not sufficient—according to the scientists' norm—another theory is chosen and tested" (p. 152). This is "learning from errors and is as old as science" (p. 152).

Tinbergen goes on to explain how to make a mathematical model, that care must be had so that the number of unknown variables equal the number of equations, and that each equation must represent a structural relation, etc. Here perhaps is the premier twentieth century methodologist in economic "science"!

This is not the place for a criticism of econometric methodology or mathematical model building; yet note: Smith was neither a budding econometrician nor a mathematical model builder.

Tinbergen suggests that future developments in economic science should work with issues of overpopulation, security, cleaning the environment, reducing inequalities in world income distribution, and preserving natural resources for future generations. Economics would cooperate with demography, technology, geology, and agronomy. It is noteworthy that Tinbergen does not mention here some of Smith's notable areas of expertise, for example, history, sociology, and ethics. Some may find Tinbergen to be mechanical, technocratic, and hence rather unSmithian in his approach (See e.g., Brown).

Wassily Leontief in "The Present State of Economic Science" laments about the lack of empirical content in modern economics, and cites the need for more actual measurement and detailed factual information. Leontief sees evidence of the ill health of economics by the popularity of the recent interest in rhetoric and economics and argues that "Rhetoric has, however, to be put aside when it comes to the pragmatic task of finding the means that have to be used to attain a given final goal" (p. 142).

There is an unfortunate misunderstanding here. Certainly for Smith, and presumably for others working in the field, rhetoric means not simply persuasion. For Smith, rhetoric means the art of communication, and for Smith the study of rhetoric and economics would quickly lead to deep, important issues of epistemology, ontology, the meaning of science, truth, and so on. Smith was a master rhetorican (see e.g., Howell), and he voluntarily taught a course in rhetoric and belles lettres throughout his academic career. For Smith, rhetoric and economics are not at loggerheads.

James Tobin in "The Invisible Hand in Modern Macroeconomics" argues that Smith's invisible hand is the ultimate inspiration for the new classical macroeconomics and real business cycle theory. The article is noteworthy for an excellent brief summary of the assumptions of the Arrow/Debreu general equilibrium model, and Tobin argues that Keynes's departures from these assumptions were legitimate and reasonable. Tobin argues that new classical macroeconomic models are oversimplied, not serious, and not relevant. He makes a shameless paradigm pitch to the "youngsters": "Younger generations of theorists will find a challenging and fruitful agenda here [neoclassical synthesis Keynesian economics] if they overcome the temptations of the new classicals" (p. 126).

Tobin has the wise sense to emphasize the ambiguity of transporting Smith to the contemporary world:

"Who knows what Smith would have thought of Walras, Arrow and Debreu, or of Lucas, Sargent and Barro? *The Wealth of Nations* is a very down-to-earth book, with a simple thematic moral, a rudimentary theoretical model, an imaginative intuition... Perhaps looser claims for the invisible hand, less sweeping, less rigorous and less abstract than general equilibrium models, would be more congenial to Smith. ... Perhaps Smith would not be altogether unfriendly to Keynes's activism against mass unemployment and to Keynes's contention that such macroeconomic activism would enable the principles of the 'Manchester School' to achieve their full potential" (p. 128).

Tobin's approach is praiseworthy: admit ambiguity where ambiguity exists. Be humble about the limits of our knowledge: it is indeed impossible to say with absolute certainty what Smith would have thought about contemporary developments.

James Buchanan is no James Tobin. In "The Supply of Labour and the Extent of the Market," Buchanan points out that Smith favored extending the market through eliminating trade restriction; this would lead to economies of scale and increased output. Buchanan argues that the market could also be extended by increasing the supply of labor, which could be accomplished by the "instillation and maintenance of a work ethic." Buchanan would like to internalize the work supply "externality" by promoting an ethic of work and he feels that "The anti-work ethic of the 1960s summarized in the admonition 'take the time to smell the flowers' involves an explicit invitation to destroy economic value for others than the addressee" (p. 115).

This seems to be a possible misuse of Smith's authority. Smith was keenly interested in botany. He enjoyed taking long walks on the beach. Smith may have felt that people needed spurs to work more, and he complained of his own indolence. But inducements to work for Smith should be done by rewarding hard work primarily with material, not spiritual rewards. Indeed, Smith tended to distrust organized religion, perhaps particularly the more work-oriented Puritan sects. According to Smith, these sects had a tendency to be unduly strict, austere, disagreeably rigorous and unsocial, and marked by melancholy and gloomy humor. Far from encouraging a work ethic for these people, the state should get people in these sects to lighten up, by the encouragement of poetry, music, dancing and drama! (*Wealth of Nations*, p. 748).

Buchanan also equates non-market work with "loafing around" (p. 115). There are many things one can do when not working in the market place besides "loafing around." It is doubtful that Smith would characterize working at home, caring for a family, cultivating friendships, or pursuing education or virtue as "loafing."

Franco Modigliani in "On the Wealth of Nations" is concerned with the decline in the saving rates between the decade of the 1960s and that of the 1980s in 21 OECD countries. He also contrasts his life-cycle model of savings with what he perceives to be Smith's theory of the determinants of saving. Modigliani "tests" his theory by running a regression where the change in savings is a function of, among other things, the change in the growth rate of the economy; he finds that his theory outperforms both a "Keynesian" and a "Smithian" theory.

There are three sets of issues with this paper: one, how skillfully does Modigliani handle his own theory; two, how accurate is his characterization and handling of Smith's theory; and three, what is the relationship between the two theories? With regards to the first issue, it appears that Modigliani does not consider that increased dissaving may occur among the elderly due to lengthening of the lifetime, especially if that lengthening is "unplanned" and a "surprise"; also, there could be unplanned, surprising life-end expenses, such as rising health care costs. Moreover, within Modigliani's model, there could be less than normal savings among the "young" if there was an extended unexpected increase in the rate of unemployment, and an unexpected decrease in temporary and lifetime income.

With regards to Modigliani's handling of Smith's savings theory, I will only say this: for Smith economic growth is largely a function of savings rather than savings is a function of economic growth. Consequently, Klein's regression was rather "Keynesian" in flavor; it was not an appropriate "test" of Smith.

Finally, the third issue: note that for Smith there is the potential for conflicts of interests and disputes over income distribution between the various social classes. By extension, there could possibly also be conflicts between generations. It is the contention of some that the current older dissaving generation has used its political power to promote policies which redistribute income from the younger saving generation, thus reducing the flow of savings (e.g., Peterson and Howe, 1989). This seems to be a promising area meriting future research.

In "Public Economic Policy: Adam Smith on what the State and Other Public Institutions Should and Should Not Do" Richard Stone emphasizes

Smith's breadth of knowledge, strong empirical streak, and general sympathy for "the underdog" in social affairs. He stresses that for Smith public expenditure and its finance are a legitimate concern of the state, points out that Smith was in favor of proportional taxation, studies the government accounts in 1776, and candidly admits when he has difficulties following Smith's arguments. Essentially, this is an excellent, thoughtful summary of Book V of the *Wealth of Nations* with a special feel for British history and institutions.

Theodore Schultz in "Adam Smith and Human Capital" concentrates on recent work in human capital theory and stresses the importance of human capital in explaining most modern economic progress. Students of Sraffa will be concerned that there will be some pretty nasty measurement problems in calculating recent increases in the stock of human capital: concerns conveniently not addressed in this essay. There are some other deep problems here as well.

Modern human capital theory starts with the neoclassical theory of prices and income distribution and tends to emphasize the demand for factor inputs: an increase in investment in human capital generates an increase in marginal productivity, which leads to an increase in the demand for the factor input, which leads to an increase in its price. Smith, on the other hand, tended to emphasize the supply side, the cost of producing and reproducing skilled workers. If skilled workers are needed in the production process, then wages must be high enough to cover for the added cost of educating and training the worker (see e.g., *The Wealth of Nations,* p. 101). Smith tended to view the economy as producing and reproducing itself through time; neoclassical economic theory (and its modern derivation, human capital theory) tends to be more concerned with scarcity and the allocation of scarce resources among infinite wants. It is not clear that the two theories necessarily reduce to one, in spite of Marshall's handy scissors (see e.g., *Dobb, Walsh and Gram*).

Similar problems concerning the compatibility of Smith with neoclassical theory arise with Maurice Allais' paper, "The General Theory of Surpluses as a Formalization of the Underlying Theoretical Thought of Adam Smith, His Predecessors and His Contemporaries." Without undue modesty, Allais explains that "the general theory of surpluses and the model of the economy of markets, which since 1943 I have been elaborating from a critical analysis of all previous works in the literature, can represent, completely and validly, the underlying fundamental theoretical framework in the works of Smith, his predecessors and his contemporaries" (p. 56). Allais' model is dynamic, with exchanges leading to equilibrium which take place successively at different prices. Allais assures us that he has "proved" that every state of stable general economic equilibrium is one of maximum efficiency; that every state of maximum efficiency is one of stable general economic equilibrium; and, that for a given structure "the working of an economy of markets tends to bring it nearer and nearer to a state of stable general economic equilibrium, and this state is a state of maximum efficiency" (p. 44). Allais also claims that one of the central ideas of Smith's fundamental economic analysis is that "all operations of exchange and production have their origin in the search for the realization of surpluses ..." (p. 38); consequently, for Smith, exchange generates surpluses.

Yet, is this so? Does "surplus" arise in exchange for Smith? This seems doubtful; for example, Smith writes of productive and unproductive labor, but never of productive versus unproductive exchange!

For Smith, humans are agitated, nervous creatures with limited rationality. In my view, Allais' work is not really a mathematization of Smith. Rather, it is more a mathematization of Hegel: a conservative non-dialectical Hegel using deductive rather than dialectical logic. For Allais and Hegel, the real is rational and the rational is real (by assumption). In this model/view, any change which takes place *must* be a change for the better: why else would people make it? It is sometimes remarked about econometric models: "garbage in, garbage out"; here, rationality in, rationality out. By the assumptions of the model, all change is progressive, and mankind is necessarily getting closer to perfection or a state of maximum efficiency.

Allais also states in a footnote that G. H. Bousquet was "right to say" that "Smith had disciples, Marx only worshippers; Smith's work was continued and developed by scientific minds, while Marx's was only expounded by theologians" (p. 57). This thoughtful concern for Marx is also evident in Paul Samuelson's paper "The Overdue Recovery of Adam Smith's Reputation as an Economic Theorist."

Samuelson objects that Smith's reputation among professional economists has been too low, perhaps partly due to Marx, even though "Marx cannot be judged by twentieth-century economists to have been competent enough in economic theory to serve as a useful judge of Smith's analytical merits" (p. 2). Samuelson refers to Samuelson's 1977 *AER* piece where he claims to have provided both a literary and a mathematical vindication of Smith's system and huffs: "So what is the problem?" (p. 4).

Samuelson defends Smith against Marx's criticism that Smith ignored depreciation of fixed capital and used-up raw materials; defends Samuelson's reading of all the classical masters as a more primitive version of the Walras-Marshall-Wicksell system; scolds historians of economic thought; wishes more of them had taken Viner's EC 301 or brooded more on Ricardo's text; and confidently proclaims that "Adam Smith is actually closer to articulated truth on many of these subtleties than those who wrote in the half century after 1776" (p. 8). Unfortunately, Smith "lived in early times and had no access to the scientific knowledge and know-how that has accumulated over the centuries" (p. 12).

The supreme self-confidence in Samuelson's writing style is, of course, reminiscent of Marx. Also, in criticizing Ricardo, Samuelson is nonetheless following Ricardo in basically treating Smith as the creator of a paradigm with nifty puzzles to solve. Samuelson disagrees with Ricardo's solution (as well as Dmitriev, Ricardo's early mathematizer), and conflates price formation via production models such as Sraffa, Dmitriev, and von Neumann with price models which derive from a Walrasian system without production. These models are different, especially with regards to profit. Samuelson's conflation of production versus non-production models manifests itself in his choice of terminology. Samuelson repeatedly substitutes interest for profit which for Smith, of course, is not the same.

In a sense, Samuelson is deficient in a sense of history (see Barth, 1973, pp. 57-59). Samuelson feels he is superior to the past; he assumes a standpoint in relation to the past from which he sets himself up as a judge according to fixed principles. For Samuelson, history is basically a matter of lightness or darkness, of truth or falseness. Samuelson takes the Hegelian view that he has access to "truth." History for Samuelson is largely a hobby or a diversion, a chance to poke fun at others. Samuelson is as Karl Barth described typical eighteenth century historians: "although as a race they were very learned in historical matters, they were at the same time singularly uninstructed, simply because their modern self-consciousness as such made them basically unteachable. But they were far from imagining themselves impoverished by this attitude, by the abandonment of all attempts at historical objectivity. On the contrary; they felt themselves to be enriched and powerful" (Barth, 1973, p. 59). Samuelson indeed appears to feel himself quite powerful. Here again, Samuelson seems much more like his arch nemesis Karl Marx, (although in my opinion, Samuelson is much funnier than Marx) than the modest, unassuming Adam Smith.

A final word on the "feel" of this book may not be entirely out of order. The book reminded me of reading a *Justice League of America* comic book. The Justice League of America, as it is relatively well known, is a group of super heroes gathered around Superman dedicated to fighting for "truth, justice, and the American way." These are ideals which this particular group of Nobel laureates would probably also support (provided "the American way" was properly specified). The essential trouble with this comic book (as with *Adam Smith's Legacy*) is that the reader gets just a little bit of action from each superhero, and then the story moves on to the next one. This generates frustration.

But the Justice League of America are just comicbook superheroes, and as of this writing, (December, 1992) Superman himself is dead. Yet, I fear the Nobel Laureate in Economic Science also has a tendency to make people unduly idolize, fetishize and hero worship the economists in the select club of Nobel Laureates. More important, Economic "Science" does not generate objective, ahistorical "truth"—at least none that the selectors of the Nobel prize have access to. The selectors of the Nobel prize have their own axes to grind, their own causes to promote. (By my relatively casual inspection, in the past they appear to have largely promoted mathematically oriented economists; and, more recently, various more or less conservative sprouts from the tree of Economics.) After reading this volume composed *only* of economists awarded a Nobel laureate in Economic Science, I am afraid that the Nobel committee may have undue influence in guiding the profession, and in promoting hero worship. At the risk of pricking a hole in our prophylactic shield, I suggest that it may be that the economics profession itself would be better off without this particular invidious distinction. A cost benefit analysis of the Nobel laureate in Economic Science Club seems overdue.

## REFERENCES

Barth, Karl. 1973. *Protestant Theology in the Nineteenth Century: Its Background and History.* Valley Forge, PA: Judson Press.

Brown, Maurice. 1988. *Adam Smith's Economics: Its Place in the Development of Economic Thought.* New York: Croom Helm.

Burkhardt, Jeffrey and Canterbery, E. Ray. 1986. "The Orthodoxy and Professional Legitimacy: Toward a Critical Sociology of Economics." Pp. 229-250 in *Research in the History of Economic Thought and Methodology,* Vol. 4, edited by Warren Samuels. Greenwich, CT: JAI Press.

Dobb, Maurice. 1973. *Theories of Value and Distribution Since Adam Smith.* New York: Cambridge University Press.

Fry, Michael, ed. 1992. *Adam Smith's Legacy: His Place in the Development of Modern Economics.* New York: Routledge.

Howell, W. S. 1975. "Adam Smith's Lectures on Rhetoric: An Historical Assessment." Pp. 11-43 in *Essays on Adam Smith,* edited by Andrew Skinner and Thomas Wilson. Oxford: Clarendon Press.

Pack, Spencer. 1991. *Capitalism as a Moral System: Adam Smith's Critique of the Free Market Economy.* Hants, England: Edward Elgar Publishing.

Peterson, Peter and Howe, Neil. 1989. *On Borrowed Time.* New York: Simon and Schuster.

Proctor, Robert E. 1988. *Education's Great Amnesia: Reconsidering the Humanities from Petrarch to Freud: With a Curriculum for Today's Students.* Indianapolis: Indiana University Press.

Smith, Adam. 1937. *The Wealth of Nations.* New York: Modern Library.

Walsh, V. C. and Gram, H. N. 1980. *Classical and Neo-Classical Theories of General Equilibrium: Historical Origins and Mathematical Structure.* Oxford: Oxford University Press.

Whitley, Richard. 1986. "The Structure and Context of Economics as a Scientific Field." Pp. 179-209 in *Research in the History of Economic Thought and Methodology,* Vol. 4, edited by Warren Samuels. Greenwich, CT: JAI Press.

# Economic Analysis in Talmudic Literature

by Roman A. Ohrenstein and Barry Gordon
(New York: Koln, 1991)

Reviewed by **Mordechai E. Kreinin**

## I. INTRODUCTION

With a considerable stretch of the imagination one can infer many phenomena from the biblical narrative. For example:

> Surgery must have been the first profession on the face of the earth, as God made Eve out of Adam's rib!

> The first psychiatrist must have been the one who treated Yitzhak after his father, Abraham, tried to sacrifice him to God. Abraham probably paid a fortune in cattle for the treatment and must have died a poor man.

> Joseph was the first macroeconomist. He dealt with aggregate magnitudes of food and populations, and was fully conversant with inter-generational transfers.

Far less imagination is needed to appreciate the fact that Talmudic and subsequent literature contain a considerable amount of economic analysis, and that this analysis found its way (in some form) into the writings of the early modern economists. After all, that literature deals with all aspects of life. Why should the economic dimension be excluded? Not only that, but rabbinical writings were always concerned with adaptation of the original text and strictures to changing circumstances and ways of life. Jewish law, as expounded in the Talmud and the subsequent medieval literature, is called *Halacha*, the Hebrew root of which is *Haloch*. It means "to walk," to be in motion, or in constant condition of change. The obvious reference is to adaptation of the

**Research in the History of Economic Thought and Methodology,**
**Volume 13, pages 359-368.**
Copyright © 1995 by JAI Press Inc.
All rights of reproduction in any form reserved.
ISBN: 1-55938-095-0

law to changing circumstances. And what dimension of life has changed more over the centuries than the economic sphere? This interpretation and modernization of the law is exemplified by the stricture: "An eye for an eye" which was later interpreted to mean: "An eye for an eye means money."

That is, one may use a monetary award to compensate for any damage (bodily or otherwise) that one has inflicted. Indeed, Talmudic writings are concerned with amounts of award needed to compensate adequately for different types of damage.

It is the purpose of the book under review (henceforth referred to as the O-B volume) to sort out the economic analysis contained in the Talmudic and subsequent rabbinical writings, and to the extent possible relate them to modern economics. This is done in a competent and highly organized manner. Most of the points made are well documented, although at times a stretch of the imagination is needed to read the economics into Talmudic writings.

There are two Talmudim (the Hebrew plural of Talmud): The Jerusalem one (100 BCE to 425 CE) and the Babylonian one (300 BCE-500 CE). Both are written in Aramaic, and the second is the fuller and more systematic. About a third of the 6,000 page text is legal (*Halacha*). Within the Talmud there are two main sections: the *Mishnah*, developed by the sages in Eretz-Israel, and the *Gemara*, written both in Eretz-Israel and Babylonia. Additional writings and legal discourse are included in various supplements. In many ways the talmudic literature was related to events and thoughts of the Greco-Roman world within which it was developed.

## A.   Talmudic Methodology

In its first chapter the volume under review is concerned with the methodology and approach of the Talmud and other biblical interpretations. The Talmud is highly analytical in its approach and dialectical in its method. The dialectics are full of endless discussions, arguments and counterarguments, development of theories and their refutations, qualifications and clarifications. Some major rules of analysis followed by the rabbis include: Inference from major to minor, inference by analogy, deduction from a general proposition to the particular circumstance, and from the particular back to the general. The analytical sharpness and ingenuity is incredible, where every phrase, word, and syllable is dissected and carefully probed. There can be nothing superfluous in biblical writings, so that if something appears redundant, there needs to be a reason for it, and the reason must be found.

A couple of examples may illustrate the latest point. The first (not contained in the O-B volume) comes from the book of Genesis, where God commands Abraham to sacrifice his favorite son Yitzhak. The text reads: "Take your son, your only son, whom you love, Yitzhak...." Why the quadruple redundancy? It remained for Rashi (Rabbi Shlomo Yitzhaki,

1040-1105 CE), the foremost interpreter of the Hebrew bible and the Talmud, to offer a credible answer. Rashi maintains that the text contains only one half of a dialogue between Abraham and God. We read only the commands of God and not the response of Abraham, who presumably knows or guesses what is coming and tries to protect his beloved son. Abraham, of course, had two sons, Yitzhak and Ishmael, each born to a different wife. Thus, the full dialogue is constructed as follows:

|          |                                    |
|---------:|------------------------------------|
| God:     | Take your son                      |
| Abraham: | I have two sons                    |
| God:     | Your only son                      |
| Abraham: | Each is an only son to his mother  |
| God:     | That you love                      |
| Abraham: | I love them both                   |
| God:     | Yitzhak                            |

A second example of the redundancy, contained in the O-B volume (pp. 84-86), relates to the dowry brought by a wife to her husband upon marriage. It became institutionalized that in return the husband was obliged to add a corresponding amount to his wife's *Ktuvah*; namely, to the settlement she could expect if widowed or divorced. There are two passages in the *Mishnah* concerning the monetary relationship between the dowry and the Ktuvah:

a. If the dowry is 1,000 denarii, the corresponding *ktuvah* must be 1,500 denarii (a denarii was a unit of currency).
b. For every 4 denarii in dowry, the corresponding sum in the *ktuvah* must be 6 denarii.

In both instances the ratio is the same: A 50 percent addition to the dowry to be included in the *ktuvah*. So why the duplication? The subsequent rabbis determined that it was necessary to highlight the fact that the principle applies both to large and small sums (more on the *ktuvah* later).

As a third illustration of the analytical approach (not related to the redundancy issue, and not contained in the O-B volume) observe the stricture in the *Mishnah*:

"Let others praise you and not your own mouth" which might be termed a principle of humility. But should not allowance be made for people's natural desire to boast about their accomplishments? Subsequent interpreters noted that by changing just one vowel in the Hebrew text (from two vertical dots to a bar under one letter) this phrase becomes:

Let others praise you and *if* not—your own mouth.

There are other examples of analytical skills, such as the 12 levels of charitable giving developed by the great medieval jurist Maimonides (Rabbi Moshe Ben Maimon, 1134-1204) of Spain, where a major criterion is the degree of anonymity of the giver and the recipient.

Other examples are discussed in the O-B volume. One of them (pp. 9ff) illustrates the principle of majority rule. Majority rule should be followed except in the case of "following to do evil." But majority rule is not observed in monetary matters. Suppose a defendant sold an ox to the claimant, and the ox was found to be a gorer. Because the presumption is that most people purchase an ox for ploughing (majority rule), the claimant wants his money back. Yet the defendant can maintain that (as in a minority of cases) the ox was sold for consumption. It is up to the claimant to prove otherwise.

It is impossible to read into the above discussion a hint of the distinction between transactions in the market sphere, where each person buys and sells what she wants, and the political sphere where the minority must follow the wish of the majority.

## B.   Economics in the Five Books of Moses

With the possible exception of the story of Joseph in Egypt alluded to above, the Bible contains strands of analysis that can be regarded strictly as microeconomic in nature. Examples, included in Chapter 2 of the 0-B volume, are the following:

> An allusion to the notion of 'consumer surplus', where a buyer is more than satisfied with his transaction, but verbally refers to it as a bad bargain.

> The idea that wants in general are insatiable ("a man's eyes are never satisfied," Proverbs 27:20), but particular wants are satiable and are subject to the principle of diminishing marginal utility (e.g., eat honey to a point of satisfaction for beyond a certain amount you would vomit it up).

> A link between wisdom and the acquisition of wealth (King Solomon), and between wealth and power.

> The role of diligence, perseverance, and investment in the creation of wealth. Furthermore, foreshadowing Adam Smith, the enlightened self interest pursued by those who accumulate capital is considered advantageous to society as a whole. ("He who creates prosperity is himself prosperous, and he who satisfies others is himself satisfied," Proverbs 11:24-25).

The Bible also:

> Counsels attention to the optimal combinations of factor inputs in the production process (alluded to in Proverbs 14:4)

Points to the risk of losing one's capital through unwise credit arrangements, since "a borrower is a slave to the man who lends" (Proverbs 22:7). Obviously this occurred before the development of huge debts that enslaved the creditor to the debtor.

Commands rest on the sabbath for workers, slaves, and animals. Orders the land to lie fallow (as well as remission of debt) every seventh year (preservation of capital), and the return of land to original owners every 50th year, the Year of Jubilee. Land is not to be sold in perpetuity.

Sets restrictions on the use of slaves, and assesses the value of slaves relative to the cost of hired servants.

For unspecified reasons, forbids the sowing of two kinds of seeds in the same field or the ploughing with an ass and an ox harnessed together.

Sanctions the use of money (silver shekels) in transactions, yet prohibits making interest-earning loans. But unlike the complete ban on interest in the Islamic tradition (in an Islamic economy other factor renumerations replace interest[1]), it appears to allow interest on certain commercial loans.

Establishes a welfare net to help widows, orphans, and other disadvantaged persons and restricts consumption behavior and worldly acquisitions by the wealthy.

While not promoting price control, the Bible assumes the existence of competitive markets, and mandates the use of fair weights, measures, and balances. It also relates the price of land to its productive potential.

But it is in the Talmud and subsequent writings that economics appears as a cogent body of analysis, to which the O-B volume is devoted. Part II of the book under review, consisting of Chapters 3 and 4, is concerned with what the authors classify as macroeconomic issues. But in fact, it contains only strands of modern macro-theory, rather than a cohesive body of analysis.

## C.   Macroeconomic Strands

While individual actions may be motivated by sympathetic feelings towards society, Talmudic scholars also view ambition, greed, avarice, passion, and envy as the vehicle of human progress. As in Adam Smith's *Wealth of Nations*, individual self interest serves the interest of society. This is documented several times in Chapter 3, to the point of being repetitive. Yet O-B do not mention a converse statement in the *Mishnah*: "Envy is the mother of all trouble." Although reconciliation of these ideas is possible, they appear contradictory.

Furthermore, self interest is pursued in the expectation of enjoying it later. It is because the individual does not know his day of death that he works hard. Had he expected to die tomorrow, why should he toil for others? Evidently the bequest motive, so evident in contemporary economics, was not part of Talmudic scholarship.

The central idea of scarcity can certainly be traced back to the garden of Eden. When Eve departs the garden, she finds the world an inhospitable place, where subsistence must be wrestled from the earth at the cost of much toil and trouble. In Talmudic writings scarcity is viewed as a social problem. It can arise either from setbacks to the distribution system which prevents adequate (unchanged) aggregate supply from reaching the consumers, or from a leftward shift in the aggregate supply function. The second cause, which can be brought about by unfavorable climatic changes, is viewed as the more serious.

Even deeper understanding is shown by the Talmudic appreciation of prosperity and depression, and the relationship between the relative abundance of commodities and money. In times of prosperity money is relatively abundant and prices rise. Inflation is characteristic of prosperity. Conversely when commodities are relatively abundant and money is relatively scarce, few people can aspire to buy goods. Both prices and personal incomes fall in a period of depression. While there exists in rabbinical writings an indication of the relationship between money prices, and income, O-B stretch the imagination when suggesting that the Talmud contains ingredients of the quantity theory of money. On the other hand, the Talmudists did appear to link prosperity and depression to the state of the weather and its effect on agricultural production.

## D.   Microeconomic Issues

Chapter 5, 6, and 7 are devoted to sorting out microeconomic issues tackled by the Talmud. As is customary in the first lecture of a principles of economics class, the Talmud recognizes the concept of opportunity cost. This is done in the context of assigning renumeration to teachers. The monetary value of their services depends on the line of work the teacher had to give up; namely, on the opportunities foregone or on the alternative uses of his time. At the very least wages must be sufficient to compensate for the foregone leisure time. In another context the Talmud attempts to establish concrete monetary equivalents for the foregone opportunities.

Beyond that, there is evidence that the Talmudists were cognizant of the potential benefit to a merchant in taking advantage of market opportunities (such as stocking up when prices are low); the distinction between price and non-price competition, where only the first type was considered a blessing because it "expands the market"; the role of knowledge of the market in executing transactions wisely; "normal profit" being part of production costs; a distinction between "fixed" and other capital; and the role of demand in determining price and market size.

There appears to be in Talmudic writing both understanding and use of game theory. The rabbis understood the difference between a zero-sum game, such as gambling where one man's loss is another's gain, and a positive-sum game where both participants gain, and which is typical of economic transactions. An example of the latter type is a loan, where the borrower expects to make profit and repay the loan on time with his collateral intact, while the lender calculates that if the borrower misses the deadline he would collect both the collateral and the full amount of the loan.

Rabbinical scholars further employed a minimax strategy to determine outcomes of uncertain situations. The context presented in the O-B volume is a case where A lends B $100 and B pledges his two fields as security. B proceeds to sell the fields consecutively to C and D for $50 each. Under the category of *Pshara* (compromise) the Rabbis analyze the various options open to the players. B, the real culprit of this affair, is deemed to be out of the picture, as the debt is uncollectible. Under strategic cooperation, A will settle for 50 percent of the debt, and C and D will receive 25 percent each. Alternative outcomes of non-cooperative strategies are discussed, leading to the *Pshara* outcome of a cooperative strategy.

Chapter 7 is devoted to consideration of risk, uncertainty, and expectations, all of which abound in Talmudic writings. Risk is first addressed in the context of the marriage contract, or *Ktuvah* alluded to earlier. In addition to recording the duties of a husband to his wife, the deed contains a provision for a financial settlement due the wife if she is widowed or divorced: It is 50 percent higher than the dowry she brings into the marriage, if the dowry was paid in cash or a highly liquid form. The 50 percent increment is justified by the fact that the husband is in a position to invest the dowry and derive a profit for the rest of his life. The wife's dowry offers the husband an opportunity for risk-taking in business ventures. Her reward is the 50 percent premium, which can be viewed as a return on risk.

*Ktuvot* (the Hebrew plural of *Ktuvah*), can be bought and sold; there exists a market for them. And in an interesting paragraph on p. 89, the authors liken a *Ktuvah* to a bond:

> A bond will mature, and so does the *Kethubah*. A bond may be redeemed before maturity, so too, the *Kethubah*. Like a bond, the *Kethubah* has two prices: a par value and a market value. Like a bond, the price of the *kethubah* is subject to fluctuation, depending on a number of variables of which some are measurable and some are subjective or psychological. Like a security, the deed can be an object of speculation with attendant potentials for gains or losses.

There is a market value for each *Ktuvah*, and it fluctuates with economic circumstances. Uncertainty enters this valuation, because one does not know whether the wife would pre-decease her husband, so that the husband would inherit from her. The value of the *Ktuvah* would then drop to zero, and its owner would lose the purchase price. Conversely, in case of a divorce, the owner of the *Ktuvah* can collect its full value. Given that it had been bought at a discount, the purchaser gains. Thus, *Ktuvot* are traded under conditions of uncertainty.

In a subsequent exercise, Rashi determines that the husband's claim would trade at a 50 percent discount, while the wife's claim would be subject to a 60 percent discount. Furthermore, the Talmud requires that a prospective purchaser of a *Ktuvah* should gather all available information concerning such factors as the wife and husband's physical health, temper, age, and social status. In this and other contexts O-B finds strands of what is currently known as rational expectations.

## E.   Human Capital

Chapters 8 and 9 are devoted to issues that later came to be labeled "Human Capital." In a society that sanctions slavery, human beings have value. The Talmud distinguishes between two types of value, a distinction which is vaguely reminiscent of that between "market value," subject to fluctuations, and "intrinsic value," which is fixed. Even an utterly disfigured person whose market value is zero, has intrinsic value (dignity of the individual). But a person who is condemned to death or is otherwise about to die has no such value. The value of men and women fluctuates over their lifecycle, reflecting their physical ability to render labor services. The following valuation table is found in O-B, p. 120-121, attributed to the Book of Leviticus:

|  | Assessed Valuation | |
| --- | --- | --- |
| *Age* | *Male* | *Female* |
| From 1 month to 5 years | 5 shekels | 3 shekels |
| 5-20 years | 20 shekels | 10 shekels |
| 20-60 years | 50 shekels | 30 shekels |
| 60 years and up | 15 shekels | 10 shekels |

While the women's movement may not like the lower valuation placed on females, it would appreciate the Talmudic answer to the question: Upon passing the age of 60, why does the value of a woman decline to a third of her prime-age value, while that of a man declines to less than a third? The specific answer given is "An old man in the house is a liability in the house, while an old woman in the house is an asset in the house." In a more general way, a female's rate of depreciation is lower than that of a male. With respect to the absolute higher evaluation of a male over a female during their prime years, probably because of greater physical vigor, it was thought that a male's worth is double that of a female, so she should have been valued at 25 shekels. The 5 shekel upgrade is offered because a women can give birth, thereby raising her productivity.

This discussion of the financial value of human beings is somewhat relevant to the contemporary debate in the health-medical economics area as to whether one can place a money value on human life. But the claim of O-B that the Talmudic scholars presaged modern welfare economics (p. 112) does not appear to rest on firm foundations.

Appreciation of human capital (the bundle of skills and abilities that an individual brings to the labor market) dates back to the Bible, especially in conjunction with the skills needed for construction of the tabernacle. The master-craftsman Betsalel (after whom a famous art school in Jerusalem is named) was later viewed by the Talmudists as having wisdom, insight, and knowledge. According to Rashi: wisdom is acquired through learning and study, insight is the intelligence to deduce independent ideas from what is learned, and knowledge comes from divine inspiration. But God helps only those who help themselves.[2] So knowledge will not drop like *Manah* from heaven to those who do not make an effort to acquire skills (imitative or educative). An attempt is further made to identify the various kinds of skills needed for construction, including planning and designing. It is understood that human capital carries a return in the form of financial compensation or payment in kind. A strong linkage is posited between education, productivity, and earnings.

Workmen's compensation is discussed in very explicit terms under the topic *nezikin* (damages). Monetary compensation is assigned for prolonged periods of inactivity caused by injury, according to the individual's economic worth and human capital. Five categories of indemnity are identified in the *Mishnah* for damaged free persons: depreciation, pain, healing, loss of time, and indignity. In other words, both physical and psychological damages are allowed for. There is an attempt to quantify some of the categories (for example, loss of time and foregone opportunities), as well as that of permanent loss of human capital. At some point the market value of slaves is used as a guide to estimating the value of foregone earnings.

There is evidence that the Talmudic tradition realized that the present economic value of a person rests upon expectation of the future stream of labor services he would generate. But there is no indication that the scholars recognized that a discount factor needs to be applied to a future stream of earnings to calculate present value.

## F. Conclusions

In the final chapter, O-B explain how Jews came to be prominent in high finance during the Middle Ages. They attribute this phenomenon to the following factors: the fact that Jewish tradition allowed them to charge interest to, and accept mortgage property (as collateral) from, non-Jews on loans for production, and that Jewish laws were continuously updated and modernized; the legal prohibition on Jews (in many countries) to engage in various occupations such as farming; the periodic expulsion of Jews (especially bankers) from certain countries which, while inflicting hardship, gave Jews a cosmopolitan outlook. Undoubtedly Jews in Europe contributed significantly to the transition from medieval feudalism to nationalistic mercantilism and to the development of capitalism. And that is documented in the O-B volume. Finally, the book suggests some channels through which Talmudic and post-Talmudic thought might have crept into the writings of the early economists.

All in all Ohrenstein and Gordon have written an impressive and an exemplary book. Talmudic writings are not easy to follow. And except in a couple of instances the authors succeeded in presenting the analysis in a well-organized fashion and with great clarity. This reviewer certainly enjoyed reading the book, and will appreciate having it on his bookshelf.

## NOTES

1.  See Karoossi (1993).
2.  Along the line of "time does not do anything for you unless you do something with it."

# NEW BOOKS RECEIVED

Anderson, Victor. *Energy Efficiency Policies.* New York: Routledge, 1993. Pp. xi + 91. $52.50, cloth; $14.95, paper.

Ankersmit, F. R., and J. J. A. Mooij, eds. *Knowledge and Language: Metaphor and Knowledge.* Boston: Kluwer, 1993. Pp. x + 213. $118.00.

Archibald, G. C. *Information, Incentives and the Economics of Control.* New York: Cambridge University Press, 1992. Pp. xv + 173. $39.95.

Backhouse, Roger E. *Economists and the Economy: The Evolution of Economic Ideas.* 2nd edition. New Brunswick, NJ: Transction, 1993. Pp. xii + 260.

Barber, William J., ed. *Economists and the Higher Learning in the Nineteenth Century.* New Brunswick, NJ: Transactions, 1993. Pp. xi + 469.

Barker, Philip. *Michel Foucault: Subversions of the Subject.* New York: St. Martin's, 1993. Pp. 229.

Baron, David P. *Business and Its Environment.* Englewood Cliffs, NJ: Prentice-Hall, 1993. Pp. xix + 698.

Benewick, Robert; and Philip Green, eds. *The Routledge Dictionary of Twentieth Century Political Thinkers.* New York: Routledge, 1992. Pp. xvii + 244. $59.95.

Bennett, Jane; and William Chaloupka, eds. *In the Nature of Things: Language, Politics, and the Environment.* Minneapolis, MN: University of Minnesota Press, 1993. Pp. xvi + 275. $44.95, cloth; $17.95, paper.

Berger, Bennett M., ed. *Authors of Their Own Lives: Intellectual Autobiographies by Twenty American Sociologists.* Berkeley, CA: University of California Press, 1992. Pp. xxviii + 503. Paper.

Research in the History of Economic Thought and Methodology,
Volume 13, pages 369-378.
Copyright © 1995 by JAI Press Inc.
All rights of reproduction in any form reserved.
ISBN: 1-55938-095-0

Bicchieri, Christina. *Rationality and Coordination.* New York: Cambridge University Press, 1993. Pp. xiii + 270. $54.95.

Blackwell, Ron; Jaspal Chatha; and Edward J. Nell, eds. *Economics as Worldly Philosophy: Essays in Political and Historical Economics in Honour of Robert L. Heilbroner.* New York: St. Martin's Press, 1993. Pp. xiii + 397.

Blau, Judith R. *Social Contracts and Economic Markets.* New York: Plenum Press, 1993. Pp. xiv + 218. $34.50.

Boggs, Carl. *Intellectuals and the Crisis of Modernity.* Albany, NY: State University of New York Press, 1993. Pp. xiv + 222. $14.95, paper.

Bottomore, Tom. *Between Marginalism and Marxism: The Economic Sociology of J. A. Schumpeter.* New York: St. Martin's Press, 1992. Pp. 150.

Brent, Joseph. *Charles Sanders Peirce: A Life.* Bloomington, IN: Indiana University Press, 1993. Pp. xvi + 388. $35.00.

Brewer, John; and Roy Porter, eds. *Consumption and the World of Goods.* New York: Routledge, 1993. Pp. xxi + 564. $59.95.

Britnell, R. H. *THe Commercialisation of English Society 1000-1500.* New York: Cambridge University Press, 1993. Pp. xiv + 273. $49.95.

Brue, Stanley L. *The Evolution of Economic Thought.* 5th ed. New York: Harcourt, Brace, 1994. Pp. xi + 563.

Brunner, Karl; and Allan H. Meltzer. *Money and the Economy: Issues in Monetary Analysis.* New York: Cambridge University Press, 1993. Pp. xvii + 392. $44.95.

Butlin, N. G. *Economics and the Dreamtime.* New York: Cambridge University Press, 1993. pp. xi + 252. $59.95.

Caldwell, Bruce J. *The Philosophy and Methodology of Economics.* Three volumes. Brookfield, VT: Edward Elgar Publishing, 1993. Pp. xxxiv + 462; viii + 475; x + 484.

Caldwell, Bruce J,; and Stephan Boehm, eds. *Austrian Economics: Tensions and New Directions.* Boston: Kluwer Academic Publishers, 1992. Pp. xiii + 283.

Cawthon, Elisabeth A.; and David E. Narrett, eds. *Essays on English Law and the American Experience.* College Station, TX: Texas A&M University Press, 1994. Pp. xiv + 135. $24.50.

Choi, Young Back. *Paradigms and Conventions: Uncertainty, Decision Making and Entrepreneurship.* Ann Arbor, MI: University of Michigan Press, 1993. Pp. ix + 184.

Clark, Charles Michael Andres. *Economic Theory and Natural Philosophy.* Brookfield, VT: Edward Elgar. Pp. x + 198. $59.95.

Coase, R. H. *Essays on Economics and Economists.* Chicago, IL: University of Chicago Press, 1994. Pp. viii + 222. $27.95.

Coats, A. W. *The Sociology and Professionalization of Economics.* New York: Routledge, 1993. Pp. xii + 642. $45.00.

Cohen, Sande. *Academia and the Luster of Capital.* Minneapolis, MN: University of Minnesota Press, 1993. Pp. xxiii + 184. $39.95, cloth; $16.95, paper.

Colander, David; and Reuven Brenner, eds. *Educating Economists.* Ann Arbor, MI: University of Michigan Press, 1992. Pp. x + 294. $15.95, paper.

Colander, David; and A. W. Coats, eds. *The Spread of Economic Ideas.* New York: Cambridge University Press, 1993. Pp. xvi + 262. $15.95, paper.

Copp, David; Jean Hampton; and John E. Roemer, eds. *The Idea of Democracy.* New York: Cambridge University Press, 1993. Pp. x + 449. $59.95.

Crabtree, Derek; and A. P. Thirlwall, eds. *Keynes and the Role of the State.* New York: St. Martin's Press, 1993. Pp. xiii + 277.

Craib, Ian. *Modern Social Theory from Parsons to Habermas.* 2nd ed. New York: St. Martin's Press, 1992. Pp. ix + 262. $18.95, paper.

Cubeddu, Raimondo. *The Philosophy of the Austrian School.* New York: Routledge, 1993. Pp. xiv + 269. $65.00.

Davis, Douglas, D., and Charles A. Holt. *Experimental Economics.* Princeton, NJ: Princeton University Press, 1993. Pp. xi + 572. $39.50.

di Leonardo, Micaela, ed. *Gender at the Crossroads of Knowledge: Feminist Anthropology in the Postmodern Era.* Berkeley: University of California Press, 1991. Pp. xii + 422.

Dintenfass, Michael. *The Decline of Industrial Britain, 1870-1980.* New York: Routledge, 1992. Pp. xi + 94. $9.95, paper.

Doering, Bernard, ed. *The Philosopher and the Provocateur: The Correspondence of Jacques Maritain and Saul Alinsky.* Notre Dame, IN: University of Notre Dame Press, 1994. Pp. xxxviii + 118. $25.95.

Dornbusch, Rudiger. *Stabilization, Debt, and Reform.* Englewood Cliffs, NJ: Prentice-Hall, 1993. pp. viii + 407.

Drake, Paul W., ed. *Money Doctors, Foreign Debts, and Economic Reforms in Latin America from the 1890s to the Present.* Wilmington, DE: SR Books, 1994. Pp. xxxiii + 270. $40.00, cloth; $14.95, paper.

Enteman, Willard F. *Managerialism: The Emergence of a New Ideology.* Madison, WI: University of Wisconsin Press, 1993. Pp. xiv + 258. $45.00, cloth; $16.95, paper.

Fabra, Paul. *Capitalism versus Anti-Capitalism: The Triumph of Ricardian over Marxist Political Economy.* New Brunswick, NJ: Transaction, 1993. Pp. xxviii + 345. $22.95, paper.

Feeley, Francis. *The French Anarchist Labor Movement and "La Vie Ourvriere," 1909-1914.* New York: Peter Lang, 1991. Pp. xix + 155. $36.95.

Ferris, David. *Theory and the Evasion of History*. Baltimore, MD: Johns Hopkins University Press, 1993. Pp. xxi + 305. $39.95.

Fisher, Donald. *Fundamental Development of the Social Sciences: Rockefeller Philanthropy and the United States Social Science Research Council*. Ann Arbor, MI: University of Michigan Press, 1993. Pp. xiv + 343. $49.50.

Fisher, William W. III; Morton J. Horwitz; and Thomas A. Reed, eds. *American Legal Realism*. New York: Oxford University Press, 1994. Pp. xvii + 326. $35.00.

Fontana, Benedetto. *Hegemony and Power: On the Relation between Gramsci and Machiavelli*. Minneapolis, MN: University of Minnesota Press, 1993. Pp. viii + 226. $44.95, cloth; $16.95, paper.

French, Peter; et al, eds. *Philosophy of Science*. Midwest Studies in Philosophy, Vol. XVIII. Notre Dame, IN: University of Notre Dame Press, 1993. Pp. 397. $49.95, cloth; $22.95, paper.

Friedman, James W., ed. *Problems of Coordination in Economic Activity*. Boston, MA: Kluwer Academic Publications, 1994. Pp. x + 230.

Fuller, Steve. *Philosophy of Science and its Discontents*. 2nd ed. New York: Guilford Press, 1993. Pp. xvi + 240. $18.95, paper.

Gay, Peter. *The Cultivation of Hatred: The Bourgeois Experience Victoria to Freud*. New York: Norton, 1993. Pp. x + 685. $30.00.

Gerrard, Bill, ed. *The Economics of Rationality*. New York: Rutledge, 1993. Pp. xv + 208. $59.95.

Goetz, Hans-Werner. *Life in the Middle Ages from the Seventh to the Thirteenth Century*. Ed. Steven Rowan. Notre Dame, IN: University of Notre Dame Press, 1993. Pp. ix + 316. $44.95, cloth; $19.95, paper.

Gibson, William. *Church, State and Society, 1760-1850*. New York: St. Martin's, 1994. Pp. x + 2099.

Grice-Hitchinson, Marjorie. *Economic Thought in Spain*. Brookfield, VT: Edward Elgar, 1993. Pp. xxix + 178. $49.95.

Grinnell, Frederick. *The Scientific Attitude*. 2nd ed. New York: Guilford Press, 1992. Pp. xvii + 180. $16.95, paper.

Habermas, Jurgen. *Autonomy and Solidarity*. Ed., Peter Dews. 2nd ed. New York: Verso (Routledge), 1992. Pp. viii + 277. $4.95, paper.

Hakken, David; with Barbara Andrews. *Computing Myths, Class Realities*. Boulder, CO: Westview Press, 1993. Pp. xiii + 251. $49.95.

Hamouda, O. F. *John R. Hicks: The Economist's Economist*. Cambridge, MA: Blackwell, 1993. Pp. xviii + 316. $39.95.

Hands, D. Wade. *Testing, Rationality, and Progress: Essays on the Popperian Tradition in Economic Methodology*. Savage, MD: Rowman & Littlefield, 1993. Pp. xiv + 238. $40.00.

Harris, Jose. *Private Lives, Public Spirit: A Social History of Britain, 1870-1914*. New York: Oxford University Press, 1993. Pp. xi + 283. $35.00.

Hoyningen-Huene, Paul. *Reconstructing Scientific Revolutions: Thomas S. Kuhn's Philosophy of Science.* Chicago, IL: University of Chicago Press, 1993. Pp. xx + 310. $40.00, cloth; $15.95, paper.

Hazari, Bharat R., and Pasquale M. Sgro. *Models of Unemployment in Trade and Economic Development.* New York: Routledge, 1992. Pp. xii + 151. $69.95.

Hebert, Robert F., ed. *Perspectives on the History of Economic Thought.* Vol. IX. *Themes on Economic Discourse, Method, Money and Trade.* Brookfield, VT: Edward Elgar, 1993. Pp. x + 214. $59.95.

Heilbroner, Robert. *The Making of Economic Society.* 9th ed. Englewood Cliffs, NJ: Prentice-Hall, 1993. Paper.

Henderson, Willie; Tony Dudley-Evans; and Roger Backhouse, eds. *Economics and Language.* New York: Routledge, 1993. Pp. x + 251. $55.00, cloth; $17.95, paper.

Hodgson, Geoffrey M. *Economics and Evolution: Bringing Life Back into Economics.* Oxford: Polity Press/Basil Blackwell, 1993. Pp. xi + 381.

Holton, Robert J. *Economy and Society.* New York: Routledge, 1992. Pp. xi + 289. $64.95, cloth; $17.95, paper.

Howson, Susan; and Donald Moggridge, eds. *The Wartime Diaries of Lionel Robbins and James Meade, 1943-45.* New York: St. Martin's Press, 1990. Pp. vii + 261.

Hughes, Jonathan; and Louis P. Cain. *American Economic History.* 4th ed. New York: HarperCollins, 1994. Pp. xxiii + 614.

Humphrey, Thomas M. *Money, Banking and Inflation: Essays in the History of Monetary Thought.* Brookfield, VT: Edward Elgar, 1993. Pp. xzi + 443. $69.95.

Hunt, E. K. *History of Economic Thought.* 2nd ed. New York: HarperCollins, 1992. Pp. xiv + 658.

Hutchison, Terence. *Changing Aims in Economics.* Cambridge, MA: Blackwell, 1992. Pp. xi + 186. $29.95.

Kadish, Alon; and Keith Tribe, eds. *The Market for Political Economy: The Advent of Economics in British University Culture, 1850-1905.* New York: Routledge, 1993. Pp. xii + 255. $65.00.

Kanth, Rajani. *Capitalism and Social Theory: The Science of Black Holes.* Armonk, NY: M. E. Sharpe, 1992. Pp. xxi + 227.

Kaplan, E. Ann; and Michael Sprinker, eds. *The Athusserian Legacy.* New York: Verso/Routledge, 1993. Pp. viii + 245. $59.95, cloth; $18.95, paper.

Kaukianen, Yrjo. *A History of Finnish Shipping.* New York: Routledge, 1993. Pp. xvi + 231. $59.95.

Kerruish, Valerie. *Jurisprudence as Ideology.* New York: Routledge, 1991. Pp. xii + 221. $16.95, paper.

Kevelson, Roberta, ed. *Law and the Human Sciences.* New York: Peter Lang, 1992. Pp. 557. $69.95.

Kramnick, Isaac; and Barry Sheerman. *Harold Laski: A Life on the Left.* London: Hamish Hamilton, 1993. Pp. xii + 669.

Lahiri, Kajal; and Geoffrey H. Moore, eds. *Leading Economic Indicators: New Approaches and Forecasting Records.* New York: Cambridge University Press, 1992. Pp. xiv + 464. $64.95, cloth; $22.95, paper.

Laidler, David E. W. *The Demand for Money.* 4th edition. New York: HarperCollins, 1993. Pp. xiv + 210. Paper.

Lamont, Michele; and Marcel Fournier, eds. *Cultivating Differences: Symbolic Boundaries and the Making of Inequality.* Chicago, IL: University of Chicago Press, 1993. Pp. xvii + 346. $49.95, cloth; $17.95, paper.

Landreth, Harry; and David C. Colander. *History of Economic Thought.* 3rd ed. Boston: Houghton Mifflin, 1994. Pp. xxii + 538.

Lehne, Richard. *Industry and Politics: United States in Comparative Perspective.* Englewood Cliffs, NJ: Prentice-Hall, 1993. Pp. xvii + 280. Ppaer.

Levin, Joel. *How Judges Reason: The Logic of Adjudication.* New York: Peter Lang, 1992. Pp. x + 267. $39.95.

Lieber, Michael D. *More Than a Living: Fishing and the Social Order on a Polynesian Atoll.* Boulder, CO: Westview Press, 1994. Pp. xx + 235. $45.00, paper.

Lukacs, Georg. *German Realists in the Nineteenth Century.* Rodney Livingston, ed. Cambridge, MA: MIT Press, 1993. Pp. xxx + 360. $35.00.

Magnusson, Lars, ed. *Mercantilist Economics.* Boston, MA: Kluwer Academic Publications, 1993. Pp. viii + 269.

Maki, Uskali; Bo Gustafsson and Christian Knudsen, eds. *Rationality, Institutions and Economic Methodology.* New York: Routledge, 1993. Pp. xi + 312. $74.50, cloth; $19.95, paper.

Margolis, Howard. *Paradigms and Barriers: How Habits of Mind Govern Scientific Beliefs.* Chicago, IL: University of Chicago Press, 1993. Pp. xii + 267. $40.00, cloth; $15.95, paper.

Martinelli, Alberto, and Neil J. Smelser, eds. *Economy and Society: Overviews in Economic Sociology.* Newbury Park, CA: Sage Publications, 1990. Pp. viii + 328. $24.00, paper.

Mayer, Thomas. *Truth versus Precision in Economics.* Brookfield, VT: Edward Elgar, 1993. Pp. x + 192. Paper.

McCormick, Thomas, J,; and Walter LaFeber, eds. *Behind the Throne: Servants to Imperial Presidents, 1898-1968.* Madison, WI: University of Wisconsin Press, 1993. Pp. xiv + 271. $45.00.

Momigliano, Arnaldo. *The Classical Foundations of Modern Historiography.* Berkeley, CA: University of California Press, 1990. Pp. xiv + 162. $12.00, paper.

Montgomeru, Scott L. *Minds for the Making: The Role of Science in American Education, 1750-1990.* New York: Guilford Press, 1994. Pp. xi + 316. $18.95, paper.

Moyer, Albert E. *A Scientist's Voice in American Culture: Simon Newcomb and the Rhetoric of Scientific Method.* Berkeley, CA: University of California Press, 1992. Pp. xviii + 301. $40.00.

Morishima, Michio. *Capital and Credit: A New Formulation of General Equilibrium Theory.* New York: Cambridge University Pres, 1992. Pp. xi + 212. $49.95.

Muller, Jerry Z. *Adam Smith and His Time and Ours: Designing the Decent Society.* New York: Free Press, 1993. pp. x + 272. $22.95.

Negishi, Takashi. *The History of Economics.* The Collected Essays of Takashi Negishi, vol. 2. Brookfield, VT: Edward Elgar, 1994. Pp. xxiv + 242. $69.95.

Negt, Oskar; and Alexander Kluge. *Public Sphere and Experience: Toward an Analysis of the Bourgeois and Proletarian Public Sphere.* Minneapolis, MN: University of Minnesota Press, 1993. Pp. xlix, + 305. $44.95.

Niethammer, Lutz. *Posthistoire: Has History Come to an End?* New York: Verso (Routledge), 1992. Pp. 158. $34.95.

Oakley, Allen. *Classical Economic Man: Human Agency and Methodology in the Political Economy of Adam Smith and J. S. Mill.* Brookfield, VT: Edward Elgar, 1994. Pp. xiv + 260.

Pasinetti, Luigi L. *Structural Economic Dynamics: A Theory of the Economic Consequences of Human Learning.* New York: Cambridge University Press, 1993. pp. xx + 186. $44.95.

Peach, Terry. *Interpreting Ricardo.* New York: Cambridge University Pres, 1993. Pp. xiv + 318.

Picchio, Antonella. *Social Reproduction: The Political Economy of the Labour Market.* New York: Cambridge University Press, 1992. Pp. xii + 193. $49.95.

Pickering, Andrew, ed. *Science as Practice and Culture.* Chicago, IL: University of Chicago Press, 1992. Pp. viii + 474. $22.50, paper.

Poggi, Gianfranco. *Money and the Modern Mind: Georg Simmel's Philosophy of Money.* Berkeley, CA: University of California Press, 1993. Pp. xi + 228. $30.00.

Pole, J. R. *The Pursuit of Equality in American History.* 2nd ed., revised and enlarged. Berkeley, CA: University of California Press, 1993. pp. xix + 498. $35.00.

Porter, Roy; and Mikulas Teich, eds. *The Scientific Revolution in National Context.* New York: Cambridge University Press, 1992. Pp. xi + 305.

Redner, Harry, ed. *An Heretical Heir of the Enlightenment: Politics, Policy and Science in the Work of Charles E. Lindblom.* Boulder, CO: Westview Press, 1993. Pp. xi + 378. $65.00.

Ricoeur, Paul. *Oneself as Another*. Chicago, IL: University of Chicago Press, 1992. Pp. ix + 363. $29.95.

Rips, Lance J. *The Psychology of Proof: Deductive Reasoning in Human Thinking*. Cambridge, MA: MIT Press, 1994. Pp. xiii + 449. $45.00.

Robbins, Bruce. *Secular Vocations: Intellectuals, Professionalism, Culture*. New York: Verso/Routledge, 1993. Pp. xiii + 263. $18.95, paper.

Roemer, Jon E. *Egalitarian Perspectives: Essays in Philosophical Economics*. New York: Cambridge University Press, 1994. Pp. xi + 356.

Rosenberg, Nathan. *Exploring the Black Box: Technology, Economics, and History*. New York: Cambridge University Press, 1994. Pp. ix + 274. $54.95, cloth; $17.95, paper.

Rothschild, Kurt W. *Employment, Wages and Income Distribution: Critical Essays in Economics*. New York: Routledge, 1993. Pp. xii + 342. $65.00.

Rubin, Leslie G., ed. *Politikos II: Educating the Ambitious: Leadership and Political Rule in Greek Political Thought*. Pittsburgh, PA: Duquesne University Press, 1992. Pp. vii + 232. $47.50.

Sargent, Thomas J. *Rational Expectations and Inflation*. 2nd edition. New York: HarperCollins, 1993. Pp. xiii + 274. Paper.

Schmookler, Andrew Bard. *The Illusion of Choice: How the Market Economy Shapes Our Destiny*. Albany, NY: State University of New York Press, 1993. Pp. xii + 349. $24.50.

Schumpeter, Joseph A. *History of Economic Analysis*. With a new Introduction by Mark Perlman. New York: Routledge, 1944. Pp. xlviii + 1260. Paper.

Scott, William G. *Chester I Barnard and the Guardians of the Managerial State*. Lawrence, KS: University Press of Kansas, 1992. Pp. xvii + 233. $27.50.

Screpanti, Ernesto, and Stefano Zamagni. *An Outline of the History of Economic Thought*. New York: Oxford University Press, 1993. Pp. xiii + 440.

Shapiro, Michael J. *Reading "Adam Smith": Desire, History and Value*. Newbury Park, CA: Sage Publications, 1993. Pp. xxvi + 140. $15.95, paper.

Shell, Marc. *The Economy of Literature*. Baltimore, MD: Johns Hopkins University Press, 1993. Pp. ix + 176. $14.95, paper.

Shell, Marc. *Money, Language, and Thought*. Baltimore, MD: Johns Hopkins University Press, 1993. Pp. xiii + 245. $15.95.

Skidelsky, Robert. *John Maynard Keyes: The Economist as Savior, 1920-1937*. New York: Allen Lane, Penguin Press, 1992. Pp. xxxv + 731. $37.50.

Smiley, Gene. *The American Economy in the Twentieth Century*. Cincinnati, OH: South-Western, 1994. Pp. x + 442.

Smith, Adam. *An Inquiry into the Nature and Causes of the Wealth of Nations*. Abridged ed. Laurence Dickey, ed. Indianapolis, IN: Hackett, 1993. Pp. xviii + 263. $7.95, paper.

Smith, Michael R. *Power, Norms, and Inflation: A Skeptical Treatment.* New York: Aldine de Gruyter. 1992. Pp. x + 307. $$4.95, cloth; $21.95, paper.

Smith, Tony. *Dialectical Social Theory and its Critics: From Hegel to Analytical Marxism and Postmodernism.* Albany, NY: State University of New York Press, 1993. Pp. vii + 173. $14.95, paper.

Snooks, Graeme Donald, ed. *Historical Analysis in Economics.* New York: Routledge, 1993. Pp. xvi + 249. $62.50.

Solo, Robert A. *The Philosophy of Science, and Economics.* London: Macmillan, 1991. Pp. 138.

Star, Leonie. *Julius Stone: An Intellectual Life.* New York: Oxford University Press, 1992. Pp. xii + 300. $55.00.

Stark, Werner. *History and Historians of Political Economy.* Charles M. A. Clark, ed. Rutgers, NJ: Transaction, 1994. Pp. xxvi + 295. $39.95.

Steele, G. R. *The Economics of Friedrich Hayek.* New York: St. Martin's Press, 1993. Pp. xiii + 262.

Stigler, George J. *Production and Distribution Theories.* With an Introduction by Douglas Irwin. Rutgers, NJ: Transaction Books, 1994. Pp. xii + 392. Paper.

Strobel, Frederick R. *Upward Dreams, Downward Mobility: The Economic Delince of the American Middle Class.* Savage, MD: Rowman & Littlefield, 1993. Pp. xv + 229. $21.95.

Sturdy, Andrew; David Knights, and High Willmott, eds. *Skill and Consent: Contemporary Studies in the Labour Process.* New York: Routledge, 1992. Pp. xi + 263. $74.50, cloth; $27.50, paper.

Swedberg, Richard, ed. *Explorations in Economic Sociology.* New York: Russell Sage, 1993. Pp. xxiv + 452. $45.00.

Thaler, Richard H., ed. *Advances in Behavioral Economics.* New York: Russell Sage, 1993. Pp. xxi + 597. $55.00, cloth; $19.95, paper.

Tsuru, Shigeto. *Institutional Economics Revisited.* New York: Cambridge University Press, 1993. Pp. 205. $44.95.

Turner, Marjorie S. *Nicholas Kaldor and the Real World.* Armonk, NY: M. E. Sharpe, 1993. Pp. xii + 235. $45.00.

van Daal, J., and A. Heertje, eds. *Economic Thought in the Netherlands: 1650-1950.* Brookfield, VT: Avebury, 1992. Pp. ix + 211. $59.95.

Van Dulmen, Richard. *The Society of the Enlightenment.* New York: St. Martin's Press, 1992. Pp. 231. $49.95.

Wagner, Steven J.; and Richard Warner, eds. *Naturalism: A Critical Appraisal.* Notre Dame, IN: University of Notre Dame Press, 1993. Pp. 342. $36.95.

Wartenberg, Thomas E., ed. *Rethinking Power.* Albany, NY: State University of New York Press, 1992. Pp. xxvi + 353. $18.95, paper.

Weintraub, E. Roy, ed. *Toward a History of Game Theory.* Durham, NC: Duke University Press, 1993. Pp. vi + 306. $35.00.

Wiggershaus, Rolf. *The Frankfurt School: Its History, Theories, and Political Significance*. Cambridge, MA: MIT Press, 1994. Pp. x + 787. $60.00.

Woo, Henry K. H. *Cognition, Value, and Price*. Ann Arbor, MI: University of Michigan Pres, 1992. Pp. 193. $34.50.

Wood, Neil. *Foundations of Political Economy: Some Early Tudor Views on State and Society*. Berkeley, CA: University of California Press, 1994. Pp. x + 319. $50.00.

Worrall, David. *Radical Culture: Discourse, Resistance and Surveillance, 1790-1820*. Detroit, MI: Wayne State University Press, 1992. Pp. ix + 236.

Zahka, William J. *The Nobel Prize Economics Lectures: A Cross-Section of Current Thinking*. Brookfield, VT: Avebury, 1992. Pp. xii + 168. $59.95.

# Research in Economic History

Editor:

**Roger L. Ransom,**
*Department of History,*
*University of California, Riverside.*

Associate Editors:

**Richard Sutch,** *Department of Economics, University of California, Berkeley* and **Susan B. Carter,** *Department of Economics, University of California, Riverside*

REVIEWS: ". . . a stimulating collection which is justifiably held by its editor to be a representative sampling of the most interesting new work ... The papers all relate to major topics in mainstream British or American economic history."

— *Economic History Review*

". . . Given the quality of essays, with their general success in meeting the initial assignment of surveying and extending recent research and providing bibliographic aid, the volume makes an excellent reference work for scholars as well as for graduate students."

— *Journal of Economic History*

**Volume 15**, 1995, 261 pp.                                    $73.25
ISBN 1-55938-604-5

CONTENTS: List of Contributors. Foreword, *Roger L. Ransom.* Methods of Analyzing Russian Peasant Household Structure in the Nineteenth Century, *I.D. Koval' chenko.* Applying Quantitative Methods: The Formation of the National Agrarian Market in Russia, 1700-1900, *L. D. Milov.* Economic Growth and Regional Economic Disequilibria in Twentieth-Century Spain, *Jose Morilla Critz.* The Geographic Mobility of Antebellum European Immigrants to the United States After Their Arrival at New York: 1840-1860, *Joseph P. Ferrie.* Immigration and the Jewish Economy in Mandatory Palestine: An Economic Exploration, *Michael Beenstock, Jacob Metzer and Sanny Ziv.* The Costs of International Disintegration: Ireland in the 1930's, *Kevin O'Rourke.* The Scale of Dutch Brewing, 1350-1600, *Richard W. Unger.*

Also Available:
**Volumes 1-14** (1976-1992)
  **+ Supplements 1-4, 6**                              $73.25 each
    **Supplement 5**   (2 part set)                     $146.50

J A I P R E S S

# Research in the History of Economic Thought and Methodology

Edited by **Warren J. Samuels,** *Department of Economics, Michigan State University*

**REVIEW:** "Methodology and the history of economic thought, two distinct but interrelated economic fields, are currently enjoying a boom, and the volumes under review afford convincing evidence of the intellectual interest and high quality of contemporary work in these areas."

— *Kyklos*

**Volume 12,** 1994, 260 pp.                    $73.25
ISBN 1-55938-747-5

**CONTENTS:** Editorial Board. Acknowledgments. Contributions as a Classical Economist, Economic Educator, Economic Popularizer and Social Economist, *William Ellis.* The History and Development of the Option Pricing Formula, *Edward J. Sullivan and Timothy M. Weithers.* Research Strategies in Economics Journals, *Rendigs Fels.* Marx's Semantics and the Logic of the Derivation of Value, *Susan Fayazmanesh.* The Interpretation of the Balance of Trade: A Wordy Debate, *Salim Rashid.* REVIEW ESSAYS. Ingrao and Israel's The Invisible Hand: Multiple Reviews, *Roger Backhouse, E. Roy Weintraub, Timonty L. Alborn, Charles J. Whalen.* Lindblom's Inquiry and Change: Multiple Reviews, *James M. Buchanan, Kenneth E. Boulding, Brian Fay.* McCarthy's Classical Ethics, Social Justice, and Nineteenth-Century Political Economy, *S. Todd Lowry.* Groenewegen and McFarlane's A History of Australian Economic Thought, *Ray Petridis.* Heertje and Perlman's Evolving Technology and Market Structure: Studies in Schumpeterian Economics, *Thomas R. DeGregori.* Berman's A History of Atheism in Britain From Hobbes to Russell, *Alon Kadish.* Swedberg's Joseph A. Schumpeter: The Economics and Sociology of Capitalism, *Charles E. Staley.* Lawson and Pesaran's Keynes Economics: Methodological Issues, *Richard X. Chase.* Little Boys on Interpreting Keynes: A Study in Reconciliation, *Allin Cottrell.* Carabellis on Keynes Method and O'Donnell's Keynes: Philosophy, Economics and Politics, *John B. Davis.* Perkin's The Rise of Professional Society, *A.W. Coats.* Books Received.

J A I P R E S S

**Archival Supplement 5,** In preparation, Winter 1995
ISBN 1-55938-094-2                          Approx. $73.25

**CONTENTS:** Readers' Guide to John R. Common's Legal
Foundations of Capitalism (1924). Introduction, *Warren J.
Samuels.* Readers' Guide to John R. Common's Legal Foun-
dations of Capitalism, *Prepared by Warren J. Samuels.* Early
Institutional Economics: Additional Materials from John R.
Common. Introduction, *Warren J. Samuels.* The Law of Col-
lective Bargaining, 20 October 1920. Notes on Analytic and
Functional Economics, May 1926. World Depressions, 9 May
1931. A Aftalion (undated). Bank Credit (undated). Economic
Cycles (undated). The Correspondence Between Clarence E.
Ayres and Waldo Emerson Haisely. Introduction, *Warren J.
Samuels.* Roswell Cheney McCrea's Course on Economic
Doctrines and Social Reform, Columbia University, 1927-
1928, *Warren J. Samuels.*

Also Available:
**Volumes 1-11** (1983-1993)
  **+ Supplements 1-4** (1989-1994)                    $73.25 each

---

**FACULTY/PROFESSIONAL** discounts are available in
the U.S. and Canada at a rate of 40% off the list price
when prepaid by personal check or credit card and
ordered directly from the publisher.

---

**JAI PRESS INC.**
55 Old Post Road # 2 - P.O. Box 1678
Greenwich, Connecticut 06836-1678
Tel: (203) 661- 7602    Fax: (203) 661-0792

# J A I   P R E S S

## Industrial Development and the Social Fabric

Edited by **John P. McKay**, *Department of History, University of Illinois at Urbana-Champaign*

**Volume 13, At the End of the Road: The Rise and Fall of Austin Healy, MG, and Triumph Sports Car**
1995, 328 pp.                                           $73.25
ISBN 1-55938-906-0

**Timothy R. Whisler**, *Saint Francis University*

**CONTENTS:** Introduction. Corporate Strategy and Structure, 1945-1971. Design and Development. Rationalization and Production Sale. Production Methods. Labor Relations. Distribution Structure. Consumer Demand, 1947-1977. Quality and Reliability. The End of Sports Car Production, 1977-1981. Conclusion. Bibliography. Index.

Also Available:
**Volumes 1-12** (1978-1990)                    $73.25 each

---

**FACULTY/PROFESSIONAL** discounts are available in the U.S. and Canada at a rate of 40% off the list price when prepaid by personal check or credit card and ordered directly from the publisher.

---

## JAI PRESS INC.
55 Old Post Road # 2 - P.O. Box 1678
Greenwich, Connecticut 06836-1678
Tel: (203) 661- 7602    Fax: (203) 661-0792